T0355767

THE LOST PEACE

THE LOST PEACE

HOW THE WEST FAILED TO PREVENT A SECOND COLD WAR

RICHARD SAKWA

YALE UNIVERSITY PRESS
NEW HAVEN AND LONDON

For information about this and other Yale University Press publications, please contact:
U.S. Office: sales.press@yale.edu   yalebooks.com
Europe Office: sales@yaleup.co.uk   yalebooks.co.uk

Set in Adobe Caslon Pro by IDSUK (DataConnection) Ltd
Printed in Great Britain by TJ Books, Padstow, Cornwall

Library of Congress Control Number: 2023945277

ISBN 978-0-300-25501-0

A catalogue record for this book is available from the British Library.

10 9 8 7 6 5 4 3 2 1

CONTENTS

PART III: WAR AND INTERNATIONAL POLITICS

ACKNOWLEDGEMENTS

My thanks as always go to my long-time editor Jo Godfrey, whose patience is matched only by her skill and enduring professionalism. Anonymous reviewers provided detailed and extremely fruitful comments, for which I am most grateful. I would like to thank my friends and colleagues in the School of Politics and International Relations at the University of Kent, which as always provided a uniquely congenial and supportive environment for research and intellectual enquiry. My thanks in particular go to the astute captains at the helm of this little platoon, latterly Hugh Miall, Richard Whitman, Ruth Blakeley, Adrian Pabst and Nadine Ansorg. Engagement with the scholars under the aegis of the Simone Weil Center for Political Philosophy in Washington DC, and those associated with Telos in New York, have been uniquely rewarding. Working as a senior research fellow in the International Laboratory on World Order Studies and the New Regionalism at the National Research University Higher School of Economics in Moscow has allowed me to present some of the ideas developed in this book, as well as providing a venue for countless rich discussions and friendships. Serving as an honorary professor in the Faculty of Political Science at Moscow State University provides an association that is as challenging as it is informative. Membership of the Valdai International Discussion Club remains a stimulating source of ideas and connections. It brings together scholars, practitioners, politicians and journalists with contrasting views from across the globe for dialogue and debate. The Center for International Security and Strategy at Tsinghua University under the wise guidance of Mme Fu Ying has allowed me to assess Chinese views on global matters, as have several visits to the China Foreign Affairs University in Beijing. The Centre for Russian Studies and the School of Advanced International and Area Studies at East China Normal University in Shanghai do a marvellous job of comparative analysis, and I have been honoured to work with the professional team there for many years. A visit to Jawaharlal Nehru University in New Delhi opened up fresh vistas for understanding. My debts and personal gratitude extend to a wide range of fellow tillers in the garden of intellectual endeavour – too numerous to name but certainly far from forgotten.

Canterbury, March 2023

ABBREVIATIONS

AA	Association Agreement
ABM	Anti-Ballistic Missile treaty (1972)
AIIB	Asian Infrastructure Investment Bank
ALCM	air-launched cruise missile
ASEAN	Association of Southeast Asian Nations
AUKUS	Australia, UK and US defence pact
BMD	ballistic missile defence
BRI	Belt and Road Initiative
BRICS	Brazil, Russia, India, China and South Africa
CAATSA	Countering America's Adversaries Through Sanctions Act
CEIW	cyber-enhanced informational warfare
CER	Centre for European Reform
CFE	Conventional Forces in Europe
CFSP	Common Foreign and Security Policy
CoP	Conference of the Parties
CPC	Communist Party of China
CPEC	China–Pakistan Economic Corridor
CPSU	Communist Party of the Soviet Union
CPTPP	Comprehensive and Progressive Agreement for Trans-Pacific Partnership
CSCE	Conference on Security and Cooperation in Europe
CSDP	Common Security and Defence Policy

CWC	Chemical Weapons Convention
DCFTA	Deep and Comprehensive Free Trade Agreement
EaP	Eastern Partnership
EEC	European Economic Community
ENP	European Neighbourhood Policy
EPC	European Political Community
ERI	European Reassurance Initiative
EST	European Security Treaty
ETIM	East Turkestan Islamic Movement
EU	European Union
EUGS	EU Global Strategy
FOCAC	Forum on China–Africa Cooperation
FONOPs	Freedom of Navigation Operations
GBSD	ground-based strategic deterrent
G7	Group of Seven advanced industrial economies
G20	Group of Twenty leading economies
IAEA	International Atomic Energy Agency
ICBM	intercontinental ballistic missile
ICC	International Criminal Court
ICJ	International Court of Justice
INF	Intermediate-Range Nuclear Forces agreement
INSTC	International North–South Transportation Corridor
IPCC	Intergovernmental Panel on Climate Change
JCPOA	Joint Comprehensive Plan of Action (the Iran nuclear deal)
LNG	liquified natural gas
MAP	Membership Action Plan
NAM	Non-Aligned Movement
NIEO	New International Economic Order
NRC	NATO–Russia Council
NACC	North Atlantic Cooperation Council
NATO	North Atlantic Treaty Organization
NPT	Treaty on the Non-Proliferation of Nuclear Weapons
NPT	new political thinking (Gorbachev)
OECD	Organisation for Economic Co-operation and Development

OPCW	Organisation for the Prohibition of Chemical Weapons
OSCE	Organization for Security and Co-operation in Europe
PCA	Partnership and Cooperation Agreement
PfP	Partnership for Peace
PGM	precision-guided munition
PGS	Prompt Global Strike programme
PJC	Permanent Joint Council
PPP	purchasing power parity
PRC	People's Republic of China
the Quad	Quadrilateral Security Dialogue
RCEP	Regional Comprehensive Economic Partnership
RFE	Russian Far East
SALT	Strategic Arms Limitation Talks
SCO	Shanghai Cooperation Organisation
SLBM	submarine-launched ballistic missile
SLCM	sea-launched cruise missile
SPD	Social Democratic Party (of Germany)
SREB	Silk Road Economic Belt
START	Strategic Arms Reduction Talks (later Treaty)
TPP	Trans-Pacific Partnership
UAV	unmanned aerial vehicle
UDHR	Universal Declaration of Human Rights
UNCLOS	United Nations Convention on the Law of the Sea
UNHRC	United Nations Human Rights Council (earlier Commission)
UNSC	United Nations Security Council
USSR	Union of Soviet Socialist Republics
WMD	weapons of mass destruction
WHO	World Health Organization

INTRODUCTION

The end of the Cold War in 1989 offered the prospect of an enduring and new kind of peace. With the world no longer torn by the harsh ideological divisions of the twentieth century, peace and reconciliation seemed possible. Global politics uniquely aligned to create a new peace order. The Soviet Union under the leadership of Mikhail Gorbachev from March 1985 repudiated much of the ideology on which the Cold War had been fought, transformed domestic politics and encouraged political reform among its allies in Eastern Europe. The Western powers overcame early doubts and engaged with the changes. A flood of declarations and agreements proclaimed an era of cooperation and development.

The beneficial effects of peace in Europe were anticipated to spread worldwide. This became the era of globalisation, the view that time and space could be conquered by new communication technologies, a thickening web of personal and business contacts facilitated by cheap air travel, and the interdependence fostered by trade and financial ties. A global middle class was coming into existence, based on similar patterns of consumption, orientations to culture and even with shared views of democracy, accountability and the rule of law. There is no automatic correlation between rising living standards and demands for democracy yet, in the long run, consumerist lifestyles generate demands for personal autonomy and the protection afforded by independent courts. When the Cold War ended in

1

Europe, China was still in the early stages of its transformation and pursuing its 'quiet rise' philosophy, yet the question of its political transformation was posed even then.

Above all, the Charter international system created at the end of World War II in 1945, based on the United Nations and its institutions, created a framework for international law, global governance and humanitarian engagement, and it was to this universal order that Gorbachev appealed. Soviet reformers believed that with the end of the Cold War this system could now come into its own, allowing multilateral cooperation to flourish while tempering traditional geopolitical and great-power rivalries. Much was achieved. The threat of an atomic Armageddon had long forced prudence in international affairs, and now the imminent shadow of nuclear war was lifted. The 'peace dividend' allowed military budgets to be slashed and the militarism that characterised the Cold War to be tempered. Globalisation and economic interdependence moderated political divisions, giving rise to 'third way' ideologies. The mystery of progress looked as if it had been resolved. With the purported 'end of history', humanity would unite on the principles of international law and market democracy.

These anticipations were disappointed, and not for the first time. The French Revolution of 1789 devoured its own and ended in military dictatorship. The Bolshevik Revolution of October 1917 inspired millions to believe that revolutionary socialism would inaugurate an era of peace and prosperity, only to be drowned in an ocean of blood. Belief in renewal once again flowered in the late 1980s, this time not through revolution but precisely through the renunciation of violence. This was a genuinely 'anti-revolutionary' moment when the logic of domestic reconciliation and international cooperation appeared in prospect. Fundamental problems of poverty, inequality, under-development, neo-colonialism, neoliberal financialisation (delinking trade from the physical delivery of commodities and services), environmental degradation and much more remained, but the conditions for their resolution appeared unusually benign. A new dawn was in prospect.

Students of the Soviet Union, including me, earnestly described the transformative potential of Gorbachev's *perestroika* (restructuring), the word he used from June 1987 to describe his programme of reform, and welcomed the easing of Cold War tensions. The achievements of that period were real, with the dismantling of the oppressive apparatus of state control, the efflorescence of debate and democratic aspirations throughout the region, and the liberation of the Soviet bloc states. In November 1989 the Berlin Wall came down, and by the end of the year the communist systems were gone. Central and Eastern European countries were free to pursue their own destinies. The Soviet Union itself was torn apart by the forces unleashed by reform, and in December 1991 collapsed. The fifteen former Union Republics emerged as independent states with relatively little violence, although the suppressed tensions would detonate in later years. The dissolution of the communist order and the disintegration of the Soviet Union were epochal events and continue to shape our 'post-Cold War' era.

The Cold War was described by George Orwell in October 1945 as a 'peace that is no peace'.[1] However, the concord that emerged after 1989–91 was at best uneasy and pregnant with new conflicts. This was a 'cold peace', in which fundamental questions of development and European security remained unresolved. The response of the French military leader Marshal Foch to the Versailles Treaty of June 1919 was unequivocal: 'This is not peace. It is an armistice for twenty years'; and so it turned out. Europe and the world once again plunged into war in 1939. Equally, the post-1989 settlement became another Versailles peace, in the sense that it was partial and ultimately led to renewed conflict, described in this book as Cold War II. This struggle is now framed as one between liberal democracy and various types of authoritarianism, with great-power contestation reinforced by cultural and civilisational mobilisation. The political West, created during and shaped by Cold War I, expanded, generating new boundaries between the enlarging liberal international order and outsiders. This was to be a democratic peace, which inevitably jarred with those who had other ideas about how best to achieve domestic development and national security. This was also to be a West-dominated peace, which added to the concerns of countries like Russia and China with great-power ambitions of their own.

3

The Charter peace order is a moderated form of great-power politics, with the lexicon of the balance of power and spheres of interest tempered by commitment to multilateral cooperation. At its core is the notion of 'charter liberalism', based on a pluralist idea of the international community. Gerry Simpson describes it as a 'procedure for organizing relations among diverse communities'. This stands in contrast to 'liberal anti-pluralism', described by Simpson as 'a liberalism that can be exclusive and illiberal in its effects', above all in its 'lack of tolerance for non-liberal regimes'. Liberalism thus divides into two traditions: 'an evangelical version that views liberalism as a comprehensive doctrine or a social good worth promoting and the other more secular tradition emphasizing proceduralism and diversity'.[2] This division took on sharper forms in the post-Cold War era. It underpins the tension between sovereign internationalism, in which respect for sovereignty is tempered by commitment to Charter values, and the more expansive view of international politics, described in this book as democratic internationalism, a radical version of liberal internationalism.

After 1989 the relatively structured bipolar Cold War I confrontation between the American and Soviet social systems shifted onto a different plane. Two peace systems – new world orders, in the jargon of the time – were on offer, and it is the clash between the two that, paradoxically, generated conflict and ultimately war. The first is the sovereign internationalism to which Gorbachev appealed in launching his reforms. This is the system that the US, the Soviet Union, China and other victors constituted in 1945 in the form of the UN and its associated body of international law, norms and practices. The international system based on the UN Charter combines state sovereignty, the right of national self-determination (which facilitated decolonisation) and human rights. The UN Charter bans war as an instrument of policy and provides a framework for the peaceful resolution of international conflicts. Unlike the ill-fated League of Nations in the interwar years, the Charter peace order was given backbone by the creation of an internal 'concert of powers' represented by the five permanent members of the UN Security Council, the P5 group comprising the US, Russia, China, France and the UK. When the Soviet Union launched its reforms in the late 1980s, it appealed to the Charter system as its model for peace and development, promoting it as a universal model for humanity.

Sovereign internationalism formally respects the interests of all powers, great and small, while committed to the multilateral resolution of the problems besetting humanity. This is the ideal, of course, and the practice of international politics typically falls far short. Nonetheless, the Charter system and its principles remain the framework for the conduct of international affairs. Although in recent years it has come under unprecedented strain, no one has come up with a serious alternative. Gorbachev appealed to this model of sovereign internationalism in putting an end to the Cold War, in the belief that it provided a common framework for a transformation in international affairs. It did not happen, but the idea of some sort of cooperative sovereign internationalism was at the core of the thinking of the Non-Aligned Movement from the 1950s and remains at the heart of various post-Western alignments today. This model of international politics eschews the creation of military alliances and blocs, and (formally at least) rejects the view that global order requires some sort of hegemon to take the lead. Commitment to the UN Charter and subsequent protocols entails allegiance to principles of human dignity and human rights, but state sovereignty and non-interference in the internal affairs of other states are prioritised.

The second 'new world order' is the narrower liberal international order created and led by the United States in the postwar years. In the nineteenth century, Great Britain acted as the champion of free trade and open navigation, a role assumed by the US after 1945. Liberal internationalism has a history reaching back at least to the Enlightenment and its views on progress, rationality, free trade and cooperation.[3] Drawing on this tradition, postwar liberal internationalism was premised on a community of liberal democracies based on two key elements: the open trading and financial system created within the framework of the Bretton Woods agreement of 1944; and the military arm that took shape as the Cold War intensified, culminating in the signing of the Washington Treaty on 4 April 1949 to create the North Atlantic Treaty Organization (NATO). The term 'liberal' in the Cold War largely signified 'anti-communist' rather than 'liberal democratic', yet it provided a powerful and ultimately successful normative framework to overcome the Soviet adversary. The interweaving of liberal internationalism with American geopolitical power and ambition meant that this was a 'hegemonic' peace order dominated by the US and its allies. Hegemony means the ability of a specific political community to exercise leadership over others and to order relations between the subordinate elements. Hegemony is achieved through a combination of coercion and consent, with the most successful establishing a common framework of beliefs and policy in which consent is genuine and freely given, with coercion applied only as a last resort.[4]

With the end of Cold War I, liberal internationalism not only proclaimed its victory but also its universality – there could be no separate 'spheres of influence' since the leadership of the US-led peace was proclaimed as a global project. Cold War bipolarity was gone and in the subsequent unipolar years there was no one left to contest the assertion. In the absence of serious competition, liberal internationalism turned into something more radical and expansive. This is described as liberal hegemony, embedding American leadership globally through democratic internationalism while entrenching its geopolitical predominance. The US emerged as a colossus bestriding the globe, fuelling hubristic illusions of omnipotence. This was couched in the benign language of human rights, democracy and open markets, but some ill-advised and unsuccessful projects of regime change in recalcitrant countries demonstrated the limits to US power and its transformative potential. The political West presented itself as a universal model for all of humanity, superior to all possible alternatives. There was much that was attractive in this model of liberal order, as long as it remained within the framework of the Charter international system. The progressive aspects of liberal internationalism won it adherents from across the globe. However, the more ambitious agenda of liberal hegemony exposed unilateral and coercive features, especially when expressed in terms of American exceptionalism. Concern turned into disquiet and ultimately resistance. In the early years, a much-weakened Moscow grumbled and insisted on the priority of Charter universalism, but was in no position to challenge US leadership, but on completing its quiet rise China became a more serious challenger.

The Charter system remains the only legitimate framework for international law and intervention, yet the radical and expansive version of the political West encroached on its prerogatives. A type of 'grand usurpation' took place, with the autonomy of the Charter system subverted by Western powers when it suited their purposes. This was accompanied by false universalism. Instead of the transformation of international politics envisaged by leaders in Moscow and anticipated by various 'progressive' movements in the West, notably peace organisations and church movements, as well as by the Eurasian powers and some countries in what is now known as the Global South (Africa, Asia and Latin America), the Western alliance system created during the Cold War (the political West) advanced globally, and in particular to Eastern Europe. This responded to the demands of the now free former Soviet bloc and some former Soviet states, but reflected the structure of choices shaped by Washington. Instead of charter liberalism, liberal anti-pluralism predominated to the exclusion of sovereign internationalism – which later returned in the form of populist challenges.

The dominance of democratic internationalism and its hegemonic institutions generated an increasingly bitter sense of betrayal and exclusion in Russia, culminating in a prolonged conflict over Ukraine. Fuelled by the commodities boom of the early 2000s, Russia reconstituted itself as an authoritarian state with the will and resources to challenge the hegemony of the political West. For Moscow, the 'grand usurpation' was considered both illegitimate and unacceptable. Instead of the impartiality and inclusivity of the Charter international system, the political West (presumptuously calling itself the 'rules-based international order') presented itself as the arbiter of the rules. Russia's resistance was stiffened by an increasingly close alignment with China. By 2014, China, in comparative pricing terms, became the world's largest economy and increasingly flexed its new power. In Europe the security order created at the end of the Cold War gradually disintegrated, accompanied by intensified conflicts along the emerging frontline on its Eastern marches. The arms control architecture painstakingly built during the Cold War was largely dismantled, various wars of choice and necessity were launched, and in the end great-power contestation returned.

The two orders – the sovereign internationalism of the Charter international system and the liberal internationalism of the US-led order – had much in common. They were both established as a response to the catastrophe of World War II and were generated by many of the same principles and aspirations. The Charter international system was broader and accommodated a diverse range of regime types (communist, Muslim traditionalist, monarchist and others). However, despite their common origins, the two were not the same. Confusion between the two entwined but separate post-Cold War orders bedevilled the post-Cold War era, and will be explored in this book. Russia openly and then China with gathering force challenged what they considered to be the usurpation of the Charter framework by US-led hegemony, which at its most expansive became the ideology of primacy. This was accompanied by a democratic internationalism that challenged the fundamental notion of sovereignty in pursuit of the undoubtedly virtuous belief in freedom and the rule of law. Two representations of international affairs, each appropriate in its own terms, clashed.

The dilemma is not a new one. Robert Kaplan refers to the Greek definition of tragedy 'not as the triumph of evil over good but the triumph of one good over another good that causes suffering'.[5] To navigate between these takes leadership of a rare quality, which has been sorely lacking since the end of the Cold War. It takes wise statecraft, too, which has also been found wanting. Max Weber distinguished between an 'ethics of conviction', in which leaders pursue noble goals irrespective of consequences, and an 'ethics of responsibility', in which statecraft is tailored to achievable benefits.[6] In our case, powers defined as revisionist condemned the perceived replacement of international law and the autonomy of Charter internationalism by America's claim to international leadership and global primacy. We describe this as the 'great substitution', and it is one of the central themes of this book. In response, the US and its allies, understandably, doubled down in defence of the liberal order, against the illiberal autocratic powers. This epic confrontation reproduced the logic of cold war. The global battle for supremacy was fought through proxy wars, information campaigns and the mobilisation of material and intellectual resources.

The relative open-endedness of the cold peace gave way to a second Cold War. The use of the term has been questioned, and for good reason. If it suggests a return to the prior pattern of relationships and a rerun of earlier contests, then it is inappropriate. The world has moved on, new concerns have emerged, innovative technologies predominate, new ideas contend and the balance of power between states has changed. Use of the term obscures what is new and distorts analysis. These criticisms are valid, yet something akin to a cold war – a permanent and entrenched great-power conflict over matters of fundamental principle, accompanied by old-fashioned but enduring struggles for power and status, unremitting information wars, the attempt to divide the world into competing ideological blocs, militarism and arms races, all overshadowed by the nuclear threat – has certainly returned. Just as Cold War I did not cover everything that mattered in international politics in the early postwar decades, Cold War II certainly does not encompass the whole spectrum of global affairs. Yet it provides not only a comprehensible framework for analysis, identifying the elements of continuity while acknowledging what makes the second conflict different from the first, but it also identifies the factors that generated renewed conflict and lost the peace.

This brings us to a fundamental question: what do we mean by peace? The Institute for Economics and Peace based in Sydney, Australia, issues the 'Global Peace Index', which scores 163 nations according to their level of peacefulness. The Index applies the concept of Negative Peace, the absence of violence or fear of violence. However, peace does not simply mean the absence of war. Sustainable peace is described as Positive Peace, which refers to the attitudes, institutions and structures that create and sustain peaceful societies.[7] Unless robust structures and principles are in place to undergird a peace order, there will always be the possibility of a relapse into war.

West Asia (encompassing what have traditionally been known as the Near and Middle East) has been prone to conflict for decades, yet despite the dense network of peace agencies in Europe it was here that the potential for a positive peace was dissipated and from 2014 turned into open confrontation. The distinction will be applied in this work.

A positive peace order in our case is one in which the actors cooperate within the framework of the broader international system guided by the principles of sovereign internationalism and international law. This accords with the point made by President John F. Kennedy in his visionary commencement address at the American University in Washington DC in June 1963, a speech that still has the power to move. We will return to the unfulfilled potential later, but his core argument was that 'peace is a process – a way of solving problems'.[8] The tragedy of the post-Cold War peace is that the 'process', in which genuine dialogue takes into account the concerns of all parties, never really started. This was really a tragedy, in the classical sense of the term, where one good is in conflict with another. On what scale can justice and freedom be measured against peace and security? All parties were convinced of the rightness of their cause, and it was logical for them to be so, yet the mutual sense of righteousness only intensified the conflict. A negative peace took hold, focused on conflict management, the classic condition of cold war. Even cold war-style conflict management proved wanting in the end.

Every game of chess is different, yet each is played according to the same rules. Just as World War II differs from the first yet stems from the way that World War I ended, so Cold War II diverges from the earlier one, yet it, too, is shaped by the way that the first Cold War ended. Many of the earlier institutions, issues and practices remained, accompanied by new actors and new lines of division. The old conflict between capitalism and socialism purportedly gave way to one between democracy and autocracy, although it can also be seen as a struggle between charter and anti-plural liberalism. Conflicts over fundamental models of societal development, human freedom, hierarchy and status once again shape international affairs. However, unlike the earlier struggle, the second Cold War in 2022 turned into a proxy war between Russia and the political West over Ukraine. A proxy war is an armed conflict fought over the territory of a third party in which a state contributes finances, arms, materiel, advisers and everything except its military. The 'proxy' character of the Ukraine conflict has been ambiguous from the outset, since Russia is a direct participant. It initially tried to limit its engagement to what it euphemistically called a 'special military operation'. On the other side, the Ukrainian Armed Forces have been supported with arms, funds and intelligence by the Western powers. They defined the conflict as a defensive war Ukraine did not start, and in which it was fighting for its very survival. The major powers sought to avoid crossing boundaries (red lines) that would escalate into direct armed confrontation and nuclear annihilation in World War III.

This is a story that begins in hope but ends in unmitigated tragedy, in both the classical and modern senses. There was a positive peace to be had after 1989 but it was squandered. This work provides an interpretive analysis, combining empirical and theoretical investigation to explain developments in these years. It is not a detailed international history, although diplomacy is part of the broader analysis, and instead seeks to explain how and why the peace was lost. On that basis the work may indicate how it can once again be found.

PART I
FROM COLD TO HOT WAR

1
THE PROMISE OF PEACE

Could it have been different? The Cold War ended in 1989, heralding the possibility of a positive peace. Instead, three decades later the world has found itself in the grip of a renewed conflict in which the Atlantic powers are ranged against a resurgent Russia and China. But was a new peace order really possible? When has a peace ever been won? Can peaceful change endure, or is it the fate of humanity to remain in thrall to conflict, with war and the threat of war forever shaping international politics and social interactions? The best minds over the ages have pondered these questions, but my starting point is narrower: the moment of perceived opportunity at the end of Cold War I. The exhaustion of the revolutionary socialist challenge to capitalist modernity and the transformation of the major geopolitical competitor to the political West was certainly epochal, but could the liminal moment become a permanent change in behaviour? We now know that the potential for some sort of new dispensation was squandered, but was there really a new peace order in prospect? No one expected the lion to lie down with the lamb, yet the Charter international system made possible (and may do so at some future point) a framework for positive peace between sovereign nations. The climate emergency and global pandemics, accompanied by a plethora of threats including nuclear annihilation and the growth of anti-microbial resistance, may force humanity to unite. In the meantime, the promised peace has been lost.

15

THE CHARTER INTERNATIONAL SYSTEM

This was not the first time that a conflict was followed by attempts to create a durable peace. The Austrian foreign minister Klemens von Metternich believed that after the upheavals of the revolutionary and Napoleonic wars, Europe required a system to connect 'the arrangements regulating the interaction between states with factors that ensured a stable social and political order within them'.[1] Metternich created such a balance at the Congress of Vienna in 1814–15, which basically survived for nearly a century, punctuated by the Crimean War (1853–6) and the wars of Italian and German unification. No such arrangement was put in place after World War I, and the interwar period represents a spectacular example of a peace that was lost. The Paris Peace Conference from January 1919 created the League of Nations, but the humiliating terms imposed on Germany in the Treaty of Versailles in June of that year stoked enduring resentments. The historian and international relations scholar E.H. Carr described the interwar era as the twenty years' crisis (1919–39), a period of 'cold peace' in which some fundamental security problems had not been resolved.[2] Similarly, 1989 was followed by a twenty-five years' crisis, what Russia's first post-communist president, Boris Yeltsin, called a cold peace (1989–2014). The shortcomings of the peace orders in both cases gave way to renewed conflict.[3]

Carr notes that the victorious allies in the interwar years were puzzled about how they had 'lost the peace'.[4] The Allied victory had been decisive although incomplete. World War I ended in an armistice rather than unconditional surrender, generating myths in Germany of a 'stab in the back'. Two decades later, the defeated powers 'made giant strides to recovery', while 'the victors of 1918 remained helpless spectators', quarrelling among themselves whether the Versailles Treaty was too punitive or not punitive enough. Following the Russian invasion of Ukraine in 2022 a similar debate was ignited. Critics, ranging from hard-line neoconservatives (neocons) to liberal interventionists, assert that a more punitive peace after the Cold War could have prevented the resurgence of Russia's great-power imperial ambitions. At the minimum, they insist that there should have been a far more robust response to Russia's annexation of Crimea and incursions into the Donbass in 2014. On the other side, international relations realists of various stripes, along with traditional conservatives, paleoconservatives and liberal pragmatists, argue that it was precisely the failure to create a viable and inclusive security order encompassing Russia that provoked the conflict. Then, as now, the issue was the character of the peace 'after victory', and the structure of international politics.[5]

The post-1989 'interwar' period lasted much longer than the one in the 1920s and 1930s, fostering illusions that indeed a permanent era of peaceful development had arrived. The enduring character of the peace was derived in part because the international system learned important lessons from the earlier failure. The Charter system was notably more ambitious in its attempt to create a durable postwar peace order.[6] The peace had been lost after 1918, and the goal in 1945 was to avoid repeating earlier mistakes.[7] The Charter international system has provided a dynamic and authoritative framework for international politics, but was threatened as never before by the Russo-Ukrainian war from 2022. However, as a sign of the maturation of the Charter system, the Global South rallied to its defence. The host of post-colonial liberated states were no longer willing to act as proxies in the struggles of the traditional great powers of the Global North and defended genuine multilateralism if not multipolarity.

The Charter international system combines respect for sovereignty while fostering the habits of multilateralism through sovereign internationalism. Sovereign internationalism represents a distinctive approach to the role of norms and power in international politics. It stands in contrast to liberal internationalism, which is predicated on the existence of a community of liberal democracies. Their security is believed to be enhanced through the expansive dynamic of democratic internationalism, achieved through democracy promotion activities, regime change operations and the delegitimation of authoritarian and non-aligned actors. At the other extreme, offensive realism and neorealism are power-based interpretations of international politics, concerned with the maintenance of hegemony and status enhancement. Sovereign internationalism represents an alternative both to neorealism, with its emphasis on the balance of power, spheres of interest, balancing and the like, and to fully fledged liberal internationalism, which includes a whole range of other attributes, including free trade and liberal democracy. The focus of neorealism is on relations between states in an anarchic global environment, whereas sovereign internationalism accepts the logic of contending states but asserts that since 1945 this is tempered by the thick normative overlay of the Charter system. Sovereign internationalism restricts itself to the legal and normative framework for the conduct of international politics, and leaves the specific content to individual states. This does not mean that sovereign internationalism is value-free. Membership of the UN means signing up to extensive commitments associated with human dignity, development and multilateralism.

ORIGINS OF THE SYSTEM

The Charter international system was born in the dark days of the Second World War. The Atlantic Charter, drafted by Winston Churchill and Franklin D. Roosevelt in August 1941 aboard the HMS *Prince of Wales* off the coast of Newfoundland, remains the keystone in the arch of the postwar international system. Its eight 'common principles' were fully in tune with the liberal universalism proclaimed by US president Woodrow Wilson (1913–21), the inspiration behind the League of Nations, hence the postwar order is often described as 'Wilsonian'. This gave expression to a radical vision of liberal internationalism that would 'transform the old global system – based on the balance of power, spheres of influence, military rivalry, and alliances – into a unified liberal international order based on nation-states and the rule of law'.[8] The vision was far-reaching and some of the ideas would not have been endorsed by Great Britain, the greatest imperial power of the time, without the overriding need to enlist the US in the struggle against Nazi Germany. In desperate circumstances, with Britain standing alone against Hitler's armies, Churchill was forced to sacrifice defence of the empire on the altar of victory over Nazi Germany. The Soviet Union was still reeling from the devastating German invasion of Operation Barbarossa of 22 June, so Churchill was willing to make compromises that threatened the integrity of the empire. The first article unequivocally declared that neither state sought territorial aggrandisement, the second expressed the 'desire to see no territorial changes that do not accord with the freely expressed wishes of the people concerned', the third committed them to 'respect the right of all peoples to choose the form of government under which they will live', while the fourth talked of all states having 'access, on equal terms, to the trade and to the raw materials of the world which are needed for their economic prosperity', which would put an end to British imperial preferences and open up the empire to American capitalism. For Churchill, the key point was the sixth paragraph: 'the final destruction of the Nazi tyranny'.[9]

The Japanese attack on the American fleet in Pearl Harbor on 7 December 1941 still lay ahead. The US was not a combatant nation, so there could be no substantive discussion of military cooperation. Instead, the focus was on general principles and the normative foundations of the future peace order. The Atlantic Charter was signed a month later by the USSR and nine governments of occupied Europe. Its combination of security and values (power and norms) later undergirded the UN Charter and the international system created after the war. These principles were incorporated into the Declaration of United Nations of 1 January 1942 in which twenty-six countries fighting the Axis powers, including the USSR and China, committed themselves to the principles of the Atlantic Charter and pledged to fight to a common victory. These states thereby became the founding members of what would become an organisation of that name.

With the support of the Allied powers, the Soviet Union turned the tide of war. The question of the postwar peace order became increasingly urgent. A series of conferences – in Casablanca, Tehran, Moscow, Yalta and Potsdam – sought, as Henry Kissinger puts in his study of world order, to 'define a concept of peace'.[10] The conferences established the foundational architecture of the postwar international system. The Allies worked to build a 'new world order' in which the Soviet Union was actively engaged. At the Casablanca conference in January and Tehran in November 1943, the outlines of the new United Nations were devised. The Dumbarton Oaks conference in Washington between August and October 1944 brought together representatives of the 'Big Four', the US, UK, the USSR and China, and some other states to formulate proposals for a 'general international organisation', and they agreed on the aims, structure and functioning of the new body. The basic outlines of the UN were adopted at the Yalta conference by the Soviet leader Joseph Stalin, Roosevelt and Churchill in February 1945.

The Yalta meeting is particularly contentious. The actual agreements were reasonable, notably on the UN and pledges for free elections in Poland and other East European states, but no mechanism was available to ensure that Stalin fulfilled his promises. Not surprisingly, Yalta is condemned in the region and symbolises the subjugation of small countries to great powers, and specifically Central Europe to Soviet security concerns. In terms of classic 'concert' politics, the great powers asserted sovereign internationalism as the foundation of the new order, which endures (with modifications) to this day. The principle of sovereign internationalism moves beyond the classic unmitigated defence of national interests, as described by classic realists, and instead combines state autonomy with multilateralism, the commitment to international treaties and processes. The world had long been moving in this direction, with the various attempts to regulate the conduct of war, if not to ban war as an instrument of policy entirely, since the late nineteenth century. Following the devastation of World War II such efforts shifted into a much higher gear. A new equilibrium was achieved between the realist pursuit of national interests and state sovereignty, and cooperation in multilateral institutions.

The adoption of the UN Charter at the San Francisco Conference on 26 June 1945 prepared the way for the organisation (following ratification by national parliaments) to be formally established that October. The five great powers of the time (France was given honorary membership) were granted the privilege of exercising the veto in the UN Security Council (UNSC), reproducing Vienna's 'concert' structure intended to keep the peace in post-Napoleonic Europe. The fundamental principle was sovereign internationalism, but the normative impulse after the mass cruelties of the war ran deep. The Charter mentions human rights seven times but does not specify what they are. This was left to the Universal Declaration of Human Rights (UDHR), adopted by the UN General Assembly in December 1948. The Genocide Convention adopted by the General Assembly the same month prohibited attempts in time of war or peace to destroy 'a national, ethnic, racial or religious group as such, in whole or in part' and outlined a range of punitive responses.[11] The 1951 UN Refugee Convention sets the rules in the field. These foundational documents are complemented by later protocols, including the International Covenant on Civil and Political Rights (ICCPR) and the International Covenant on Economic, Social and Cultural Rights (ICESCR), both of which were adopted in 1966 and came into force in 1976. These are flanked by regional agreements, notably the European Convention on Human Rights, adopted in 1950.[12] The Charter system and associated conventions are far from becoming a world government. The great powers continue to compete in what realists call the 'anarchic' (that is, without an overriding authority) international arena.[13] International politics retains its competitive character, but the legitimacy of their actions is derived from conformity to the standards established by the Charter system. Power still trumps norms, yet the norms in the final analysis act as a constraint.

COLD WAR I

The UN developed in the shadow of a deepening conflict between former allies. The Cold War was a traditional conflict between the great powers bound up in a struggle between contending ideologies. According to John Lewis Gaddis, it was 'a necessary contest that settled fundamental issues once and for all'.[14] With victory in 1945, Stalin wanted 'security for himself, his regime, his country, and his ideology, in precisely that order'.[15] Gaddis argues that there was little prospect of maintaining the wartime alliance, since Soviet goals were fundamentally incommensurable with those of the West.[16] Others argue that the Cold War was precipitated by a misreading of Soviet intentions, and that ultimately Stalin was amenable to continued cooperation with the nascent political West, as long as Soviet security concerns were respected.[17] In the Greek Civil War, the USSR kept its part of the bargain that consigned the country to the West's sphere of interest.[18] All this was overshadowed by the onset of the nuclear age. The US deployed nuclear weapons against Hiroshima on 6 August 1945 and on Nagasaki three days later. The Soviet threat became more palpable when it tested its first atomic bomb in August 1949 and its first thermonuclear device (hydrogen bomb) in November 1955. Early attempts to place the entire military and civilian nuclear cycle under an international agency, the UN Atomic Energy Commission (the Baruch Plan of 1946), came to naught. Instead, the accelerating nuclear arms race heralded the era of mutually assured destruction, the MAD doctrine at the heart of deterrence.

In response to the Soviet threat, the US devised three strategies. The first was to rely on the UN and the predominance of allies in the Security Council to constrain Moscow. Even before the US entered World War II its elites were thinking how the country would institutionalise its enhanced power and interests. A new type of international society was formulated, with isolationism condemned as a useful foil to sideline opponents.[19] America had long presented itself as a uniquely virtuous state, but this was now combined with a new sense of global mission. Stephen Wertheim argues that one of the features of American exceptionalism is the belief that 'peaceful interaction would transcend the system of power politics emanating from the Old World'.[20] US primacy would not be of the classical imperial type but embedded in a set of multilateral institutions, above all in the UN.

The second was the containment strategy advocated by the diplomat and scholar George Kennan. In his 'long telegram', dispatched from Moscow on 22 February 1946, Kennan argued that Soviet intransigence stemmed from the internal dynamics of the Stalinist regime. There was nothing that the West could do to alleviate that fundamental fact. Hence, the West had to wait until some other Kremlin leader redefined the country's priorities (an argument later made about Vladimir Putin). In the meantime, in a more developed version of his telegram, he advocated the 'long-term, patient but firm and vigilant containment of Russian expansive tendencies'.[21]

This approach was considered too passive for the likes of Dean Acheson and his associate Paul Nitze (who replaced Kennan in the State Department's Policy Planning Staff). They advocated a more robust third approach, asserting that containment would only work if the US rallied the free world under its leadership, 'uniting the whole of Europe and Japan *against* the USSR on the basis of power-politics and by way of *exaggerating* the Soviet threat'.[22] Together they devised National Security Council paper NSC-68 in April 1950, one of the most influential US government documents of the Cold War era yet only declassified in 1975. It outlined a militarised strategy for American primacy couched in ideologically charged language. The authors warned of a growing Soviet military threat, and called for the massive build-up of the US military and armaments. This hawkish line prefigured that of the neocons later.

The US emerged from World War II by far the most powerful state, but how would it manage the peace? In the end, it co-created the Charter international system while fostering interlocking networks of power of its own, which together with its allies became the political West. The US played a central part in devising the Charter international system, but it was a cooperative endeavour and remains the property of the entire 'international community'. Indeed, it is the most vivid manifestation of the existence of such a community. During the war, 'a political consensus emerged that a peaceful, law-governed world order was a sufficiently important national interest to warrant making lasting commitments to other countries and accommodating America's own actions to the requirements of such an order'.[23] Rather than going it alone or returning to prewar isolationism, postwar American elites understood that rooting hegemony in a broader multilateral order would endow it with greater legitimacy and efficacy. There would inevitably be tension between the exercise of US sovereignty and the constraints of multi-lateralism, yet ultimately both legs helped maintain US hegemony. During the Cold War and after the US engaged in coups and wars to defend its power, using the UN as a source of legitimacy when it could, but otherwise going it alone or in concert with its allies in the political West. The exercise of veto powers in the UNSC ensured that Charter multilateralism would not challenge national interests.

In parallel, Washington created the Atlantic alliance, the military arm of the nascent political West.[24] The wartime alliance between the USSR and the Western powers was already under strain as the final battles against Nazi Germany were fought in early 1945, and it was not to endure long into the postwar era. Facing an economic crisis, the UK in 1947 effectively transferred its responsibilities to the US, and thereafter Washington took the lead in the struggle against communism in Greece, Turkey and elsewhere. The Truman Doctrine announced to Congress in March 1947 pledged support for nations struggling against communism, while the Marshall Plan from April 1948 helped rehabilitate the economies of seventeen Western European nations. By 1948, Cold War I was in full swing, with the Berlin Airlift preserving the Western part of the divided city while the Soviet satellite states became increasingly Stalinised. The Cold War soon assumed truly global dimensions.[25] The People's Republic of China (PRC) became part of the communist alliance following Mao Zedong's victory in October 1949. The Korean War the following year pitted Allied forces fighting in the name of the UN against the Soviet Union and China. By late 1950, the Allies had successfully prevented the Korean People's Army from taking over the South, but the war dragged on until 1953 and the divided country is still technically at war. France's defeat in May 1954 at Dien Bien Phu led to the division of Vietnam. America's defence of South Vietnam lasted until defeat in 1975 and the reunification of the country. The Korean War was the only US military intervention during the Cold War that took place under UN auspices.

Postwar Atlanticism combines hard power with the normative principles of democracy and human rights outlined in the Atlantic Charter. Article 1 of the Washington Treaty commits signatories 'to settle any international dispute in which they may be involved by peaceful means in such a manner that international peace and security and justice are not endangered', while Article 2 commits them to 'contribute toward the further development of peaceful and friendly international relations by strengthening their free institutions, by bringing about a better understanding of the principles upon which these institutions are founded, and by promoting conditions of stability and well-being', and only then moves on to Article 5 commitments to collective defence.[26] In other words, as Kissinger puts it, the Atlantic community represented a new combination of power and legitimacy. Values were central to the rhetoric legitimating the Cold War, although obscured by the logic of military confrontation. In the post-Cold War era the merging of security and values made democratic internationalism the operative norm for the entire system.[27] It justified a continuing role for NATO and prompted various regime-change and nation-building endeavours in Kosovo, Afghanistan, Iraq and Libya.

The final ingredient of postwar US power focuses on international political economy, the other half of the liberal international order. It was designed to avoid the mistakes of the interwar period, when a boom in the mid-1920s was followed by the bust of the Wall Street crash of October 1929, mass unemployment and the rise of fascism. The US sponsored an open economic order based on free trade and democratic principles. The Bretton Woods institutions (the World Bank and the International Monetary Fund, IMF) tied the dollar to gold as the benchmark against which other currencies were valued. The Paris Agreement of 1971 ended the Bretton Woods system of fixed currencies, opening the door to financialisation and an era of recurring financial crises. The rules of the General Agreement on Tariffs and Trade came into force in 1948, and in January 1995 GATT became the World Trade Organization, regulating international trade and some services. The struggle against communism encouraged the creation of welfare states, described by John Ruggie as a form of 'embedded liberalism', accompanied by social democratic ideas of equality and social justice.[28] However, even before the fall of communism, the tide had turned. Neoliberal orthodoxies from the 1980s pushed back against the welfare state, industrial policy and corporatism and instead favoured privatisation, financialisation and flexible labour markets.

In Europe a new political order was created within the framework of a larger Atlantic community.[29] As the ideological struggle against communist ideas intensified, one of the conditions for the disbursement of Marshall Aid was that European states cooperate. This encouraged the creation of the European Coal and Steel Community in July 1952, followed in 1957 by the establishment of the European Economic Community (EEC) by Germany, France, Italy and the Benelux states of Belgium, the Netherlands and Luxembourg. US economic and normative power were institutionalised in these expressions of economic internationalism. After 1989 this was universalised in the form of globalisation accompanied by the neoliberal 'disembedding' of markets from the earlier forms of social democratic social control. The postwar European order was based on legitimacy and respect for international law and various humanitarian objectives, but it was also part of an Atlantic security community forged during the Cold War. This helps explain why after 1989 Atlanticism failed to give way to pan-continental unification, as proposed by Gorbachev and his successors as well as by Europeans loyal to the Gaullist vision of a Europe acting as a third force between the US and the USSR. Instead, post-Cold War liberal hegemony sought to create a new world in its image, advancing American national interests through the major security, economic and normative institutions of our era.[30]

HELSINKI AND HUMAN RIGHTS

The Soviet Union was a founding member of the Charter international system, but like the US it also established a sub-order of its own. The Cold War froze the dividing line between the two along a jagged 'iron curtain ... from Stettin in the Baltic to Trieste in the Adriatic', as Winston Churchill put it in his landmark 'Sinews of Peace' speech in Fulton, Missouri, on 5 March 1946.[31] The continent thereafter was 'overlain' by what became the two superpowers at the head of their respective alliances. The Soviet bloc reached as far as Berlin and Prague, while a network of communist and socialist-oriented movements spanned the globe. Presented as a revolutionary model of world order, Soviet state socialism's narrow dogmatism undermined its transformative potential. Revolutionary activism was overshadowed by traditional diplomatic forms of interaction with the world of states. As revolutionary zeal waned, the Soviet Union behaved pre-eminently as a traditional state, although it continued to support foreign communist parties and various national liberation movements. Gorbachev completed the transition from revolutionary to sovereign internationalism, accompanied by a vigorous recommitment to Charter principles. Tragically for him, the ambitious transformative agenda was derailed by the triumphant US-led liberal order.

To understand how this came about we need to go back to the emergence of contrasting security models in the latter stages of the Cold War. As détente, a period of easing of Cold War tensions, took hold in the early 1970s, European and North American foreign ministers gathered in Helsinki in July 1973 to discuss security matters. The outcome was the Conference on Security and Cooperation in Europe (CSCE), which included the entirety of security, political, economic and humanitarian issues. The process culminated in the Helsinki conference of August 1975, bringing together thirty-three European states (all except Albania) plus the US and Canada. The goal was to create a comprehensive and inclusive security order stretching 'from Vancouver to Vladivostok'. This was the postwar conference long sought by the USSR to ratify the 1945 borders, accompanied by a range of economic and security agreements.[32]

The Helsinki Final Act consisted of three 'baskets': political and military, including ratification of postwar territorial boundaries; economic, trade and scientific cooperation; and human rights, freedom of emigration and cultural exchanges. The first 'basket' outlined ten fundamental principles covering 'sovereign equality' of states, 'refraining from the threat or use of force', 'inviolability of frontiers', 'territorial integrity of states', 'peaceful settlement of disputes', 'non-intervention in internal affairs', 'respect for human rights and fundamental freedoms, including the freedom of thought, conscience, religion or belief', 'equal rights and self-determination of peoples', 'cooperation among states' and 'fulfilment in good faith of obligations under international law'.[33] Helsinki codified the existing state of affairs, but also opened the door to radical change. The core postulates represented a significant extension of the values underpinning the Charter system. However, the Final Act reproduced in new forms the tension embedded in that system, in particular between the sovereignty vested in nation states and the commitment to universal values that transcends the logic of state sovereignty. The Soviet Union achieved its fundamental goal – the formal recognition of the borders established in 1945, thus confirming the outcome of the Yalta conference – but at the same time, the logic of great-power sovereignty was challenged.

Moscow's endorsement of 'third basket' human rights principles provided a legal framework for human rights dissident movements within the country to hold the Soviet government to account. Soviet achievements in social modernisation and planned economic development were delegitimated as the normative foundations of Soviet rule became the focus of debate. This in turn provided a powerful tool for external powers to exercise leverage over Moscow. The shift from sovereign to democratic internationalism was not universally welcomed, even in the West. The realist Kissinger, President Gerald Ford's secretary of state, famously dismissed the idealism of third basket provisions. He acerbically observed that they could be written 'in Swahili for all I care'.[34] Despite Kissinger's misgivings, a fundamental shift had taken place. Samuel Moyn describes the new focus as the 'last utopia'. Socialist concerns with social and economic justice were displaced by the prioritisation of human rights. Instead of the earlier focus on modernisation and development, the concern now was 'democracy' and the 'rule of law'.[35]

The Helsinki CSCE was followed by eight review conferences on European security. The three held during the Cold War (Belgrade 1977–8, Madrid 1980–3 and Vienna 1986–9) provided an institutional framework for new thinking to flourish. In the short term, however, the spirit of détente did not last long, and by the late 1970s the Cold War was back in full swing, prompting talk of a second Cold War.[36] Fearing that Afghanistan would fall into the American orbit, Moscow sent in a 'limited military contingent' in December 1979, inaugurating a war that lasted nine years, costing the Soviet Union 15,000 lives and incalculable resources. It became a classic proxy war as the US and its allies armed and supported the mujahideen resistance.[37] The Soviet – Afghan war presaged the fall of the Soviet Union, inevitably drawing comparisons with Russia's 'special military operation' against Ukraine launched forty-two years later.

NEW POLITICAL THINKING

Change in the Soviet Union was long delayed, but when it came it was with the characteristic frenzy of a Russian spring. After a long sequence of geriatric mismanagement, Gorbachev took over as Soviet leader in March 1985. His grand ambition was to 'normalise' Soviet foreign policy within the framework of Charter internationalism. The strategy was directed towards New York, as the seat of the UN, and not Washington, the heart of the political West, although inevitably the latter acted as the main interlocutor. Gorbachev appealed to the multilateralism at the heart of the Charter system, and certainly did not envisage submission to the political West.

Most of the Soviet elite recognised that reform was long overdue, although the goal was to save rather than to subvert the Soviet system. Gorbachev firmly believed in the potential for Soviet rejuvenation based on the renewal of socialism through perestroika. Gorbachev's *reform communism* drew on a long intellectual tradition. As a student in Moscow State University in the early 1950s he met Zdeněk Mlynář, who went on to become one of the leaders of the Prague Spring in 1968. Under the leadership of Alexander Dubček, 'socialism with a human face' sought to combine political freedoms with socialist market mechanisms. The reform movement proclaimed loyalty to the Soviet Union, but the Kremlin leadership under Leonid Brezhnev was not convinced. On the night of 21 August, the Warsaw Treaty Organization (the Warsaw Pact) invaded Czechoslovakia, eventually sending in 500,000 troops and 6,000 tanks from all 'fraternal' socialist states, with the exception of Romania and Albania.[38] This represents the greatest self-invasion in history. It not only crushed the Czechoslovak reforms but also stymied attempts at renewal within the Soviet Union, setting the stage for what came to be known as the era of stagnation (*zastoi*) in the 1970s. This was the period when the young Vladimir Putin came to political maturity. In the wake of the crushing of reform communism, his generation lacked the idealism of the *shestdesyatniki* (people of the 1960s, like Gorbachev), who believed in the reform potential of Leninist socialism. Instead, the 1970s generation were hard-nosed and materialistic, even cynical and nihilistic, concerned with defending the power of the state rather than communist ideology.

Political dissent was suppressed, but reform ideas were brewing within the system. This took the form of 'new political thinking' (NPT), a term which Gorbachev first used in his report to the 27th Congress of the Communist Party of the Soviet Union (CPSU) on 25 February 1986, and which he then developed eighteen months later in his book *Perestroika: New Thinking for Our Country and the World*.[39] New thinking sought to build on the achievements of Soviet socialism while removing what were believed to be its ideological dogmatism, anti-market rigidity and superfluous restrictions on individual freedoms.[40] These reformist and cosmopolitan views developed in the context of deteriorating relations with China and the potential for renewed détente with the West.[41] The NPT was the product of a period of intellectual gestation in Soviet intellectual life, notably in the various institutes of the Academy of Sciences.[42] Gorbachev developed his own concept of new thinking, although early on it still contained many orthodox ideological precepts.[43] The NPT rejected class principles in favour of 'all-human' interests and values. Its fundamental idea was the demilitarisation of international relations. Conflicts were to be resolved by political rather than military methods, a core postulate of the Charter system. This entailed ending the division of the world into blocs, removing the threat of nuclear war, and greater focus on the environment and development. International politics would be conducted on the basis of the balance of interests and mutual benefit rather than the balance of power. Sovereign internationalism would do away with the remnants of revolutionary socialism and the Soviet Union would join, in the language of the time, the mainstream of human civilisation.

The NPT represented a radical repudiation of the classical Marxist – Leninist foundations of Soviet foreign policy. The predominance of classic geopolitical ideas such as spheres of influence, power politics, the correlation of forces and power vacuums gave way to a more benign and cooperative perception of international affairs. This did not go so far as to believe in an essential harmony of interests, but the view that the capitalist states were inherently aggressive and militaristic, ready to take advantage of any weakness, was jettisoned. Communist ideology was losing its grip on the Soviet imagination and earlier aspirations to 'catch up and overtake' Western capitalism had long become a pipe dream.[44] The new thinking abandoned the idea of class struggle and world proletarian revolution. The classic elements of Marxist historicism (the view that the meaning and purpose of history is knowable, and thus manageable) were forsaken and thereby claims of historical infallibility and inevitability. The determinism of ideological thinking gave way to a new openness at home and abroad. Paradoxically, just as the classic postulates of Marxist historicism were being abandoned in the Soviet Union, Western liberalism advanced its own version. This fuelled optimism that an era of 'perpetual peace' based on the 'end of history' was in the offing.[45]

New thinking drew on the ideas of the nuclear physicist Andrei Sakharov, who became one of the leaders of Russia's democratic revolution during perestroika. In the late 1960s he argued that communism and capitalism could 'converge' on some humane middle ground and thereby overcome nuclear confrontation.[46] Gorbachev revived the idea of convergence in his landmark speech to the UN on 7 December 1988. He declared the Cold War over, repudiated the Brezhnev Doctrine of limited sovereignty for East European states and outlined the consequences of his new thinking. He argued, 'Further world progress is now possible only through the search for a consensus of all mankind towards a new world order.' He continued, 'It is a question of cooperation that could be more accurately called "co-creation" and "co-development." The formula of development "at another's expense" is becoming outdated.' He stressed the importance of 'freedom of choice' and the 'de-ideologisation of inter-state relations', as well as their demilitarisation. He outlined a comprehensive agenda on which the new peace order should be based, including strengthening the centrality of the UN, the renunciation of the use of force in international relations and a concern for environmental issues. The fundamental principles were pluralism, tolerance and cooperation.[47] This was a bold restatement of charter liberalism.

Rather than ever-swelling defence budgets, the principle was now to be 'reasonable sufficiency' (*razumnaya dostatochnost*), enough to ensure security and no more. The new thinking opened the door to the principle of 'freedom of choice' for Soviet bloc countries, rendering bloc discipline redundant. The repudiation of the Brezhnev Doctrine of limited sovereignty for Warsaw Pact allies opened the way to the revolutions of 1989 and the end of the Soviet bloc in its entirety. Already in Poland the ruling party had abandoned its monopoly on power in April, and the negotiated transition saw free elections to parliament and the senate in June. In November the Berlin Wall came down, paving the way for German reunification. By the end of the year, 'velvet' revolutions had swept communist administrations from power in Czechoslovakia, Hungary and Bulgaria, while in Romania in December a more violent struggle overthrew the dictatorial regime.

The revolutions exposed Gorbachev to the charge that he was betraying not only communist ideals but also Soviet state interests. Critics condemned him for giving up hard-fought Soviet achievements and getting nothing but vague promises of cooperation in return.[48] This later came to a head over the issue of NATO enlargement, and in particular the principle of 'freedom of choice' conceded at the time of German unification in 1990. Moscow believed that the classic image of the Atlantic power system as perennially hostile was false, giving way to the view that a constructive relationship was possible. This became the guiding principle of the nascent 'democratic' Russian foreign policy, under the guidance of foreign minister Andrei Kozyrev, and it predominated until the mid-1990s.[49] Thereafter an increasingly hard-nosed defence of Russian sovereignty and perceived state interests predominated. This was fuelled by a sense that the positive peace agenda outlined by the Moscow leadership had been betrayed, and that the political West had taken advantage of Russia's good will.

TOWARDS A POSITIVE PEACE

The political West took shape during Cold War I, but it was far from monolithic. Disquiet with the militarism associated with the Cold War had long been voiced. The greatest US leaders since 1945 repeatedly turned to the question of how a common peace order could be devised, accompanied by concern about the heavy burden imposed by the arms race. President Dwight D. Eisenhower was one of the first to enunciate themes that would resonate later, drawing on his experience as the supreme commander of Allied forces in World War II. His 'Chance for Peace' speech delivered on 16 April 1953, just three months into his presidency and three weeks after Stalin's death, described how US and Soviet forces met on the Elbe on 25 April 1945, inspiring a 'common purpose' but which 'lasted an instant and perished' as the two countries parted ways over their visions of peace and security. He warned that 'the Soviet Union itself has shared and suffered the very fears it has fostered in the rest of the world. This has been the way of life forged by 8 years of fear and force.' If no way could be found of turning from this 'dread road', the worst to be feared was atomic war, but the best was not great: 'a life of perpetual fear and tension; a burden of arms draining the wealth and labour of all peoples'. He described arms spending as stealing from the people: 'Every gun that is made, every warship launched, every rocket fired signifies, in the final sense, a theft from those who hunger and are not fed, those who are cold and are not clothed.' He described how, 'Under the cloud of threatening war, it is humanity hanging from a cross of iron.' He offered the post-Stalin leadership an opportunity to turn away from the path of confrontation and create a new peace order.[50]

His aspiration came to naught. Instead, an unprecedented arms race built up a global nuclear stockpile that at its peak in 1985 reached 63,662 weapons. In the US a ramified war economy developed in parallel with the civilian economy to create the consumer society that we know today. It was in these years that the Cold War 'Trumanite' militarised state was created, which overshadowed the 'Madisonian' constitutional state. Michael Glennon describes how the Trumanite state forged resilient connections between the various branches of the military and intelligence agencies, the political class, the media, think tanks and some universities. This represented a structural transformation of the American state, in which military contractors, the armed services and their civilian acolytes play an outsize role, to the detriment of diplomacy and traditional statecraft. Constitutional control withered because of the inherent complexity of national security issues as well as the enduring bipartisan ideological consensus on America's primacy and hegemony in world affairs.[51] Eisenhower referred to this in his farewell address on 17 January 1961. He warned against the corrupting influence of what he described as the 'military-industrial complex', the combination of 'an immense military establishment and a large arms industry', which he noted was 'something new to the American experience'. He warned that 'the potential for the disastrous rise of misplaced power exists and will persist'.[52] Eisenhower warned against the creation of a permanent war economy, which would skew the priorities of American foreign policy and divert resources from domestic needs.[53] Instead, as Glennon argues, the bipartisan consensus of a militarised US grand strategy endures despite the regular turnover in political leadership.

This did not go unchallenged. Scathed by the failure of the invasion of Fidel Castro's Cuba in the Bay of Pigs in April 1961 and scarred by the world coming to the brink of nuclear war in the Cuban missile crisis of October 1962, President John F. Kennedy turned to the question of 'world peace'. In his commencement address at the American University in Washington DC in June 1963, he asked:

What kind of peace do I mean? What kind of peace do we seek? Not a Pax Americana enforced on the world by American weapons of war. Not the peace of the grave or the security of the slave. I am talking about genuine peace – the kind of peace that makes life on earth worth living – the kind that enables man and nations to grow and to hope and to build a better life for their children – not merely peace for Americans but peace for all men and women – not merely peace in our time but peace for all time.

Kennedy spoke of peace because of the 'new face of war', in which 'a single nuclear weapon contains almost ten times the explosive force delivered by all of the Allied air forces in the Second World War'. Peace therefore was 'the necessary rational end of rational men', and it was achievable: 'Let us examine our attitude toward peace itself. Too many of us think it is impossible. Too many of us think it is unreal. But that is dangerous, defeatist belief. It leads to the conclusion that war is inevitable – that mankind is doomed – that we are gripped by forces we cannot control.' He was open-hearted towards Russia:

> No government or social system is so evil that its people must be considered as lacking in virtue. As Americans, we find communism profoundly repugnant as a negation of personal freedom and dignity. But we can still hail the Russian people for their many achievements – in science and space, in economic and industrial growth, in culture and in acts of courage.

We have seen how he insisted that 'peace is a process – a way of solving problems' and urged practical steps in the spirit of what we call sovereign internationalism, including a ban on nuclear tests.[54] Kennedy was assassinated in November, and America slid further into the morass of the Vietnam War.[55] A later attempt to ease tensions during the détente of the early 1970s gave way to renewed Cold War in the Jimmy Carter years, intensified by the Soviet invasion of Afghanistan in December 1979. Positive peace was as elusive then as it is now.

2
TIME OF GREAT HOPES

The new political thinking returned to the issues raised by Eisenhower and Kennedy: how to end the arms race and militarism, and to grasp the prospect of a positive peace. Although welcomed as an indication that the Soviet Union was renouncing its hostility, sceptics in Washington perceived Gorbachev's agenda as a threat to US leadership. This prompted an ideological counter-offensive to seize the conceptual high ground. In the end two models of the post-Cold War order clashed, both with their roots in developments since 1945. The first appealed to Charter principles and sovereign internationalism, which in the regional context was formulated as the common European home. This encompassed the idea of the indivisibility of security – that no state could achieve security at the expense of another. The second drew on the undoubted achievement of the political West in emerging intact and unscathed from the Cold War. In the regional context this was formulated as Europe whole and free, and advanced in terms of the enlargement of the political West and the universal applicability of liberal internationalism. There appeared to be no limits to the Atlantic power system and democratic internationalism, generating an expansionary dynamic that was welcomed by the former Soviet bloc states but which increasingly alarmed Moscow. The two approaches engaged in an oblique yet acknowledged struggle, with both sides aware of the high stakes. However, one side was disarmed by its conviction that the Cold War really had ended, while the other continued the struggle – for the best and worst of motives – in new forms. This distorted endgame shaped the whole post-Cold War era, warping reality and the terms used to describe it.

NEW THINKING BEARS FRUIT

President Ronald Reagan's sunny optimism in the 1980s shrugged off the defeat in Southeast Asia and restored confidence in America's future. He built up American military power and condemned the Soviet Union as an 'evil empire', yet was receptive to the lure of new thinking, and worked with Gorbachev and other leaders to end the Cold War.[1] Gorbachev found a ready interlocutor in Reagan, and the joint statement following their first meeting in Geneva in November 1985 declared that 'a nuclear war cannot be won and must never be fought'.[2] At their meeting in Reykjavik in October 1986, Gorbachev proposed eliminating all nuclear weapons by the end of the century. The two came surprisingly close to agreeing on that, although in the end the idea was rejected as unrealistic by the US side, and no doubt Soviet military strategists would have baulked as well. Nevertheless, it prepared the ground for the Intermediate-Range Nuclear Force (INF) treaty signed in December 1987, which for the first time banned a whole category of strategic weapons. The US and USSR each eliminated missiles with a range of 500 to 5,500 kilometres and agreed to limits on the deployment of land-based cruise missiles.

The Strategic Arms Reduction Treaty (START), signed in July 1991, was the most ambitious arms control treaty ever, limiting each side's number of long-range missiles to 1,600. For Moscow, these agreements not only restrained the arms race but also reduced costs at a time of budgetary crisis. Economic factors were important, but most significantly Gorbachev shared Reagan's belief that nuclear weapons were an abomination, an unusable threat to humanity that should be eliminated as a category. The various agreements allowed the world's nuclear stockpile by January 2022 to fall to 12,705, 90 per cent of which belonged to the US and Russia. Limits were also placed on conventional deployments. The Conventional Forces in Europe

(CFE) treaty was signed in November 1990 between NATO and the Warsaw Pact, limiting the number and types of conventional weapons deployed in European Russia and Western Europe. The cuts fell disproportionately, with the Warsaw Pact destroying over 30,000 weapons and the Western allies hardly any. As a sign of coming troubles, this was 'the kind of settlement that would normally be imposed on a defeated state after a war'.[3] The same month the CFE was complemented by the CSCE's Vienna Document, implementing confidence-and security-building measures through the exchange of information and inspections. Periodically updated, the 2011 version became defunct following the onset of Cold War II in 2014.

In keeping with the postulates of the NPT, the Soviet Union adopted the doctrine of 'defence sufficiency', accompanied by cuts to deployed forces and defence expenditure, which at the time was running at some 15 to 20 per cent of Soviet GDP. A few months after his UN address, Gorbachev delivered his landmark 'common European home' speech at the Council of Europe in Strasbourg on 6 July 1989. He stressed the openness of the historical moment and the possibility of the Soviet Union joining a peaceful Europe:

> Now that the twentieth century is entering a concluding phase and both the postwar period and the Cold War are becoming a thing of the past, the Europeans have a truly unique chance – to play a role in building a new world, one that would be worthy of their past, of their economic and spiritual potential. . . . We are convinced that what they need is one Europe – peaceful and democratic, a Europe that maintains all its diversity and common humanistic ideas, a prosperous Europe that extends its hands to the rest of the world. A Europe that confidently advances into the future. It is in such a Europe that we visualise our own future.[4]

He talked of creating a single political community from Lisbon to Vladivostok, but he also stressed ideological pluralism and the coexistence of states with different social systems. The house that he envisaged would be a home with many different rooms. The European (Economic) Community, which would become the

European Union by the February 1992 Treaty of Maastricht, was to be part of a larger pan-continental entity. Although the details were vague, Gorbachev was calling for a new world order that was not ideologically homogenous but pluralistic and diverse. He called for 'a restructuring of the international order existing in Europe that would put the European common values in the forefront and make it possible to replace the traditional balance of forces with a balance of interests'. When Putin assumed the presidency in 2000, this was recast as the project for a 'greater Europe'. In the event, Euro-Atlanticism squeezed out Gorbachev-style pan-continentalism.

The ideological innovations of the NPT enhanced Moscow's status and reinforced its position as one of the main poles in international politics.[5] By placing the Soviet Union at the head of the movement towards the end of the Cold War, Gorbachev changed the terms of the debate. This 'shortcut to greatness' can be considered instrumental, as a way of boosting Moscow's status by shifting the focus away from hard economic power to the more intangible aspirations for a new peace order. This is often dismissed as naïve idealism, yet it was rooted in the same aspirations that had given rise to the Charter international system in the first place – to rid the world of the scourge of war and to create a more cooperative international order. This was accompanied by the dismantling of the institutions of communist rule within the Soviet Union and the creation of new instruments of democratic representation. Gorbachev's misfortune was that his challenge to Soviet-style state socialism was superseded by Yeltsin's separate challenge based on the national reawakening of the republics, with Russia in the lead. Gorbachev repudiated the logic of cold war, but Yeltsin repudiated the logic of the Soviet Union itself.

CHINA'S COMMUNISM OF REFORM

China's path to greatness was grounded on more solid political and economic foundations. China also supports the Charter peace order as the universal framework for international politics and development, and on that basis aligns with Russia to reject the 'monist' view that the liberal international order is the only viable one on offer. Monism in this context simply means the rejection of the pluralist view (advanced by Gorbachev) that the world is made up of different types of legitimate social systems (regime types), reflecting societies at different levels of development and with different historical trajectories and needs. Instead, post-Cold War democratisation theory restored the idea of unilinear development that was redolent of the discredited modernisation ideas of the 1950s and 1960s, in which the more advanced societies purportedly show the less developed their future. Modernisation at the time was taken to mean Westernisation on the US model. Although some fundamental traits are common to all developed societies, the rise of China demonstrates that modernity can take different forms.[6] From this perspective, there is no single 'right side of history'.

China always rejected the view that modernisation would make everyone look like America, but it also rejected what it considered the naivety of Gorbachev's reform communism. His ideas found little support among China's leaders, and in fact reinforced their view that ideological revisionism and reforms of the Gorbachev type were dangerous and destabilising. Relations between the PRC and Moscow were never smooth, although the Soviet Union contributed much to China's early development. The Moscow – Beijing axis dissolved following Soviet leader Nikita Khrushchev's condemnation of Stalin in his 'secret speech' in February 1956. Amid intensifying recriminations, border clashes on Damansky Island in 1969 brought the two communist powers to the brink of war. By 1973, adroit diplomacy by Washington brought China into closer alignment with the US, while Moscow countered with détente. In July 1986, Gorbachev's 'common Asian home' speech in Vladivostok announced concessions, including the withdrawal of Soviet troops from Mongolia, the Russian Far East (RFE) and Afghanistan, and recognition of the Chinese definition of the border along the Amur and Ussuri rivers.[7] Beijing opened a consulate in Leningrad, and the USSR in Shanghai, and there were also economic and cultural agreements. The damaging Sino-Soviet split began to heal and the two countries set out on a path towards alignment that has deepened ever since.

This set the stage for Gorbachev's state visit to Beijing in 1989, the first by a Soviet leader since Khrushchev in 1959. At the summit on 15–18 May, state-to-state relations were normalised, and connections between the two ruling parties restored. The Chinese side insisted that there could be no return to Soviet dominance and instead relations would be based on equality, independence and sovereignty. There was also talk of a common front against the US, although disagreement over Cambodia remained. The two sides agreed to reduce military tensions along the border and signed some economic agreements. However, while rapprochement was achieved in the international sphere, the political trajectories of the two countries were very different.

Under the leadership of Deng Xiaoping from 1978, China pursued a unique developmental path, the *communism of reform* in which the Communist Party of China (CPC) applied market mechanisms to achieve economic modernisation. China avoided Russian-style economic reforms, which in the absence of a supportive geopolitical environment had catastrophic social and political effects, and instead devised a unique combination of statism and marketisation, with spectacular results.[8] This model of authoritarian state capitalism was in sharp contrast to the disastrous economic reforms pursued by Gorbachev. His model of reform communism fizzled out amid widespread alienation from any form of socialist renewal. By contrast, the communism of reform proved successful in modernising the country, although it left unresolved questions about democratic citizenship and political inclusion. The Chinese model of bureaucratic modernisation installed a relatively unaccountable and irremovable politicised technocracy. Its meritocratic ethos was unable to overcome the 'Leninist trap', in which stability is mechanical and requires ceaseless interventions. The system can deliver enormous public goods, yet organic and spontaneous forms of social integration are suppressed. Gorbachev's visit encouraged those who sought to apply his principles of reform communism, including greater openness and democratisation, to break out of the trap. Student demonstrations catalysed by the death of the reformer Hu Yaobang on 15 April were inspired by Gorbachev's visit to call for democratic reforms.

The Chinese leadership had other ideas, and crushed the Tiananmen Square protest encampment in the centre of Beijing on 4 June. The dominance of the CPC was reasserted. Although since then there have been moments of relative democratisation, the overall strategy remains that of the communism of reform and Leninist CPC leadership. This delivered economic growth and the transformation of the country, but political liberalisation is not on the agenda. Socialism 'with Chinese characteristics' left party rule intact. The country avoided the fate of the Soviet Union, but it also foreclosed greater openness and a new relationship between the state and society. China's rejection of new political thinking and bureaucratic consolidation achieved unprecedented economic growth, but also insulated it from the euphoria that accompanied the end of the Cold War in Europe.

THE CONTESTED PEACE

As the military contest receded in the late 1980s, the field of struggle shifted to the concepts and ideas that would shape the new order. Reagan's successor, George H.W. Bush, and his national security adviser, Brent Scowcroft, argued that America should counter Gorbachev's transformational initiatives, otherwise the Europeans would lose their orientation to the US.[9] Bush was condemned for his lacklustre response to the Soviet reforms, but in fact he seized the diplomatic and ideological initiative. He was criticised for failing to formulate a long-term vision for US strategic leadership, but in practice he successfully re-imposed US discursive hegemony. He regained the intellectual initiative by challenging the common European home rhetoric, and thus the pan-continental perspective. The White House perceived desperation in Gorbachev's manoeuvres and was irked by the 'bold public proposals or acts of "one-upmanship" designed to portray Washington as the recalcitrant party'.[10] A battle of ideas ensued. This was an exercise in intellectual hegemony with profound implications for the type of peace that would emerge. Gorbachev's urge to transcend the Cold War was based on a genuine dialogical transformation of the relationship between Soviet Russia and the West – one in which both sides changed, rather than one simply being taught by the other.[11] The Soviet Union/Russia was ready to learn, but resolutely refused to become part of a master – student relationship. By contrast, the Western perspective meant that there was little scope for such pluralism. There was a conscious attempt to retake the initiative and to reassert American leadership in shaping the terms on which the new peace order would be built. This was driven in part by Cold War hegemonic ambitions, but it was also shaped by an understandable (although blinkered) sense that there was little that the political West could learn from Russia.

The competitive logic generating cold war was not transcended. The US was not ready to cede the ideological initiative to Moscow. While welcomed by Western public opinion, Washington feared that Moscow was seeking to gain geopolitical advantage in advancing its ideas on a new type of post-cold war peace. As far as the US was concerned, this was a 'propaganda effort ... timed to create and exploit divisions in NATO'.[12] A famous article in *Time* magazine argued that Gorbachev's initiatives could entice 'Western Europe into neutered neutralism'. The piece went on to note that there was a danger that the Soviets would gain the moral initiative, and that Gorbachev's new world order would make security alliances such as NATO and the Warsaw Pact redundant, shift resources from the military to domestic needs and, sin of sins (the Gaullist 'heresy'), encourage moves towards European integration on a pan-continental scale. Gorbachev appealed to a strengthened Charter international system, but Washington countered by advancing its own model of liberal internationalism. Gorbachev's 'common home' rhetoric was to be challenged by a narrative of 'common ideals', rendering the alliance of necessity into one of shared values.[13]

This was a remarkably prescient analysis. The struggle now became one not only over models of world order, but who had the right to set world order agendas. Gorbachev eloquently set out his view of a transformed model of international politics based on trust and pluralism. What was to become the European Union busied itself with its own transformation from a largely economic association into a more political body, but ultimately failed to support

Gorbachev's pan-continental agenda. This is hardly surprising, since it would inevitably have diluted the centrality of Brussels institutions and forced it to share agenda-setting with Moscow. Instead, it became trapped in a cycle of subordination to Washington's concerns, despite striving for what would later be called 'strategic autonomy'.[14] France as usual took the lead in the autonomy strand of European thinking, and during the presidency of François Mitterrand (1981–95) advanced the idea of a 'confederation of Europe', which took up earlier Gaullist ideas of a Europe 'from the Atlantic to the Urals'. This chimed with broader ideas for pan-continental unification, but the perceived imperative of Euro-Atlantic unity (defended above all by the UK) stymied such initiatives.

Bush outlined his ideas in a speech in May 1989 in Mainz, where he talked of a 'Europe whole and free'. He argued: 'The forces of freedom are putting the Soviet status quo on the defensive. And in the West we have succeeded because we've been faithful to our values and our vision. And on the other side of the rusting Iron Curtain, their vision failed.' The observation was certainly correct, but it reinserted the logic of victory (and commensurately defeat) into the Cold War endgame. Talk of victory generated resentment on the side of the alleged 'losers', thus in the end undermining the putative victory itself. This sort of language was explicitly avoided by Gorbachev and the Soviet leadership, framing it as a common victory for all – a view adopted by all subsequent Russian leaders. A gulf opened up between Gorbachev's pluralist vision of a Europe in which different social orders could amicably coexist and the Bush model of a Europe united on the principles of liberalism and competitive markets, and ultimately a US-dominated security order. The division would later tear the continent apart.

Cold War I ended in the competitive spirit of cold war, which naturally was no end at all. The struggle assumed a new aspect and was conducted with different methods, but the result was the perpetuation of negative peace in new forms. Bush insisted that 'The Cold War began with the division of Europe. It can only end when Europe is whole.' He repudiated the transformative agenda and instead advanced a programme based on enlargement. The peace would be liberal democratic or there would be no peace at all. At the core of his vision was the proposal to 'strengthen and broaden the Helsinki process to promote free elections and political pluralism in Eastern Europe. As the forces of freedom and democracy rise in the East, so should our expectations. And weaving together the slender threads of freedom in the East will require much from the Western democracies.'[15] This represented a powerful vision of European unity, but it was based on the extension of an existing order rather than the transformation of that order in light of the changed historical context. Gorbachev's dialogical approach was rejected and instead an expansive logic was applied, based on the view that history was on the side of the West, and all that now had to be done was to implement an already proven model. The 'end of history' imposed a logic that was as implacable as the Marxist – Leninist dialectic that it replaced. The seeds of renewed conflict fell on fertile soil.

TOWARDS VICTORY

A few months later the communist systems in Eastern Europe collapsed, and it soon became clear that the Soviet bloc as a whole was doomed. The coercive aspect of the post-1945 Yalta – Potsdam international settlement was repudiated. The Malta summit between Bush and Gorbachev of 2–3 December 1989 tried to make sense of it all. Focusing on the future of the two Germanys, the meeting represented not only a 'power transition', when the US realised that the Soviet Union was no longer a credible rival, but also a shift in models of world order.[16] Bush and Scowcroft describe how they planned to flood Gorbachev with proposals to confuse the Soviet team and to shift the initiative to the American side. In this way Gorbachev's transformative ideas would be sidelined.[17] However, containment was to give way to cooperation accompanied by the transformation of NATO into more of a political agency, and there was even talk of its dissolution. The Malta summit represents 'the real end of the Cold War'.[18] Key security issues were discussed, but political issues were also prominent, including a commitment to 'democratic values'. By then Gorbachev had fully embraced these values, but they were embedded in an expansive US-led power system, a matter of increasing concern in Moscow.

At the time this was lost in the tumultuous and urgent flow of events. The old bloc politics were dissolving and it seemed that everything was possible. Yet one bloc reconstituted itself in a more vigorous form. In substantive terms Malta offered little more than a modification of the status quo.[19] The meeting was followed by epochal discussions over whether a united Germany would join NATO in whole or in part, accompanied by an enduring debate whether Western leaders promised that NATO would not move beyond the united Germany, an issue to which we will return. The promise of 1989 for Gorbachev and later Russian leaders was an entirely new logic of power in Europe and the world. It appeared that there was a unique opportunity to overcome not only the specific forms of Cold War confrontation but to transcend the logic of ideological conflict that had given rise to it in the first place. Europe would be united as a political community of free nations based on sovereign internationalism, transforming international politics to advance the Charter system and its values.

Bush had rather different ideas, calling for a 'new world order' in his address to the US Congress on 11 September 1990. Bush stressed that there was 'no substitute for US leadership'. In the context of the crisis provoked by Iraq's seizure of Kuwait the previous month this was understandable, but he insisted that, even in 'troubled times', a

> new world order . . . can emerge: a new era – freer from the threat of terror, stronger in the pursuit of justice, and more secure in the quest for peace. An era in which the nations of the world, East and West, North and South, can prosper and live in harmony. A hundred generations have searched for this elusive path to peace, while a thousand wars raged across the span of human endeavor. Today that new world is struggling to be born, a world quite different from the one we've known. A world where the rule of law supplants the rule of the jungle. A world in which nations recognize the shared responsibility for freedom and justice.[20]

This was a powerful vision of a new type of peace. In the First Gulf War the US and Soviet leaders came together to reverse Saddam Hussein's occupation and the independence of Kuwait was restored. This was sovereign internationalism at work, founded on the assertion of Charter values. For Moscow (although not without internal divisions) this was an example of the cooperative management of global affairs, but for Washington US leadership and its necessity was reasserted. The 'new world order' proposed by Bush 'meant simply that the old Western one would be extended worldwide'.[21] The USSR, and later Russia (and indeed Europe), were consigned a subordinate role in this system.

WHEN A PROMISE IS NOT A PROMISE

The question of German reunification quickly came to the fore. In his meeting with Gorbachev on 9 February 1990, the US secretary of state, James Baker, posed the fundamental question that has provoked a torrent of commentary. He asked: 'Would you prefer to see a united Germany outside of NATO, independent and with no US forces, or would you prefer a unified Germany be tied to NATO, with assurances that NATO's jurisdiction would not shift one inch eastward from its present positions?' It was a question rather than a pledge, and Gorbachev agreed that, put that way, he preferred the latter, although he insisted, 'It goes without saying that a broadening of the NATO zone is not acceptable.' While Baker may have posed the question, it was part of a cascade of at least thirty assurances by Western leaders, including the German chancellor Helmut Kohl, the German foreign minister Hans-Dietrich Genscher, French president Mitterrand and British prime minister Margaret Thatcher to the effect that NATO would not move beyond the enlarged Germany.[22] Gorbachev agreed to the Two plus Four (the two Germanies and the four allied powers – the US, UK, France and USSR) formula, and after intense negotiations agreed to German reunification largely on Western terms. He accepted the Western proposition that it would be better to have all of Germany in NATO than a neutral Germany outside. But did the Western powers agree that there would be no enlargement beyond the united Germany?[23] The Atlantic allies feared that a neutral Germany would mean the end of NATO. Soviet agreement that the unified Germany would be part of NATO represented a major victory. This was accompanied by verbal assurances that the alliance would not move to the east to absorb former Warsaw Pact countries and that it would be transformed to reflect the end of the Cold War.[24] However, there was no clear prohibition on NATO adding new members.

According to Mary Elise Sarotte, who has written an important work on the subject, the earlier promises were tempered by the Final Settlement treaty on German unification of 12 September 1990. There was discussion about including a 'not one inch' stipulation, but the treaty in the end allowed NATO to encompass Eastern Germany. Expansion at this point was confined to the eastern part of the united Germany, but the settlement did not explicitly preclude further enlargement. Once the precedent of enlargement had been established, the US assumed this allowed further expansion, whereas Moscow took the narrow view that the agreement was limited to Germany.[25] Advocates of expansion stress that the promise was made to the leader of a defunct state, and therefore it no longer applied. However, Moscow was still Moscow, the capital of the continuer state, Russia, that assumed the legal status of the Soviet Union. There was no formal agreement prohibiting further expansion, yet by any normal standards a promise is a promise, and it is an exercise in bad faith to suggest otherwise.[26] The perceived betrayal permanently poisoned relations between Russia and the West.

The deception appears to have been strategic and deliberate. This was obscured by the fast pace of events at the time. How the non-enlargement promise could apply to countries still part of the Warsaw Pact has cast doubt on what Baker and other Western leaders had in mind.[27] Joshua Shifrinson argues that US leaders repeatedly raised the issue of NATO enlargement during the unification negotiations, promising Moscow that the new European security architecture would have a place for the Soviet Union. The assurances were designed to exploit Soviet weaknesses and American strengths to ensure that the US would have a 'free hand in Europe following German unification – allowing it to decide whether and how to expand the US presence on the continent – even while telling Soviet leaders that Soviet interests would be respected'. The US assurances were part of a ploy to get Gorbachev to endorse unification, hence the later expansion could not have violated the 'spirit' of the agreements, since the whole exercise was conducted in the spirit of duplicity. 'Baldly stated', Shifrinson concludes, 'the United States floated a cooperative grand design for postwar Europe in discussion with the Soviets in 1990, while creating a system dominated by the United States.'[28]

Moscow was outwitted in the negotiations. The tactical victory opened the door to NATO enlargement, but this represented a catastrophic strategic blunder. The opportunity for creating a transformed, equitable and durable European security order was squandered, and instead the fragile negative peace would sooner or later be challenged. In the end, revision took the most catastrophic form possible. Putin bears responsibility for pulling the trigger on 24 February 2022 when Russian forces invaded Ukraine, but the gun was primed by the European security impasse of the preceding three decades.

NATO membership for Soviet bloc countries at the time was almost inconceivable. Nevertheless, Gorbachev is held responsible for failing to secure this agreement in writing, and thus opening the door to NATO's enlargement to what the later US secretary of defence, Robert Gates, called 'the suburbs of Moscow'. The Kremlin failed to negotiate a better post-Cold War peace because the 'Soviet leaders genuinely embraced utopian ideas about a new welcoming European community, failing to conceive of any alternatives', accompanied soon after by the Soviet collapse.[29] Gorbachev himself made contradictory statements, complaining to the *Bild* newspaper in 2009 that the West had tricked Russia: 'Many people in the West were secretly rubbing their hands and felt something like the flush of victory, including those who had promised us "We will not move 1 centimetre further east"'. However, in October 2014 he told the *Kommersant* newspaper that in 1989–90, 'The topic of "NATO expansion" was never discussed; it was not raised in those years. I am saying this with a full sense of responsibility.'[30] However, numerous Western leaders promised that NATO would remain largely as it had historically taken shape, which clearly implies no enlargement, although this was nowhere formulated in formal terms. It was a commitment but not a formal promise.

THE CLASH OF NEW WORLD ORDERS

At the Malta summit on 3 December 1989, Bush and Gorbachev announced that the Cold War was over. Bush promised that the US would not respond 'with flamboyance or arrogance that would complicate USSR relations', and instead noted the opportunities:

> For forty years, the Western alliance stood together in the cause of freedom, and now with reform under way in the Soviet Union, we stand at the threshold of a brand-new era of US – Soviet relations. And it is within our grasp – to overcome the division of Europe and end the military confrontation there.[31]

In July 1990, the leaders of NATO met in London and declared:

> Europe has entered a new, promising era. Central and Eastern Europe is liberating itself. The Soviet Union has embarked on the long journey toward a free society. The walls that once confined people and ideas are collapsing. Europeans are determining their own destiny. They are choosing freedom. They are choosing economic liberty. They are choosing peace. They are choosing a Europe whole and free. As a consequence, this alliance must and will adapt.[32]

In the same month, the former enemies agreed on the unification of Germany. For so long stuck in rigid confrontation and divided by the iron curtain, Europe was changing. New ideas and leadership opportunities provided a unique opportunity for the creation of a positive peace order. Various 'new wars' within states and over borders continued and West Asia remained locked in conflict, but relations between states at the global level entered a new phase.[33] International politics appeared on the cusp of transformation.

However, two models of post-cold war order – sovereign and liberal internationalism (now recast as liberal hegemony) – were on offer, presented in the idiom of the day as a 'common European home' or 'Europe whole and free'. Both drew on the postwar settlement, and Charter principles were incorporated into the various documents of the time. However, the contradiction between the declared sovereign right of nations to choose their own security alignment and the indivisibility of security was present in the founding document of what was to become the new era, the Helsinki Final Act of August 1975. This contradiction was then repeated in all the fundamental documents of the post-Cold War era. The Charter of Paris for a New Europe, adopted on 21 November 1990, heralded 'a new era of democracy, peace and unity', stressing that 'Europe is liberating itself from its past'.[34] The focus was on the temporal challenge – overcoming the past – but the new spatial order entailed the logic of enlargement. The tension between these two logics, each rational in its own terms, contained the seeds of later conflicts.

At the time there were 'great hopes' for a new peace settlement.[35] On 1 February 1992, just a month after the independent Russian state was formally born, Bush and Yeltsin signed the Camp David Declaration proclaiming that 'Russia and the United States do not regard each other as potential adversaries. From now on, the relationship will be characterised by friendship and partnership'.[36] The Charter for American – Russian Partnership and Friendship signed in Washington on 17 June 1992 characterised the relationship as a 'strategic partnership'. However, this was already belied by the imperatives of US domestic politics. Facing a tough re-election fight that year, in his State of the Union Address in January Bush repudiated the notion of a common victory and instead argued, 'The Cold War didn't end; it was won.'[37]

The language of 'mature strategic partnership' assumed that some sort of US – Russian condominium would jointly manage global affairs. This was certainly Moscow's view. As a former superpower endowed with a nuclear armoury matching that of the US and as the 'continuer state' inheriting the Soviet Union's permanent seat on the

UNSC, as well as its rights and obligations, there were grounds for such a belief. This was reinforced by the moral credit that Moscow assumed that it had earned in voluntarily ending the Cold War and dismantling 'imperial Russia'. However, such moral credit weighs little in the scales of international politics. In his typically unsentimental manner, Zbigniew Brzezinski, President Jimmy Carter's national security adviser from 1977 to 1981, punctured such pretensions, arguing that 'it was devoid of either international or domestic realism'. America 'was neither inclined to share global power with Russia nor could it, even if it had wanted to do so'.[38] The new Russia was far too weak and diminished to be a real partner for Washington. By the time Russia became stronger it was perceived as less an ally than a rival. The rhetoric of partnership remained until 2012, although Russia's slide into authoritarianism rendered the country a less appealing collaborator. The relationship became marked by hostility and confrontation.

Old battle lines were restored across Europe and shaped a global second Cold War. This is the 'lost peace' referred to in the title of this book. Sceptics argue that these aspirations were from the outset an illusion, reminiscent of earlier promises that a new era had dawned. When the US entered World War I in 1916, President Wilson averred that this was 'the war to end all wars', only for the world to be engulfed in conflict again little more than two decades later. After the terrible devastation of that war there was a new commitment after 1945 to create an international system that could avert another catastrophe, compounded by the growing shadow of a nuclear apocalypse. The year 1989 was another such juncture, although there was no institutional or conceptual innovation. Instead, the principles and norms at the heart of the system created in 1945 were affirmed. This was to be the 'new world order' much spoken of at the time.

However, the Charter system harbours two versions of a more cooperative multilateral order. After 1989, two new peace orders were on offer, both drawn from the 1945 settlement and subsequent agreements but emphasising different aspects. While the US and its allies stressed the 'democratic' character of a post-Cold War world, emphasising the rule of law, competitive markets and globalisation, Russia looked to the sovereignty side of the equation and the autonomy that it had recently gained through the collapse of the Soviet Union. This pitched democratic against sovereign internationalism. Both drew on Charter-based multilateralism, but the one focused on the application of universal rules and freedom of choice while the other warned against interference in the internal affairs of states and stressed the indivisibility of security. The competing formulations were explicit in the Helsinki Final Act and the Charter of Paris. Democratic internationalists insisted on the right of the newly freed post-communist states to choose their own allies and alliance system; whereas Russia insisted on the principle that one state should not enhance its security at the expense of another. This inevitably raised the spectre of old-style spheres of influence, buffer states and limited sovereignty for countries caught in between, all ideas that had been discredited by the twentieth-century wars. Moscow countered that the bloc politics associated with the right to choose membership of an alliance system reproduced Cold War thinking and old-style hostilities. The great hopes were dashed.

3
HOW THE PEACE WAS LOST

The common victory at the end of Cold War I soon dissolved into conflicting interpretations over what type of peace would emerge. This was also the case after World War II, and in both cases the outcome was cold war. The international system established in 1945 provides the overarching framework for international politics, but within the larger system a number of sub-orders were created. Up to 1989 the Soviet Union had its own bloc of allies, while the US sponsored a liberal international order combining the Atlantic military alliance and an economic system based on open markets and economic interdependence. This was the political West, a distinctive creation of the Cold War era but with roots reaching back at least to Wilsonian internationalism of the interwar period. The Soviet collapse now opened up unparalleled opportunities for the political West, which if used wisely and with restraint could have become a fundamental pillar of a positive peace order. Instead, the more ambitious factions of the political West (neoconservatives and liberal interventionists) combined to assert a one-sided victory discourse. The Cold War was perpetuated in new forms. The year 1989 did not in retrospect mark such a decisive break. Instead of a transformative shift towards 'peace as a process' within the framework of sovereign internationalism, cold war practices generated a negative peace – a peace defined as the expansion of a specific order, rather than the end of all sub-orders (blocs) in their entirety. The liberal anti-pluralism of the expansive political West was associated with political freedom, competitive markets and the rule of law, but it was also a geopolitical power system focused on the US. This provoked the resistance of sovereign internationalists and charter liberals. An epochal confrontation was in the making.

THE ARC OF AMBITION

Who would define the character of the peace? The two peace orders offered at the end of the Cold War were rooted in associated but separate projects. One claimed universality through its institutionalisation in the Charter international system, while the other sought to generalise the experience of the political West as a model for successful political and economic development. The political West is the security community that took shape during the Cold War, but represents only the most recent and contingent component of 'the West' as a whole. The cultural West reaches back into antiquity, while the civilisational West came to dominate the world for 500 years in the age of imperialism. The political West is a geopolitical construct though is not limited by geography to the Atlantic region but includes Asian and other allies. At its heart is the US power system, which after 1989 believed that its triumph over the Soviet adversary demonstrated the need to spread its power and values globally. The project was rich in hubris and was ultimately doomed not only to fail but also to corrupt the heartlands of the political West itself.[1]

The implication took some time to emerge. At first the two peace orders – the sovereign international and liberal hegemonic – appeared compatible and even mutually reinforcing. The two had much in common, and it was on this basis that Gorbachev's reforms were conducted. He believed that the common commitment to the Charter system would allow different countries and social systems not only to coexist but to thrive together. Theoretically attractive, this failed to take into account the fact that the US after 1945 had created its own sub-order within the Charter system, as had the Soviet Union. Just because Moscow gave up on its own system, largely because of the failure of that order to deliver the public goods that it had promised, did not mean that Washington had to do the same. In fact, the chaos that attended the final Soviet years and the disintegration of the country in December 1991 only confirmed the superiority of the US-led system. The Russia that emerged out of the debris of the Soviet Union was a much-reduced power, and only after a decade of travails could it reassert itself.

The US and its European allies were triumphant, but the victory scattered the seeds of hubris.[2] Power and values were mutually reinforcing, with ideas of freedom, democracy and open markets reinforced by a dominant security system. The package proved irresistible to the other side of the former 'iron curtain'. The liberal peace order after 1989 expanded ideologically politically and later militarily to the East. Emerging from its long immersion in the Soviet communist project, Russia also sought to become part of the liberal peace, but advanced its own ideas about how the new peace should be shaped. Russia was a much-weakened power, but it insisted then (and later with increasing vigour) on a model of peace that referred to sovereign rather than liberal internationalism. Moscow argued that the Charter international system was not the property of any single state or constellation of states, however attractive and successful they may have been, but the patrimony of all of humanity. The impartiality and universality of the principles embedded in the UN Charter and the body of international humanitarian law developed on its basis was asserted. This stance later became the basis of Russia's neo-revisionism: condemning the perceived usurpation of universal principles by a particular power system, while asserting continued loyalty to the Charter system itself. This long-term attempt to thread the needle of resistance to the political West while appealing to the universalism of Charter internationalism in the short-term failed to find an effective political formulation.

The NPT envisaged a new sort of international politics, but the realities of power hit home as the Soviet Union disintegrated. Russia painfully transformed its economy and society in a decade of turmoil accompanied by repeated political crises. The armed confrontation in October 1993 between Yeltsin and parliament was followed by the Kremlin ramming through a hyper-presidential constitution in

December of that year. The brutal war in Chechnya from December 1994 exposed the weakness of the Russian military and the shoddiness of its politics. Russia could hardly be reckoned the equal of the Soviet Union let alone comparable to the political West, hence the patronising and denigratory stance adopted by the latter. Russia became the continuer state, assuming the Soviet Union's permanent seat on the UNSC as well as its legal and financial obligations. Although armed with nuclear weapons, its claims to great-power status lacked the economic and political muscle of its predecessor.

The unilateralism of the liberal peace order was condemned as usurping the prerogatives of the Charter system. The credibility of the critique was undermined by the brutality with which Moscow prosecuted the two Chechen wars (1994–6, 1999–2002), domestic chaos and disorder in the 1990s and then the growing authoritarianism of the 2000s. The transition to the market led to large-scale immiseration, accompanied by repeated loss of people's savings (1992 and 1998). The poverty, insecurity, criminality and corruption was made all the starker by the rise of the oligarchs – individuals who took advantage of their proximity to government to carve out business empires based on the appropriation of former Soviet assets. The democratic aspirations of 1991 were further subverted when in 1996 Yeltsin was up for re-election. By then he was physically debilitated, but after a ferocious campaign (supported financially by the oligarchs and by American election technologists) he was duly re-elected.[3] Yeltsin repeatedly railed against American high-handedness and opposed NATO enlargement, but the US president, Bill Clinton, understood that he would be more malleable than his communist adversary. Despite the travails, by the late 1990s the rudiments of a market economy had been established. In the 2000s Russia enjoyed unprecedented economic growth of 7 per cent per annum as it benefited from the rise in global commodity prices fuelled by China's insatiable demand. The boom ended with the global financial crisis of 2008–9, and thereafter Russia's growth never returned to previous levels, indicating the need for a less statist economic paradigm. That entailed structural reform, something that Putin refused to undertake since it would inevitably challenge his model of managed democracy.

Russian foreign policy developed in the shadow of this reality. For the next three decades, policy veered between acquiescence and resistance, but over time cooperation gave way to an entrenched conflict. The relatively peaceful transition from the Soviet to the Russian polity perpetuated traditional geopolitical and statist impulses. The strategic culture is shaped by an overriding concern with security derived from the country's vulnerable geographical position on a vast plain with few defensible and stable borders. Security concerns naturally rank higher in countries not protected by oceans and friendly neighbours. Russia had been repeatedly invaded from the west (Poland, Sweden, France, Germany twice, plus the Allied intervention during the Civil War of 1918–20), accompanied by various proxy conflicts during the Cold War. Soviet elite structures were inherited almost in their entirety, especially in the security and military establishments, ensuring a high degree of continuity with earlier traditions. Domestic transformation did not become a peace project of its own, and instead security concerns predominated. An administrative regime consolidated its power by presenting itself as the defender of the state, but in so doing it undermined the autonomy of constitutional procedures and rules. Democracy was increasingly managed, while the rule of law gave way to the instrumental use of law to achieve regime goals. The consolidation of authoritarianism at home reinforced distrust abroad.

HOSTAGES TO GEOPOLITICS

The US revelled in the sort of dominance it had never enjoyed before. In 1945 the US was by far the most powerful state, but it was challenged by the Soviet Union and, after 1949, by China and the communist world. Communism as an ideology and its geopolitical manifestation in Europe now dissolved, and liberal democracy appeared to be the wave of the future. The democratisation literature of the time was suffused with the linear view of history, whereby sooner or later all countries would end up as democracies. There was much discussion of the best institutional arrangements to achieve the transition, accompanied by a literature on the advantages of open economies rather than state-directed economic development. These were important issues and the arguments in favour of democracy and competitive markets were well made and retain their relevance to this day. However, the practice of democracy turned out to be far messier than envisaged.

In Russia, status concerns and the yearning to be recognised as a great power of the first rank were never abandoned. Stephen Kotkin argues that geopolitics will predominate until 'Russian rulers make the strategic choice to abandon the impossible quest to become a great-power equal of the West and choose instead to live alongside it and focus on Russia's internal development'.[4] In starkly pragmatic terms, the argument is right – resistance to the expanding political West perpetuated cold war behaviours. From this perspective, the idea of some sort of substantive Western – Russian partnership was no more than a 'mirage'.[5] If leaders from Gorbachev to Putin had accepted that they had lost the Cold War, then there was nothing to stop Russia joining the West and enjoying its benefits. The price would have been the reduced status of a legacy great power, like France, Germany or Japan.

Three factors prevented Russia acquiescing in this manner. First, the Gorbachevian perspective asserted that the universal principles embodied in the Charter international system provided the framework for some sort of positive peace, in which Russia would become part of a transformed European community. In other words, the resistance was ideologically and normatively grounded, imbuing the Russian leadership with the sense that they stood on the moral high ground. From this perspective, increased demonisation by the West simply did not make sense. It was, as the Kremlin repeatedly argued, the political West that was acting as the revisionist power in its unilateral attacks on Serbia, Iraq and Libya, whereas Russia's intervention, as in Syria from August 2015, was at the invitation of the Damascus leadership. Second, even when Russia did try to join the institutions of the political West, above all NATO and the EU, it was rebuffed. Russia was not like the other post-communist countries, and its size, traditions and potential meant that Moscow would demand a leadership role that the Western powers, above all

Washington, were not willing to grant. In part this was prompted by the third factor, Russia's failure to undergo a democratic transformation of the sort required by the Atlantic alliance. Russian democracy in the 1990s was brutal and unforgiving, but it existed. Putin's model of 'sovereign democracy' eroded many of the earlier gains, such as competitive elections, executive accountability and relative judicial independence.

Auguries of renewed conflict were present from the beginning. The NPT's critics accepted some of its postulates, including the need to wind down the Cold War in conditions of relative economic stagnation and competition with China, but they rejected what they argued was the naïve view of the possibility of some essential harmony between the Soviet Union and the Western states. Gorbachev was condemned for giving up the hard-won achievements of the Soviet Union, and before that the Russian Empire, for negligible if any gains. The overall picture is well presented by Jack Matlock, US ambassador to the USSR from 1987 to 1991, who worked closely with President Ronald Reagan and Gorbachev to bring the Cold War to an end. He notes how 'myths and false ideologies' led the US astray:

> Instead of working to create an international order that would address the issues most important to its own security – an order in which power and responsibility would be shared, local conflicts contained, and weapons of mass destruction brought under reliable control – the United States allowed itself to be distracted. It involved its military forces in struggles hardly relevant to American well-being . . . The Clinton administration's decision to expand NATO to the east rather than draw Russia into a cooperative arrangement to ensure European security undermined the prospects of democracy in Russia.[6]

Despite the numerous declarations of friendship, the institutional and ideological framework remained that of a negative peace. The spectre of the Cold War had not been laid to rest but haunted the shadows. Moscow came to the view that a new type of 'victor's peace' had been imposed, as Germany believed after 1918 (*Das Diktat*), spawning once again the 'Versailles syndrome' of resentment and sense of betrayal. Just as sections of postwar German society believed that the November 1918 armistice represented a betrayal, so part of the Russian elite nurtured festering grievances. The political West remained much the same as it had been during the Cold War and expanded to the east, encroaching on what Russia considered its sphere of security if not interests. Nothing approximating a 'common European home' had been established, and instead new dividing lines emerged as the East European states joined the expanding West.

WORLD ORDER INSIDE OUT

John Ikenberry argues that the postwar liberal order did not begin as a global order but was created 'inside' half of the bipolar system, part of the 'larger geopolitical project of waging a global Cold War'. Its institutions and arrangements were thereby part of the development of what we call the 'political West', the unique combination of power and norms tied to the emergence of the US as a global power. Ikenberry then makes the crucial point: 'When the Cold War ended, the inside order became the outside order'. The Soviet collapse removed the other half of the bipolar system, and allowed liberal internationalism to globalise: 'the American order expanded outward'.[7] A sub-order designed to fight the Cold War now claimed to be the system itself. This gave birth to the 'great substitution', with fateful consequences for post-Cold War international politics and for liberal internationalism itself. It meant that power and norms became entwined, displacing sovereign internationalism in favour of democratism – the instrumental application of democracy promotion to achieve geopolitical goals. This does not mean that the struggle for democracy, human dignity and constitutional government – the core principles of Charter internationalism – became any less important, but it was now entwined with considerations of American power.[8] Anti-hegemonic alignments seek to return the US-led rules-based international order to its 'insider' status: as one sub-order among others, subordinate to the imperatives of the Charter system and its associated charter liberalism.

The apparent triumph of the political West and the absence of ideo-logical and geopolitical alternatives radicalised American hegemony. No longer constrained by its 'inside' character, it sought to become the entirety of the 'outside'. The neoconservative perspective was expressed by Charles Krauthammer in his lecture of 18 September 1990, later published as 'The Unipolar Moment', in which he talked about American primacy. He curtly dismissed the view that the bipolar struc-ture of the Cold War would give way to multipolarity, and instead argued that the US had become the unchallenged superpower.[9] This was, as David Calleo argues, a 'revolutionary' proposition, since a world domi-nated by a single superpower 'would mean . . . for the first time in modern history a world without a general balance of power'.[10] If multipolarity is derived solely from the distribution of material capacities, then US primacy was unquestionable. A decade later Krauthammer argued that he had been too modest to posit a 'unipolar moment': it was in fact a 'unipolar era'.[11] In practice, this 'era' came to an end as US primacy was contested by Russia and China, inaugurating something akin to multipolarity, while domestic political polarisation undermined confi-dence in hegemonic ambitions abroad.[12] As Calleo puts it, the US was 'slow to see, let alone accept, what to many others seems a more probable and desirable future – a plural world with several centres of power'.[13]

Krauthammer dismissed 'pious talk about a new multilateral world and the promise of the United Nations as a guarantor of a new post-Cold War order'.[14] Instead, he argued:

International stability is never a given. It is never the norm. When achieved, it is the product of self-conscious action by the great powers, and most particularly of the greatest power, which now and for the foreseeable future is the United States. If America wants stability, it will have to create it. Communism is indeed finished; the last of the messianic creeds that have haunted this century is quite dead. But there will constantly be new threats disturbing our peace.[15]

The threats he identified included the proliferation of weapons of mass destruction (WMD) and the emergence of rogue states, such as

Iraq, North Korea and Libya. His conclusion was unequivocal: 'the alternative to unipolarity . . . is not a stable, static multipolar world. It is not an eighteenth-century world in which mature powers like Europe, Russia, China, America, and Japan jockey in the game of nations. The alternative to unipolarity is chaos.'[16] This is a stark representation of hegemonic peace. Only a dominant power can impose order on international politics, and the alternative was not genuine multilateralism within the framework of multipolarity, but anarchy.

A decade later, he returned to the question but now spoke of the emergence of resistance to American unipolarity. In the 1990s, 'it was mainly China and Russia that denounced unipolarity in their occasional joint communiqués', but in the 2000s the chorus now even included France.[17] French foreign minister Hubert Védrine popularised the term *hyperpuissance* (hyperpower) to describe a state surpassing all others in military and cultural domains.[18] Krauthammer rejected critiques of the unipolar thesis, and agreed with the formulation provided by the secretary of defence in the George W. Bush administration (2001–9), Donald Rumsfeld, who argued during the 'war on terror' and the invasion of Afghanistan in 2001 that 'the mission determines the coalition'.[19] Krauthammer was scathing about the liberal internationalist school that believes multilateralism is the core of US policy. Instead, he stressed that multilateralism and the alliance system was intended to ensure that allies did not go their own way and leave the US 'isolated', and hence were subordinated to US strategic goals. In Krauthammer's words, this was 'in service to the larger vision: remaking the international system in the image of domestic civil society' – the goal of democratic internationalism. As far as neocons and the more robust liberal interventionists were concerned, this sometimes had to be achieved at the point of a gun.[20] The ambition was breathtaking:

The multilateralist imperative seeks to establish an international order based not on sovereignty and power but on interdependence, a new order that, as Secretary of State Cordell Hull said upon returning from the Moscow Conference of 1943, abolishes the need 'for spheres of influence, for alliances, for balance of power'.

Instead, Krauthammer asserted the prerogatives of the nation state and condemned liberal internationalism for trying 'through multilateralism to transcend power politics, narrow national interest and, ultimately, the nation-state itself'. Liberal internationalists saw the nation state 'as some sort of residue of an anarchic past, an affront to the vision of a domesticated international arena'.[21]

Russia, China and even France could sympathise with his defence of great-power politics and opposition to the erosion of national sovereignty, but his brutal rejection of multilateralism exposed the dual character of postwar US leadership. The principles and institutions of the Charter international system were dispensable when they clashed with US national interests. Krauthammer stressed that liberal internationalists, especially in Europe, sought to enmesh the US in an 'entangling web of interdependence', and he dismissed the liberal principle of 'goo-goo one worldism' represented by 'paper' agreements in favour of the reality of 'power'.[22] The goal was clear:

> [the] principal aim is to maintain the stability and relative tranquillity of the current international system by enforcing, maintaining and extending the current peace. The form of realism that I am arguing for – call it the new unilateralism – is clear in its determination to self-consciously and confidently deploy American power in pursuit of these global ends.[23]

The 'new unilateralism' required 'explicitly and unashamedly ... maintaining unipolarity, for sustaining America's unrivalled dominance for the foreseeable future'.[24] In other words, the unipolar moment of 1990 was to become permanent. The al-Qaeda strike on the Twin Towers in New York and the Pentagon in Washington on 11 September 2001 (9/11) shattered some of the illusions. They were further stripped away when the Anglo-American invasion of Iraq in March 2003 went ahead despite the lack of a UN mandate, unleashing years of chaos and destruction in the region. Slavoj Žižek argues that in the 'new world order' emerging after 9/11, 'the USA basically wrote off the rest of the world as a reliable partner'. The ultimate goal was 'no longer the Fukuyama utopia of expanding universal liberal democracy, but the transformation of the USA into ... a lone superpower isolated from the rest of the world' to protect its security and economic interests.[25] This answered Krauthammer's question on what should be done 'if the Security Council refuses to back you'. The answer was simple: go it alone. This was the 'great substitution' in action, in which the US arrogated the right to stand above international law and the constraints of the post-1945 international system when necessary. It entailed the non-negotiable assertion of the 'right to choose' principle, thereby undermining the 'indivisibility' of European security.

PARADOXES OF ENLARGEMENT

The events of 1989 were consequential but did not mark a decisive break with the pattern of politics established in 1945. The institutional framework remained the same, namely the Charter international system; and the dominant framework of international politics also endured, the struggle between the assertion of hegemonic power represented by the US and its allies against the resistance of other putative great powers. Non-aligned nations remained on the sidelines, although occasionally exploiting the divisions. This deeper continuity also ran though the policies of all post-Cold War US presidents, operating within the framework of the same structural constraints. Individual preferences matter and styles differ, but all broadly perpetuated the Cold War struggle for US pre-eminence within the political West while containing potential adversaries. The collapse of the Soviet Union changed the rhetoric, yet underlying patterns endured. The Soviet Union may have gone, but the institutional structure of the Cold War remained.[26] NATO's eastward enlargement became integral to the political West's peace project and was considered 'a means to end the Cold War once and for all'.[27] In practice, expansion only fostered a new cold war and ran into Russia's alternative view of how the peace should be organised. In a classic case of how tragedy plays out in life, the clash of peace orders generated war.

Postwar confrontation was not a 'proper war', hence the peace that followed was not a 'proper peace'.[28] This is the negative peace, as defined earlier. Cold War I was accompanied by various proxy wars punctuated by moments of détente. The absence of any real means of transcending the conflict meant that these were no more than moments rather than culminations. As far as Washington was concerned, détente in the early 1970s was a 'tactical manoeuvre' and did not represent a 'permanent strategic change in the US – Soviet relationship'.[29] The same logic in the end applied to the post-1989 period in which the language of reconciliation failed to transcend the logic of contestation. After 1989 no substantive peace conference was convened and instead Cold War institutions and practices assumed new forms, accompanied in the early years by ringing declarations of strategic partnership and new peace orders. The jarring incompatibility of perspectives soon became apparent. The expansive ambitions of the Atlantic powers encountered the resistance of states defending traditional interpretations of sovereign internationalism. The strategic stalemate of Cold War I was reproduced in new forms, giving rise to the cold peace. As in the interwar years, this was little more than the negative peace of an armistice.

This was the context in which NATO enlarged. There was and remains a genuine demand from candidate states, generated by the bitter experience of subjugation by the USSR/Russia as well as the incomplete and contested character of the negative peace. Demand was further motivated by the intensifying security dilemma. It made sense for insecure countries to join an alliance that had demonstrated its strength and viability. However, this did not come cost-free. Without some sort of overarching security arrangement, expansion alienated Russia and generated a cold peace that turned into a new Cold War. The universalism of the Charter peace order came into stark contradiction with the Atlantic power system, which came to describe itself as the 'rules-based order'. The indivisible security promised by the former ran into the exclusivity of the latter. The logic of this hierarchy was challenged by Gorbachev and the NPT, and it was on this basis that Russia consistently opposed NATO enlargement.

Following Gorbachev's death in August 2022, he was feted in the West as the man who brought the Cold War to an end and presided over the relatively peaceful collapse of the Soviet Union. However, the other side of his legacy was forgotten: his condemnation of US foreign policy, particularly towards Russia, and his view that decision-making in Washington destabilised the international system. On the eve of the Ukraine war, he criticised the 'triumphant mood in the West, especially in the United States', after the disintegration of the Soviet Union: 'They grew arrogant and self-confident. They declared victory in the Cold War.' The result, he stated elsewhere, was the US claim to monopoly leadership in world affairs. The end of the Cold War was equated with the break-up of the Soviet Union, whereas in fact the conflict had ended two years earlier.[30] Hubris provoked conflict, which in the end undermined the security of all.

For Bush senior and his advisers, NATO was more than just a military alliance, but 'the primary vehicle for continued American involvement in Europe ... the emerging European security identity would be coordinated with and subordinated to NATO'.[31] Against realist expectations, the NATO alliance survived and became the cornerstone of Western primacy. In the absence of a unifying threat, balance of power theory anticipated the unravelling of Cold War alliances. The Warsaw Pact had been created in May 1955 in response to West Germany's accession to NATO, but barely outlasted German unification in October 1990. East Germany immediately withdrew and, at a meeting in Hungary in February 1991, the six other members declared the alliance over. The Warsaw Treaty Organization formally came to an end on 1 July. With its demise, the doyen of neorealism, Kenneth Waltz, repeatedly predicted the commensurate break-up of NATO. He anticipated that the US would retreat to become an offshore balancer – intervening like Great Britain earlier in regional affairs if one power threatened to become so strong as to endanger the security of others.[32] Instead, the US remained committed to its regional alliances. Equally, the much-anticipated balancing against US power was long delayed and took the form of informal alignments rather than counter-alliances. In this respect at least, Cold War II – so far – differs from the first.

The logical correlate of new thinking was pan-continentalism. The territorial dispensation agreed at the Yalta conference in

February 1945 was confirmed by the Helsinki Final Act, but in the same breath the logic of Yalta – in which the fate of small powers and citizens was disposed of by great powers – was transcended. This launched an all-European process with the potential to become the foundation of a post-Cold War security order. The CSCE in December 1994 in Budapest was transformed into the Organization for Security and Co-operation in Europe (OSCE), although it retained elements of its conference structure. Russia hoped to turn the OSCE into a genuinely comprehensive and inclusive security organisation to rival NATO, accompanied by the creation of some sort of security council. The OSCE's members are considered equal and the organisation works by consensus. It serves as a model of the transformative approach advanced by Gorbachev and later Russian leaders, but it also serves as an exemplary case of resistance to radical change. The logic was impeccable. After all, Western democracy had triumphed and its military alliance withstood the Soviet challenge. Why should Brussels, the capital of both the EU and NATO, be 'decentred' by such a vague formulation as the 'common European home' or an amorphous body like the OSCE?

The Soviet Union's demise fostered the view that NATO's long-term military and political containment strategy had been responsible. The enemy collapsed and successor states clamoured to join the opposing alliance. This certainly looked like victory, but it always had a deceptive quality. The peaceful end of the Cold War had been achieved because of some brave leadership choices, but it was always fragile. The 'victory' discourse undermined the achievement that it celebrated. The substantive victory – the end of the Cold War – would be squandered unless it was formalised in binding agreements and institutions. Instead, the Western security order was consolidated on a selective and exclusive basis, and no new inclusive security system was established. The Gaullist view that NATO expansion could undermine European security was ignored. Instead, US-led hegemonic internationalism predominated, leaving 'no place for Russia': 'neither Russia, the major European powers, nor the United States have been successful since 1989 in defining a place for Russia in the European or Euro-Atlantic security architecture or in integrating Russia into the major European security institutions'.[33] In the ensuing mimetic cold war, opposing conceptions of European international order clashed.[34]

NATO EXPANDS

There were substantive achievements in establishing a new peace order at the end of the Cold War, but the tension between transformation and enlargement fuelled tensions that in the end provoked Cold War II. The Atlantic powers set on the path of expansion, but the potential for transformation became part of the mythology of Russian foreign policy. It appealed to Charter universality against the enlargement of liberal hegemony.

At first Russian membership of NATO was not excluded. When in December 1991 NATO created the North Atlantic Cooperation Council (NACC) as a forum for dialogue and cooperation with NATO's former Warsaw Pact adversaries, Yeltsin addressed a letter outlining his position. He argued that Russia's transition to democracy established a new relationship based on mutual trust and common values, and he concluded: 'Today we do not ask for Russian membership in NATO, but regard it as our long-term political objective.'[35] Yeltsin sought to join what he called the 'civilised community' of nations, 'his term for the peaceful and economically developed countries of the West'.[36] The obvious question then arose: what if Russia's democratic transition stalled – what then would be the relationship? Even before that Russia's first post-communist foreign minister, Andrei Kozyrev, provides vivid examples of how the concerns of an ostensibly democratic but weak Russia were ignored. He recalls one CSCE ministerial meeting in 1992 in which Russia was not even mentioned. The topic was the Nagorno-Karabakh conflict between Azerbaijan and Armenia and the role of peace-keeping forces, a subject of vital concern to Moscow. Kozyrev remonstrated with Western ministers, arguing that they 'should have been above such treachery'. He warned that 'Attempts to isolate Russia would only serve the interests of the Russian imperialists, who challenged the policy of partnership with the West.'[37] He voiced the perennial fear that unless the West accommodated the concerns of the existing leadership in the Kremlin, they could face a far more aggressive nationalistic alternative.

One of the 'imperialists' whom he had in mind was the veteran Soviet diplomat and scholar, Yevgeny Primakov, who succeeded him as foreign minister in January 1996. Primakov argued 'that the basic national interests of Russia remained the same as they were before', and thus rejected Kozyrev's notion of 'reinventing' Russia's 'interactions with the West and East'.[38] The scholar Sergei Karaganov argued that Russia had to avoid repeating Gorbachev's mistakes and needed to 'act and think in a systematic manner'. He warned that 'current policy-making weaknesses must not be misused by the outside world to exacerbate the feeling of national weakness and humiliation within Russia', and identified a growing 'Versailles syndrome' among the population.[39] Instead, Kozyrev tried to persuade Yeltsin to 'stop playing old-style global hegemony games' to focus on 'the hard work of building trust and practical partnerships with the West'.[40] This was an admirable strategy, but it exposed Kozyrev to the criticism (like Gorbachev earlier) that it placed Moscow in the position of a supplicant. As he was soon to learn, 'hegemony games' and 'trust' were a two-way affair. Traditionalists like Primakov argued that it made little sense to give up long-term relationships to please the West, with no guarantee of any benefit other than what they considered the dubious privilege of becoming Washington's junior partner.[41]

The enlargement agenda shaped the relationship of Bill Clinton's presidency (1993–2001) and that of his successors with Russia until Donald Trump disrupted the narrative. Clinton delegated responsibility for Russia to vice president Al Gore, deputy secretary of state Strobe Talbott, and Treasury Department official Lawrence Summers.[42] Together they devised policies that shaped Russia's economic reforms in the 1990s, condemned at the time and later as an act of wanton irresponsibility that triggered one of the most profound economic and social crises in history, accompanied by the creation of a class of oligarchs who captured parts of the state.[43] The Putin restoration is founded on this narrative of exclusion from global decision-making and the terrible 1990s.[44] The political harm done to the trust required for cooperative international relations is an enduring legacy, exacerbated by the overriding issue of NATO enlargement. NATO launched the Partnership for Peace (PfP) programme in 1994 as a series of bilateral agreements with individual countries in which they choose the level and intensity of cooperation. Yeltsin believed that PfP would act as the alternative to enlargement, but when it became apparent that this was not the case, he felt betrayed. The Clinton administration came to pose the question of NATO enlargement in terms of 'not whether, but when'.[45] As far as critics were concerned, by signing up to PfP, Russia legitimised NATO's continued existence.[46]

Clinton and Yeltsin enjoyed a strong personal relationship, giving rise to the 'Bill and Boris' double act, but Clinton always had an eye on his domestic audience. In the end, 'Subordination of foreign policy to the swinging fortunes of partisan domestic politics prevented him from being the kind of consequential friend President Yeltsin desperately needed.'[47] Russia was offered 'schoolbook' advice on the basics of a market economy, when what the country needed was practical assistance.[48] Worse, American financial assistance was meagre and the practical assistance boiled down to giving advice that only exacerbated economic problems and social injustice, all 'accompanied by self-congratulatory remarks on having won the Cold War', a view that was seized on by traditionalists to argue that Russia was being treated 'not as an equal partner in building a new world but as a defeated enemy that had to submit to the victor's intentions'.[49] This was starkly apparent in the Balkans, where Lord David Owen notes that Russia's proposals to regulate the Bosnian crisis were killed off 'because it was a Russian initiative, and they [the Americans] were suspicious of Russian motives'.[50] Kozyrev insisted that, 'as a great power, Russia needed a visible place in world affairs'.[51] According to him, the conservative view in Moscow was that the US 'would always discriminate against Russia, no matter what reforms Russia undertook or how many concessions it made in foreign policy'.[52] Kozyrev himself provides much evidence to justify that view.

The US blocked Russian attempts to upgrade the CSCE, and Yeltsin also felt deceived on this account by Clinton.[53] That is why at the December 1994 summit, Yeltsin warned that if NATO were to overshadow all other organisations and enlarge its membership, 'the new Europe would be thrown back, if not to the Cold War, to a cold peace'.[54] Kozyrev believed 'that until Russia and NATO worked out a firm partnership or better mutual alliance, no new members should be admitted'.[55] The sense of disappointment, and even betrayal, in Moscow was palpable. Yeltsin was unequivocal when he told Clinton: 'For me to agree to the borders of NATO expanding to those of Russia would constitute a betrayal on my part of the Russian people.' The conversation is recorded by William Burns, at the time the political counsellor at the US embassy in Moscow. Soon after, he reported to Washington that 'Hostility to early NATO expansion is almost universally felt across the political spectrum here.'[56]

A passionate advocate of enlargement, Brzezinski understood the implications of carving up European security, contrary to the promises of 'indivisibility' in the Helsinki Final Act, the Paris Charter and innumerable other texts. He argued that Russia should have been offered 'a deal it could not refuse', namely 'a special cooperative relationship between Russia and NATO'.[57] His idea was to 'create a new transcontinental system of collective security, one that goes beyond the expansion of NATO proper'.[58] This would have been a genuine expression of the 'mature partnership' and would have allayed Moscow's sense of exclusion. The point is also made by Burns, who observed 'mounting Russian concern about expansion of NATO'. One of the ablest American diplomats of his generation, he urged 'caution on NATO enlargement' and argued: 'Before thinking seriously about extending offers of formal NATO membership to Poland and other Central European states, we recommended considering other forms of cooperation with former Warsaw Pact members and perhaps a new "treaty relationship" between NATO and Russia.'[59]

In a cable a month after Clinton's visit to Moscow in May 1995, Burns noted that 'nowhere are Russian sensitivities about being excluded or taken advantage of more acute than on the broad issue of European security. There is a solid consensus within the Russian elite that NATO expansion is a bad idea, period.'[60] William J. Perry, who later became secretary of defence, was concerned that 'formal enlargement of NATO would undermine hopes for a more enduring partnership with Russia, undercutting reformers who would see it as a vote of no confidence in their efforts, a hedge against the likely failure of reform'.[61] As he later put it, he opposed expansion not only because of its damaging effects on Russo-US relations but also because of what it represented: 'a general failure by Western governments to respect the vital importance of this nuclear power to the world order'. Before enlargement, the two nations were developing 'a relationship that could have resulted in a true global partnership', but as enlargement gathered momentum, 'Russia began to withdraw from its cooperative programs with NATO'. What made it worse was that renewed confrontation was unnecessary since, as far as he was concerned, 'There is no organic reason why Russia should be our enemy.'[62]

Despite the warnings, after Yeltsin's re-election in June–July 1996 and Clinton's return to the White House in November of that year, NATO enlargement rose to the top of the agenda. The US Committee to Expand NATO, headed by Bruce P. Jackson, director of strategic planning for Lockheed, took the lead in mobilising political and corporate support for expansion.[63] The course was set, and the signing of the NATO–Russia Founding Act on Mutual Relations in May 1997, along with the creation of a Permanent Joint Council (PJC), managed the symptoms rather than the problem. By signing the Founding Act, Russia in fact paved the way for NATO enlargement. The historic Madrid NATO summit in July issued the first invitations. Article 10 of the North Atlantic Treaty states that membership is open to any 'European State in a position to further the principles of this Treaty and to contribute to the security of the North Atlantic area'. In 1949 there were twelve founding members, Greece and Turkey joined in 1952, West Germany in 1955, Spain in 1982, and now the gates were opened to the former communist states. The Czech Republic, Hungary and Poland joined in the first wave in March 1999, against the backdrop of NATO's bombing of Serbia, in which some 500 civilians were killed. The creation of the NATO–Russia Council (NRC) in May 2002 was yet another attempt to assuage Russian concerns, but while Moscow may have gained a voice it increasingly lacked a stake in the US-centred security system.

Despite declarations of partnership, European security was increasingly built against rather than with Russia. Four more waves of expansion followed: the 'big bang' enlargement of 2004 brought in Bulgaria, Estonia, Latvia, Lithuania, Romania, Slovakia and Slovenia, Albania and Croatia joined in 2009, Montenegro in 2017 and North Macedonia in 2020, bringing the total to thirty. In response to Russia's invasion of Ukraine in 2022, Finland and Sweden applied to join.

Various alternatives had been mooted, including a special treaty of alliance. Instead, membership doubled and the cold peace became a reality. Notwithstanding the 1997 PJC and the 2002 NRC, 'the Russians stewed in their grievance and sense of disadvantage, a gathering storm of "stab in the back" theories slowly swirled, leaving a mark on Russia's relations with the West that would linger for decades'.[64] As far as Burns was concerned, he considered NATO enlargement 'premature at best, and needlessly provocative at worst'.[65] The Russian version of the Versailles syndrome fed on the belief that the Western powers had betrayed Moscow, taking advantage of the country's weakness to expand despite assurances that it would not do so and contrary to the spirit of the cooperative peace order anticipated at the end of the Cold War. Karaganov argued that the post-1989 peace order was built against Russia: 'We tried to integrate in it but we saw that it was a Versailles system number 2.'[66] Moscow believed that the cooperative idea was never given institutional form. As both Brzezinski and Burns stressed, if NATO enlargement had been mediated by some sort of pan-continental framework, then the hard edge with Russia could have been avoided and with it renewed European war.

A similar argument is made by Sarotte, who argues that NATO 'expansion itself was a justifiable response to the geopolitics of the 1990s', but 'What was unwise was expanding the alliance in a way that took little account of the geopolitical reality.' The closer NATO moved its infrastructure, including bases, troops and even nuclear weapons, to Moscow, 'the higher the political cost to the newly-cooperative relationship with Russia'.[67] Two realities were important. The first is that there would be no shared leadership in NATO, an issue that also affects France and other countries with aspirations to leadership of their own, as well as the EU's later striving for 'strategic autonomy'. The US was certainly not ready to grant a weakened and chaotic Russia veto power over issues of European security, something that it has not been willing to grant even to its allies; and even more so since Russia did not recognise the need for an enduring American political and military presence in Europe. Second, America was committed to maintaining the larger Euro-Atlantic system, and if this meant sacrificing a better relationship with Russia, then 'the former has to rank incomparably higher to America'.[68] These priorities were applied in the management of the various conflicts in the former Yugoslavia and in global affairs more generally. This fed into the 'widespread disappointment with the consequences of the end of the Cold War. Instead of a "new world order" based on consensus and harmony, "things which seemed to belong to the past" have all of a sudden become the future.'[69] The opportunity for genuine reconciliation was destroyed and the peace was lost.

4

THE ROAD TO WAR

In 1998 the Russian scholar Sergei Kortunov argued that the Cold War never ended. In defence of this claim, which at the time was shocking although later became commonplace, he argued that Moscow won World War II 'as Great Russia, not as a Red Empire'. He asserted that after 1945 neither the Soviet Union nor Stalin had any ambitions other than recovery, but that the West rejected all of Moscow's attempts to ease conflict and the struggle continued, no longer centred on Berlin but on Washington. Thus to concede that the West had been 'right' during the Cold War meant not simply 'the renunciation of communism' but the acceptance of 'the fallacy of the entire Russian historical idea – of the entire Russian Orthodox idea in history'. This in turn would mean accepting the Western view of Russia as an 'evil empire', and even Brzezinski's rather extreme view of Russia as 'a redundant country'. He regretted the fact that 'most democrats' in Russia did not deny Russia's 'defeat' in the Cold War, turning a blind eye to the West's 'unrelenting struggle against our former motherland, Russia-USSR, and that it was only by our own efforts that we destroyed the "evil empire"'. Russia had been 'fighting' against the USSR on the side of the West, and only after the Soviet collapse in 1991 did some Russians recognise that they had been helping the West pursue an anti-Russian rather than an anti-Soviet strategy.[1] From this perspective, cold war would only end when the West accepted Russia's legitimacy as a moral equal. By questioning the character of the 'victory' at the end of the Cold War, and to whom it properly belonged, a national narrative of a wrong to be righted was forged.

THE LOGIC OF CONFLICT

The 'pull' factor in the NATO enlargement process was crucial, and was magnified in the absence of any convincing alternative. The former Soviet bloc countries and some former Soviet states sought to join NATO to ensure their security and to hedge against the potential resurgence of Russian imperialism. Given the history of conflict in the region and the experience of Soviet domination, this is understandable. A case in point is Václav Havel, the playwright who became the last president of Czechoslovakia and served as president of the Czech Republic from 1993 to 2003. He was initially sceptical about NATO enlargement, believing that a genuine post-Cold War peace order made such alliances redundant. This was in line with the common European home concept and represented the transformation to which Gorbachev aspired. This vision of European pan-continentalism marginalised the US, and instead the 'Europe whole and free' model of peace came to predominate. As early as March 1991, Havel cited insecurity as the grounds to expand Western institutions:

It is in the West's own interest to seek the integration of Eastern and Central Europe into the family of European democracy because otherwise it risks creating a zone of hopelessness, instability and chaos, which would threaten Western Europe every bit as much as the Warsaw Pact tank divisions of old.[2]

He was right, but integration only later came to mean NATO enlargement.

Ambiguity about what precisely was promised at the time of German unification generates a continuing debate. Robert Gates, CIA director at the time, later argued that 'Gorbachev and others were led to believe that [expansion] would not happen'.[3] Gorbachev's later commentary on the issue was contradictory, but on the substance, he was unequivocal: 'The decision for the US and its allies to expand NATO into the east was decisively made in 1993. I called this a big mistake from the very beginning. It was definitely a violation of the spirit of the statements and assurances made to us in 1990.'[4] Enlargement was condemned in Moscow but also by some leading figures in Washington. George Kennan in February 1997 delivered a prescient and powerful warning:

> Why, with all the hopeful possibilities engendered by the end of the Cold War, should East – West relations become centred on the question of who would be allied with whom and, by implication, against whom in some fanciful, totally unforeseeable and most improbable future military conflict? . . . bluntly stated . . . expanding NATO would be the most fateful error of American policy in the entire post-Cold War era. Such a decision may be expected to inflame the nationalistic, anti-Western and militaristic tendencies in Russian opinion; to have an adverse effect on the development of Russian democracy; to restore the atmosphere of the Cold War to East – West relations, and to impel Russian foreign policy in directions decidedly not to our liking.[5]

A group of fifty American politicians from across the political spectrum condemned NATO expansion as 'a policy error of historic proportions'.[6] This was not the first time that experienced professionals warned against NATO's eastward expansion. In May 1995, a group warned that the policy:

> risked endangering the long-term viability of NATO, significantly exacerbating the instability that now exists in the zone that lies between Germany and Russia, and convincing most Russians that the United States and the West [were] attempting to isolate, encircle, and subordinate them, rather than integrating them into a new European system of collective security.[7]

Enlargement was opposed by members of the US establishment with 'impeccable Cold War credentials', including Paul Nitze, a long-standing hawk, Sam Nunn, an influential hardliner in Congress, Senator Daniel Patrick Moynihan, a former US ambassador to the UN, and even the Russophobic Harvard historian Richard Pipes. They all argued that expansion would poison relations with Russia and foster hard-line and reactionary forces there.[8] Kennan later called it 'a tragic mistake', warning during the Congressional ratification process that 'references to Russia as a country dying to attack Western Europe' were misguided: 'Don't people understand? Our differences in the Cold War were with the Soviet Communist regime. And now we are turning our backs on the very people who mounted the greatest bloodless revolution in history to remove that Soviet regime.'[9] He warned that Russia would sooner or later respond. Once again, he was proved right.

Gorbachev added his voice to the general condemnation of NATO enlargement, arguing that it was both unnecessary and destabilising. In a speech in Washington in 1997, he argued, 'I believe it's a mistake. It's a bad mistake', and added, 'I'm not persuaded by the assurances that we hear that Russia has nothing to worry about.' He warned of a backlash in Moscow, and viewed expansion as the attempt to build a new empire. Looking back in 2021, he noted that 'we had 10 years after the Cold War to build a new world order and yet we squandered them' because 'the United States cannot tolerate anyone acting independently'.[10] By then Gorbachev was critical of the authoritarian path in domestic politics, but on foreign policy he was of one mind with Putin. In 2016 he argued that 'a democratic and unaligned Ukraine is in the interests of the Ukrainian people', and called for neutrality to be enshrined in the Ukrainian constitution. Instead, in 2019 Ukraine's future entry into NATO was codified in the constitution. All this represented a betrayal of Gorbachev's multilateral perspective, in which NATO's expansion and 'its transformation from a defensive alliance to a vehicle for proactive military force' represented 'a blow to a budding world order where problems would be resolved via international law, diplomacy, and institutions like the United Nations'. As he put it in 2011, NATO's expansion to Russia's borders while presenting itself as a 'pan-European or even a global policeman ... usurped the functions of the United Nations and thus weakened it'.[11] This is an eloquent restatement of the grand substitution argument outlined in this book.

NATO enlargement exposed the contradiction between the two peace orders and is the most concentrated expression of that tension. In the end, both were found wanting. The model based on sovereign statehood protected by the Charter international system was not enough unless reinforced by some specific structure and the commitment of the great powers to its human rights and legal norms. The PfP combined with the OSCE could have filled the security gap, but instead NATO expansion became the main item on the menu. The Charter of Paris proclaimed the right of all states to choose their own security arrangements, and the East European states now sought to exercise that prerogative. The Charter also stressed the indivisibility of security, hence enlargement inevitably fostered conflict with Russia. Enlargement generated precisely the security threats that it was intended to avert. Eastern European countries may have individually increased their security by allying with like-minded states in NATO and formally coming under the protective umbrella of the US, but enlargement contributed to the long-term collective degradation of European security. Collective defence undermined common security.

The architects of enlargement were well aware of the problem, and although dismissive of Russian security concerns, sought to allay Russian fears. Since NATO was a defensive alliance, Russia had nothing to worry about. There was little engagement with the core Russian argument – that European security should be indivisible and inclusive, although palliative measures were adopted. Some of Moscow's concerns may have been self-serving and self-aggrandising, especially when they affected the security of neighbours, yet ultimately it was for Russia to decide what threatened its security rather than the West. Hence Moscow repeatedly appealed to the other half of the Paris Charter, which argued that the security of one state should not be to the detriment of another. Proponents of NATO enlargement believed that the two principles could be applied simultaneously, since there was no intention to exclude Russia entirely. There would be no going back on the principle of enlargement, however, but this would be tempered by special arrangements. Thus the May 1997 NATO–Russia Founding Act brought Russia formally into alliance councils for the first time, in the form of the PJC, accompanied by a ban on the permanent deployment of NATO forces in the new East European member states.[12] However, the declaration that 'NATO and Russia do not consider each other as adversaries' was soon to be tested.

The US campaign in Bosnia in summer 1995 was authorised by the UN, and suggested that humanitarian intervention with UN sanction would be the path of the future. For some, like Samantha Power, the engagement was too little, too late.[13] For others it exposed an anti-Serb bias, yet in general the conventions of international law were observed and enforced. By the time it came to the intervention in Yugoslavia in 1999, the divergence between the self-defined goals of the Atlantic powers and the multilateral legal order was exposed. Ignoring Russia's objections, NATO launched its bombing of Serbia on 4 March without UN sanction. The crisis took place against the background of the induction of Poland, Hungary and the Czech Republic into NATO at the anniversary summit in Chicago. The seventy-eight-day campaign was justified by the need to avert genocide in Kosovo, yet the diplomatic route had not been exhausted. The Rambouillet Agreement of early 1999 imposed onerous terms on Serbia, including the stationing of 30,000 NATO troops in Kosovo, the unhindered passage of NATO forces in Serbia and immunity for NATO forces in Yugoslav law, provocative conditions that the Serb leader, Slobodan Milošević, predictably refused.

The bombing campaign forced Serbia out of Kosovo along with at least 200,000 Serbian refugees. The violation of Serbian sovereignty and disregard for international law reflected the new paradigm of 'sovereignty as responsibility' rather than the traditional model of 'sovereignty as autonomy'.[14] For British prime minister Tony Blair and Clinton, 'the demands of international morality' trumped the instrument of international legality, the UN.[15] This represented a new form of the doctrine of limited sovereignty, of the sort instituted by Brezhnev after the invasion of Czechoslovakia in 1968. More disturbingly, it appeared that NATO had supplanted the UN as the arbiter of international law. The proclaimed goal was to avert a humanitarian catastrophe but also to demonstrate NATO's credibility. In the end it did neither. It undermined the claim that NATO was a purely defensive security alliance and raised fears in Moscow that Russia could one day be the object of similar high-handed behaviour. The Kosovo campaign was a critical turning point in Russia's relations with the West.

The journalist David Ignatius argued, 'What makes the Russia case so sad is that the Clinton administration may have squandered one of the most precious assets imaginable – which is the idealism and goodwill of the Russian people as they emerged from 70 years of Communist rule. The Russia debacle may haunt us for generations.'[16] NATO enlargement was a calculated risk, and one that in the end failed to deliver security for the continent. The facts of geography forced Finland after 1945 to eschew military alliances although it enjoyed complete domestic autonomy, and in 1955 the Austrian State Treaty allowed Soviet and Allied occupying forces to leave, and saved Austria from the fate of Berlin. Neutral states such as Austria, Ireland and Finland thrived in such a framework, with complete domestic sovereignty and autonomy. Instead, after 1989, the option of neutrality was dismissed and the concerns of a weakened Russia ignored. NATO enlargement alienated Russia from its neighbours and imposed new dividing lines in Europe.

NATO had been established as an anti-Soviet alliance, and it was now perceived as an anti-Russian one as well. As the bombing began, Yeltsin warned:

A dangerous precedent has been set creating a policy of diktat through force, placing in jeopardy the entire contemporary frame-work of international law. In fact, we speak of an attempt by NATO to enter the 21st century in the uniform of a world policeman. Russia will never agree to this. The UN Security Council should consider this increasingly troubled situation and call for an immediate halt to the military activity of NATO.[17]

Hill notes that this was 'by far the single greatest act and the single most important factor in eroding the trust that served as the basis of

Russia's relations with the West and the European security system in the 1990s'.[18] The acknowledged limitations of the Founding Act were ostensibly remedied in 2002 through the establishment of the NATO–Russia Council, a forum for joint decision-making in matters of common security concern. In the formula of the time, Russia was given a voice but not a veto. However, the NRC proved an inadequate forum even for Russia's voice to be heard, hence Putin's repeated appeals for the West to listen more attentively to Russian concerns.

The divergence between the exercise of power and the proclaimed norms was once again on display in the invasion of Iraq in March 2003 and in Libya in 2011. As far as Moscow was concerned, this bifurcation between what the Atlantic powers called the 'rules-based international order' and the UN-grounded system of international law defined the lost peace. Conflict was built into the very logic of enlargement, although there were attempts to mitigate the consequences. Russian membership was excluded for geographical and normative reasons, and this explains why Putin's early explorations of the possibility of Russian joining were rebuffed. He sought to defuse the tension between an expanding military alliance and the exclusion of a major neighbour. Washington would have none of it, and when wind of the informal contacts in Brussels in 2000–1 became known, put a stop to discussions.[19] There was still talk of some sort of treaty relationship between Russia and NATO, which would have established the basic ground rules for security in the Euro-Asian region. NATO and Russia would have been treated as equals, and various pathways elaborated for security cooperation. This idea was also stillborn, and instead various mitigation strategies were adopted. None resolved the underlying dilemma of a club of insiders creating an outsider, with all of the physical and ideational bordering and 'othering' this generated. The OSCE was not transformed in the way that Russia had hoped, and no new security institutions were established. Partnership for Peace would have created a common security umbrella to transform the European geopolitical landscape. Russian fears of exclusion would have been allayed and the practice of 'peace as a process' fostered. Critics argued that it would have failed to offer the security guarantees sought by former Warsaw Pact members. The decision was taken to enlarge the NATO alliance to the east, undermining the very peace order that it claimed to represent.

FATEFUL STEPS

The tension between the open-door policy (freedom of choice) and the indivisibility of security became the defining issue of the era. The Istanbul OSCE meeting in November 1999 adopted a Charter for European Security, restating the fundamental principles of the Paris Charter.[20] The seventh OSCE heads of state in December 2010 adopted the commemorative Astana Declaration, which talked in terms of the establishment of a security community. Meeting in the Kazakhstan capital eleven years after the Istanbul summit, the leaders recommitted themselves 'to the vision of a free, democratic, common and indivisible Euro-Atlantic and Eurasian security community stretching from Vancouver to Vladivostok, rooted in agreed principles, shared commitments and common goals'.[21] Russian foreign minister Sergei Lavrov repeatedly stressed that both declarations committed member states 'to indivisible security and their pledge to honour it without fail'. The freedom of states to choose their military alliances was balanced by the 'obligation not to strengthen their security at the expense of the security of other states'.[22]

Membership in NATO did little to temper the animosity of former Soviet and Soviet bloc members, and in fact hostility was intensified. With a safe berth under the American protective umbrella, they were free to perpetuate old grievances in new forms. This only exacerbated the abandonment of the 'indivisible security' framework in favour of a one-sided assertion of the expansion agenda. Neither the 1997 nor the 2002 institutions transcended the conflictual logic inherent in expansion. They were propitiatory rather than transformative, intended to keep Russia on board a vessel moving towards a destination not of Russia's choosing. Kosovo's unilateral declaration of independence in February 2008 and its immediate recognition by the US and some other leading powers, although significantly not by some NATO states with secessionist problems of their own, such as Spain, further exacerbated the tensions.

Nikolai Sokov, a former Russian diplomat who served in the foreign ministry between 1987 and 1992, argues that neither the PJC nor the NRC prevented the alliance from taking actions 'that affect Russian or regional security of the alliance or with ensuring security in Europe without consulting Moscow ... NATO makes a decision and then tries to convince Russia that [the] decision is good and should be accepted. The latter is a formula for disaster.' Nevertheless, it had been possible both to enlarge NATO and avoid conflict by establishing some sort of overarching compact between NATO and Russia, of the sort suggested by Brzezinski and Burns, with genuinely equal decision-making. One can understand the reluctance to give Moscow such power, since it would have involved a fundamental transformation of NATO and could potentially have diluted its democratic standards. Hence Sokov recognised that 'NATO expansion ... represents a serious provocation that reduces the level of mutual trust.'[23] The West did not set out to deceive but, like all dominant powers, it believed that enlargement was in the best interests of all, while coincidentally advancing its own interests. Euro-Atlanticism assumed an enduring interconnection between NATO and the EU, something that Euro-continentalists disputed. In the event, the expansion of the political West reproduced the logic of cold war in Europe.

The political West was far from monolithic, with the 'old Europe' powers of France and Germany opposing the invasion of Iraq in 2003, while the so-called 'new Europe' in the east welcomed it. Another endemic division was the question of burden sharing within NATO. The US traditionally bore a disproportionate share of the costs, providing three-quarters of all NATO capabilities, allowing the European countries to focus on developing welfare states. The 2006 Riga summit adopted the 2/20 formula, with NATO countries committed to allocate at least 2 per cent of GDP to defence, with 20 per cent of this to be devoted to defence technology. The most contentious issue, however, was the enduring debate over the limits to NATO enlargement. This came to a head over the prospects for Georgian and Ukrainian membership. Burns, who by now had returned to Moscow as ambassador, warned that:

> Ukrainian entry into NATO is the brightest of all redlines for the Russian elite (not just Putin). In more than two and a half years of conversations with key Russian players, from knuckle-draggers in the dark recesses of the Kremlin to Putin's sharpest liberal critics, I have yet to find anyone who views Ukraine in NATO as anything other than a direct challenge to Russian interests. . . . Today's Russia will respond. Russian – Ukrainian relations will go into a deep freeze. . . . It will create fertile soil for Russian meddling in Crimea and eastern Ukraine.[24]

Putin also warned that the recognition of Kosovan independence 'encourages conflict' and set a precedent for other multi-ethnic states.[25] He was dismissive about Ukraine, warning in March 2008 that NATO enlargement could trigger instability: 'Doesn't your government know that Ukraine is unstable and immature politically, and NATO is a very divisive issue there? Don't you know that Ukraine is not even a real country? Part of it is really East European, and part of it is really Russian.'[26] For the first time Putin voiced doubts about the integrity of Ukrainian statehood, which would be amplified later.

Despite the warnings, the NATO summit in Bucharest in April 2008 resolved that 'NATO welcomes Ukraine's and Georgia's Euro-Atlantic aspirations for membership in NATO. We agreed today that these countries will become members of NATO.' The resolution spoke of the national desire to join NATO, but this was misleading since no more than 20 per cent of Ukrainians at the time were in favour.[27] Putin repeated his lecture on the unreal character of Ukraine, while German and French opposition prevented Membership Action Plans being issued. As Burns notes, the Bucharest summit 'left us with the worst of both worlds – indulging the Ukrainians and Georgians in hopes of NATO membership on which we were unlikely to deliver, while reinforcing Putin's sense that we were determined to pursue a course he saw as an existential threat'.[28] Burns later noted that Russia 'fears unpredictable and uncontrolled consequences' because of the 'strong divisions in Ukraine over NATO membership, with much of the ethnic-Russian community against membership'. He warned that this could lead to a major split resulting in violence or even civil war, in which case, 'Russia would have to decide whether to intervene; a decision Russia does not want to have to face.'[29] If Burns's analysis is correct, then Russia was reluctantly drawn into the Ukrainian imbroglio rather than seeking to fulfil some sort of predetermined mission to restore imperial greatness.

The immediate effect was to encourage the Georgian leadership into an ill-advised attempt to reclaim the breakaway province of South Ossetia on 7 August, provoking a five-day war with Russia. This resulted in the permanent alienation not only of South Ossetia but Abkhazia as well, some 20 per cent of Georgia's territory. In a premonition of later events in Ukraine, Russia recognised the independence of the two republics on 26 August. The unilateral declaration of independence of Kosovo in February that year was cited as a precedent. More broadly, the prospect of Ukraine in NATO raised fears similar to those provoked by the deployment of Soviet missiles to Cuba in October 1962. It came to a head in 2014, and then again from 2021. By then Burns was director of the CIA, and one of the few people in Biden's Washington foreign policy establishment with a deep understanding of the region.

The expanding Atlantic power system would sooner or later run up against the realities of Eurasian geopolitics. Its leading edge would encounter resistance in Eastern Europe or in the steppes of Asia. In the event, the jagged frontline ran between the Masurian lakes across the Carpathians to the Caucasian mountains. Gorbachev hoped to transcend the iron curtain by transforming European security, but the spatial logic of enlargement predominated. Despite warnings that the model was exclusionary and would provoke resistance, the Clinton team convinced themselves that the problem was a managerial one, as Strobe Talbott describes in his memoirs. They believed that Russian concerns could be allayed not by a genuine debate over the structure of post-Cold War order but by symbolic concessions, such as membership of the G8 and the PJC.[30] This failed to address the fundamental power consequences of enlargement. As Noam Chomsky argued, instead of a new world order, the post-Cold War era was one in which the new world gives the orders.[31]

NATO enlarged to Russia's borders, accompanied by a discursive style that focused on bloc unity and cohesion. The primary concern was the survival of the military alliance, transcending even the purpose for which alliances are created – namely, to maximise the security of all. This was balanced by political changes that emphasised the peace-making functions of the alliance and its contribution to out-of-area nation-building, as in Afghanistan. At the same time, the coercive factor was unleashed in the bombing campaign of Serbia in 1999 and the extensive aerial bombardment of Libya that far exceeded the no-fly mandate of UN resolution 1973 of 17 March 2011. Europe meantime enjoyed an unprecedented period of peace. European states cashed in the peace dividend to slash defence spending, allowing military capability to atrophy. US troop levels in Europe declined from 300,000 in 1989 to the low point of 61,000 in 2014. British and Canadian troops left the continental mainland entirely. Most countries ended conscription, while Germany cut its force numbers by two-thirds and allowed its military capabilities to degrade. The Ukraine crisis of 2014 signalled a sharp reversal and troop commitments rose in step with the intensification of Cold War II, although NATO still struggled to build mainland military capacity. The Russo-Ukrainian war from 2022 has signalled the full-scale return to armed confrontation.

THE SECURITY DILEMMA

NATO pursued an open-door policy to all countries in the region except one – Russia. This was a 'club' that Russia could not join.[32] Moscow's various proposals to associate substantively with NATO were rebuffed, almost guaranteeing that at some time there would be a backlash. The doubling of NATO membership had fateful consequences for European security and Russo-US relations. No substantive security relationship was established. Instead, as Bill Clinton put it later, 'My policy was to work for the best, while expanding NATO to prepare for the worst.'[33] Advocates of NATO enlargement saw it as a 'means of building democracy, market economies, ethnic peace, and stability in Central and Eastern Europe', but they 'essentially hoped to have their cake and eat it too'; to achieve all of this and, at the same time, despite all the warnings, somehow include Russia in the process, 'without irreparable damage to relations with Russia or the process of reform within Russia'.[34] Enlargement sought to hedge against the return of Russia as a hostile great power; but the very act of enlargement, as Kennan presciently warned, all but guaranteed precisely such a return.

A deepening security dilemma was set in motion. Measures taken to increase the security of one side are perceived as detrimental to the other, which responds to intensify the initial dilemma. As the originator of the term, John Herz, notes, where groups 'live alongside each other without being organized into a higher unity', a condition of anarchy prevalent since the dawn of recorded history, they are concerned about being attacked by others:

> Striving to seek security from such attack, they are driven to acquire more and more power in order to escape the impact of others. This, in turn, renders the other more insecure and compels them to prepare for the worst. Since none can ever feel entirely secure in such a world of competing units, power competition ensues, and the vicious circle of security and power competition is on.[35]

Europe was once again trapped in a cycle generated by the assumption that there was no exit from the impasse without the defeat or systemic transformation of the other. The fatalism that gripped Europe in 1914 was again evident. Even 'the most aggressive initiatives [were presented] as essentially defensive'.[36] As earlier, decision-makers 'hide, even from themselves, their responsibility for the outcomes of their actions'.[37] NATO's eastern members demanded 'reassurance' against the perceived threat, which could never be enough, ramping up 'deterrence' measures to ensure 'credibility' but thereby provoking commensurate responses. The logic was later applied to the South China Sea region, where China armed to ensure its security, raising fears in other actors who correspondingly sought to reinforce their security. The defensive actions of one side exacerbate the fears of the other, whose further defensive moves raise the threat perception on the other side, thus establishing a destructive cycle.[38] The absence of trust provoked the original Cold War, but confidence in the sincerity of the negotiating partners allowed Gorbachev and Reagan/Bush to bring it to an end. 'Trust but verify' was Reagan's mantra, but today there is no trust and nothing left to verify.

How then can we explain why aspirations for peace ended up fostering war? At least four factors can be identified. The first is the failure to create an overarching ideological and organisational 'higher unity' between the two contrasting visions of post-Cold War security in Europe. Different representations of international politics generated conflict. Moscow's proposal to create a European security council under the aegis of the OSCE would have given it a veto over fundamental security decisions in Europe.[39] The idea was firmly rejected by the Atlantic powers, considering that this would represent a reconstitution of Yalta-style dominance over smaller states and give Russia veto rights in the new European security order. This would have run firmly against the logic of enlargement, which was premised on the homogenisation of political space. NATO (and to a lesser degree the EU) in effect became the European security system, where 'Russia has no vote and no chance of ever getting one'.[40] Equally, neo-Gaullist ideas about establishing some sort of overarching pan-European 'union of unions', encompassing the entirety of Europe's 800 million people, were given short shrift, since it would have decentred Brussels and marginalised Washington. It was assumed that Moscow's logic in advancing such ideas was to drive a 'wedge' between the two wings of the Atlantic system. Two power systems came into confrontation, each nurtured with passion, idealism and fear.

The second factor is the radicalisation of liberal hegemony, an inherent consequence of a unipolar system order. The Cold War stabilised as a bipolar system, but with the Soviet collapse the US emerged as the single pre-eminent power. It remained committed to the maintenance of its unrivalled supremacy. This in the end led to 'over-balancing' against a threat from Russia that at the time did not exist, but which the very process of balancing helped bring into existence. Over-balancing was encouraged by most of the former Soviet bloc communist states, fearing a revival of Russian imperialism, exacerbating the security dilemma that ultimately undermined their security. Gorbachev's idealism was condemned not only as unworkable but also as disruptive of the triumphant expansiveness of liberal order, thus threatening accustomed patterns of hegemony and hierarchy in international politics. Under-balancing against a potential threat is undoubtedly a risk, but over-balancing by maintaining an alliance system devised for other times and other threats generated its own dangers. Comparable alliance formation in the period before World War I led to catastrophe.

The third factor is 'transdemocracy' – the combination of security and democracy within the framework of democratic peace theory. If democracies indeed do not go to war with each other, then it makes sense to create as many democracies as possible, and thereby ensure Euro-Atlantic security. This combination of harsh realism and democratic idealism became bound up with liberal interventionism and democracy promotion. As part of the grand substitution, democratic internationalism supplanted sovereign internationalism. The liberal international order effectively repudiated the pluralism that had once been characteristic of liberalism, the liberal anti-pluralism identified earlier. Interventions precipitated state failure in Iraq and Libya, and engulfed Syria and Ukraine. When the defence of democracy is couched in terms of a struggle to turn back an 'authoritarian tide', geopolitical risks are multiplied and the finer points of statecraft and diplomacy blunted. International politics becomes a crusade, in which geopolitics is recruited to serve purposes antithetical to the 'higher idealism' it purportedly practises. Yascha Mounk argues that 'Any attempt to halt the authoritarian resurgence must simultaneously stop embattled democracies such as India and Poland from joining the ranks of the world's dictatorships and prevent countries such as China and Russia from reshaping the world order.'[41] India and Poland had moved in an illiberal direction, but it is not clear how this could be stopped.

The final factor is Russia as the bone in the throat of liberal hegemony, later joined by China. In the 1990s, Russian concerns about NATO enlargement and US intervention in the various Balkan conflicts could be ignored. However, as Russia benefited from windfall commodity prices in the 2000s and revived its power capacity, the Kremlin became more assertive. However, it was liberal hegemony that was challenged but not the international system in which it was embedded. This represents *neo-revisionism*, the attempt to change how a system operates rather than a full-blown revisionism that seeks to change the system itself. There is remarkable continuity in the strategy, with Yeltsin in December 1994 condemning the nascent unipolar model of international politics as a 'cold peace', but Putin had the power (or so he thought) to do something about it. Despite Putin's reputation as a hard-headed realist, up to 2012 his foreign policy remained within the bounds of the Gorbachevian matrix, still loyal to some version of a transformative and idealistic post-Cold War security order based on rapprochement with the West. The failure to reconcile the two visions of security ramped up the security dilemma.

TWO RIGHTS MAKE A WRONG

For an approach focused on power balances and capabilities, the advocates of expansion were remarkably negligent about the power consequences of their actions. Power is never absolute but relational. An action on one side will have consequences on the other, including asymmetric responses. Reactions are also shaped by how actors view international affairs. Russia and its allies (notably China) believe that the international system is bigger than any particular order within it, whereas partisans of liberal hegemony believe that their particular order is universal and applicable globally, with a special mission for the US in that order. As Bill Clinton's secretary of state, Madeleine Albright, memorably put it, the US was the 'indispensable nation. We stand tall. We see further into the future.'[42]

In Russia, too, the tide ran in favour of self-affirmation. The Atlanticism of the Kozyrev era was long over, and his successor as

foreign minister, Primakov, revived a version of the theory of coexistence popular in the 1950s. *Competitive coexistence* assumed that the
struggle with the Atlantic powers was far from over but could be
managed to avoid conflict. Opportunities for cooperation should be
exploited, but ultimately Russia had to find allies in the Global South
and assert its hegemony in Eurasia. On coming to power in 2000,
Putin believed he could do better, and in his typical manner sought to
reconcile competing viewpoints. His policy of *new realism* announced
that foreign policy would work to achieve economic development
and modernisation, a stance that endured (with declining conviction;
see Chapter 7) until 2012. The policy was new to the degree that it
tempered Primakov's traditional hard-nosed realism to argue that
some sort of substantive relationship could be achieved with the
West, and in that Putin remained in the tradition of Gorbachev's new
thinking. It was realist, however, because the policy had a more
substantive and assertive view of Russia's national interests, and thus
lost some of what had been perceived to be Gorbachev's excessive
idealism. An activist foreign policy does not necessarily equate to
revisionism – the attempt to change the rules of the game. It was in
this spirit that Putin understood that the issue of NATO enlargement had to be tackled head on. If not, then there would be new
dividing lines in Europe, and it was inevitable that Russia would be
on the other side. Putin repeatedly suggested that Russia could join
NATO, or at least become part of some sort of expanded security
community uniting Russia and NATO. These initiatives as we have
seen were rebuffed.

After the al-Qaeda attack on the US on 11 September 2001
(9/11), Putin was the first to call President Bush to offer support.
Against the advice of the military, Putin agreed to intelligence
sharing, US bases in Central Asia, and other assistance.[43] The terrorist
attack catalysed the most ambitious elements of US policy, shifting
international politics towards a more militaristic frame. The 'global
war on terror' (GWOT) was launched as a civilisational struggle
against the forces of evil (in this case in the form of Islamism), with
whom there could be no compromise, rather than as a police operation to deal with a gang of criminals. The very notion of a war against

such a nebulous adversary as 'terror' meant that the struggle was diffuse and practically endless (later repeated in the war on 'disinformation'). It also meant that the struggle would be conducted through emergency methods, which made possible the subversion of the very principles in whose name the war was being waged. That is also the logic of cold war, and another layer was added to the crusading dimension of international politics.

Support for the mujahideen insurgency against the Soviet forces in Afghanistan in the 1980s generated the Taliban, who took power in Kabul in 1996, which in turn unleashed Islamic terrorism that struck the US.[44] Afghanistan was invaded in autumn 2001 in the hunt for Osama bin Laden, the mastermind of 9/11, but he escaped and hid in Pakistan before being hunted down by US forces and killed in April 2011. The Taliban government was overthrown but, before Afghanistan was even moderately stabilised, Washington turned its attention to Iraq. The invasion in March 2003 soon dislodged Saddam Hussein, but the dismantling of the army, the Ba'ath party and other instruments of Saddam's rule plunged the country into decades-long chaos from which it has still not recovered. In both Afghanistan and Iraq, dogged resistance movements were catalysed, drawing the US and its allies into what came to be known as 'forever wars'. The so-called Islamic State swept across northern Iraq and Syria in summer 2014, leaving a trail of destruction in its wake. By the time the Taliban retook Kabul in August 2021, it was clear that the war on terror had been a monumental – and expensive – failure.[45]

Burns considers the period following 9/11 and the invasion of Iraq eighteen months later a 'hinge point in history'. If the US had avoided 'the debacle in Iraq, instead projected American power and purpose more wisely, it seems obvious today that American interests and values would have been better served'.[46] As Putin told Burns, US ambassador in Moscow from August 2005, 'You Americans need to listen more.' 'You can't have everything your way anymore. We can have effective relations, but not just on your terms.'[47] Instead, the radicalised liberal order overshadowed the international system and looked for new enemies to vanquish, which it found in the guise of

Islamic fundamentalism and authoritarianism. It also helped rekindle old-style great-power confrontation. The litany of Russian complaints grew ever longer. The NATO bombing campaign against Serbia in 1999 had already set off alarm bells. Now the list included America's unilateral abrogation of the 1972 Anti-Ballistic Missile (ABM) treaty in June 2002, the lack of significant strategic cooperation following Russia's support for the war on terror after 9/11, the invasion of Iraq in 2003 without a formal UN mandate, Washington's support for the various 'colour revolutions', including the Rose Revolution in Georgia in December 2003, and the Orange Revolution in Ukraine in late 2004, and the 'big bang' NATO and EU enlargements of that year, followed by the plan to deploy ballistic missile defence (BMD) installations in Eastern Europe.

Putin's Munich Security Conference speech in February 2007 outlined his grievances. He affirmed the 'universal, indivisible character of security' and condemned attempts to establish a 'unipolar world . . . in which there is one master, one sovereign. And at the end of the day this is pernicious not only for all those within this system, but also for the sovereign itself because it destroys itself from within.' He noted that 'those who teach us [about democracy] do not want to learn themselves' and condemned the marginalisation of the UN while warning that NATO enlargement represented 'a serious provocation that reduces the level of mutual trust' accompanied by the 'almost uncontained hyper use of force – military force – in international relations, force that is plunging the world into an abyss of permanent conflict'. He warned, 'We are seeing a greater and greater disdain for the basic principles of international law.'[48] Putin spoke in defence of the autonomy of the Charter international system against the arbitrariness of the Atlantic powers, but his pushback against the politics of substitution further alienated Russia from the West.

The BMD programme became a matter of increasing concern. In 2007, Washington announced that it would install European Interceptor Sites in Poland and the Czech Republic as part of the array to defend against a putative missile attack from Iran. Moscow considered the plan the thin end of a wedge that could threaten Russian intercontinental ballistic missile (ICBM) bases in Kozelsk and Tatishevo. In response to Russian concerns, in September 2009 Obama announced the European Phased Adaptive Approach, with installations in Turkey and Spain as well as Eastern Europe. Major BMD sites were built in Romania and Poland, equipped with what Russia feared was the nuclear-capable Mk-41 Aegis Ashore system, deploying the Aegis Standard Missile-3 (SM-3) missile interceptor. The Radzikowo site in Poland is just 300 kilometres from the Russian border (Kaliningrad) and 1,300 kilometres from Moscow. NATO insisted that BMD was intended to defend against potential threats from outside the Euro-Atlantic area and 'is not directed against Russia and will not undermine Russia's strategic deterrence'.[49] Moscow was not convinced. Ostensibly intended to guard against Iranian missiles, Moscow feared that it could be used against Russian second-strike capabilities. In the event of a conflict, it would be impossible to know whether the missiles were loaded with conventional or nuclear weapons. By the time they found out, it would be too late. Even the most benign and democratic Russia would express de Gaulle-style pique at the situation.

Distrust came to permeate the relationship. In his Munich speech, Putin noted that the CFE treaty, adapted at the Istanbul CSCE summit in November 1999 to take into account the elimination of the Warsaw Pact and including new flank limits, had so far been ratified by only four states, including Russia, on the grounds that Russian forces had not been removed from Georgia and Moldova. That year, Russia suspended its participation, and in March 2015, citing NATO's failure to ratify the amended treaty, pulled out entirely. NATO expansion provoked a qualitative change in the security system itself. The accession of a cohort of countries morbidly suspicious of Russian intentions and aspirations worsened the tone of the relationship. Moscow viewed it as an increasingly anti-Russian organisation. This was exacerbated by the appointment of a succession of general secretaries from small countries, who lacked the heft or ability to sustain diplomatic initiatives of their own. Moscow considered that the organisation had become hermetic – impervious to its concerns and increasingly radical in its rhetoric. Although the Bucharest promises to Georgia and Ukraine were not followed up by accession strategies, repeated assurances of membership fed into the deepening security dilemma, especially when Ukraine after 2014 was rearmed by NATO states.

EUROPEAN SECURITY TREATY

Having come to the end of his two constitutionally mandated successive terms, Putin in 2008 made way for President Dmitry Medvedev. Before leaving, Putin directed the foreign ministry to draft a proposal to enshrine in international law the 'principle of international security, a legal obligation, under which no state or international organisation in the Euro-Atlantic area could strengthen their security at the expense of other countries and organisations'.[50] The directive specifically called for the proposal to be in conformity with the UN Charter. Medvedev in Berlin in June called for a European Security Treaty (EST). He proposed that the OSCE should take priority over NATO to ensure 'the unity of the entire Euro-Atlantic space'. He proposed transforming 'the OSCE into a fully-fledged regional organisation'.[51] Medvedev provided more details of his envisaged treaty in a speech in Evian in France. He stressed the renunciation of the use of force in international politics and reiterated the principle of 'indivisible security' based on 'three nos': 'no ensuring one's own security at the expense of others'; no acts by military alliances or coalitions that would undermine the unity of the common Euro-Atlantic space; and 'no development of military alliances that would threaten the security of other parties to the [proposed new security] treaty'. This was reinforced by the injunction that 'no state or international organisation can have exclusive rights to maintaining peace and stability in Europe'.[52]

The draft version presented in November 2009 appealed to the principles outlined in the UN Charter and the Helsinki Final Act, clearly signalling that the goal was to restore the primacy of sovereign internationalism within the framework of Charter principles. The immediate political goal was to manage (if not to stymie) NATO enlargement, with Article 1 appealing to 'principles of indivisible, equal and undiminished security'. It went on to declare: 'Any security measures taken by a Party to the Treaty individually or together with other Parties, including in the framework of any international organization, military alliance or coalition, shall be implemented with due regard to security interests of all other Parties.'[53] On the face of it, this was a reasonable proposition, but by effectively granting Moscow veto rights on NATO enlargement, it was clearly unacceptable to the Atlantic powers. The point was reiterated when a conference of signatory parties was mooted as a mechanism of conflict adjudication, with binding decisions taken by consensus (Article 6.3). There was some engagement through the 'Corfu process', a forum for OSCE states to discuss the proposal, but the initiative soon ran into the sands. The proposal reflected Russia's readiness to challenge the existing model of European security, something that it would do more forcefully later.[54] The goal was to shift the normative parameters away from expansive liberal hegemony back to sovereign internationalism, and thus to return to the greater Europe model and away from 'Europe whole and free'. Moscow's attempt to broaden the European security agenda was an obvious challenge to US regional hegemony. The paradox of the post-Cold War European security was also evident. The focus on US – Russian relations demonstrated that Europe was definitely not a power when it came to the issue of global and even European security.

THE RESET AND BEYOND

It was not all downhill. On 7 February 2009, Vice President Joseph Biden at the Munich Security Conference delivered the new Obama administration's first major foreign policy statement. He argued, 'It's time to press the reset button and to revisit the many areas where we can and should be working together with Russia.'[55] The two countries disagreed over NATO enlargement and policy in the South Caucasus, but the subsequent Reset registered some significant achievements. These included the New START Treaty, limiting strategic nuclear weapons, although as a condition of ratification the US Senate imposed a multi-trillion-dollar nuclear modernisation programme. Russia supported sanctions against Iran, and the subse-

THE ROAD TO WAR

quent Joint Comprehensive Plan of Action (JCPOA) of July 2015 constrained Tehran's ability to develop nuclear weapons. Between 2009 and 2015, the Northern Distribution Network facilitated material to transit from Afghanistan across Russia and Central Asia. The US supported Russia's accession to the WTO, which finally (the initial application was registered in June 1993) took place in August 2012. The Reset nevertheless failed to overcome the deeper sources of distrust, exacerbated by intensifying disagreements over the Arab Spring and the conservative turn within Russia itself.[56]

NATO's *Strategic Concept* of 2010 reflected the cooperative spirit of the Reset but also its limitations. The *Concept* reaffirmed the founding principles of democracy and security and noted, 'Today, the Euro-Atlantic area is at peace and the threat of a conventional attack against NATO is low.' The alliance claimed credit for itself: 'This is an historic success for the policies of robust defence, Euro-Atlantic integration and active partnership that have guided NATO for more than half a century.'[57] The report urged the further reduction of nuclear weapons and greater transparency over Russia's strategic weapons in Europe. The 'open door' policy was reiterated amidst the contentious assertion that 'NATO's enlargement has contributed substantially to the security of allies'. The strategy declared:

NATO–Russia cooperation is of strategic importance as it contributes to creating a common space of peace, stability and security. NATO poses no threat to Russia. On the contrary: we want to see a true strategic partnership between NATO and Russia, and we will act accordingly, with the expectation of reciprocity from Russia.[58]

The character of 'strategic partnership' was never fully articulated and it was not enough fundamentally to reset relations. The goal remained 'a Europe whole and free', which 'would be best served by the eventual integration of all European countries that so desire into Euro-Atlantic structures'.[59] The logic was impeccable and, as far as the Atlantic powers were concerned, the expansion of the security pact enhanced Russia's security by tying its neighbours into a robust peace order. By contrast, Moscow considered the advance of a military alliance which had bombed Serbia, destroyed Iraq and Libya, waged a futile and ultimately ineffectual war in Afghanistan and sought to turn its neighbours away from Moscow as rather less than benign. This is the logic that led to the breakdown of European security in 2014 and to war in 2022.

The Obama administration made no secret of its preference for Medvedev and his modernisation programme, with Obama going so far as to argue that Putin was a man of the past. This alone would have been enough to scupper Medvedev's chances of running for a second term. However, for Putin the last straw was the overthrow of Muammar Gaddafi in Libya. Medvedev's order for Russia to abstain in the UN vote in March 2011, imposing a no-fly zone in Libya, created an open rift with Putin, who considered the move reckless. Putin ultimately was proved right since, under the guise of humanitarian intervention, the Anglo-French forces, with the US 'leading from behind', quickly destroyed the Libyan air force and installations, and enabled insurgent forces to overthrow the government and brutally to kill Gaddafi in October. Libya had enjoyed the highest living standards in Africa but was now plunged into civil war. The resulting lawlessness affected neighbouring countries as a tide of arms and unemployed fighters spread across the region and opened an immigration route to Southern Europe. Regime change 'may have achieved important security objectives' for the West, but by its actions the 'Alliance intensified and accelerated the deterioration of its relations with its largest and arguably most important European partner – Russia'.[60]

After his meeting with Putin in Slovenia in June 2001, Bush stated: 'I looked the man in the eye. I found him to be very straightforward and trustworthy. We had a very good dialogue. I was able to get a sense of his soul; a man deeply committed to his country and the best interests of his country.'[61] He came to regret his comment, but Biden later took up the theme, allegedly telling Putin in 2011, 'I don't think you have a soul', to which Putin apparently replied, 'We understand one another.'[62] If this bizarre exchange really did take place, then it reflected a breakdown in relations deeper than geopolitics to encompass an existential dimension. The collapse was confirmed when Putin accused secretary of state Hillary Clinton of stirring up the 'white ribbon' protests against vote falsification in the December 2011 parliamentary elections. In the largest political demonstrations of the Putin era, marchers called 'for fair elections' and 'Russia without Putin'. The March 2012 presidential election brought Putin back to the Kremlin, and he rolled back even the modest political liberalisation of his predecessor.[63]

The Reset failed to address the underlying issues that continued to poison the relationship. Russia's litany of complaints continued to grow, but critics argue that these structural and policy issues are not fundamentally causative. For them, the key issue is Russia's domestic system. From that perspective the authoritarian power elite fostered neo-Soviet great-power pretensions, corrupt social relations and the drive to establish internal legitimacy through external adventurism. This 'diversionary' reading of Russian foreign policy includes the attempt to create a 'sphere of influence' in post-Soviet Eurasia while pursuing aggressive policies further afield, including the subversion of Western polities through 'active measures' of disinformation and social media 'discord' campaigns.[64] The academic-turned-diplomat Michael McFaul supported the Reset as a member of the Obama administration but once in Moscow in 2012 as ambassador he presided over its demise. In McFaul's view, Putin is motivated by ideological factors rather than material or security interests. He argues that the costs and benefits of various interventions in Ukraine, Syria as well as the US were discounted in pursuit of the intangible benefits of status, prestige and legitimacy.[65] The survival strategy of the administrative regime is certainly part of the story, and its manipulations and suppressions to hold on to power intensified over the years. The independence of the institutions of the constitutional state was commensurately reduced.

However, this view is itself part of the Cold War narrative about Russia, and too readily discounts structural approaches to Russian foreign policymaking. This sees the country facing genuine challenges from the expansive and radicalised post-Cold War Atlantic power system approaching its borders from several directions.[66] From this perspective, it was the deepening security dilemma rather than Russia's neo-imperial and increasingly conservative and repressive domestic politics that fed the geopolitical crisis. It also discounts genuine policy differences over appropriate actions in the Middle East and elsewhere. For example, Russia's military intervention in Syria in September 2015 came on the back of intense diplomatic engagement with all the parties concerned, and in the face of the imminent danger of insurgent Islamist forces defeating Damascus, with incalculable but undoubtedly damaging consequences for Russia itself.[67]

The liberal order considers itself guided by benign motives, hence any dissent is not only mistaken but inherently malevolent. On the other side, Russia's tightening authoritarianism undermined the credibility of its defence of the Charter international system. In the absence of some sort of overarching European security structure its security concerns were not unfounded. The tension between the principle of 'Europe whole and free' and its accompanying insistence that states could join the alliance system of their choice was countered by 'greater Europe' notions and insistence on the 'indivisibility of security'. Both drew on the repertoire of norms enshrined in the Charter international system and post-Cold War declarations, but emphasised different aspects. The differences became embedded in what turned out to be irreconcilable geopolitical ambitions and a deepening existential alienation. The road to war was not straight but it was sure.

PART II
GREAT-POWER CONFLICT

5
AMERICA BETWEEN LEADERSHIP AND PRIMACY

There is an enduring debate about the ends and purpose of US foreign policy.[1] The US came to embrace global supremacy during
World War II but this was neither a long-harboured ambition nor a
reluctant acceptance of some manifest destiny. It was a policy option
shaped by the war.[2] The plan for US ascendancy took shape as early
as 1940, and in the end was formulated in terms of advancing the
American conception of order globally, backed by overwhelming military power. US policy and public opinion were transformed, with
opponents branded as 'isolationists'. In fact, they were mostly conservative internationalists, engaging prudentially in international
affairs but focused above all on domestic development. The new globalists shaped a novel form of internationalism combining leadership
in multilateral institutions and dominance at the head of an order of
its own. This expansive globalism was held in check by the existence
of a powerful alternative order, the military and ideological bloc
headed by the Soviet Union. Wartime cooperation gave way to confrontation. The end of Cold War I in 1989 and the collapse of the
Soviet Union in 1991 gave free rein to the expansive ambitions of
postwar globalism. The 'American century' came into its own.[3] However, unipolar predominance proved fleeting, and Washington's ability to impose its will on other countries was increasingly constrained
by the 'rise of the rest'.[4]

US GRAND STRATEGY

One of the enduring themes of US grand strategy is exceptionalism, the view that Americans are a chosen people with a unique mission to civilise the rest of the world. This can take the form of the US as a model, in which case the focus is on domestic development and the struggle to live up to its stated ideals, described by John Winthrop in 1630 'as a city upon a hill' for others to learn from and observe. This is the hegemonic version of US leadership, where it convinces by the power of example. Alternatively, there is the more active interventionist version, that later took the form of a struggle for primacy. It was first evoked by those calling for the US to aid the Greek struggle for independence in the 1820s. This prompted John Quincy Adams to argue in his famous 4 July 1821 address that America 'has abstained from interference in the concerns of others, even when conflict has been for principles to which she clings . . . she goes not abroad, in search of monsters to destroy'. He ended by asserting that America's 'glory is not *dominion*, but *liberty*'.[5] The Monroe Doctrine of 1823 declared the Americas off-limits to other powers, asserting that the whole region was to be an exclusive American 'sphere of influence'. After 1989, democratic internationalism applied the principle globally. The whole world was effectively treated as a single sphere of interest, and any attempt to carve out a zone of 'privileged interests' by other powers was perceived as a challenge to US supremacy.

The concept of containment shaped the grand strategy of the Cold War era, although it provided little guidance on concrete policies. The Soviet launch of the Sputnik satellite in 1957 provoked a moment of self-doubt accompanied by exaggerated fears of a 'missile gap', while the lessons of defeat in Vietnam were shrugged off by Reagan. The end of the Cold War re-energised American conceptions of global leadership. American power was restored and it appeared that the unipolar moment would endure indefinitely. However, the fundamental question remained unresolved, namely the appropriate relationship between the three components of American power: the multilateralism of the Charter international system, which endowed American power with legitimacy and a grounding in international law; and the two legs of its hegemonic power, the Atlantic power system, and the increasingly globalised economic order. Post-Cold War presidents emphasised different aspects but all agreed on American leadership, until Donald Trump recast this in more crudely material and transactional terms. The Trump phenomenon reflected underlying concern about what globalisation had done to America, accompanied by fears about what sort of society America had become.[6]

Grand strategy describes the overarching purpose and definable goals of foreign policy, combining defence, security and national aspirations with the means and plans to pursue them. In the postwar era, US grand strategy comprised two fundamental elements: the maintenance of US primacy, constrained in the Cold War years but more expansive thereafter; and maintenance of the post-1945 international system, which it had done so much to create and which legitimised US hegemony. This entailed a permanent tension between commitment to multilateralism and the pursuit of narrowly defined national interests, a contradiction defined as one between hegemonic leadership and primacy. Hegemony relies primarily on consent and belief in the values proclaimed by the hegemon, whereas primacy entails predominance and the conscious attempt to thwart the ambitions of others. These aspects of postwar US power have been mutually nourishing and reinforcing.[7] If one grows excessively at the expense of the other, then US grand strategy is thrown into turmoil. The struggle to maintain primacy in the post-Cold War era represented precisely such a period of turmoil, coming perilously close to dominion. Rational statecraft and the realistic appraisal of America's core national interests were questioned. This in turn provoked calls for 'restraint', an issue to which we will return.[8]

Primacy was maintained by a network of security alliances and raw economic and financial power. This represented a consistent strategy to defend US dominance across the most strategically relevant regions of the world: Europe, the Middle East and East Asia.[9] Hegemony was maintained by commitment to multilateral institutions and procedures as well as pervasive cultural influence. The latter is defined as 'soft power', the ability to attract and co-opt and thus to project power without recourse to military means.[10] This was accompanied by the creation of a global network of some 800 military bases in 80 countries, reinforced by numerous multilateral and bilateral security treaties. According to Stephen Brooks and William Wohlforth, there are no real challenges to US primacy and the two postwar constants remain: the US as the world's most powerful state; and its strategic choice to remain deeply engaged in the world. Despite domestic calls for restraint, they argue that retreat from this deep but judicious model of globalism would threaten US security and economic interests and imperil what they call 'world order'.[11] They rightly stress the importance of US leadership, but when untethered from Charter norms it runs the danger of undermining the very order that it seeks to defend.

Scowcroft argued that the Soviet collapse and the dissolution of its empire 'brought to a close the greatest transformation of the international system since World War I', but the contradiction remained.[12] Bush senior argued that the US bore a 'disproportionate responsibility to use [US] power in pursuit of a common good. We also have an obligation to lead'. He noted that the US 'is mostly perceived as benign, without territorial ambitions, uncomfortable with exercising our considerable power ... We need not, indeed should not, become embroiled in every upheaval, but we must help develop multilateral responses to them.' However, his view of the international scene as 'about as much of a blank slate as history ever provides' was an early warning of the potential for overreach.[13] As liberal order became liberal hegemony, the prerogatives of the international system were usurped. The defence of primacy prevented Russia developing a regional hegemony, and later sought to restrain the exercise of Chinese power. In sharp contrast to Bush's benign view, critics argue that US foreign policy since 1945 has been one long 'miscue', leading to much suffering and failed costly military interventions. A policy of complacency and appeasement would have worked better.[14] As Kennan argued, 'In a less than perfect world ... it is natural that the avoidance of the worst should often be a more practical undertaking than the achievement of the best'.[15] From this perspective, there is nothing virtuous about the US bipartisan foreign policy consensus. Instead, a return to the pre-Wilsonian American tradition of republican liberalism, an early version of sovereign internationalism, would have better served US national interests.[16]

The great substitution entailed a linguistic shift from 'international law' to the 'rules-based order', accentuating the contradiction between the impartiality of the international system and the particularity of US primacy. The universalism proclaimed by the liberal international order entailed imposition of the hegemonic norms represented by that order, undermining the formal equality enshrined in the Charter international system. US primacy entailed the containment of other powers, a situation obviously unacceptable to Russia and China and only reluctantly accepted by non-Atlantic states (and even at various times by some within the Atlantic system). The hermetic character of the liberal international order – the liberal antipluralist view that there cannot be anything legitimate outside of it – reduced all 'others' into potential antagonists or outright adversaries. The choice appeared to be subordination to the US-led liberal order, as a 'responsible stakeholder' or some other formulation, or resistance, in which case the entire armoury of coercion and demonisation would be deployed. Traditional forms of diplomacy were marginalised and the conduct of international affairs coarsened. Cold War I was far from a golden age of diplomacy, but at least a certain etiquette was observed and proprieties respected. By contrast, Cold War II is accompanied by sharp denunciations, sanctions and corrosive propaganda campaigns, which are typically portrayed as the exposure of misinformation, fake news and disinformation. The contending power systems portray their own truth, and impartiality gives way to polarisation and partisanship.

LIBERAL HEGEMONY AND AMERICAN PRIMACY

Neoconservatives believe that the maintenance of US primacy is an end in itself, while liberal interventionists seek to deploy US power to advance liberal and human rights. Power and norms converged with devastating effect. The language of hegemony – rules, norms and the prevention of harm – disguised the idiom of primacy. In the former, the US is constrained by the multilateral bodies that it has taken such care to create, whereas the latter prioritises national security interests. The merger allowed the US to interpret the rules in a manner that suited its purpose. Both exalted American exceptionalism, although for different purposes: liberal interventionists to maintain US hegemony, and the neoconservatives to ensure US dominance.

The Bush junior administration was packed with exponents of neoconservative ideas, including Donald Rumsfeld, Richard Perle, Michael Ledeen, Paul Wolfowitz, Elliott Abrams and Scooter Libby, with the militant Dick Cheney as vice president acting often as if he were president. The enduring self-certainty and overweening confidence in America's power to change the world took a peculiar turn in this 'faith-based' presidency. Intuition and certainty took the place of rationality and doubt.[17] As Kaplan puts it, Washington lost the 'tragic sensibility' and failed to understand that, in international affairs, 'all things cannot be fixed', so the world should be accepted as it is.[18] Wise leaders must 'think tragically in order to avoid tragedy'.[19]

The *National Security Strategy* of September 2002 reflected what became known as the Bush doctrine, noting that the US enjoyed 'a position of unparalleled military strength and great economic and political influence'. It licensed pre-emptive military action against hostile states and groups seeking weapons of mass destruction. The US would not allow any hostile foreign power to challenge it militarily. Although affirming its commitment to multilateralism, the *Strategy* made clear that the US 'will not hesitate to act alone, if necessary'. The document also proclaimed the goal of spreading democracy and human rights globally, to develop 'free and open societies on every continent'.[20] It licensed the preventive war against Iraq the following year, violating the fundamental Charter norm of war only in self-defence. This was democratic internationalism in action. In this spirit, Ledeen advised that, 'Every ten years or so, the United States needs to pick up some small crappy little country and throw it against the wall, just to show the world we mean business.'[21] The journalist Ron Suskind quotes an anonymous White House official shortly after the war:

The aide said that guys like me were 'in what we call the reality-based community', which he defined as people who 'believe that solutions emerge from your judicious study of discernible reality'. I nodded and murmured something about enlightenment principles and empiricism. He cut me off. 'That's not the way the world really works anymore', he continued. 'We're an empire now, and when we act, we create our own reality. And while you're studying that reality – judiciously, as you will – we'll act again, creating other new realities, which you can study too, and that's how things will sort out. We're history's actors . . . and you, all of you, will be left to just study what we do'.[22]

The Obama presidency shifted towards the more cautious exercise of liberal hegemony. He followed the lead of secretary of state Hillary Clinton in 2011 in the Libya intervention, but resisted calls to bomb Syria, even after Damascus apparently crossed his 'red line' in using chemical weapons in Ghouta in August 2013. Trump had little truck with the democracy-promotion activities of his predecessor, but he packed his national security team with exponents of neoconservative primacy while marginalising the liberals. Trump couched American primacy in terms of American 'greatness' but the result was much the same. When it came to hegemony, he had no understanding of its subtle relationship to primacy and in the end undermined both. For Trump, rules represented constraints on America's ability to exercise power in the pursuit of 'deals' that were uniquely advantageous to the US, but this shallow mercantilism served neither primacy nor hegemony.

There is a remarkable continuity in US grand strategy.[23] Voices urging restraint were drowned out by those insisting that America was a 'superpower, like it or not'.[24] For Robert Kagan, a US retreat from global responsibilities would mean the world would revert to disorder and chaos. The 'jungle', in his words, would grow back.[25] He failed to distinguish between leadership, which for a major power is appropriate, and primacy, which was increasingly contested. For Glennon, as we have seen, the explanation lies in the creation of a Trumanite 'deep state' as a function of the Cold War, expanding the intelligence services and corporate militarism.[26] The vast military-industrial complex and the ramified alliance system abroad not only persisted but were enhanced after the original cause – the Cold War with the Soviet Union – had gone. Obama White House staffer Ben Rhodes explains this policy continuity in terms of 'the blob', the enduring influence of the foreign policy establishment.[27] This group, mostly located in Washington and its environs, seeks to prevent the erosion of American primacy, which they see as being under permanent threat. Hence the perennial need to ramp up military spending to fill some or other 'gap': missiles, ships or planes. According to Rhodes, the blob 'has been distinguished by its unwillingness, or inability, to reconsider or reprioritize national interests that were first defined after World War II, and then continued, by and large, on auto-pilot after the end of the Cold War'.[28]

At that time, the former US ambassador to the UN, Jeane Kirkpatrick, called on the US to become a more 'normal' power. She urged a greater focus on domestic concerns, because 'a good society is defined not by its foreign policy but its internal qualities … by the relations among its citizens, the kind of character nurtured, and the quality of life lived'.[29] Instead, the Washington foreign policy establishment's 'groupthink' continued to advance an 'exceptionalist' view of US power. From this perspective, the US is always on the side of the good. The country's primacy is inherently benign, even when it makes 'mistakes' and millions die. As classical realists like Hans Morgenthau stressed, even the most benevolent of policies can generate catastrophic outcomes.[30] From a very different perspective, the benign view was challenged by Trump. His critique was based on a narrow mercantilist and semi-isolationist position, hence was easy to discredit. The failure to generate a more substantive and popular critique of American exceptionalism, and its associated militarism, is one of the factors that perpetuated the worst aspects of the post-Cold War negative peace.[31] Patrick Porter is right to note the 'tragic nature of international life', where 'In an inherently insecure world, to order is an illiberal process', in which there have to be compromises 'between liberal values and brutal power politics'.[32] The issue, however, is the character of that order. Compromise is an essential feature of statecraft based on the 'ethics of responsibility', but good leadership also requires the capacity for restraint.

PRIMACY BECOMES DOMINANCE

The rise of al-Qaeda and the Islamist attack on America in 9/11 heralded a new era of global military activism. The 'war on terror' took many forms, including the invasion of Afghanistan in autumn 2001, the war in Iraq in 2003, the attack on Libya in 2011 and support for insurgent forces in Syria from 2011. This helps explain the inflexibility of American policy. Sanctions on Cuba and Iran, with variations in tempo, have endured for decades. Cuba, a country of 11 million people, has endured an illegal embargo imposed by the US for over six decades. In its final days, the Trump administration returned Cuba to its state sponsor of terrorism list, even though Havana had facilitated the peace process in Colombia.[33] Russia joined the 'axis of evil' in 2014 because of its actions in Ukraine. Moscow acknowledged US leadership and even hegemony on certain issues, but refused to accept a dominance that was perceived as threatening to national sovereignty. US postwar grand strategy, the ideational networks that it fostered and the security establishment that it sustains have created a system resistant to change. In keeping with the radicalisation of democratic internationalism, in the post-Cold War era the Trumanite state retained its domestic primacy, now recast as the struggle of democracies versus autocracies.

Trump challenged what he considered to be the anachronistic multilateral formats of the national security state abroad, notably NATO, but his mercantilist critique did not extend to challenging the structures and privileges of the Trumanite state. The military corporations continue to fund think tanks such as the New York-based Atlantic Council, established in 1961 to promote, as its name suggests, the transatlantic community, as well as analogues abroad, such as the Australian Strategic Policy Institute (ASPI), which took the lead in ramping up the containment rhetoric against China. Many of the Democrat members of the relevant profile committees in Congress are funded by the same corporations. There is a 'revolving door' between employment in defence corporations, politics and think tanks. The Trumanite state persists, and although after 1989 there was some retrenchment in military expenditure accompanied by the withdrawal of the bulk of US forces from Europe, the network of US bases abroad was barely trimmed. New justifications were found to maintain overwhelming US military predominance.

As Cold War II intensified, US ideological structures were restored to their earlier centrality. These include the US Agency for International Development (USAID), the Peace Corps, Voice of America, Radio Free Asia, Radio Free Europe-Radio Liberty (RFE/RL), the National Endowment for Democracy (NED) and many more, all of which advance democratic internationalism in one form or another.[34] Carl Gershman, the president of NED, was disarmingly open about his regime-change ambitions, admitting in September 2013 that Ukraine was 'the biggest prize'.[35] What the CIA had earlier tried to achieve by subversion was now done overtly. As a study written soon after the failure of the August 1991 coup in Moscow put it:

> Preparing the ground for last month's triumph of overt action was a network of overt operatives who during the last 10 years have been quietly changing the rules of international politics. They have been doing in public what the CIA used to do in private – providing money and moral support for pro-democracy groups, training resistance fighters, working to subvert communist rule.

The subversive functions of the CIA had been transferred to advocacy institutions such as the NED. The former Soviet dissident Allen Weinstein, a co-founder of a committee to monitor the Helsinki Accords and who in 1984 founded the Center for Democracy, agreed: 'A lot of what we do today was done covertly 25 years ago by the CIA.'[36] Instead of coups, regime-change operations were conducted within the framework of what later came to be known as 'colour revolutions'. Russia claimed that the NED was involved in the overthrow of the Ukrainian president, Viktor Yanukovych, in February 2014.[37]

The US Agency for Global Media (USAGM) was reconfigured and generously refinanced to wage new battles against the soft power and ideology of perceived adversaries. Russia and China were accused of promoting authoritarian governance, hence the perceived need to defend 'human rights, freedom, and democracy as universal values'.[38] These countries responded in kind. China established Confucius Institutes in over a hundred countries, while the cultural work of the Russkiy Mir (Russian World) Foundation was reinforced by the Rossotrudnichestvo (Russian Cooperation) organisation. Moscow and Beijing no longer propound communism, but they do condemn democratic internationalism. From the US perspective, their stance in defence of the Charter principles was no less guilty of double standards than it was accused of itself. Fundamental human rights are traduced and (for Russia) a crabbed conservative illiberalism advanced.[39] The accusation is fair, but when this spilled over into the denigration of alternative policy perspectives on global affairs or views on appropriate models of development and economic policy, then hegemony gave way to domination, and the lauded freedom to intolerance. Legitimate policy differences seen through a Manichean cold war prism become hostile and subversive acts.[40]

The bipartisan defence and security consensus endures. Obama and Trump, in their different ways, challenged elements of the consensus but failed to generate coherent alternative grand strategies. In the end, both bowed to continuity and the 'deep state'. As the price for getting the Senate to ratify the Start-2 treaty with Russia, Obama authorised the most extensive and expensive modernisation of US strategic forces since the 1960s. Trump ramped up the military budget and neglected his campaign promise to shift resources into infrastructure modernisation. The debate over whether the US should exercise 'restraint' and limit itself to 'offshore balancing' – intervening only when a regional balance of power is threatened – or maintain its Cold War commitments is far from resolved. The American 'exit from hegemony' under Trump was partial, while the assertion of primacy endures.[41]

THE TRUMP DISRUPTION

Trump's election to the American presidency in November 2016 dealt a major blow to the consensus. It was interpreted as the end of the Wilsonian era.[42] Trump was an outsider to the political establishment, having never served in an elected office before his unexpected victory. He advanced an ill-defined yet powerful 'America first' agenda, condemning the deleterious effects of globalisation on American jobs and the economy. His slogan of 'make America great again' promised investment in American infrastructure and support for suffering industries (such as coalmining) to usher in a new era of prosperity. In foreign policy, the 'Trump doctrine' combined 'America first' with 'principled realism', whereby states would pursue their own interests while respecting common principles of international behaviour.[43] This came close to sovereign internationalism, but the populist inflection and readiness to use trade wars and other coercive policy instruments repudiated multilateralism.[44] As far as the Trump White House was concerned, the US had become 'hostage to the international order it created, and liberation [was] overdue'.[45] This threatened the foundations of hegemonic stability theory, which asserts that the benevolent leadership of a dominant state is a necessary and sufficient condition for an open and liberal world economy.

Trump's rise reflected a long-term shift 'away from the engaged internationalism that characterized the previous 75 years ... toward something closer to isolationism'.[46] The trend had been apparent during the presidency of Bush junior, when many administration officials were 'outright hostile to the multilateral, rule-based system that the United States has shaped and led'.[47] However, Trumpian nationalism represented something new: the fundamental repudiation of the liberal internationalism that had dominated US foreign policy in the postwar years. It questioned not only the hegemonic form of liberal hegemony that predominated after 1989, but also the fundamental premises of US grand strategy as practised since the war. Trump's approach represented not a return to the sovereign internationalism of the Charter system but to something more visceral and nationalistic, reminiscent of Charles Lindbergh's prewar isolationism or even the pre-1914 era of great-power competition and imperialism. The US was becoming a revisionist power.[48]

Trump's assault on 'globalism' was comprehensive. In October 2018 he argued:

We're putting America first, it hasn't happened in a lot of decades, we're putting them first, we're taking care of ourselves for a change, but radical Democrats want to turn back the clock and restore the rule of corrupt, power-hungry globalists. You know what a globalist is right? A globalist is a person that wants the globe to do well, frankly, not caring about our country so much. We can't have that. They have a word, it sort of became old fashioned – it's called a Nationalist. Really, we're not supposed to use that word, you know what I am? I'm a nationalist, okay? I'm a nationalist, use that word.[49]

As if to confirm the point, two of Trump's leading advisers asserted 'that the world is not a "global community" but an arena where nations compete for advantage . . . Rather than denying this elemental nature of international affairs, we embrace it'.[50] The fundamental premise of liberal internationalism was questioned, the view of 'multilateral regimes, democratic institutions, economic interdependence, and the export of American values and norms as the most effective and appropriate means to advance US interests and to get others to do and want what Americans want'.[51] The whole package was now rejected and the unalloyed assertion of America's interests advanced. Trump's supporters question the post-Cold War 'revisionism in the guise of liberal hegemony'. In that model, 'All states, including authoritarian major powers such as Russia and China, would become supplicants in an American-dominated world order'.[52] In effect, Trump advocated 'offshore balancing', whereby the US would no longer act as the universal policeman and instead intervene strategically to pre-empt the rise of coalitions of regional rivals.[53] At home, Trump's economic nationalism resonated with working-class Americans as well as a middle class whose real incomes had stagnated for a generation.

The reassertion of sovereignty was the guiding principle of the Trump administration. This did not mean the renunciation of US primacy, but this was no longer couched in terms of leadership or even hegemony. To assert primacy, Trump used brutal methods, spurning allies and engaging in high-risk personal diplomacy with adversaries. He denounced nation-building, demanded that allies pay more for their own defence, but built up what he claimed was an underfunded US military. Trump eschewed the language of 'exceptionalism', and thus repudiated the messianism that dominated Bush junior's foreign policy and the more pragmatic version that characterised Obama's leadership. In June 2017, Trump announced that the US would leave the 2015 Paris Climate Agreement, the commitment to reduce carbon emissions to prevent a catastrophic rise in the earth's temperature over 2°C. He also pulled the country out of UNESCO (the UN Educational, Scientific and Cultural Organisation), and in May 2018 he withdrew from the Iran nuclear deal (JCPOA), negotiated by Obama and which had come into effect in 2015. In June 2018, the US left the UN Human Rights Council (UNHRC, up to 2006 the Human Rights Commission) halfway through its term, the first country ever to do so. The US ambassador to the UN, Nikki Haley, argued that the Council was a 'protector of human-rights abusers, and a cesspool of political bias', and therefore 'America should not provide it with any credibility', citing its alleged bias against Israel.[54] In May 2020 Trump announced that the US would stop cooperating with the World Health Organization (WHO), just as the country entered a devastating phase of the Covid-19 pandemic. By mid-2022, SARS-CoV-2 had killed a million Americans, over double the 416,800 US military deaths in World War II.

The Trumpian disruption not only undermined US leadership in global affairs but also potentially turned it into a 'rogue' power, defecting from the global liberal order that it had so assiduously built. His policies even threatened the foundations of the postwar international system, which provided the normative framework for the management of international affairs. Trump's readiness to challenge the postwar consensus raised hopes in Moscow that he would bring new ideas to the table. Russian elites were well aware that he was unstable in his views, temperamental and disloyal in personal relations, and unpredictable in his behaviour, yet his leadership appeared to offer an alternative to renewed cold war. His Democratic opponent, Hillary Clinton, by contrast represented policy continuity and unremitting hostility towards Russia.[55] Trump observed that 'NATO is obsolete and it's extremely expensive for the United States, disproportionately so', and 'it should be readjusted to deal with terrorism'.[56] He later warned that he would only assist European nations during a Russian invasion if they first 'fulfilled their obligations to us'. He also noted that the US had 'to fix our own mess before trying to alter the behaviour of other nations': 'I don't think we have the right to lecture.'

He argued that his 'America first' slogan was a 'brand-new, modern term', and did not signal isolationism of the sort advocated by Lindbergh.[57] Above all, Trump adopted a radical position:

> We desire to live peacefully and in friendship with Russia. . . . We have serious differences . . . But we are not bound to be adversaries. We should seek common ground based on shared interests. Russia, for instance, has also seen the horror of Islamic terrorism. I believe an easing of tensions and improved relations with Russia – from a position of strength – are possible. Common sense says this cycle of hostility must end. Some say the Russians won't be reasonable. I intend to find out. If we can't make a good deal for America, then we will quickly walk from the table.[58]

In the event, the Russiagate allegations of collusion between Putin and Trump and of Russian interference in the 2016 election threatened the legitimacy of his presidency and narrowed Trump's room for diplomatic initiatives.[59] The perception of Russia as a malevolent actor was confirmed, and the drift towards full-blown cold war accelerated.

The US *National Security Strategy* unveiled on 18 December 2017 (NSS-2017) represented a return to elements of the 'Bush doctrine' of American primacy, including a wider role for nuclear weapons against 'non-nuclear strategic attacks'. The document warned against the 'revisionist powers of China and Russia', ranked alongside the 'rogue powers of Iran and North Korea' and the 'transnational threat organisations, particularly jihadist groups'.[60] The previous version issued by Obama listed Russia as a threat, alongside the Ebola virus and so-called Islamic State, but now its elevation to join the company of 'rogue states' reflected the shift from liberal international moralism towards the realism of great-power conflict. The *Strategy* reflected the concerns of the traditional Republican national security establishment over those of the neoconservatives and liberal interventionists. The new strategy had nothing to say about promoting democracy, a key theme of the Bush and Obama presidencies, and instead reflected Trump's anti-globalist 'America first' concerns. The document outlined four pillars of US national security: protecting the homeland; promoting US prosperity; preserving 'peace through strength', a theme earlier advanced by Reagan and Bush senior; and US influence. Although critical of Russia, the document reserved its harshest language for China.

Presenting the document, Trump reaffirmed his desire to 'build great partnership' with Russia and other countries, 'but in a manner that always protects our national interest'. He acknowledged Putin's call, thanking him for the information provided by the CIA that averted a terrorist attack in St Petersburg, noting, 'That is the way it is supposed to work.' He insisted that 'we do not seek to impose our way of life on anyone', and added that he would 'not allow inflexible ideology to become an obstacle to peace'.[61] He reiterated the theme of 'peace through strength', and emphasised his military build-up, which raised the US defence budget for 2018 to $700 billion.[62] The Russian defence budget for that year was only $46 billion, 2.8 per cent of GDP.[63] The document was prepared by H.R. McMaster, Trump's national security adviser, and one of his key deputies, Nadia Schadlow. In response, the Kremlin spokesman Dmitry Peskov noted, 'Looking through [the strategy], particularly those parts concerning our country, one can see the imperial nature of the document, as well as persistent unwillingness to abandon the idea of a unipolar world and accept a multipolar world', and he rejected the country's designation as a threat to US security.[64] China also opposed America's globalist and interventionist agenda, rejecting the insinuation that it was a 'revisionist state' and urged the US to 'abandon its cold war mentality'.[65]

These themes were prominent in the *National Defense Strategy*, an eleven-page unclassified version of which was issued on 19 January

2018. The document noted that in the unipolar decades the US 'enjoyed uncontested or dominant superiority in every operating domain', followed by a period of 'strategic atrophy'. The US faced 'increased global disorder' in which 'inter-state strategic competition, not terrorism, is now the primary concern in US national security'. Top of the list of challengers was China, which was characterised as 'a strategic competitor using predatory economics to intimidate its neighbours while militarizing features in the South China Sea'. As for Russia, 'it has violated the borders of nearby nations and pursues veto power over the economic, diplomatic, and security decisions of its neighbours'.[66] The two states, as in NSS-2017, were labelled 'revisionist powers'. The list of charges against Russia was far-reaching:

> Russia seeks veto authority over nations on its periphery in terms of their governmental, economic, and diplomatic decisions, to shatter the North Atlantic Treaty Organization and change European and Middle East security and economic structures to its favour. The use of emerging technologies to discredit and subvert democratic processes in Georgia, Crimea, and eastern Ukraine is concern enough, but when coupled with its expanding and modernizing nuclear arsenal the challenge is clear.

The document noted the 'resilient, but weakening, post-WWII international order', and warned that competition with China and Russia threatened America's global predominance and eroded its military advantage.[67] The document made no bones about its concern over the loss of American military superiority, which used to be total and unquestionable: 'We could generally deploy our forces when we wanted, assemble them where we wanted, and operate how we wanted. Today, every domain is contested – air, land, sea, space, and cyberspace.'[68] Such days would not return, and Russia and China were indeed the main challengers.

The *Nuclear Posture Review*, revealed on 27 January 2018, once again lamented that the US had 'continued to reduce the number and salience of nuclear weapons', while others, 'including Russia and China, have moved in the opposite direction'.[69] The document asserted that 'The United States does not wish to regard either Russia or China as an adversary and seeks stable relations with both.'[70] However, it went on to outline an ambitious programme for the modernisation of US nuclear forces (begun under Obama), which fuelled a new arms race. Enhanced flexibility of US nuclear options included low-yield options in its submarine-launched (SLBM) warheads and the development of nuclear-armed sea-launched cruise missiles (SLCM). The threshold for the use of nuclear weapons remained ambiguous. In keeping with long-standing US policy, there was no commitment to no first use, forcing Russia and other countries to maintain permanent nuclear readiness. The strategic thinking was redolent of the worst periods of the Cold War, asserting, 'These supplements will enhance deterrence by denying potential adversaries any mistaken confidence that limited nuclear deployment can provide a useful advantage over the United States and its allies.'[71] We will return to the issue of arms control, or the lack thereof, in Chapter 9.

BUSINESS AS USUAL

Biden came to the presidency committed to 'standing up' to Russia and all its works.[72] He had long been closely involved in Ukrainian matters, in particular during the latter stages of the Euromaidan insurgency of 2013–14 and then in curating the new pro-American administration. His son, Hunter, was on the board of Burisma, a Ukrainian energy company owned by the controversial oligarch Mykola Zlochevsky. In their first telephone call in July 2019, Trump asked the newly elected Ukrainian president, Volodymyr Zelensky, to investigate whether any malfeasance had been involved. The implication that arms transfers depended on Zelensky acquiescing in the attempt to discredit Biden, his potential opponent in the 2020 presidential election, led to Trump's impeachment. On the campaign trail, Biden promised:

The Biden foreign policy agenda will place the United States back at the head of the table, in a position to work with its allies and partners to mobilize collective action on collective threats. The world does not organize itself. For 70 years, the United States, under Democratic and Republican presidents, played a leading role in writing the rules, forging the agreements, and animating the institutions that guide relations among nations and advance collective security and prosperity – until Trump.[73]

The return to liberal hegemony was welcomed by partisans of American foreign policy activism.[74] The bipartisan policy of US primacy was restored, accompanied by the now ritual condemnation of Russia and China – the language of 'partnership' had long gone. Biden pledged 'to impose real costs on Russia for its violation of international norms and stand with Russian civil society, which has bravely stood time and again against President Vladimir Putin's kleptocratic authoritarian system'.[75] He warned that rules of the digital age should not be written by China and Russia and, instead, 'It is time for the United States to lead in forging a technological future that enables democratic societies to thrive and prosperity to be shared broadly.'[76] Biden's foreign policy, he promised, would be driven by domestic concerns and the interests of the American middle class and recovery from the Covid-19 pandemic. The priority was to create jobs, promote economic growth and modernise the country's decayed infrastructure. To this end the ambitious 'build back better' agenda envisaged spending $1.9 trillion on Covid relief, $2.3 trillion on infrastructure and climate, and nearly $2 trillion extra for education, families and healthcare. Following the chaotic withdrawal from Afghanistan in August 2021, the earlier 'nation-building' agenda, the attempt to remake states and societies, was abandoned, but the ideology of democratic internationalism was not. At home, the ambitious but misnamed Inflation Reduction Act of August 2022 provided $490 billion in spending and tax breaks to support energy security and green technology, including subsidies for electric vehicles. This was an industrial strategy the like of which had not been seen for decades.

Biden faced a fundamental choice between restoration and renewal, both dependent on rebuilding American credibility.

Although the foundations of US grand strategy endure, actual US foreign policy changes with every leader. This generates 'a dangerous game of American roulette, dealing with a United States that can flip unpredictably from one foreign policy posture to its opposite'.[77] Some issues persist, such as a renewed nuclear arms race with China and Russia accompanied by what had become the $1.7 trillion nuclear modernisation programme.[78] The 'Russia syndrome', whereby policy lacked strategic direction and typically overreacted to events as a result of partisan domestic in-fighting, was repeated with China. Neither country would let the US speak to them 'from the position of force', as Lavrov put it. When it came to China, the options were to replay the Cold War and depict the struggle as an ideological one, or 'to identify China's legitimate interests in Asia and around the world and determine what Washington should accept, where it should try to outcompete, and what it must confront'.[79] When it came to Russia, the choice depended on

> how deftly the Biden administration defines its fundamental interests – either as a hegemonic democratic empire, determined and obliged to implement the international rules of the game; or as a leading but restrained geopolitical and economic power prepared to define those interests more narrowly that allows other nations, as long as they do not directly challenge America, to live more or less according to their own standards.[80]

In other words, to use the language outlined earlier, the choice was between democratic internationalism (liberal anti-pluralism), the attempt to reshape the world in America's image, or sovereign internationalism (charter liberalism), in which the US exercises restrained leadership in cooperation with others while respecting their autonomy and choices. This offered an escape from the 'unipolar predicament', in which the assertion of primacy stymied domestic development while undermining cooperative relations with other powers.[81]

Biden's inauguration speech on 20 January 2021 promised to 'repair our alliances', a theme he developed in his State Department address on 4 February. Biden outlined his administration's major foreign policy goals and declared that 'America is back'. This included the restoration of the Iran nuclear deal and a return to the Paris Climate Agreement and WHO. He worked to rebuild relations with NATO and European partners, promising to restore 'the muscle of democratic alliances that have atrophied over the past few years of neglect and, I would argue, abuse'. He also halted Trump's planned troop withdrawals from Germany, retaining the whole complement of 38,000. He called China 'our most serious competitor', but much of the speech was devoted to Russia, insisting that the US would stop 'rolling over in the face of Russia's aggressive actions'.[82] It is hard to make sense of this, since the Trump administration could hardly be accused of 'rolling over' to Russia, despite Trump's laudatory personal comments about Putin. America's re-engagement with multilateral agencies and policies restored the status quo, but the Trump phenomenon exposed elements of crisis in the old order.

There could be no simple return to business as usual. While some of the damage to the alliance system inflicted by the previous administration could be repaired fairly easily, the deeper sources of the Trumpian disruption remained. Advocates of restraint were disappointed, with Biden promising more of the same for an already overstretched country. The pledge to maintain US forces in Saudi Arabia and the arrival of more troops in north-east Syria kept the US engaged in the various conflicts across the Middle East: 'Policymakers must stop the endless occupation of the Middle East and prioritize America's own interests rather than a global force posture acting as an enforcer of liberal hegemony.'[83] His order to withdraw US forces from Afghanistan in 2021 revealed an unexpected radicalism. However, the precipitate and chaotic manner in which it was conducted allowed the Taliban to occupy Kabul on 15 August, accompanied by scenes reminiscent of America's evacuation from Saigon in April 1975. This blow to the credibility of the Biden administration may well have influenced policymaking over Ukraine in the following months. Defeat in Afghanistan represented yet another failure of ambitious post-Cold War nation-building efforts. America's longest war raised some fundamental questions about the overall coherence of US grand strategy.

Addressing the Munich Security Conference in February 2021, Biden pledged 'unshakable' support for the Atlantic alliance, as part of the era-defining struggle to safeguard democracy. He once again proclaimed 'America is back', and he even used the term 'Europe whole and free', the watchword of US hegemonic leadership in the post-communist era. He renewed the commitment to the Atlantic alliance and to work with European partners to face common challenges. He warned that the world was at an 'inflection point' between those who viewed 'autocracy' as the way forward and 'those who understand that democracy is essential – essential to meeting those challenges'. Among the challenges was 'long-term strategic competition with China', including pushing back against 'the Chinese government's economic abuses and coercion that undercut the foundations of the international economic system'. As for Russia, he noted that 'The Kremlin attacks our democracies and weaponizes corruption to try to undermine our system of governance.' He warned that 'Putin seeks to weaken European – the European project and our NATO Alliance. He wants to undermine the transatlantic unity and our resolve, because it's so much easier for the Kremlin to bully and threaten individual states than it is to negotiate with a strong and closely united transatlantic community.' He pledged continued support for Ukraine, although cautioned there could be no return to the reflexive 'opposition and rigid blocs of the Cold War'. Competition should not 'lock out cooperation on issues that affect us all', and he listed the Covid pandemic, Ebola, climate change and nuclear proliferation.[84]

The *Interim National Security Strategic Guidance* of March 2021 outlined the administration's priorities.[85] The document combined the need to 'build back better' following the pandemic and the Trumpian disruption with the renewal of American global leadership. This involved revitalising 'America's unmatched network of alliances and partnerships', as Biden put it in the introduction. The document described 'a world of rising nationalism, receding democracy, growing rivalry with China, Russia, and other authoritarian states, and a technological revolution that is reshaping every aspect of our lives' (p. 6). Three key goals were outlined: first, the US had to 'Defend and nurture the underlying sources of American strength'; second, this would allow the US to 'Promote a favourable distribution of power to deter and prevent adversaries from directly threatening' the US and its allies; and third, the US would 'lead and sustain a stable and open international system, underwritten by strong democratic alliances, partnerships, multilateral institutions, and rules' (p. 9). In short, the document returned to enduring post-Cold War themes. While seeking to undo the damage wrought by Trump to US prestige and relationships, it offered very little in the way of rethinking US grand strategy. This model of liberal hegemony was already running into the sands before Trump. The refusal to envisage a cooperative model of world order based on collaboration with other sovereign powers and not just allies reproduced Cold War attitudes. More dangerously, the triumphal spirit induced a hubristic ethos and blunted sensitivity to the risks.

In keeping with Trumpian priorities, much attention was devoted to China, characterised as 'the only competitor potentially capable of combining its economic, diplomatic, military, and technological power to mount a sustained challenge to a stable and open international system'. Russia was substantively mentioned only once, described as 'determined to enhance its global influence and play a disruptive role on the world stage'. The two countries 'have invested heavily in efforts meant to check US strengths and prevent us from defending our interests and allies around the world' (p. 8). In other words, there was not much sign of new thinking, and instead the logic of substitution and cold-peace thinking was intensified. The document claimed that the US 'cannot return to business as usual, and the past order cannot simply be restored' (p. 8), but this was precisely what was on offer. It did indicate some awareness of the need for change, above all ending what it called 'forever wars' (p. 15) and recognising that strategic competition did not 'preclude working with China when it is in our national interests to do so' (p. 21), although the commitment to 'revitalize democracy the world over' at a time when 'authoritarianism is on the global march' (p. 19) suggested a Cold War-style ideological offensive.

The *National Defense Strategy* of March 2022 focused on China, even as the war was raging in Ukraine. The document justified the

$773 billion defence budget for 2023 by prioritising the Chinese threat in the Indo-Pacific, while Russia was presented as an acute threat.[86] China remained enemy no. 1, despite the war in Europe. The point was reiterated by a leading figure in the Atlantic Council who argued that the US had to prepare for war with both Russia and China.[87] The immediate issue was the Iran nuclear deal. Trump had brusquely pulled the US out of the JCPOA in May 2018, as part of the strategy of 'maximum pressure', while promising to negotiate a 'better deal', although typically none was forthcoming. Iran turned to China and negotiated a twenty-five-year strategic partnership, including economic cooperation of some $400 billion, throwing Iran an economic lifeline. In addition, in October 2019 Iran signed a preferential trade agreement with the Eurasian Economic Union (EEU), significantly boosting exports despite the US economic blockade. Work began on constructing a second nuclear reactor at the Bushehr power plant in November 2019 to add 1,000 megawatts to Iran's power grid. The visit of Iranian president Ebrahim Raisi to Moscow in January 2022 was accompanied by declarations of 'strategic cooperation' and condemnation of what was described as the US strategy of domination. In his address to the State Duma, Raisi mercilessly condemned NATO enlargement and outlined a joint strategy of resistance.[88]

By then it was clear that a return to the JCPOA was unlikely. In November 2020, the Iranian parliament passed a law obliging the government to restore elements of the country's nuclear programme that had been halted as part of the JCPOA. More advanced centrifuges were installed at the Natanz and Fordow facilities, which by late 2022 had raised uranium enrichment to 60 per cent, with 90 per cent the threshold to make an atomic bomb. The law also mandated the government to stop implementing the International Atomic Energy Agency (IAEA) Additional Protocol, which guaranteed extensive verification over Iran's nuclear programme. While Moscow sought to restore the JCPOA, it rejected US attempts to add other issues, such as Iran's missiles or support for regional proxies, which it considered extraneous matters.[89] In the negotiations in Geneva, Iran demanded the wholesale lifting of sanctions and for any agreement to be enshrined in international law. It no longer trusted Washington to keep its word. The US argued that some of the sanctions were not associated with the nuclear deal but human rights and terrorist abuses. With the onset of war in Ukraine, Russia was less willing to see Iranian oil back on the market, and called on the US to pledge not to impose sanctions on any trade between Russia and Iran if the agreement was restored. As the war progressed, Russia and Iran forged closer military and economic ties.

WARNING SIGNS

On entering office in 2021, the secretary of state, Antony Blinken, talked of a reset of relations with China and a 'strategic dialogue' with Russia. The Biden administration combined pushback strategies with diplomacy. In April 2021, he invited Putin and Xi to an online conference on global environmental challenges. At the same time, the president doubled down on support for Ukraine. In March 2021, the Pentagon announced a new $125 million package for the supply of 'defensive lethal weapons' within the framework of the Ukraine Security Assistance Initiative, in addition to the $150 million already allocated by Congress. Between 2014 and 2021, the US supplied over $2 billion in 'security assistance'.[90] Ukraine was granted the status of NATO Enhanced Opportunities Partner in recognition of the progress made in defence reform, and the NATO summit in June 2021 reaffirmed the strategic commitment to membership. By then Ukraine had 250,000 personnel under arms, defence spending was running at 6 per cent of GDP, and over 400 kilometres of complex engineering structures had been built along the line of contact in the Donbass, along with a second line of fortifications.[91] Confrontation assumed a harsh personal edge amid remarkably undiplomatic language. In a TV interview on 16 March, Biden agreed that Putin was 'a killer', and reprised his notion that he had 'no soul'. This was accompanied by the threat that Russia 'would pay a price' for allegedly helping Trump in the 2020 presidential election. The director of national intelligence issued an Intelligence Community Assessment asserting that at Putin's direct behest Russia had conspired to help Trump and to denigrate Biden.[92]

The general coarsening of the conduct of international affairs was on display shortly afterwards at the first meeting in the Biden era of top US and Chinese officials in Anchorage, Alaska, on 18 March. The Chinese foreign ministry issued a statement setting the terms, calling on the US to 'discard cold war and zero-sum thinking'.[93] Although China was reluctant to categorise the confrontation as a cold war, it increasingly used the term, as on this occasion. Blinken opened the session by raising 'deep concerns with actions by China, including in Xinjiang, Hong Kong, Taiwan, cyberattacks on the United States and economic coercion against our allies. Each of these actions threatens the rules-based order that maintains global stability.' The Chinese foreign minister Wang Yi was in no mood for lectures and riposted with uncustomary lack of finesse: 'We do not believe in invading through the use of force, or to topple other regimes through various means, or to massacre the people of other countries, because all of those would only cause turmoil and instability in this world.'[94] The point was reiterated by Yang Jiechi, Politburo member and director of the CPC's Central Foreign Affairs Commission Office, in words that echoed the earlier foreign ministry statement. He asserted that China would do whatever it takes to resist US bullying and interference in its internal affairs, and demanded that the US maintain normal standards of courtesy in diplomatic affairs: 'I think we thought too well of the United States. We require the US to treat China and Sino-US relations in an objective and rational manner, discard the cold war and zero-sum thinking, and respect China's sovereignty, security, and development interests.'

This reflected a historical shift in the Chinese approach and profound disillusionment with US behaviour amid what were perceived to be double standards. Yang did not mince his words:

> So let me say here that, in front of the Chinese side, the United States does not have the qualification to say that it wants to speak to China from a position of strength. The US side was not even qualified to say such things even 20 years or 30 years back, because this is not the way to deal with the Chinese people. If the United States wants to deal properly with the Chinese side, then let's follow the necessary protocols and do things the right way.

The key point was that he defended the autonomy of the international system: 'What China and the international community follow or uphold is the United Nations-centred international system and the international order underpinned by international law, not what is advocated by a small number of countries of the so-called rules-based international order.'[95] US global interventionism and anti-diplomacy here encountered serious and substantive resistance. Despite Trump's departure, the US stance had not changed. This proved the rule that Democratic administrations, 'by a long tradition, assume they must be still more hawkish than Republican opponents so as to deflect any charge they are "soft" on national security questions'.[96]

The pushback against the US resonated 'with the belief of many Chinese that their country has found its voice on the global stage'. The new tone reflected a 'paradigm shift' in which 'China believes that its rise to great-power status entitles it to a new role in world affairs', one that was incompatible with US dominance.[97] It was a view long held by Moscow. Russian foreign minister Lavrov visited China shortly afterwards to celebrate the twentieth anniversary of the 2001 Russo-Chinese friendship treaty. Meeting in Guilin City, Lavrov's opening statement declared, 'We need to mobilise our supporters while defending justice and the principles of the UN Charter which, as I have repeatedly said, are being increasingly ignored by Western colleagues. They are trying to invent their own rules and to impose them on all others.' He insisted that the US-led liberal order 'does not represent the will of the international community'.[98] The two sides condemned 'hegemonic bullying' and in a joint statement declared that no country should seek to impose its form of democracy on any other: 'Interference in a sovereign nation's internal affairs under the excuse of "advancing democracy" is unacceptable.'[99] They agreed to stand firm against Western sanctions and to reduce dependence on the dollar in international trade settlements. Lavrov noted that 'We both believe that the US has a destabilising role. It relies on Cold War military alliances and is trying to set up new alliances to undermine the world order.'[100] Both sides acknowledged that this was a cold war of a new kind although reproducing features of the original.

NEW CHALLENGES

The reassertion of American leadership was in for a rough ride. The post-Cold War balance was giving way to a more competitive situation. Even some US allies, including France, Hungary and Italy, were wary of being trapped in the logic of US hostility to Russia and China. Germany in particular pushed back against American attempts to block the 1,230-kilometre (764-mile) Nord Stream 2 gas pipeline from Ust-Luga in Leningrad region to Pomerania, an issue that was 'shaping up as the biggest clash between Europe and the United States since the end of World War II'. Washington continued its Cold War policy of opposition to an energy partnership between Russia and Western Europe, fearing that it would heighten Moscow's economic and political influence in Europe while providing resources for military modernisation.[101] German chancellor Angela Merkel's support for the project did not waver, on the grounds that it was a purely commercial venture, despite political pressure to cancel. Her resistance was taken as an indication that 'European countries are steadily less subservient to Washington'.[102] In the end, to help improve relations with Germany, a presidential waiver in May allowed the pipeline to be completed by September 2021. However, as Merkel's leadership gave way to a coalition government headed by the Social Democrat Olaf Scholz later that year, the certification process was halted. The project was frozen in response to Russia's invasion of Ukraine, and then on 26 September 2022 both strands of Nord Stream 1 and one of Nord Stream 2 were blown up in an act of sabotage by unknown parties.[103]

In its quadrennial review of global trends issued in March 2021, the US National Intelligence Council warned that, in the coming decades, 'the world will face more intense and cascading global challenges'.[104] Russia and China were categorised as 'rising and revisionist powers ... seeking to reshape the international order to be more reflective of their interests and tolerant of their governing systems ... for an order devoid of Western origin norms that allows them to act with impunity at home and in their perceived spheres of influence'. The report also noted intensifying ideological competition with

China, which in the 'evolving geopolitical competition' was unlikely to gain the same intensity as in the Cold War, but 'China's leadership already perceives it is engaged in a long-term ideological struggle with the United States'.[105] Russia was categorised as 'likely to remain a disruptive power for much or all of the next two decades even as its material capabilities decline relative to other major players'. Its advantages included 'a sizable conventional military, weapons of mass destruction, energy and mineral resources, an expansive geography, demographics, and a willingness to use force overseas, [which] will enable it to continue playing the role of spoiler and power broker in the post-Soviet space, and at times farther afield'.[106] The administration's *Global Posture Review* reported in November 2021, but added little to the existing mix of policies. It reaffirmed the US commitment to strengthen NATO, but left open the strategic question of balancing commitments between Europe and Asia and the stationing of new land-based weapons in Europe. US military infrastructure across the region was to be enhanced, including in Australia, Guam and the Pacific islands, while the 25,000 cap on active troops in Germany was lifted.[107]

On coming to power, Biden declared that the US was 'not looking to kick off a cycle of escalation and conflict with Russia. We want a stable, predictable relationship'.[108] Moscow was receptive but sceptical, by now believing that the US had become a 'rogue' state. Deputy foreign minister Sergei Ryabkov insisted that the 'American narrative' had not only lost touch with reality but it had also 'lost signs of common sense'. He sought to normalise relations, but 'it will not be possible to conduct a conversation with Russia from a position of strength'.[109] Moscow by now was convinced that it was impossible to reach any agreement with Washington. The US in its view had become 'undealable with' (*nedogovorsposobnyi*). Biden initiated the Reset, but had become extremely critical. Russia was also adopting a more uncompromising stance. The impasse reflected not only policy failures, susceptible to change through negotiation, but a more profound existential separation. The two sides lacked a common language. Western commentary that the UN system was failing was interpreted in Russia as yet another indication that the political West sought to free itself of postwar multilateral constraints. Nevertheless, when Biden suggested a summit meeting, after some hesitation Moscow accepted.

The contradictions between the two countries were not 'antagonistic' in the earlier Cold War manner, when their respective social systems were based on fundamentally different values and principles. Compromises and agreements should have been easier, but contrasting interpretations of post-Cold War order led to a deepening estrangement. Russia's slide into authoritarianism did not help, but the US maintains cordial relations with any number of authoritarian systems – if the geopolitics align. Strategic differences were compounded by subjective factors, including personal animosities and perceptions.[110] Conflict became entrenched and the scope for diplomacy constrained. At home, Biden was accused of 'going soft on Putin'.[111] The radical democrat and former chess champion Garry Kasparov warned that 'History has demonstrated time and again that appeasing a dictator only convinces him you're too weak to oppose him, provoking further aggression.'[112]

The summit meeting in Geneva on 16 June 2021 did not hide the differences yet signalled constructive engagement. Working groups were established to discuss strategic arms and cyber issues, and the joint statement reaffirmed the principle (in language used by Reagan and Gorbachev at their meeting in Geneva in 1985) that 'a nuclear war cannot be won and must never be fought'. Unlike the earlier Cold War, the two powers no longer shape international politics alone. Nevertheless, Biden explicitly recognised Russia as a 'great power', a much-delayed acknowledgement of reality. It appeared that a return to a cold war-style relationship, in which conflict was accepted and managed, would stabilise the relationship and lower the ideological temperature. The two countries would focus on their respective concerns. The US would concentrate on consolidating the political West against authoritarian challenges, deal with its domestic problems and redefine its global leadership in the struggle against China. However, for Russia there was a major piece of unfinished business – the inadequacy of the European security system and the impasse in Ukraine. Moscow refused to join the political West as a subordinate, although history may well judge this to have been a mistake of historic proportions. Alliance with a dynamic and innovative system would have allowed the country to focus on domestic development. Instead, the Kremlin turned to a forceful resolution of the perceived security dilemma.

The National Defense Authorization Act (NDAA) of December 2021 allocated $778 billion to defence in 2022, a 5 per cent increase over the previous year. Congress added several anti-Russian amendments, including $4 billion to 'deter' Russia in Europe, to support Ukraine and to prevent Russian meddling in Interpol. Attempts to have Russia declared a state 'sponsor of terrorism', however, failed to pass. The conditions were created for a proxy war between Russia and the political West. America had 'squandered its Cold War victory'.[113]

6
GLOBAL CHINA

China seeks to avoid making the mistakes that destroyed the Soviet Union. Marxist – Leninist ideology had turned into stultifying dogma and failed to provide an adequate framework to analyse the challenges facing the country. Moscow repeatedly missed opportunities to conduct reforms that could have rejuvenated the Soviet economy and society. Instead, Gorbachev's transformational but confused reforms in the late 1980s precipitated the dissolution of the communist system and the disintegration of the country. The political West will not be so fortunate in its new protagonist, and China is unlikely to give up in like manner. China will prove a more enduring and formidable challenge than the Soviet Union ever was.[1] Beijing has been more skilful in defining and advancing its interests while adapting to technological and societal challenges. China has become the leading alternative to liberal hegemony, bending with the wind when necessary but firm in resolve when it comes to core principles and interests. This derives in part from the civilisational self-confidence lacking in the Soviet Union, as well as from changes in international politics. Robert Gilpin argues that as a country increases in power it will seek to shape its environment.[2] Instead of the liberalisation anticipated by some Western observers, the political regime consolidated its power.[3] There would be no Gorbachev-style reform communism, let alone Western-style democratisation here – at least, not for the foreseeable future. Party-led communism of reform remains the ruling ideology, and in various original formulations reinforced its hold. This does not mean that China will avoid the problems that gave rise to reform communism in the Soviet Union. One-party dominance can deliver public goods, but the Leninist trap does not thereby disappear. Problems of political inclusion, accountability and non-corrupt governance remain. Critics argue that China could ultimately suffer a fate similar to that of the Soviet Union, although by a different route.[4]

CHINA COMES OF AGE

Xi Jinping was appointed general secretary of the Communist Party of China in November 2012 and president of the country in March 2013. In 2016 the CPC anointed Xi 'core' leader and thereby elevated him above his immediate predecessors to a status equal to that of Mao Zedong and Deng Xiaoping. In the previous five years, Xi's harsh anti-corruption campaign had felled potential rivals and consolidated power in his hands. On assuming office, he set two main goals: to make China a 'moderately prosperous society' by doubling its 2010 per capita GDP to $10,000 by the time of the centenary of the CPC's foundation in 2021 (in Covid conditions it reached just under $9,000); and for China to become a 'fully developed, rich and powerful' nation by the centenary of the establishment of the People's Republic of China in 2049.[5] Xi's speech to the opening of the 19th Party Congress on 18 October 2017 outlined global ambitions for a re-emerging China that had entered a 'new era' and would move 'closer to centre stage' in world affairs. In his four-hour address, Xi described 'a new historic juncture in China's development'. He defined the 'principal contradiction' (using a Maoist term) as that 'between unbalanced and inadequate development and the people's ever-growing needs for a better life'. At the closing ceremony on 24 October, it was announced that Xi's 'Thought on Socialism with Chinese Characteristics for a New Era' had been written into the CPC's Charter. He was thereby elevated to the pantheon of great leaders.[6] With the abolition of the formal limit of two five-year presidential terms in the state constitution and the suspension of the Party's informal convention about reappointment, the 20th Party Congress in October 2022 extended Xi's leadership.

Xi believes that Chinese ideology is superior to that of the USSR, which failed to understand Marxist methodology and the character of the threat from the West. Underestimation of the ideological character of national security and 'ideological confusion', above all through the acceptance of 'universal values', undermined the CPSU's 'leading and guiding' role and provoked the Soviet collapse. China's communism of reform reinforced the leading role of the Party and avoided the dogmatic and ultimately self-destructive Soviet form. Xi at the 19th Party Congress formulated this as a fourteen-point plan to turn China into a 'great modern socialist country' that was 'prosperous, strong, democratic, culturally advanced, harmonious and beautiful', while its foreign policy defended sovereign internationalism. In his opening speech, Xi argued that as China became 'a moderately prosperous society' at home, in international affairs, 'It will be an era that sees China moving closer to centre stage and making greater contributions to mankind', and he called on the 'peoples of all countries to join China's effort to build a common destiny for mankind and enduring peace and stability'.[7]

The 'dual circulation' strategy, unveiled in May 2020, sought to reduce dependence on foreign markets. Domestic demand and import substitution would increasingly balance 'external circulation' (that is, international trade and economic ties). Rather than allowing globalisation to hollow out the domestic economy, China would once again 'walk on two legs' (Mao's attempt to balance industry and agriculture). China was proposing its own set of norms and sought to shape the global agenda. Giovanni Arrighi famously argued that it was only a matter of time before economic power was converted into global order-making ambitions, and he was right.[8]

The Chinese government launched a number of initiatives to increase its 'soft power', although the instrumental use of the term misrepresents its character.[9] The emphasis shifted from soft to 'discursive power'.[10] Confucius Institutes were created in 2004, and by 2021, 516 had been established in 140 countries. The internationalisation of Chinese higher education saw tens of thousands of

Chinese students study abroad, although financial and other impediments, including security service surveillance in the US and elsewhere, reversed the trend even before the Covid-19 pandemic struck in early 2020. This was accompanied by tightening social controls at home. The anti-corruption campaign removed Xi's rivals, while media and political freedoms were limited. Reform initiatives were firmly suppressed. Russia meanwhile moved closer to China in political terms, with both concerned about protest from below and democracy promotion from abroad. Internal developments in China and its more assertive stance abroad, as with Russia earlier, provoked a backlash. Some genuine concerns were addressed, while threats were exaggerated. Clive Hamilton, for example, argues that China is exporting its authoritarianism to Australia and infiltrating the West to subvert liberal democracy.[11]

In structural political terms there are similarities with the USSR, above all the political dominance of the 92-million-strong CPC, which under the leadership of Xi intensified its control over society and restricted the earlier modest liberalising measures. However, China is a far more effective developmental state than the USSR ever was. It is far more integrated into the global economy and more of a 'peer competitor'. The US government estimated that at its peak in late 1975 the USSR's GDP reached 57 per cent of America's, but thereafter the Soviet economy grew more slowly and the proportion fell back.[12] With the USSR committed to self-sufficiency, in 1984 foreign trade comprised only 4 per cent of Soviet GDP, most of which was conducted with other Soviet bloc countries.[13] By contrast, when China overtook the US in purchasing power parity (PPP) terms in 2014, it had a GDP of $17.6 trillion, compared to America's $17.4 trillion.[14] By late 2020, China's nominal GDP reached 71 per cent of America's. The fourteenth five-year development plan, 2021–5, anticipated that by 2027–8 China would overtake the US to become the world's largest economy in nominal terms, although it will take longer to achieve parity in per capita incomes. The plan envisaged a doubling of GDP by 2035 compared to 2020 to achieve the status of a high-income country. China also rapidly gained in military power. Nominal Chinese defence spending is a quarter that of the US (in

2020 $178.2 billion compared to America's $738 billion), but spending is more focused and in purchasing terms is much greater.

CHINA AND WORLD ORDER

The question then appears to be the one posed by Ikenberry: 'Will China overthrow the existing order or become part of it?'[15] This is a fundamentally misleading way of posing the question. China already considers itself a member of the international system by right, so there can be no question of 'joining' anything else. Nevertheless, Ikenberry is right to question how China will behave within the international system. After 1945, the US took the lead in creating the institutions of the liberal international order, which later provided the framework for globalisation – thus fostering China's rise. The liberal order is a power system, but it also has its own rules, which are mostly compatible with the larger international system within which it is nested. China stands accused, above all by the US, of violating some of these rules. These infractions include the poor defence of intellectual property rights, unfair access to the Chinese domestic market, the dominance and distorting effect of state-owned enterprises (SOEs), militarising the South China Sea and intimidating countries in which it has invested to prevent them criticising China.

In addition, there has been heavy repression in the Xinjiang Uyghur Autonomous Region, justified by Beijing as being in response to acts of terrorism by the al-Qaeda-affiliated East Turkestan Islamic Movement (ETIM). The repression has affected great swathes of the Islamic population who had nothing to do with secessionist militancy.[16] International lawyers debate whether actions there, including the incarceration of up to a million people in 're-education' camps, the destruction of mosques and abuse against women, amounts to genocide.[17] Xinjiang is crucial for China's development, with three of the Belt and Road's (see below) six main corridors passing through the region, including the $60 billion China–Pakistan Economic Corridor (CPEC) that provides China with access to the Indian Ocean through the BRI-financed port of Gwadar. In July 2020, a draconian national security law was imposed on Hong Kong in response to unrest provoked by the attempt to introduce a new extradition law in 2019. The earlier 'umbrella' protests in 2014 defended more open elections but in Beijing's view overstepped the bounds of the 1997 transfer agreement with the UK. Taiwan is an enduring bone of contention with the West. When the Nationalist forces under the leadership of Chiang Kai-shek retreated to the island in 1949 after losing the civil war, all sides considered it part of the Chinese state. The US committed itself to the One China principle when it signed the Shanghai Communiqué in 1972. The Republic of China (as Taiwan is officially known) has enjoyed extraordinary economic success, and in the 1980s transitioned to democracy. The PRC is committed to peaceful reunification by the anniversary year of 2049, but the military option cannot be discounted. A series of provocative visits by senior American officials from summer 2022 aggravated the situation, as did the passing of the $10 billion Taiwan Enhanced Resilience Act in December of that year. The US has maintained a degree of 'strategic ambiguity' over how far it would go in the island's defence, but in recent years has come close to a military commitment.

Beijing's early success in containing the Covid-19 pandemic was accompanied in spring 2020 by the radicalisation of China's foreign policy rhetoric (the so-called 'wolf warrior' diplomacy), which trumpeted China's successes while hitting back hard against critics, an approach that proved deeply counter-productive. China moved beyond the legitimate striving for parity of esteem in the international system, and advanced its governance model as superior to what it perceives to be a declining political West. The more assertive China of Xi amounts to what Elizabeth Economy calls a 'third revolution', a new phase in communist China's development following the revolutionary élan of Mao Zedong and the 'quiet rise' masterminded by Deng Xiaoping. She notes that on becoming leader Xi talked about the rejuvenation of the 'Chinese Dream', which was defined not as political reform or constitutionalism but 'a call for a CCP-led China to reclaim the country's greatness'.[18] Economy argues that Beijing seeks a radical change in international politics whereby the US is essentially pushed out of the Pacific and becomes merely an Atlantic power.[19] Given the economic weight of the Asia-Pacific region, this would turn China into the new global hegemon.[20] The goal is no longer simply to exercise China's increased economic muscle; Xi's vision of the centrality of China 'connotes a radically transformed international order'.[21]

This may be the ambition, but its accomplishment is far from assured. There are simple physical constraints on further development, with climate change and water shortages affecting China's urbanisation, while the demographic consequences of the one-child policy imposed between 1980 and 2016 entails an ageing population with greater healthcare needs and a declining workforce.[22] The structural factors that prevented Russia becoming part of the expanding political West after 1989 apply with even greater force to China, which never considered itself part of the historical let alone the political West. Ikenberry called for the liberal order to become 'so expansive and so institutionalized that China has no choice but to become a full-fledged member of it', but the conditions of entrance into 'liberal order' were problematic for Russia and are prohibitive for China. Beijing will not enter into a hierarchical relationship with Washington, let alone become a subaltern like the postwar European states. Ikenberry is right to call for China's power to be exercised within 'the rules and institutions that can protect the interests of all states in the more crowded world of the future'.[23] These are the rules not of the US-led liberal order but of the international system, which in large part overlap: but the other part is a US-dominated power system that China and Russia will resist joining as 'vassals'. The former provides a broad framework for sovereign development and a common peace order, working in partnership with the US and the political West – if an appropriate formula for cooperation can be found.

CHINA'S HORIZONS

The 'third revolution' is premised on overcoming the weakness and humiliation endured by China from the mid-nineteenth century. Its relatively low international status is considered a 'historical mistake' that has to be corrected.[24] China's distinctive developmental path comes over forcefully in Zhang Weiwei's spirited defence of China's approach to domestic and international affairs. The central theme of his famous trilogy *The China Ripple*, *The China Wave* and *The China Horizon* is that China is a civilisational state with a continuous history that can be traced back 5,000 years, in comparison with which all other states pale.[25] This enormous cultural and political resource is now combined 'with a super-large modern state', 'new model of development' and a 'new political discourse'.[26] Although critics condemn China's institutional arrangements, above all the continued leadership of the CPC, Zhang considers them a source of strength, especially in comparison with the dysfunctionality of what in his view passes for democracy in the West. He stresses the wise leadership of Deng Xiaoping, which allowed China to enter the ranks of the major powers. In line with Zhang's argument, Daniel Bell in his *The China Model* provides a sophisticated analysis of the Chinese approach to political meritocracy and the limits of democracy.[27]

Zhang condemns 'market fundamentalism' and 'democracy fundamentalism', and painstakingly demonstrates their failings. He describes the general decline in the quality of governance, particularly in the US.[28] This critique is no longer couched in the stale ideological language of Marxism – Leninism, but in the vigorous language of a confident power drawing on its demonstrable achievement in transforming a largely peasant country into an industrial and technological giant in the space of two generations. In fact, in a neat reversal, Zhang condemns the way that 'the foreign policies adopted by the Western countries, especially by the US, are heavily ideological', no longer imbued with the spirit of 'seeking truth from facts'.[29] From this perspective, it is the West that has become revolutionary, while Russia and China were conservative status quo powers.

Above all, Zhang advances a vigorous defence of the CPC's role, which he argues provides long-term effective leadership as a 'state party . . . that represents the interests of the overwhelming majority of the Chinese population'.[30] It provides long-term developmental planning, social and political stability, and a meritocratic framework for career development. He rejects the 'autocracy vs. democracy discourse', arguing that it should be replaced by that of 'good governance vs. bad governance'.[31] When it comes to human rights, he raises the enduring question whether such rights are above state sovereignty, stressing that interventions should only be exercised in conformity with 'the procedures stipulated in the international law and by the United Nations'. There was no room here for human rights as the 'last utopia' (taking priority over social rights); instead, China devised a utopia of its own. In words that echo Moscow's sentiments, Zhang notes: 'Some Western countries have, however, attempted to act as both the judge and the gendarme of the world, and intervene in the internal affairs of other countries and readily launch wars against others on the pretext of "humanitarian intervention".'[32] In his view, 'it is perhaps time for the West to think beyond the Cold War mentality and move along with the changing times'.[33]

The point is reiterated by the Singapore diplomat Kishore Mahbubani. He notes that Trump's trade and technological war against China became the consensus view in Washington, with China condemned as a revisionist power. However, he argues that 'America is making a big strategic mistake by launching this contest with China without first developing a comprehensive and global strategy to deal with China'.[34] The struggle will last many years, and he raises the fundamental question whether 'America's primary goal would be to improve the livelihood of its 330 million citizens or to preserve its primacy in the international system'.[35] He argues that the great democracies in the region, such as India or Indonesia, do not feel threatened by China, and that the CPC functions not as the vanguard of Marxism – Leninism but as the 'Chinese *Civilisation* Party', reinforcing the point made by Zhang.[36] He stresses above all that 'there is no fundamental conflict of interest between the United States and China', underlining the common interest in keeping waterways free for navigation.[37] He also notes that China's population of 1.4 billion and America's still add up to only 1.74 billion, less than a quarter of the world's total.

He notes the strategic mistakes made by China, above all in failing to register 'the strong convictions among leading American figures that China has been fundamentally unfair in many of its economic policies: demanding technology transfer, stealing intellectual property, imposing nontariff barriers'.[38] In the South China Sea there is a web of conflicting island and maritime claims involving China, Taiwan, Brunei, Indonesia, Malaysia, the Philippines and Vietnam. The latter four claimants allegedly started reclaiming land and the like, but when China got involved it did so aggressively, making the 'South China Sea a useful propaganda tool to use against China'.[39] He advises China to 'abandon its two-thousand-year Middle Kingdom mentality and decide to become the most open society in terms of economic engagement with the rest of the world'.[40] As for America's 'strategic mistakes', they were numerous and potentially turned the US into a 'rogue superpower'.[41] In sum, Mahbubani argues that 'a major geopolitical contest between America and China is both inevitable and avoidable'.[42] China had alienated the American business community, while the US needed an external scapegoat for its profound domestic problems. China's leaders sought to rejuvenate Chinese civilisation, but 'they have no missionary impulse to take over the world and make everyone Chinese'.[43] There are no fundamental contradictions between the two countries, hence in his view there is room for hope if not optimism.

Martin Jacques develops the theme of China as a civilisation-state and argues that expectations of China developing as a classic European-style nation state were always fanciful. China's rise would raise some enduring issues. Jacques advances three crucial arguments. First, that China's challenge will be far more than economic in character, but will spill over to encompass cultural issues, the character of political authority and the quality of relations in international affairs. Second, the idea that a modernised China will become more 'Westernised' and gradually adopt liberal democratic norms is fundamentally misconceived. Instead, the potency of the authority of the CPC will endure. Third, that China's rise could be incorporated into the international system as presently constituted. By this Jacques means the US-led liberal world order but as we have seen, the international system is something different, in which China is already happily accommodated, above all as a permanent member of the UN Security Council. In fact, China fights to advance and preserve the autonomy of the international system. Nevertheless, his fundamental point is correct: 'The rise of China will change the world in the most profound ways.'[44] The change will be to the way that international politics are conducted, given China's emergence as a near-peer competitor to the US, and not to the system in which it is embedded.

Jacques argues that China most fully exemplifies the idea of alternative modernities – there can be a variety of ways in which to be modern.[45] As he notes, 'Chinese modernity will be very different from Western modernity.'[46] This was already illustrated by Japan, which is both highly developed while at the same time deeply traditional.[47] The multiplicity of civilisations will give rise to multiple modernities, a point made in a different way by Samuel Huntington.[48] With its long history, China runs on a different calendar to that of the West and other civilisations. The Chinese alternative modernity is more highly ramified, prompting suggestions that it may become a model of international order in its own right. The China-centred tributary system could be reinvented in new forms. Tributary trade 'is an ancient Chinese ruling strategy' and is better suited to describe China than the American concept of 'soft power'.[49] The instruments of such power are trade and investment in transport and manufacturing infrastructure, and conversion of economic strength into influence.

POWER AND PURPOSE

China has its own model of political legitimacy (the 'mandate from heaven'), suggesting that CPC rule will endure as long as it adapts and remains flexible, like successful dynasties in the past, while delivering the public goods that the mandate requires. The sheer scale, power, sense of purpose and historical grounding will make China a far more formidable power than the Soviet Union ever was. China is potentially the centre of its own model of world order, incorporating a modified version of sovereign internationalism into some sort of recreated tributary system. This China-centred order will subtly but corrosively subvert the norms and principles of the Charter international system, although not formally repudiating it. This is the fundamental charge advanced by China's critics in the West. Undoubtedly,

China's return to global pre-eminence is a paradigm-shattering process. However, although China strains at the limits of the Charter international system, it still remains within it, defending globalisation and international law while enjoying the privileges and protections they afford. The US–China clash so far is between interpretations of order *within* the international system, but the conflict erodes the viability of that system.

If China is beginning to create its own model of world order, what does this mean for its partners? China remains part of the alignment with Russia and some other states in defence of sovereign internationalism, but is this model rather too thin to describe the enormity of the challenge that China's power poses to the functioning of the international system? Is a new model of globalism emerging, centred on China and functioning as some sort of analogue to the tributary system? In that case, we would have to rethink some of our assumptions. First, the alignment with Russia takes on a different hue. From an association of equals, Russia is relegated to a tributary. Second, the confrontation with the US becomes even more systemic: an upstart nation state would face a powerful and historically grounded civilisation-state, whose power and coherence will gradually put the US in the shade. No measure short of war can stop the process – the so-called 'Thucydides trap'. Third, the principles governing relations between Beijing and the rest of the world, although formally still conducted within the framework of the Charter international system, will assume a different character. Fourth, the relevant time frame from 1945 is far too short to encompass the system-changing qualities of China's re-emergence. The 200 years of European military supremacy and 500 years of cultural dominance are undoubtedly coming to an end, but even this is put in the shade by China's 3,000 years of demonstrable cultural continuity. The 'American century' after 1945 and its period of unparalleled primacy between 1989 and 2014 was not 'some kind of natural state' but 'a historical anomaly': 'The longer-term movement toward a post-Western world was interrupted, but not fundamentally dislodged by the brief and fleeting period of US unipolarity.'[50] Extending the time horizon changes perspectives on the great-power conflicts of our day.

Does that make China (like Russia) a revisionist power (if the term has any meaning in this longer time frame)? In its rhetoric, the opposite is the case and Beijing seeks to ensure that the international system becomes less hierarchical and more balanced. That means challenging liberal hegemony, and thus China (like Russia) becomes neo-revisionist: defending the international system against the encroachments of a particular sub-order. China is a staunch defender of post-1945 sovereign internationalism, and thus condemns forced regime change. Xi stressed that China was a 'participant and builder' of the international system, but in the same speech in September 2015 he emphasised that 'China merely seeks to reform and perfect the existing international system, and this does not mean fashioning a new order but only moving toward a more just direction'.[51] This was a point Xi made at the January 2017 World Economic Forum in Davos, when he explicitly defended globalisation and once again proclaimed that China was a defender of the existing international system, and thereby asserted China as a core leader in international politics.[52] This entailed challenging the selectivity and arbitrariness of liberal hegemony – hence the conflict with the US.

It also forced China to assume a stronger leadership position, even though the country had been hesitant to do so earlier. The Trumpian disruption made this more urgent, throwing liberal internationalism into disarray while weakening traditional consensual forms of US leadership – thus creating space for China. However, Trump's response was only an episode in the broader shift in US thinking. China's ability to benefit from the liberal order while maintaining its state-regulated model of the market economy, accompanied by market-distorting restrictions and regulations, quite apart from resistance to political change, undermined the earlier domestic consensus on relations with China. As for Beijing, it certainly chafed against the expansive agenda of democratic internationalism, and even more so against liberal hegemony, but it was quite comfortable with the more modest framework of the Charter international system, and hence defended its principles.[53] The war in Ukraine from 2022, however, threatens the viability of the Charter international system more than any event since 1945, with an interstate war provoked by a clash between interpretations of that order, prompting a return to the brutal great-power politics that Charter multilateralism was precisely designed to avert. China is caught between its alignment with Russia and its declared commitment to Charter norms.

The war takes place against the background of a growing narrative of the decline of the political West in Beijing and Moscow. The global financial crisis from 2008 exposed enduring problems in US social and political development, prompting some in China (as in Russia) to exaggerate the decline of the capitalist West. If the tide of history was turning, then why not push against a fading political order? The danger of overreaction was clear, accompanied by some rowing back on the technical reforms launched in response to justified Western criticisms of Chinese trade, investment and economic behaviours. As trust evaporated it became more difficult to resolve these issues through negotiation and compromise. This reflected the profound consequences of the shift in the balance of power. As Jacques notes, 'hegemonic powers seek to project their values and institutions on to subordinate nations and the latter, in response, will, depending on circumstances, adapt or genuflect towards their ways; if they don't, hegemonic powers generally seek to impose those values and arrangements on them, even *in extremis* by force'.[54] China began to exert a force field of its own, offering a putative alternative to the US-led liberal hegemony. Given that the liberal order was so deeply interwoven into the postwar international system, it would not be easy to reject the one while defending the other. Neo-revisionism by definition has the potential to spill over into full-scale revisionism.

CHINA IN THE WORLD

In the early post-Mao period of reforms from 1978, the traditional centre-of-the-world mentality gave way to the search for 'legitimate recognition from the international society'.[55] This was accompanied by a raft of assertions of modesty: 'lie low, bide our time', 'responsible power', 'peaceful rise', 'peaceful development' and many more. Deng's economic reforms repudiated revolutionary radicalism and represented a pragmatic turn in foreign policy that took advantage of multipolarity to ensure China's independence and 'peaceful development'.[56] The elite view was that China was regaining its accustomed international status rather than winning something new, hence the preferred term was 'return' rather than the 'rise' of China. Reference to the 'century of humiliation' not only reinforced the CPC's nationalist legitimacy but also painted Western hostility as part of the historical pattern whereby it refused to accord China the status it deserved.[57]

In keeping with sovereign internationalism and the non-alignment principles of the Bandung Declaration (April 1955), in 2018 Xi announced the Five Nos policy: 'no interference with development paths, no interference in internal affairs, no imposing one's will on others, no attaching political conditions, and no political self-interest in investments and financing'.[58] Above all, China (like Russia) considers itself a founder member of the Charter international system. After all, as foreign minister Wang Yi reminded his audience at the 2020 Munich Security Conference, China was a founder member of the UN and 'has stayed true to the UN's founding aspirations and firmly defended the purposes of the UN Charter and international law. The mission of China's foreign policy is to promote world peace and common development'. China would not copy the Western model but would continue 'the path of socialism with Chinese characteristics' and 'not seek hegemony even when it grows in strength'.[59]

Deng's injunction to 'rise quietly' was discarded as China leveraged its vast economic gains into greater influence in its region and beyond. Xi expanded what he considered China's 'core interests' and asserted them robustly. Building on earlier plans, the Belt and Road Initiative was at the heart of the new globalism. Xi Jinping announced the Silk Road Economic Belt (SREB) on 7 September 2013 in a speech at Nazarbayev University in Astana in Kazakhstan.[60] A month later, on 3 October in the Indonesian capital, Jakarta, he reinforced this with a 'Maritime Silk Road'. Together they became known as BRI, now simply called the Belt and Road, a vast infrastructure plan to connect China with the rest of the world through ports, railways, highways and energy installations. This was an ambitious attempt to promote regional cooperation, economic integration, and communication and transport networks. The accompanying maritime belt was to be supported by upgrades to ports and transport hubs.[61] It filled the gap in global development finance and, by January 2023, 151 countries had joined by signing a memorandum of understanding. This was accompanied by the establishment of regional nodes such as the 16+1 partnership in Central and Eastern Europe in 2012, since then reduced with the defection of Lithuania. The Belt and Road soon outgrew its original regional corridors to cover the world. It now includes a Digital Silk Road to improve telecommunications, artificial intelligence, cloud computing and e-payment systems in partner states as well as, more controversially, surveillance systems. There is also a Health Silk Road to advance Chinese ideas on global health governance, with hundreds of projects falling into this category. These programmes met 'a legitimate need around the world for new infrastructure and to fill the gap in infrastructure financing and construction in a way that benefits it', amid the failure of Washington-based institutions to provide such support. There were calls in the US to force China to change its Belt and Road practices and for Washington to provide an 'effective alternative'.[62] This was to become yet another arena of contestation.

The grandiose plan sought to link China with the rest of the world through land and maritime 'silk routes'. The Belt and Road reflected the needs of the Chinese economy, looking for new investment opportunities for the enormous accumulation of capital, although the dual circulation strategy later sought to ensure that domestic investment was also boosted. Relations were based on connectivity rather than integration, allowing entities to come together while maintaining their separate identities; whereas integration suggests some ultimate end point of fusion and becoming one.[63] This approach is in keeping with sovereign internationalism, in which countries engage with others but maintain their autonomy. However, critics also detect elements of the light-touch imperialism of the tributary system, in which suzerainty requires only formal obeisance rather than the full-scale renunciation of sovereignty. Despite Western criticism, this was a grandiose and transformative project. In his *China Connects the World*, Wang Yiwei argues that Belt and Road gives rise to a whole 'new human civilisation' and the taming of Western 'dualism', which is stuck in a cycle of 'estrangement and confrontation'. Instead of 'the curse of US hegemony', Belt and Road opens up the prospect of a world without hegemony. Different states and cultures would be connected but separate.[64] The ambition is vast and trans-regional, creating a new spatial and developmental order while defending postwar sovereign internationalism. This is internationalism of a new type, while remaining traditional in form.[65]

Belt and Road is condemned on a number of grounds, including the controversial and contested charge of 'debt-trap diplomacy', whereby recipient countries are rendered beholden to China, as well as neglecting environmental safeguards and economic sustainability. China was accused of 'extractivism', the ripping out of natural resources in self-enclosed bubbles of little benefit to host communities, and of arrogant high-handedness in supplying its own workers, security guards, raw materials and even cooks. The contrary view argues that in fact recipient countries actively shape their involvement in the programme, and rather than being part of a consistent strategy to trap countries in the Chinese web, BRI advanced incrementally and in a piecemeal fashion. There were some poorly conceived and badly managed projects, notably in Sri Lanka and Montenegro, but the appropriate response was better risk management and project evaluation.[66] The Asian Infrastructure Investment Bank (AIIB), established in 2013, had already moved in this direction, incorporating good governance demands into its lending practices. The US opposed its establishment, but Washington failed to stop allies joining. By 2022 the AIIB had eighty-six members and had become one of the world's major infrastructure investment banks.

The Obama administration negotiated the Trans-Pacific Partnership (TPP), but it was summarily cancelled by Trump on his first day in office. Its putative members went ahead without the US to create the eleven-country Comprehensive and Progressive Agreement for Trans-Pacific Partnership (CPTPP), encompassing a market of 500 million and 14 per cent of the global economy. It modified controversial provisions that allow businesses to sue governments if they can show that a change in government policy caused material damage. This is the notorious investor – state conflict provision of the hyper-globalisation period, which fundamentally undermines economic sovereignty in favour of transnational corporations. Overall, it was less ambitious than the projected TPP but marked an important step in regional integration. This was complemented in November 2020 when the Association of Southeast Asian Nations (ASEAN), as well as five partner countries (China, Japan, South Korea, Australia and New Zealand), signed the Regional Comprehensive Economic Partnership (RCEP), an ASEAN idea first mooted in 2011. Less ambitious than the projected TPP, RCEP nevertheless created the world's largest free trade zone. It provides a framework for China to resolve contentious regional issues, including provisions on intellectual property, telecommunications, financial flows and e-commerce. It excludes uniform labour and environmental standards and preserves vulnerable areas of national economies. Although India did not sign, it played an active part in devising the agreement. US-led economic integration was now systemically challenged by an alternative model of globalisation.

China strives to become a full-spectrum and self-sufficient economy, thereby reducing exposure to external pressure. Trump's ban on the export of semiconductor technology to China acted as a warning that dependence on external suppliers rendered the country vulnerable to sanctions. China had long encouraged technology transfer from Western companies (by fair means or foul), but this assumed new forms when Beijing announced the 'Made in China 2025' programme, establishing ten priority areas for the Chinese economy, including aerospace and aviation, machine-tools and robotics, new energy vehicles, advanced information technology, high-performance medical devices and more.[67] The aim was to create an indigenous base for the major technologies of the future within the framework of the Fourth Industrial Revolution. China accelerated domestic innovation to compete on the global level, while reducing dependence on foreign technologies. This was accompanied by a push for greater state control over the economy and the tightening of the 'social credit' system, more severe cyber laws and a renewed emphasis on the role of CPC cadres on company boards. Cold War practices of separation, condemnation and domestic control were intensified.

SINO-US RELATIONS

In 2005, the US public official who went on to head the World Bank, Robert Zoellick, famously argued that China should become a 'responsible stakeholder' in the international system. This reflects the conundrum at the heart of US–Chinese relations. As far as Beijing is concerned, it was always a stakeholder in that system, and indeed was a founder member (although its seat at the UN was held by Taiwan until 1971). What China had reservations about was its status in the US-led liberal international order, and here some of the same issues as with Russia come to the fore. Both countries globalised their economies, although China became integrated into the world economy to a far greater extent, but both rejected US primacy. Washington argues that it facilitated China's rise in the expectation that it would abide by the rules of competitive market economies, respect intellectual property rights and abandon anti-competitive state subsidies and export dumping. This is a fair point, although China would counter-argue that as a developing economy it needed to support its industries to allow them to compete on an even footing with more advanced societies. Catch-up development requires a degree of protectionism to shield nascent industries from the fierce competition of more established economies. However, these non-competitive practices were now viewed as a threat to US interests, precipitating a fundamental shift in US strategy.

As China gained in power, Brzezinski argued that the only relationship in international politics that really mattered was the one between the US and China. In 2009, in his characteristically robust manner, he called for a Group of Two (G2) to run the world together.[68] History, however, took another turn. In October 2011, secretary of state Hillary Clinton announced the birth of 'America's Pacific century', portraying the Asia-Pacific region as one requiring US 'leadership'.[69] A few months later, the Pentagon issued its *Defense Strategic Guidance* that outlined a 'pivot to Asia', calling for 'credible deterrence' and the need to 'project power despite anti-access/area denial [A2/AD] challenges', soon followed by military exercises with Japan, the establishment of a US Marines base in Australia, increased arms sales across the region, more frequent 'Freedom of Navigation' operations (FONOPs) and much else, all naturally perceived as threatening to China. This came on top of the American B-2 bomber attack on the Chinese Embassy in Belgrade on 7 May 1999, killing three Chinese journalists and wounding twenty-seven people, an incident that has still not been fully explained.

The status of Taiwan is an enduring bone of contention. Since Nixon's visit to China in 1972 and the signing of the Shanghai Communiqué, the US has been committed to the 'one-China' policy, accompanied by, as we have seen, strategic ambiguity when it came to the island's defence. US relations with Taipei were severed in 1979 and the PRC recognised as the only legitimate Chinese state, and in 1982 Washington agreed to end arms sales to Taiwan, an implicit acknowledgement that ultimately the island would reunify with the mainland. In the Trump years, however, high-level contacts with Taipei suggested sympathy for Taiwanese independence, a threat to what Beijing considers its 'core interests'. Elements of the mutual defence treaty that had lapsed in 1979 were restored. For Beijing this appeared to be part of a larger pushback against Chinese interests. The attempt to convert the Quadrilateral Security Dialogue (the Quad), comprising the US, India, Japan and Australia, into a military alliance patently directed against China only added to Beijing's concerns.

Exercising China's new-found strength, Xi advanced the idea of 'building a new type of major power relations' with the US and other states.[70] On his visit to Washington in 2012, Xi proposed 'a new type of relationship between major countries in the 21st century'. This was in keeping with the principle of sovereign internationalism, in which countries coordinate their actions in international affairs while pursuing their own interests. The US refused to accept this model, and instead insisted on its leadership and set about containing

China.[71] At first Chinese analysts assumed that this reflected only the preference of individual US leaders, but later understood that the problem was systemic.[72] The lack of empathy (not the same as sympathy) for Chinese sensibilities repeated the pattern with post-Cold War Russia and resulted in the same action/reaction security dilemma escalatory cycle. The veteran diplomat Fu Ying noted that the question for China was 'how to evaluate the US's strategic change', and stressed that, 'based on its fundamental foreign policy principles, China would want the relationship to be one of effective cooperation', with competition kept within limits and 'benign'. However, she warned that 'China must also prepare for the possibility of wider confrontation'.[73]

The Biden presidency considered the relationship the defining issue of the era. On the eve of the G7 Cornwall summit in June 2021, Biden wrote, 'Will the democratic alliances and institutions that shaped so much of the last century prove their capacity against modern-day threats and adversaries?'. Competition between the world's democracies and authoritarian regimes – with China in the vanguard of the latter – defined the period, and the president believed that, to win, 'the democratic camp will have to show greater cohesion and ambition in response to the world's biggest problems – climate change and the pandemic'.[74] But what does 'win' mean in this context? On the other side, the Chinese foreign ministry issued a series of hard-hitting critiques of US policy, which made Putin's criticisms seem tame in comparison. The document 'US Hegemony and its Perils' of February 2023 catalogued US misdemeanours since its foundation, and in particular the abuse of its hegemonic position in all spheres, including a pattern of regime subversion and interventions. The US was accused of exercising double standards in international rules, 'Placing its self-interest first', turning its back on international organisations that it could not control and reneging on international obligations. The US was condemned as 'the most warlike nation in the history of the world'. Since 2001, the US 'war on terror' claimed 'over 900,000 lives, some 335,000 of them civilians, and creating some 37 million refugees worldwide'. The US was also accused of abusing its economic and financial pre-eminence, with the dollar enjoying the 'exorbitant privilege' (the term coined in the 1960s by Valéry Giscard d'Estaing when he was French minister of finance) of collecting 'seigniorage'.[75] Countries need dollars to conduct international trade, which the US 'sells' by issuing Treasury debt.

The US repeated with China the pattern of relations that had so disastrously failed with Russia. Many of the same factors were at work. The relationship had been based on two key principles. First, that China's development would also benefit the West. For many years this was indeed the case, with China the locomotive for a sustained period of global economic growth in the 2000s and pulling the world out of recession after the 2008 financial crash.[76] China's rise lifted millions out of poverty, but it also benefited the broader international community. However, common economic self-interest is not enough on its own to overcome diverging political and strategic imperatives. The second postulate was that engagement would lead to system transformation in China, along the lines of Germany's 'change through trade' strategy with the Soviet Union from the 1960s. The limitations of such an approach were exposed when Xi changed China's grand strategy from an essentially defensive posture to one actively advancing China's global interests.

The first position is broadly correct, but the second is more contentious: China is not the Soviet Union and is built on much firmer foundations. Soviet ideology, after all, was ultimately a renegade version of European modernity, hence would always be susceptible to liberal democratic values, just as Russia was in the 1990s and will probably be once again. In the Chinese case, belief in the ultimate triumph of Western-style democracy is based on a faulty strategic perception. In a country where the source of legitimacy has for hundreds, if not thousands, of years operated according to a different logic, it could hardly be expected that there would be systemic convergence. Whether this should take the specific form of CPC rule is certainly debatable. Issues of human dignity, the rule of law, legitimate governance and constitutionalism have long been part of Chinese political discourse, but it was clearly a mistake to believe that China would turn into some sort of pale imitation of the historic

West, let alone the political West as constituted during the Cold War. In the end, the two pillars crumbled: economic relations with China became increasingly perceived as zero-sum; and disappointment with China's failure to 'reform' in a Gorbachev-like manner fostered suspicion and ultimately hostility.

THE LOGIC OF CONFLICT

Unlike Japan, China was not a defeated power and was far from being part of the US alliance system. China's rise would inevitably sooner or later challenge Washington, as the principal architect and guardian of a liberal order that acted as a potential rival to the autonomy of the Charter international system. Graham Allison notes that the idea of an era of great-power competition, equating Russia and China as major players, fails to capture the unique character of the Chinese challenge, which is something that the US has never before faced. In his view, China is more than just another great-power competitor (into which category Russia falls), but a genuine Thucydidean rival – the analogy being the perceived challenge posed to Athens by the rise of Sparta, as described in Thucydides' *History of the Peloponnesian War*. Allison defines such a rival as a state with the capacity not only to change the global balance of power but also to challenge the identity of the ruling power and its conception of global order.[77] The Soviet collapse removed a geopolitical competitor but above all a geo-ideological one and seemed to confirm the American creed that 'political freedom and prosperity came as a package. There could be no enterprise without markets, no markets without fair rules, and no enforceable rules without democracy'. The novelty of the situation now was that 'The Communist Party of China's hybrid model of authoritarian capitalism appears to have disproved that theory'.[78]

In keeping with his model of offensive realism, John Mearsheimer goes further and stresses not only the possibility but also the inevitability of conflict. The structural logic of international politics forces states to pursue competitive politics against each other, to ensure that the balance of power remains skewed in their favour. Mearsheimer has no time for the idea of an international system, let alone an international society, since for him great-power relations *are* the system.[79] The purpose of American foreign policy is to maximise its security and prosperity, and the best way to achieve that is to remain a regional hegemon, defined as dominating its area of the world, and to prevent the emergence of another regional hegemon that could act as peer competitor. Mearsheimer argues that this could best be achieved through offshore balancing, and thus after Cold War I there was no need to maintain the grand strategy of primacy or global hegemony.[80] The challenge for America is that China represents such a competitor, which in Mearsheimer's view would emulate US behaviour by trying to dominate Asia in the way that America dominates the Atlantic world. As Mearsheimer predicted, Beijing rapidly built up a blue-water navy and global power projection capabilities and positioned itself to challenge US dominance in the Gulf and elsewhere.

Mearsheimer applauds the US intolerance for peer competitors and insists that this derives not from any unique exceptionalism but from the rational and ruthless pursuit of great-power politics, just as any other traditional great power in its position would do – something that the Chinese in his view well understand. In the twentieth century, the US confronted four potential regional hegemons: imperial Germany, imperial Japan, Nazi Germany and the Soviet Union, and it was instrumental in overcoming all four. From this cold-blooded perspective, the US had mistakenly helped China grow and had thus nurtured precisely what it should have avoided. For good measure, he adds that the US had been misguided in trying to spread democracy across the world, a fool's errand that was not only doomed to fail but also provoked chaos and mayhem across the Middle East and alienated Russia. The US failed to foster its own growth as a nation state, and its neglect of nationalism undermined its ability to defend its security and prosperity.[81] The grandiose ambitions of the liberal international order were 'bound to fail'.[82]

Trump responded to the challenge, but in an inchoate and incoherent manner. Trump in the 1980s warned against Japan's rise and its threat to American economic interests, but as president he turned his fire on China. Trump's second speech to the UN General

Assembly on 25 September 2018 asserted, 'We reject the ideology of globalism and accept the doctrine of patriotism.'[83] At a meeting of the UNSC the next day, to the evident consternation of the Chinese delegation, Trump claimed that

China has been attempting to interfere in our upcoming [midterm] 2018 election . . . against our administration. They do not want me or us to win because I am the first president ever to challenge China on trade. And we are winning on trade. We are winning at every level. We don't want them to meddle or interfere in our upcoming election.[84]

The attack was resumed by Vice President Mike Pence in a hard-hitting speech to the Hudson Institute on 4 October 2018. He held China responsible for half (amounting to $375 billion) of the US global trade deficit, for the theft of technology, foreign policy aggression, a clampdown on religious freedom and the mobilisation of 'covert actors, front groups, and propaganda outlets to shift Americans' perception of Chinese policies', as well as influencing voters. In his view, Russia's alleged US election interference 'pales in comparison' to China's, with Beijing even trying to eject Trump from the presidency.[85]

If this is the case, then it was China rather than Russia that got Trump elected: 'China's economic attack on America caused US voters to turn to Trump.'[86] Instead of focusing on Russian 'meddling' in the 2016 election, China's alleged predatory trading policies 'ate America's lunch', including 'currency manipulation, unfair trading practices and, most damaging of all, intellectual property theft', leading to the enormous trade deficit which in 2022 approached $1 trillion. The Democrats had done nothing as jobs moved offshore, and it was Trump who recognised the plight of workers in America's manufacturing industry, so they voted for him in even traditionally 'blue' (Democrat) states.[87] Typically, Trump was ungrateful. The Trump administration ordered the closure of the Chinese consulate in Houston to protect 'American intellectual property and private information'. The consulate, serving several southern states, was alleged to be an 'espionage hub'. Beijing condemned the move as 'outrageous' and unprecedented, and accused the US of restricting its diplomats, including opening their pouches without permission.[88] Personnel were given only seventy-two hours to move out, much the same period allowed for staff in the Russian consulate in San Francisco when it was closed in September 2017. In response, China closed the US consulate in Chengdu. The repeated attack on diplomatic facilities and practices distinguishes the second Cold War from the first.

The US 'Indo-Pacific Strategy' was approved by Trump in February 2018. This included the US-led Free and Open Indo-Pacific Strategy (FOIP), which sought to counter China's Belt and Road challenge. As part of this, Japan embraced Washington's Pacific Deterrence Initiative, the positioning of precision-strike missiles against China. America's Indo-Pacific strategy drew criticism from both Moscow and Beijing. The formulation was controversial, indicating a shift away from the neutral 'Asia-Pacific' terminology (which excludes South Asia) towards one that ties India into a new geopolitical construct. There were even calls for NATO to extend its reach into the Asia-Pacific, raising the prospect of importing divisive Europe-style bloc politics into the region.[89] Only in 2021 was a Cold War I-type hotline established between Washington and Beijing to lessen an accidental miscalculation in one of the periodic crises over Taiwan or the South China Sea. In February 2022 the Biden administration released its Indo-Pacific Strategy which once again stressed that the region was 'vital to our security and prosperity', and reiterated the 'free and open' perspective. The strategy described a 'collective lattice-work of reinforcing coalitions', all directed towards the containment of China. The PRC was described as 'combining its economic, diplomatic, military, and technological might as it pursues a sphere of influence in the Indo-Pacific and seeks to become the world's most influential power'. The five regional mutual defence treaties – with Australia, Japan, South Korea, the Philippines and Thailand – were to be deepened, while the security partnerships with many other regional states, including Taiwan, were to be strengthened.[90]

More sober voices called for restraint, noting that the US had patiently handled the threat from the Soviet Union, and a similar approach would work for China.[91] However, the scale and character of the challenge in this case was different, and so was the response – although it drew on the Cold War toolkit. Since the 2011 'pivot to Asia', the US 'resisted the expansion of even entirely legitimate Chinese economic influence in the world'. This included 'the blank refusal to allow China a say' in the World Bank and IMF 'commensurate with its economic weight in the world'.[92] China is not interested in exporting its ideology, but it does defend its positions and principles. It increasingly believes that the US response is no longer a matter of improving its bargaining position to reach some compromise in the future but 'is aimed at isolating China, ousting it from added value high-tech chains, slowing down its growth, drawing it into an arms race and marginalising it in international affairs'.[93] This certainly was the sentiment of the 2020 Trump White House *Strategic Approach* to China, which lamented that forty years after the restoration of diplomatic relations Washington could no longer expect China to become a fully fledged market democracy. Instead, China had become a threat to the US economy, values, security and leadership, and the response had to be a more competitive approach and pressure to defend US prosperity, although this should not cross the line to open conflict.[94]

DECOUPLING

An epochal separation is under way. The Chinese and American economies had become entwined and even interdependent, but now with brutal resolve the divorce began. In his landmark speech on 23 July 2020, secretary of state Mike Pompeo outlined the rationale for the policy, arguing that 'Communist China' threatened the free world's future. He noted, 'We stopped pretending Huawei is an innocent telecommunications company that's just showing up to make sure you can talk to your friends. We've called it what it is – a true national security threat – and we've taken action accordingly'.[95] The 'clean networks' policy he announced in August 2020 sought to guard 'our citizens' privacy and our companies' most sensitive information from aggressive intrusions by malign actors', such as the

CPC. A comprehensive programme of technological decoupling was envisaged, with Huawei in the sphere of communications excluded from 5G development and Chinese media and chat platforms, such as TikTok, constrained. China was excluded from US-based cloud-based storage systems, undersea cables and even from US mobile app stores.[96] Trump banned the supply of microprocessors, forcing China to develop a more self-sufficient technological base but causing untold economic damage in the meantime. Biden's CHIPS Act in 2022 committed $50 billion to 'reshore' microchip manufacturing from Asia. Four decades of engagement based on cooperation and mutual benefit came to a shuddering end.

A full-scale ideological offensive was launched, including condemnation of Belt and Road as part of China's 'debt-trap diplomacy'. Washington sought to create a broad anti-Chinese alliance, particularly in the Asia-Pacific region. At the 6 October 2020 meeting of the Quad in Tokyo, Pompeo tried to convince the foreign ministers of Australia, India and Japan to commit to a military alliance, to evolve into what he suggested could become an 'Asian NATO'. The Quad is a loose grouping established in 2004 to address the devastating effects of the Boxing Day tsunami that swept across the Indian Ocean. It first met formally in May 2007 in the Philippine capital Manila, but in 2008 the newly elected Labor Party prime minister, Kevin Rudd, withdrew Australia. Pompeo's opening statement talked in apocalyptic terms about a life and death struggle not just between the US and China, but a critical struggle 'to protect our people and partners from the CPC's exploitation, corruption, and coercion'.[97] The other foreign ministers were not ready to go as far in ramping up confrontation, and no joint closing communiqué was issued. Ministers feared that talk of an 'Asian NATO' represented a dangerous escalation and would reduce the centrality of ASEAN. Even India, embroiled in a territorial conflict, refused to commit itself to a crusade against China. The Trump administration questioned the constraints that NATO imposed on the US in the West, but Pompeo now implied that the US was ready to commit itself to such constraints in the Pacific. The 24 May 2022 meeting of the Quad in Japan demonstrated a lack of consensus on counterbalancing China, despite

Biden's best efforts. Biden stated that the US would intervene militarily in defence of Taiwan, thus weakening the long-standing US policy of 'strategic ambiguity'. India maintained a neutral stance on the Ukraine war, while the new Labor administration in Australia from May 2022 tempered the hard-line anti-China stance pursued by the previous Liberal – National coalition under Scott Morrison. Nevertheless, the Quad remains the kernel of an Asian NATO.

The US slid 'into open-ended conflict with China with eerily little debate'. Politicians in Washington competed to show their toughness. The underlying rationale was that 'pre-Trump Washington was a place of Whiggish credulity, forever betting on material enrichment to make of China a vast Japan or South Korea: a democracy, a friend. In this account, its admission to the World Trade Organisation [in December 2001] was the inadvertent crowning of a rival by American enablers'. In this reading, the only options were 'liberal naïvete and a second Cold War', when in fact a succession of American leaders had imposed sanctions and other restrictions on China. The absence of a debate now was 'disconcerting'.[98] There were dissenting voices arguing that there was no need for the US to become trapped in the logic of great-power conflict, and the US should avoid a policy of containment, prevent decoupling and avert a new Cold War. Instead, a policy of 'conditional competitive cooperation' with allies and China should lead rather than destroy the global economy.[99] The contrasting view argued that the West had been caught unawares in helping China develop, failing to take seriously the CPC's commitment to maintain its power, allowing China to exploit the policy of engagement to build up national power to pursue its geopolitical goals.[100]

China's spectacular rise caught the US unprepared, and 'American political culture has never been particularly apt dealing with foreign adversaries' as equals. With the US accustomed to post-Cold War unipolarity, China's emergence as a peer competitor found America trapped in a 'very precarious, painful and incoherent process' of adjusting to a new global balance of power. Some in Moscow considered an extended US–China confrontation would benefit Russia as it raised Russia's value as Beijing's strategic partner and, while true to an extent, wiser voices argued that 'Russian – Chinese cooperation should have its own foundation, not a common enemy', a version of the Chinese 'endogeneity' stance.[101] This is certainly the case, but the intensification of Sino-US rivalry revealed the common concerns. Beijing and Moscow complemented each other in their critiques of US behaviour. The pandemic saw a further downward spiral in relations, as Beijing was accused of covering up the source of the Covid-19 virus and mishandling its early stages.

In the Russo-Ukrainian war, Beijing treads a delicate line, calling for peace and diplomacy, while at the same time making it clear that it will maintain alignment with Russia.[102] It does not identify with Russia's war, yet the war has only deepened China's mistrust of the West, especially since the US was effectively supporting Taiwan's international recognition. Beijing's stance evolved from studied impartiality to the denunciation of the sanctions as 'financial terrorism' and 'economic weaponisation', fearing that one day such measures could be deployed against it. Hard-liners argue that even if Beijing supported US sanctions, the relationship would not fundamentally change and would only prepare the path for such sanctions to be applied against Beijing. In a famous tweet on 19 March 2022, the broadcaster Liu Xin stated that the US position amounted to the proposition: 'Can you help me fight your friend so that I can concentrate on fighting you later?' Blinken's statement in June that Washington would 'shape the strategic environment around Beijing' confirmed such fears.[103] Nevertheless, even though the Joint Statement of 4 February 2022 talked about 'no limits', the war demonstrated that there were constraints. Chinese companies were unwilling to risk sanctions by working with Russia, hence limiting the sale of aircraft parts, while Sinopec (China Petroleum and Chemical Corporation) pulled out of a $500 billion investment in SIBUR, Russia's largest petrochemical producer.[104] Russia lost some of its value as a strategic partner, yet Beijing's 'credibility' (to use the term favoured by Washington) would be on the line if it distanced itself from Moscow.[105]

Beijing was brutal in its assessment of Washington's behaviour. In July 2020, Chinese foreign minister Wang Yi told his Russian counterpart, Lavrov, that the US had 'lost its mind, morals and credibility', and urged Beijing and Moscow to work together on issues of global importance, such as Covid-19 and regional security. Wang Yi asserted, 'The US has bluntly pursued its "America first" policy, pushing egoism, unilateralism and bullying to the limit, and that's not what a great power should be about.' In a separate statement, Wang argued that the US had adopted a Cold War mentality, revived McCarthyism and 'intentionally stirred up ideological opposition, which breaches the bottom line and basic norms of international laws and international relationships'. Wang stressed that China's strategic relationship with Moscow was a 'priority', asserting that the US had 'failed in its duties as a great power by shirking its responsibilities and trying to discredit other nations'.[106] Senior Chinese officials usually refrain from criticising other countries, but 'wolf warrior' diplomacy no longer held back. The various tensions mutated into a full-blown Sino-US cold war. A cold war entails the management of entrenched hostility, and is certainly preferable to a hot war, but it would be wiser to avoid both.[107]

7
THE RUSSIA QUESTION

As Russia recovered from the doldrums of the 1990s and rebuilt its economy and military, it asserted its voice in international affairs.[1] The country was one of the founder members of the Charter international system and enjoys permanent membership of the UN Security Council. Russia never doubted that it was a great power, but recognition encountered institutional and ideological resistance. Even in its region, its hegemony was challenged. The Eurasian Economic Union was formally established on 1 January 2015, but its five members (Armenia, Belarus, Kazakhstan, Kyrgyzstan and Russia) were far from agreeing on 'ever closer union', the ambition of the EEC when it was created in 1957. As the political West consolidated and expanded, Russia at first adapted and then resisted. Moscow opposed the power implications of the Atlantic alliance's advance and called for 'multipolarity', a model of international affairs based on traditional great-power politics at odds with the idea of a US-led rules-based order. From 2012, Russia began to define itself as a 'civilisation-state'.[2] It devised a set of 'exceptionalist' (*Sonderweg*) principles that increasingly diverged from European modernity. The attempt to create an 'equal partnership of unequals' generated tension and mistrust. By most standards, Russia lacks the resources to sustain its challenge to the political West. Critics argue that the country will be forced down the path of economic stagnation, technological degradation, political repression and dependence on uncertain allies in the East. However, supporters assert that a self-reliant and resilient Russia will emerge strengthened from the confrontation.

FORTRESS RUSSIA

Russia's collapse as a power in the 1990s was so profound that the prospect of the 'reconstitution of its Cold War military capabilities and return to policies guided by long-standing security requirements and threat perceptions' was inconceivable, and hence its concerns could be ignored.[3] The legacy of such assessments remain. The 'declinist' view suggested that Russia was a marginal and waning power, with its economy stagnating, its population falling, its institutions dysfunctional and the legitimacy of the regime eroding. The decrease in national power was taken to be permanent, and hence there was no pressing need to address Moscow's concerns. Russia's assertive foreign policy, moreover, was discounted as little more than the impotent thrashing of a regional state fuelled by memories of past grandeur (notably the obsession with victory over Nazi Germany in 1945), and a regime desperate to cling on to power, reinforcing the return of neo-Soviet social and political authoritarianism. In 2014, Obama dismissed Russia as 'a regional power that is threatening some of its immediate neighbours, not out of strength but out of weakness'.[4] Serious politics would be conducted with Beijing, while Moscow was not much more than a distraction and 'spoiler'. Russian policy in Syria, Ukraine and elsewhere was thereby denounced as little more than the deluded ambitions of a failing power.

The main driver of Russia's foreign policy was viewed as a 'patronal autocracy', in which the national interest was subordinated to the domestic political needs of a corrupt authoritarian government devoted to personal enrichment.[5] From this perspective, 'power projection abroad ... has become necessary to maintain regime support at home'.[6] This is the 'diversionary' model, mentioned above. Any 'off-ramps' out of confrontation would provide the kleptocratic regime with unwarranted breathing space amounting to appeasement. Pressure had to be maintained and regularly escalated – through sanctions, military deployments, intelligence leaks, arms to

Ukraine, propaganda campaigns and much else out of Cold War I's playbook – until the whole rotten edifice collapsed.[7] 'Wedges' needed to be driven between Russia and China and the alignment destroyed.[8] As in the conflict with the Soviet Union, and even the longer tradition of hostility to Tsarist autocracy, the assumption was that there could be no serious prospects for normalisation as long as the old regime remained in place. This deterministic account had little room for the complexities of Russian statecraft or for nuanced diplomatic engagement. From this essentialist perspective, Russia is irremediably imperialist and expansionist. If correct, this is a fight to the death in which only one side can emerge victorious. The end of Cold War I indicates that in fact a negotiated outcome is possible, although the prospect for some sort of positive peace in this case had long been irretrievably lost.

An active state with ambitions to rise in the global hierarchy requires at least three elements: economic resources, military capacity and 'narratives about becoming a great power'.[9] Russia enjoyed an abundance of the latter (its critics argue rather too much); its military was significantly strengthened following the reforms from autumn 2008 and equipment modernisation programmes; but its aspirations rested on a rather slender economic base.[10] Russia's national power was rising in the period 1999–2014, although it continued to trail well behind the US, China and India in absolute terms. According to IMF data, in 2019 Russia's nominal GDP was just $1.5 trillion, eleventh in the world and accounting for just 1.8 per cent of global GDP, with per capita income of $11,600. However, in comparative purchasing power terms, with the data adjusted for different living costs between countries, GDP was over $4 trillion, accounting for 3.5 per cent of global GDP, making Russia the world's sixth-largest economy with per capita income at just over $28,000. Russia's share of global GDP has been in steady decline, but that holds for most of the Global North. Between 2014 and 2019, the US share fell from 16.6 to 15.3 per cent, while India's rose from 5.9 to 7.0 per cent and China's from 14.9 to 17.3 per cent.[11]

Most importantly, Russia was a full-service economy integrated into the global system, with supremacy in hypersonic and hi-tech weaponry. Its anti-missile systems, the latest being the S-500 Triumfator-M, were best in its class. Russia enjoyed an advanced IT sector, developed aircraft and shipbuilding industries, factories producing 10 per cent of the world's power turbines, a nuclear industry building 40 per cent of the world's commercial power stations, the world's only nuclear-powered ice breakers and ship-board small modular reactors (SMRs), along with advanced urban infrastructure and a well-educated population. It had a number of e-commerce giants and the world's largest digital bank (TCS Group, better known as Tinkoff Bank). Yandex parallels the work of Google, with cloud services, AI and self-driving cars, along with a host of service facilities (taxis, search engines, mapping and much more). Russia produced the world's first anti-Covid-19 vaccine (Sputnik V) by August 2020, which was then delivered to much of the non-Western world as well as some European countries (Serbia, Hungary and Slovakia). By 2011, the GLONASS geospatial positioning system had restored its full complement of twenty-four orbiting satellites with a network of ground receiving stations outside Russia, allowing global coverage to rival America's GPS. When foreign companies cut the provision of data in 2022, the Russian government provided additional resources to the complementary 'SFERA' (Sphere) programme, which provides geo-navigational and internet services. In 2019, a convoy led by the missile frigate *Admiral Gorshkov* circumnavigated the globe, the first time a Russian naval fleet had done so since the nineteenth century.

Russia demanded 'a status and rights in the international order equal to those of the West'.[12] Putin's landmark Munich speech in February 2007 condemned US unilateralism and its 'uncontained hyper use of force'. Recognition by most major Western powers of Kosovo's declaration of independence on 18 February 2008, despite Moscow's vigorous objection, confirmed Russian complaints that its views were ignored, and that decisions were taken 'outside the international institutions where discussion had been going on and in which Russia had a vote'.[13] In its submission to the UN's International Court of Justice (ICJ) Russia did not deny Kosovo's right of self-determination and even secession, but repudiated the argument that it was a 'special' case that could not be compared to other secessionist conflicts. The Russo-Georgian War later that year 'marked a failure on all counts' of the European security order.[14] Russia recognised the independence of South Ossetia and Abkhazia on 26 August, on the grounds that self-determination allowed secession in 'extreme situations'. The neo-revisionist stance from 2012 assumed that the demand for status and equality would have to be asserted rather than negotiated. The Kosovo precedent and the perceived breakdown of European security provoked the annexation of Crimea in March 2014. Moscow argued that the February 'coup', the change of regime in Kiev and the flight of Yanukovych, created an 'extreme situation' allowing Crimea to exercise the right of self-determination that could no longer be exercised within Ukraine's constitutional framework.[15] More broadly, the Charter system, to which Russia repeatedly appealed as the unique source of authority in international politics, appeared unable to provide a framework for the deepening European security dilemma.

A 'fortress Russia' mentality predominated. When, in April 2014, some Russian banks were blacklisted by the US and Visa and MasterCard suspended their services, the National Payment Card System, later known as 'Mir' ('World'), wholly owned by the Central Bank of Russia (CBR), was created. By 2021, Mir handled a quarter of Russian card transactions with 73 million users, although coverage outside the country was limited. Surprisingly, nearly one-third of the 30 million daily financial messages on the Brussels-based Society for Worldwide Interbank Financial Telecommunications (SWIFT) international payment system (essentially a notification and communications network) involved Russia. Fear that the country could be disconnected accelerated decoupling from Western-dominated globalisation processes. The CBR is on the board of SWIFT, but in 2014 it developed its System for Transfer of Financial Messages (SPFS), analogous to SWIFT, allowing financial institutions to communicate with each other. By 2021, some 400 domestic users had signed up, including most licensed lenders, but very few foreign subscribers. Only one Chinese bank had joined, since Chinese financial institutions prefer their home-grown alternative, the Cross-Border Interbank Payment System (CIPS). Both sought to reduce the dominance of Western institutions in the global economy, a process of directed deglobalisation.[16] Russian businesses preferred SWIFT (in particular oil and gas companies) because of its greater capacity and permanent operation (SPFS only works during office hours). In 2020, SWIFT still carried 80 per cent of messages.[17] SWIFT is incorporated in Belgium (hence the US has no jurisdiction over it) and must adhere to rules made there. It was an EU decision that disconnected Iran in 2012. Prime Minister Medvedev in 2019 warned that blocking Russia's access to payments would 'in fact, be a declaration of war – but nevertheless it was being discussed'.[18] In 2022, the majority of Russian banks were disconnected from SWIFT.

Speculation about Russia's demise as a great power was tempered by the recommendation that 'Russia's competitors and partners would do well to shape their policies towards this country on realistic assessments of its actual power rather than on some far-flung forecasts of its "inevitable collapse"'.[19] Russia returned to its historical situation of being an independent actor in the European state system, with all of the ambivalence that attended this status in the nineteenth century. Russia had been extraneous to the European state system then, and it became so now. Vilified and feared because of its 'reactionary' stance, with its relative power exaggerated in the popular imagination and dismissed by elites, there was no model for how relations should be conducted. Otto von Bismarck, at the head of the newly united Germany, believed that the secret to a successful foreign policy was a strong treaty with Russia, but his successors from 1890 thought otherwise. This propelled Russia into an entangling alliance with France and Great Britain, with disastrous consequences in World War I; a salutary lesson that the post-communist elite has taken to heart. Russia avoided alliance commitments, except with its closest neighbours in the Collective Security Treaty Organisation, and was hesitant to trigger collective security operations. The only occasion the CSTO was mobilised was to help quell the unrest in Kazakhstan in January 2022, repeating the pattern of the Warsaw Pact, which had also been used in policing operations rather than against external enemies. There was no formal security alliance with

China, and it would only be struck under intensified pressure from the political West. This would signal the return to pre-World War I levels of rivalry and Cold War bloc politics.

Russia adroitly managed power asymmetries to become a significant global actor. It became a power broker in West Asia and to a degree in Africa. The Wagner Group private military company was active at various times in Syria, Libya, Mali, Chad, Mozambique and the Central African Republic, and then in Ukraine. Trade relations with Africa returned to Soviet levels, although nearly two-thirds of Russia's trade was with Egypt, Algeria and Morocco. As relations between France and Mali deteriorated after the August 2020 coup in Bamako, Russia stepped up its anti-colonialist rhetoric to fill the vacuum, much to France's displeasure. Russia mobilised its diplomatic, military, energy and economic resources to reassert itself in the Eastern Mediterranean and across the world. Policy has been remarkably consistent, reflecting elite consensus over the underlying grand strategy of restoring Russia as a great power. This was more than improvisation; it was the mobilisation of the various tools of statecraft to achieve defined goals. Russia became more than a short-term challenge to the West.

The extent of Russian decline may have been exaggerated, but the country was hard-pressed to maintain its position. There are enduring demographic challenges, with the long cycles of falling birth rates associated with World War II losses and the social devastation of the 1990s. The focus on rearmament and the hoarding of resources after 2012 depressed economic growth. Preparations for a long siege prompted import substitution policies accompanied by domestic repression. The sharp fall in energy prices in 2014 and again in 2020 exposed vulnerabilities and a stagnating economy. While sanctions up to 2021 had little effect on Russian foreign policy behaviour, they did suppress growth – by most estimates at around 0.2 per cent annum. However, by early 2022, healthy growth of some 3 per cent had been restored, which makes the subsequent economic travails all the more poignant. The sanctions imposed after February were on an unprecedented scale. This triggered an economic recession, but instead of the anticipated disaster, the shift to a more state-directed mobilisational model saw GDP drop by only 2.1 per cent that year. Whether this could be sustained in the face of an unprecedented sanctions regime would prove the decisive test of Russian resilience.

IS RUSSIA REVISIONIST?

The assertion of multipolarity and sovereign internationalism turned Russia into a *neo-revisionist* power: defending Charter principles, but condemning the universal pretensions of the political West.[20] Russia's defence of the Charter international system against the supposed expansive ambitions of liberal hegemony turned the argument on its head. It was the US and its allies that had become revisionist, not Russia, and hence Russia at the time defined itself as a conservative status quo power. China and Russia positioned themselves as defenders of the established system and challenged only the expansionist practices of the political West. This took the form of the struggle against what was perceived to be the usurpation by a group of states of the prerogatives that were held to be the property of the system as a whole. They challenged not the international system but the practices of liberal hegemony – or so they claimed.

Russia's democratic revolution from the late 1980s transformed the polity and society, but its incomplete character allowed neo-Soviet features to reassert themselves. These included an outsize role for the security apparatus and the bureaucracy, which gradually tempered the early gains of freedom and political expression. The trauma of the 1990s, when Boris Yeltsin's dysfunctional administration oversaw a chaotic and damaging transition to the market, cast a long shadow over subsequent developments. Oligarchs took advantage of state weakness to seize profitable parts of the economy, while the mass of the population endured poverty and insecurity. Already in the 1990s a 'regime-state' was forged to manage public affairs, in a manner reminiscent of the old party-state. In the post-communist dual state, the administrative regime stood over and assumed a tutelary relationship with the institutions of the constitutional state (the rule of law, competitive elections, the free media, parliament and the federal system).[21] One of Putin's first acts was to curb the power of the oligarchs. In a famous meeting with leading business representatives in July 2000, he outlined the new ground rules: property gained through dubious means in the 1990s, including through the loans-for-shares scheme in 1995–6, could be kept, but in return the tycoons had to stay out of politics. An oligarch is someone with wealth and privileged access to political power, but in the Putin era the term applies less to the class than to a select group with long-standing personal ties to the leader.

Putin's programme focused on the assertion of state sovereignty at home and abroad. Putin's reassertion of state power was embellished for a time by the term 'sovereign democracy', the insistence that Russia would move towards democracy in its own time and in its own way, or not at all. In practice, it was not so much the state and its institutions that were strengthened but the network of regime relations focused on Putin personally and the Kremlin's administrative system. In foreign policy, the assertion of sovereignty was nourished by the perceived threat posed by democratic internationalism. After the Orange Revolution in Ukraine in late 2004, which saw Moscow's favoured candidate, Viktor Yanukovych, defeated by the 'pro-Western' candidate Viktor Yushchenko, the regime doubled down to defeat the threat of a 'colour revolution'. Further restrictions were imposed on civic activity and party-political life. In geopolitics, Putin's condemnation of Western unilateralism became increasingly shrill, condemning NATO's domination of the European security system. Putin's Russia may have been 'neither uniquely evil nor threatening', but its refusal to accept liberal hegemony generated tensions both at home and abroad.[22] These burst into open conflict with Russia's invasion of Ukraine in February 2022. Domestic repression foreshadowed adventurism abroad.[23] Discussion of whether Russia was rising or declining gave way to fears of political catastrophe and economic degradation as the country became bogged down militarily amid draconian sanctions targeting its elites, economy and society.

Russia (and China) by then had long been accused of being more than spoilers but outright disruptors. US strategic documents argued that Russia had become a revisionist power, intent on destroying the foundations of post-Cold War order. But what precisely did Russia seek to revise? Russia, along with China, sought to change the conduct of international politics, and thus challenged the global ambitions of the US and its allies. If the world was indeed becoming multipolar, the dominance of a hegemonic power would become redundant. However, at a more profound level, neither country sought to destroy the Charter international system as it had developed since 1945. Both enjoyed a privileged position within that system as veto-wielding permanent members of the UN Security Council. It would be irrational to destroy a system that guaranteed their great-power status. However, their attempt to revise the conduct of international politics challenged the usurpation of international law and Charter principles by Washington and its liberal allies, dubbed the 'collective West' in Russian jargon.

This was accompanied by disillusionment with international institutions. Moscow continued to criticise the liberal world order, but its neo-revisionism now became alienated from some of the institutions of the Charter system on the grounds that they had become subordinated to liberal hegemony. Russia thus drifted towards a more consistent revisionism. The 2020 constitutional amendments changed 206 articles of the 1993 constitution and confirmed the primacy of Russian domestic norms over international provisions, affecting in particular relations with the Council of Europe. It also soured relations between Russia and the Organisation for the Prohibition of Chemical Weapons (OPCW). In 2013, Russia helped the body win the Nobel Peace Prize, largely as a result of the joint work conducted with the US to destroy Syrian chemical weapons. However, following the Sergei Skripal poisoning in March 2018 and the poisoning of Russian opposition leader Alexei Navalny in August 2020, relations rapidly deteriorated. Lavrov argued that 'The OPCW has been de facto privatised.'[24] As far as Moscow was concerned, 'The OPCW firmly steers its way fully in line with Western countries' policy, Moscow lacks influence and tools needed for adjusting this course for its own benefit.' Russia had to return to its 'age-old habit of relying primarily on itself'.[25]

PATTERNS OF ALIENATION

The lack of a 'single and consolidated peace at the Cold War's end' provoked an intensifying security dilemma. For Russia, the terms of the settlement 'became harsher with that passage of time'.[26] A respected Russia was more likely to be cooperative, thereby reducing conflicts and tensions.[27] As Larson and Shevchenko argue, Russia (and China) 'have been more likely to contribute to global governance when they believed that doing so would enhance their prestige'.[28] Instead, status and security concerns combined to provoke the 2014 Ukraine crisis. The conflict represented an inflection point reflecting a qualitative change in relations, but it came in the context of a long slide towards hostility. By the time of his return to the presidency in 2012, after the four-year Medvedev interregnum, Putin had lost all trust in the Western powers, a feeling that was mutual. Obama offered Putin a visit to the White House in May 2012, on the eve of the G8 summit that was moved to neighbouring Maryland for his convenience, but he refused to attend. Putin had given up on the possibility of equitable integration and felt that he had been 'stabbed in the back by the West repeatedly' by three consecutive US presidents.[29] As far as Washington was concerned, Moscow's expectations were unrealistic. After all, Brzezinski stressed that the relationship between the US and its allies in Europe was essentially one between a 'hegemon and its vassals'. He noted that 'a democratic Russia would be more sympathetic to the values shared by America and Europe and hence also more likely to become a junior partner in shaping a more stable and cooperative Eurasia'.[30] This model had been tried in the early 1990s and found wanting. The alternative was not the revival of neo-imperial ambitions to recreate some sort of 'greater Russia' but the establishment of a new regional balance in which the sovereignty and integrity of the independent states was affirmed while recognising Russia's concerns and interests. No such balance was achieved and the destructive logic of the security dilemma led to disaster.

Andrei Tsygankov identifies three 'schools' or fundamental orientations in Russian foreign policy: Westernism, statism and civilisationism. In his view, they provide a better guide to analysis than classic Western international relations models.[31] Westernists, usually categorised as liberals, believed that the benefits of aligning with the political West would be enormous and to Russia's long-term benefit. They argued that instead of clinging to the fading hope that the Atlantic powers would somehow transform to become a greater West (appealing to the broader conception of the civilisation of the historical West, of which Russia considered itself to be a core member), Russia should simply accept membership on the terms offered by the actually existing West and focus on domestic development. The terms for integration were not generous but far from punitive. This strategy was predicated on the view that there was no security challenge from the political West. For an unconfident regime with a strategic culture that was historically insecure, such an approach was perceived to endanger not only the polity but above all the sovereign existence of the state.

This helps explain why in the Putin years statism came to predominate, although in the early period this was tempered by a strong dose of Westernism. Putin's 'new realist' strategy was predicated on the belief that there was a better alternative to the 'competitive coexistence' advanced by Primakov in the late 1990s, a policy harking back to the Cold War 1950s. To this end, Putin sought to enter the political West while retaining Russia's autonomy and status. In the end, no formula could be found to combine the two. Hard-headed strategists like Brzezinski were unrelenting, and even Putin's offer of cooperation after 9/11 was taken as a forced choice and 'provided the West with a strategic opportunity. It created the preconditions for the progressive geopolitical expansion of the Western community deeper and deeper into Eurasia.'[32] Brzezinski argued that to survive with its territory intact, 'Russia has no choice but to realign itself as the West's junior partner.'[33] This was not a view shared by the Kremlin.

The gradual drift away from Westernism gave way to the view of Russia as a separate and distinct civilisation. The ambitious goal of transforming the political West into a greater West was abandoned, but the need for some new European security arrangement and substantive post-Cold War political settlement remained. The former socialist states joined NATO in 2004 before joining the EU, which Putin interpreted to mean that it was 'necessary to become anti-Russian to be European. He understood that Europe had been vassalized by the United States.'[34] In the context of the US abrogation of the ABM treaty, Putin increasingly viewed NATO enlargement in existential terms, a perspective that would end in war with Ukraine. As noted, a chorus of commentators warned that 'expanding NATO without Russia runs the risk of creating a severe security dilemma for both the East and the West'.[35] The circle of NATO enlargement could not be squared, but Russia's repertoire of responses was extremely limited. Putin had earlier explored the option of Russian membership, but initiatives in this direction had been stymied. The impasse forced Moscow back onto classic realist options: going along with the West (bandwagoning) or enlisting allies to resist (counterbalancing). Even the Munich speech in February 2007 represented not so much a repudiation of this strategy as a plea for Russian concerns to be heeded.

The appeal for the West to 'listen' to Russian concerns was enduring and bathetic. The Medvedev period from 2008 differed in style and substance from the Putin years, but it was shaped by similar structural constraints.[36] Medvedev represented the liberal end of Putinism and not its repudiation (as desired by Obama and other Western leaders). Even Medvedev's emollient approach was unable to crack the code, and tensions were exacerbated by ill-judged personal condemnation of Putin by both Obama and his vice president Biden, humiliations that Putin was slow to forgive. Disagreement over Libya in 2011 brought the differences into the open. The US administration made no secret of its preference for Medvedev to return to the Kremlin for a second term – effectively precluding it from happening. The protests against fraud in the parliamentary election of December 2011 were the final straw, which Putin considered were sponsored from abroad. The popular mobilisation in his view served American foreign policy goals. It was an embittered Putin who returned to the Kremlin in 2012. Policy reverted to the classic Cold War version of peaceful coexistence in which competition was intense but managed.

Dmitri Trenin, the head of the Carnegie Moscow Center from 2008 until its closure at the beginning of the Ukraine war, argues that Russian foreign policy after 1991 rested on Gorbachev's shoulders, based on integration with the West and a cooperative relationship with the Atlantic powers. The enduring goal was to find the optimum balance between domestic imperatives and external realities, encompassing the appropriate balance between security and development. This period conclusively ended in 2014, and instead a distinctive 'Russian project' took shape. Integration with the West was abandoned and the shift to the Global South intensified. Russia emerged as a separate global pole, which Trenin labels 'the North', looking for constructive partnerships in Eurasia and the broader 'non-West', such as the SCO.[37] This fulfilled Brzezinski's warning about the danger to US power of what he called an anti-hegemonic front. Presciently, he had in mind China, Russia and possibly Iran.[38] Statists in Russia called for reversion to a nineteenth-century type of concert-based global order, while pragmatists appealed to a more defensive yet muscular approach to stop the political West's relentless expansion. Primakov today is held in such high esteem in Russia because he recognised that, as long as the political West existed in its Cold War format, then conflict was inevitable. Coexistence could be cooperative but in a multipolar world it could not be transcended.

The strategy of resistance and separation was supported by Eurasianists, the most coherent and vocal of the civilisationist faction. The political theory of Eurasianism emerged in the nineteenth century but took recognised form as an alternative to Soviet communism in the 1920s among Russian émigrés in Western Europe. For Eurasianists, Russia represents a formation separate and distinct from Western and Asian civilisations, a unique multi-ethnic and multinational community forged in the vast Eurasian landmass.[39] Imperial expansion across the vast North Eurasian plain assimilated many different peoples and cultures, creating a unique civilisation. Eurasianism draws on nineteenth-century romantic nationalism but stresses not racial differences but pluricultural 'ethnogenesis', the making of a new people through combination rather than division. The ethnographer Lev Gumilëv argued that the historic symbiosis between Russians and other native peoples created a unique Eurasian cultural and spiritual identity.[40] On this reading, Russia represents a separate world combining distinct ethnocultural entities. The leading theorist of this separate developmental path is Alexander Dugin, who argues that Russia and China represent the vanguard of multipolarity as Western-led unipolarity collapses.[41]

Eurasianists welcomed the neo-revisionist turn but argued that it did not go far enough – they favoured full-blown revisionism. Even statists were giving up on anything approaching a 'strategic partnership' with the EU, while relations with the US became increasingly frosty, even if tempered by moments of cooperation over issues of common concern (cyberattacks, arms control, the environment, Afghanistan, and non-proliferation in Iran and North Korea). Putin's frustration at the West's failure to recognise Russia as an appropriate interlocutor and strategic partner pushed him towards more radical positions. Westernism was not entirely abandoned, above all in macroeconomic policy, in keeping with Putin's proclivity to keep all options open. This was matched by his refusal to allow Russia to become a subaltern to the political West, even if this provoked strategic isolation. As early as 2007, after *Time* magazine had named him man of the year, Putin noted that:

> Sometimes one gets the impression that America does not need friends. . . . [but] some kind of auxiliary subjects to take command of, and this gave rise to a dismissive attitude towards Russia, that they are a little bit savage still or they just climbed down from the trees, you know, and probably need to have their hair brushed and their beards trimmed.[42]

For hawks in the security apparatus, the *siloviki*, the issue was rather more straightforward – the long-term attempt to weaken if not to destroy Russia as a great power. Nikolai Patrushev, the former head of the Federal Security Service (FSB) who in 2008 became secretary of the Security Council, argued in a manifesto of October 2014 under the title of 'Cold War Two' that the Western goal was to dismember Russia by supporting its enemies and sponsoring hostile movements. He quoted Madeleine Albright to the effect that it was 'unjust' that such vast, resource-rich areas as Siberia and the Russian Far East should be 'under Moscow's rule'.[43] The statement is apocryphal but has entered Moscow lore as evidence of the conspiracy against Russia.[44] Patrushev was at the head of the anti-Western faction and by 2020 his views predominated.

RUSSIAN POST-WESTERNISM

Political resistance was reinforced by a cultural critique of the political West, driving a conservative turn at home. The new traditionalism stressed Russia's cultural specificity and diversity in a plural world. In 2012, Putin argued, 'For centuries, Russia developed as a multi-ethnic nation, a civilisation-state bonded by the Russian people, Russian language and Russian culture native for us all, uniting us and preventing us from dissolving in this diverse world.'[45] In his Valdai speech in September 2013, Putin's tone was more strident, warning about the degeneration of the West. This was based on a religious-conservative ideology, presenting Russia as a moral bastion against the decadence, sexual licence, porn and gay rights of the West. He presented Russia as a 'state-civilisation' in these graphic terms:

> Russia – as philosopher Konstantin Leontyev vividly put it – has always evolved in 'blossoming complexity', as a state-civilisation, reinforced by the Russian people, Russian language, Russian culture, Russian Orthodox Church and the country's other traditional religions. It is precisely the state-civilisation model that has shaped our state polity. It has always sought flexibly to accommodate the ethnic and religious specificity of particular territories, ensuring diversity in unity.[46]

The definition of a 'civilisation-state' in the Russian context is unclear.[47] When applied to China, it refers to millennia of history, whereas Russia developed in fits and starts, repeatedly returning to first principles and lacking a self-confident national identity. The philosopher Vadim Tsymbursky used geopolitical thinking to critique spatial analysis, arguing that Russia would only become free when liberated from imperial thinking and the sterile Russia–Europe dichotomy. He advanced the notion of 'island Russia', an entity sufficient unto itself.[48] This 'isolationist' trend in Russian thinking was taken up by Russian commentators, notably by Vladislav Surkov (the former deputy head of the Presidential Administration responsible for political affairs between 1999 and 2011). In his 'The Loneliness of the Half-Breed' in 2018, he argued that Russian elites for 400 years had unsuccessfully tried to Westernise the country. He announced, 'Russia's epic Westward quest is finally over.' Failure in one direction did not necessarily entail a turn to the East. Instead a generations-long period of 'geopolitical loneliness' (*odinochestvo*) lay ahead.[49] This was not isolation, since Russia would maintain a strong international presence, but it would do so on its own.

The 'cultural turn' had immediate policy consequences. First, a renewed emphasis on Eurasian economic integration (the EEU), as well as aspirations to develop Eurasia as a self-sufficient geopolitical entity. This was couched in the language of complementing rather than challenging the EU, but the creation of an alternative pole of integration generated a competitive dynamic. A struggle ensued over what was termed the 'shared neighbourhood', precipitating the Ukraine crisis. Second, the conservative turn was given legislative form in a number of laws from 2012, notably the ban against the propagation of homosexuality among minors and a law criminalising 'offending the feelings of religious believers'. Third, there was a renewed interest in 'Eurasia' as a distinct subject of history and as a region with its own concerns. Russia's neo-revisionism devised a 'heartland' strategy to prevent Eurasia becoming an enormous 'fracture' zone, torn between the rising power of China in the East and the established Atlantic powers in the West. In 1995, Kissinger warned that the domination by a single power of Eurasia's two main spheres, Europe or Asia, would represent a strategic danger to the US.[50] This was the argument made by Brzezinski when he stated that after 500 years as the centre of world power, Eurasia remained 'the chessboard on which the struggle for global primacy continues to be played . . . It is imperative that no Eurasian challenger emerges, capable of dominating Eurasia and thus also of challenging America.'[51]

Eurasia is part of a single vast landmass, with no clear natural borders. A narrow definition of Eurasia focuses on Russia and post-Soviet republics (excluding the Baltic), while the more expansive version runs from Shannon in the West to Shanghai in the East. This fluidity is reflected in the work of Dugin, Russia's leading 'geopolitical' thinker, even though his interests range widely. Dugin's influence has been exaggerated, but his neo-Eurasianist view that Russia has a special mission to preserve the world from the corrupt values of Western liberal democracy resonates with the public. Tsargrad TV, a religious-patriotic channel funded by the Kremlin-aligned investment banker Konstantin Malofeev, enjoys surprising popularity. Appearing on this station, Dugin declared:

In this epoch of cyborgs, hybrids, mutants, chimeras and virtual reality, mankind will only be saved by tradition . . . all modernism – the idea of progress, development, the so-called scientific view of the world, democracy and liberalism [is] a Satanic idea that spells a death sentence for humanity . . . the only defence is asserting God, the church, the empire, the congregation of the faithful, the state, and the people's traditions.[52]

Such views undermined attempts to create a more vibrant educational sector and dynamic economy. State-sponsored puritanism fostered intolerance of diversity and difference and undermined the pluralism enshrined in the first two chapters of the 1993 constitution. This was evident in the 2020 constitutional amendments, the great majority of which reflected the conservative turn, including a ban on same-sex marriage.

The Ukraine crisis from 2014 marked the end of greater Europe aspirations, and Moscow thereafter focused on various Eurasian integration projects and the broader goal of creating some sort of Greater Eurasian Partnership (GEP). The *National Security Strategy* of 31 December 2015 starkly warned about the threat: 'Expanding the force potential of NATO and endowing it with global functions that are implemented in violation of international legal norms, the bloc's heightened military activity, its continued expansion and the approach of its military infrastructure to Russia's borders, all create a threat to national security.'[53] The *Strategy* presented Russia as a global actor with legitimate regional concerns, and condemned attempts at renewed containment. It defined confrontation with the West as a threat, and warned against the 'hybrid' wars allegedly conducted against Russia. The country's self-reliance and self-sufficiency was stressed, accompanied by the 'securitisation' of new policy areas, both in Russia and the West. According to the Copenhagen School, securitisation is the way that 'normal' politics is subsumed into national security discourses, which then shape policy.[54] After 2014, NATO abandoned the language of 'strategic partnership' as policy also underwent a creeping securitisation, including the monitoring of the media to counter 'Russian propaganda' and 'fake news'.[55] The process was uneven and partial, with most European countries reluctant to engage in wholesale securitisation, but the US went the furthest. Its NSS-2015 warned that it 'will continue to impose significant costs on Russia through sanctions' to 'deter Russian aggression'.[56] Trump talked of improving relations but during his presidency sanctions and associated coercive measures far exceeded those imposed during the original Cold War.

The shift towards domestic conservatism was not immediately reflected in foreign policy. The revised *Foreign Policy Concept* issued on 30 November 2016 was remarkably emollient and denied any imputed condition of 'war' between Russia and the Atlantic community. The *Concept* stressed Russia's desire for good relations with all of its 'partners', the continued commitment to multilateral organisations and international economic integration, the supremacy of international law, the central role of the UN, the importance of democracy and Russia's contribution to peace and security in Europe. The general stance remained the same: 'The contemporary world is going through a period of profound changes, the essence of which is the formation of a polycentric [multipolar] international system.' The West's attempt to impede this natural shift generated instability in international relations. Russia would 'resist the attempts of individual states or groups of states to revise the generally recognised principles of international order', for instance, using Responsibility to Protect (R2P) to intervene in the internal affairs of other countries. The document asserted Russia's independent status and indicated a reluctance to be drawn into any alliance or bloc. It also called on the news media 'to convey the Russian viewpoint to broad circles of the world community'. Russia had been embroiled in the Syrian conflict since September 2015, but the Middle East was ranked behind the post-Soviet space, Europe, the US and Asia-Pacific in its regional priorities.

No alternative ideological project for the creation of some sort of Eurasian civilisation was outlined, but instead the *Concept* reiterated Russia's support for 'universal democratic values'. Regional integration would be in conformity with WTO rules, and there was no suggestion that Russia would turn its back on globalisation. Instead, the document stressed Russia's desire to establish 'constructive, stable and predictable cooperation' with the countries of the EU. The greater Europe ambition was voiced in terms of Russia's wish 'to create a common economic and humanitarian space from the Atlantic to the Pacific Ocean on the basis of the harmonisation of the processes of European and Eurasian integration'. The document condemned 'NATO's expansion and the alliance's military structure approaching Russia's borders', but Russia still sought 'an equal partnership' while establishing 'mutually beneficial relation with the United States'. The *Concept* accused the US and its allies of undermining 'global stability' by trying to 'contain' Russia and reserved the right to 'react harshly to any unfriendly' moves. Cooperation was only possible on the basis of 'equality, mutual respect of interests, and non-interference in one another's internal affairs'. Russia's goal was good relations with all states based on 'mutual respect'. There was no talk of an anti-hegemonic strategy, although 'polycentrism' was defended and 'full-scale' partnership and cooperation with China stressed. The tone overall was defensive but reflected confidence that the tide of history – what in Soviet parlance had been called the 'correlation of forces' – was running in Moscow's favour. The document stressed Russia's enduring commitment to universal principles, as long as these were not abused to justify interference in the internal affairs of states.[57]

Putin's annual address to the Federal Assembly on 15 January 2020 took up the theme. He called on the permanent members of the UNSC to reboot world order within the multipolar paradigm: 'I am convinced that it is high time for a serious and direct discussion about the basic principles of a stable world order and the most acute problems that humanity is facing', and called for a new system based on the UN Charter.[58] Putin repeatedly drew on the experience of the 1990s. In his 2020 Valdai speech, he argued, 'We have always considered a strong state a basic condition for Russia's development. And we have seen again that we were right by meticulously restoring and strengthening state institutions after their decline, and sometimes complete destruction in the 1990s.'[59] He noted that 'Ever since the cold war model of international relations, which was stable and predictable in its own way, began to change (I am not saying that I miss it, I most certainly do not), the world has changed many times', and warned how some countries sought 'to take advantage of the benefits the end of the cold confrontation brought'. Instead, he appealed to the postwar world order established by the three victorious countries at Yalta, but recognised that 'The role of Britain has changed since then, the Soviet Union no longer exists, while some try to dismiss Russia altogether':

> Let me assure you, dear friends, that we are objectively assessing our potentialities: our intellectual, territorial, economic and military potential. I am referring to our current options, our overall potential. Consolidating this country and looking at what is happening in the world, in other countries. I would like to tell those who are still waiting for Russia's strength to gradually wane, the only thing we are worried about is catching a cold at your funeral.

Following this rather chilling warning, he disagreed with 'the assumption that existing international structures must be completely rebuilt, if not dismissed as obsolete and altogether dismantled'. Instead, he stressed the maintenance of the basic structures established in 1945, with the UNSC at its head, although he accepted that the changed 'correlation of forces, potentialities and positions of states' allowed some adjustment of 'the institutional arrangement of world politics' as well as breathing 'new life into multilateral diplomacy'. This was a classic restatement of the neo-revisionist position: a defence of the international system established in 1945, but with some adjustments. As he argued, 'We cannot do without a common, universal framework for international affairs.'[60]

The *National Security Strategy* of July 2021 was predicated on continuing confrontation as the West tried to 'maintain its hegemony'. Amid growing international tension, Russian foreign policy would seek to 'stabilise international relations based on international law and the principle of general, equal and indivisible security'.[61] The West was to be balanced by closer economic, political and military ties with the non-Western world, in the first instance China but also India, Turkey and Iran. These countries did not threaten Russia's security but represented the core of the emerging multipolar and multilateral international community.[62] Moscow intensified its criticism of the 'rules-based international order' as subverting the impartiality of the international system. The Hague-based OPCW came in for particular criticism, which from Moscow's perspective singled out US adversaries such as Iran and Syria for condemnation while being indulgent to US allies. Moscow argued that in the 'rules-based order' the US made up the rules as it saw fit, generating disorder. Karaganov argued that Russia should adopt 'neo-isolationism' to reinvigorate its national spirit. He framed this as a new 'assertive ideology' to reflect Russia's character as a 'liberating people' who freed the world from 500 years of Western tyranny and a 'victorious people' who defeated hegemons from Genghis Khan to Uncle Sam. He called on the Kremlin to assume a 'psychological offense' against the West, asserting that Europe and the US would never forgive Moscow for challenging their dominance. NATO in his view should be treated as 'an aggressive alliance'.[63]

Russia found no place in the 'liberal world order'. It acknowledged the reality of US-led military power but, unlike West European states and Japan, it refused to become a 'legacy' great power. Liberal critics argue that this was derived from the demands of the repressive power system, requiring a foreign enemy to consolidate power at home.[64] This 'diversionary' model is not convincing. Even a perfectly democratic Russia would defend its sovereignty and interests in a world of competing nation states. The cost of excluding Russia from the expanding Atlantic alliance was high, but the price of premature Russian inclusion entailed the dilution of EU and NATO principles. More adroit leadership may have handled the challenge better, but the dilemma would not thereby have disappeared.

RUSSIA LOOKS EAST

The Soviet – Chinese Joint Communiqué of December 1991 included an 'anti-hegemony' provision, which set the tone for later relations.[65] In December 1992, Yeltsin visited Beijing and signed a declaration that Russia and China were 'friendly states' and would 'develop relations of good-neighbourliness, friendship and mutually beneficial cooperation', the foundation for later interactions. In April 1997, a 'strategic partnership' was declared between the two countries based on the Russo-Chinese 'Joint Declaration on a Multipolar World and the Establishment of a New International Order', and agreed to limit troop numbers on their mutual border. The two countries united in opposition to US-led unipolarity. This stage culminated in July 2001 with the signing of the 'Treaty of Good Neighbourliness and Friendly Cooperation' (renewed in 2021), and in 2008 a treaty ratified the Russo-Chinese border demarcation settlement of 2004. Given the long history of border contestation, which still simmers among nationalists on both sides, this was a major achievement. In 2015, the bilateral relationship was elevated to a 'comprehensive strategic cooperative partnership in a new era'.

The Sino-Russian alignment is one of the most important global developments in the twenty-first century, but will it last?[66] Does Russia underestimate the strategic dangers of great-power competition and, blinded by historic grievances with the West, underrate the dangers of the Chinese embrace? Will it escape from the Western frying pan only to be burnt in the Chinese fire? Gorbachev healed the Soviet-era split, Yeltsin signed the Friendship treaty and started border demarcation, and in the early Putin years the relationship was cordial and professional. However, the warm personal relationship between Putin and Xi Jinping is of an exceptional historical character. On the eve of his June 2019 visit to Moscow, Xi declared, 'I have had closer interactions with President Putin than with any other foreign colleague. He is my best and bosom friend. I cherish dearly our deep friendship.' He noted that he had met with Putin nearly thirty times and regularly communicated by letter and telephone, and that both were committed to maintaining and deepening the China–Russia relationship.[67]

This naturally raises the question of whether such warm relations will endure following the end of their respective leaderships. There are good economic and strategic reasons to believe that this will be the case. Russia provides China with an increasing proportion of its energy and agricultural products. Defence cooperation turned their long border into a source of security rather than confrontation. Sino-Russian alignment became a major strategic asset and 'strengthens their respective status on the international stage and provides basic support for the diplomacy of both countries'.[68] China became the core of Russia's Asian strategy, although tempered by continued close links with other regional states, notably India, Indonesia, South Korea and Vietnam. Despite the growing asymmetry in the relationship, Russia tried to keep open its hedging options.[69] Beijing considered Moscow a legitimate partner that posed no threat to regime security, while Russia proved a stable and reliable partner. However, neither country sought a bloc-type alliance, with Russia seeking to avoid the fate of the Soviet Union, while in China, 'alliance has gradually been framed as a negative political concept'.[70] Russia has sought to avoid being drawn into the US–China conflict, while from 2022 China has been wary of being dragged into the proxy war between Russia and the West.

Views of the relationship are torn between those that consider it a tenuous 'marriage of convenience' and others who wish 'to create an anti-US, anti-Western alliance due to heavy pressure on both countries from the United States'. Instead, according to the former head of the National People's Congress standing committee on foreign relations, Fu Ying, 'Neither argument accurately captures the true nature of the relationship. [The] China–Russia relationship is a stable strategic partnership and it is complex, sturdy and deeply rooted.'[71] Although the relationship between Putin and Xi Jinping is exceptionally warm, there has long been a solid consensus in Beijing on the need for a strong relationship with Russia, shared by Xi's predecessors, Hu Jintao and Jiang Zemin. The relationship today is based on six pillars.[72]

First, defence of a common normative understanding of the international system, and thus joint resistance to the great substitution. The two are fundamentally conservative status quo powers, repeatedly affirming their commitment to the fundamental principles of sovereign internationalism, the core of the Charter international system. These include the primacy of state sovereignty, territorial integrity, the supremacy of international law and the centrality of the UN and its Security Council. On this basis the two countries coordinate their diplomatic activities on major international issues. A study in 2018 found that they voted together 98 per cent of the time in the UN, and Russia backed every Chinese Security Council veto since 2007.[73] However, both became neo-revisionist powers, challenging hegemonism in international affairs.

Second, the energy relationship has been steadily deepening. By 2018, Russia had become China's major oil supplier. In that year a second branch of the East Siberia – Pacific Ocean (ESPO) pipeline doubled Russia's direct oil exports to China, and at the same time Beijing purchased oil from the pipeline's Pacific terminal at Kozmino. The Power of Siberia pipeline started pumping gas in late 2019 and soon reached its full capacity of 55 billion cubic metres (bcm) a year, while Gazprom conducted feasibility studies for a Power of Siberia 2 pipeline (Soyuz Vostok) across Mongolia. In 2019, Novatek sold 19 per cent of its Arctic liquified natural gas (LNG-2) project to the China National Petroleum Corporation (CNPC) and the China National Offshore Oil Corporation (CNOOC). Between 2011 and

2020, China invested some \$36 billion in Russia, with the greatest share devoted to raw materials and energy enterprises. Under sanctions from 2022, Russia has diverted its energy exports from Europe to Asia, and above all China.

Third, in terms of trade, in 2010 China overtook Germany as Russia's single largest trading partner and became the primary supplier of industrial goods. China's share in Russia's external trade increased from 10.5 per cent in 2013 to 20 per cent in 2022, by the end of which year mutual trade had reached \$190 billion. Much of this was attributable to Russia opening up hitherto protected sectors of the economy, including the upstream energy sector and digital infrastructure. Raw materials and resources, primarily energy, account for 70 per cent of Russia's exports, although China is now a growing market for Russian agricultural goods. While China is Russia's largest trading partner, Russia only in 2022 entered China's top ten.

Fourth, in terms of security and defence, Chinese forces regularly take part in Russia's annual military exercises. It participated in twenty-eight between 2002 and 2012, while in 2014 alone it took part in thirty-one. From 2018 this became a more formal annual occurrence, beginning with the Vostok military exercise that year. As part of China's 'going out to the world', in 2019 and again the following year, the two countries conducted a joint bomber patrol along the East Asian coast. There was even talk of China relaxing its traditional hostility to joining military alliances.[74] Arms sales to China played an important part in preserving Russian defence industries in the 1990s, but exports peaked in 2005 and by 2020 volumes were less than a fifth of what they had been earlier. Sales of military technology slowed as China developed its own defence production.[75] China overtook Russia to become the world's second-largest arms manufacturer and competed for the same global markets. Beijing had apparently reverse-engineered the Sukhoi SU-27SK and SU-33 fighters to create the J-11B and J-15, respectively. Moscow was now ready to share its technologies in exchange for high-quality Chinese goods. China became a key supplier of parts, components and avionics for the advanced SU-35S fighter jet, and in November 2015 the People's Liberation Army became the first export customer for the plane. Russia also supplied kilo-class submarines and the S-400 anti-aircraft missile system.

Fifth, the two countries generated an alternative globalisation. From May 2015, the two countries agreed to the 'conjugation' (*sopryazhenie*) of the EEU and BRI, and numerous commissions were established to deepen relations. A year later, Putin broadened the terms of the docking to encompass the Greater Eurasian Partnership. The two countries accelerated their technological and financial decoupling from the Atlantic powers. Prompted by security concerns, in May 2019 US companies were prohibited from doing business with Huawei and banned the export of advanced semiconductors. Putin condemned the American actions as the 'first technological war of the coming digital era'.[76] Russia became one of Huawei's fastest-growing markets. Huawei and ZTE were at the heart of Russia's plans to develop 5G networks, accompanied by extensive technological localisation.[77] In June 2019, Huawei and the Russian telecommunications giant MTS agreed to build the 5G network in Russia; in March 2020, Huawei agreed with Sberbank to create a cloud platform for Russian businesses; and in October, Huawei agreed with Avtodor to build roads capable of supporting autonomous vehicles. Russian and Chinese engineers combined to develop the Harmony operating system (OS) to replace Google's Android OS (Google had been forced to suspend Huawei's Android licence in 2019).[78] Other plans included the exploitation of the GLONASS and BeiDou satellite navigation systems, and cooperation with Huawei in shipbuilding (with the Russian United Shipbuilding Corporation). There were clear synergies between the two countries, with Russia strong in basic science, military and dual-use technologies, while China had an impressive record in infrastructure development, transport and civilian technologies.[79]

Sixth, as we shall see in Chapter 12, the two countries sponsored post-Western regional associations. These multilateral bodies institutionalise multipolarity and thereby potentially reinforce the autonomy of the international system. They were not so much anti-Western as anti-hegemonic. An alternative architecture of global governance and associations was being created, tangible evidence of a world moving out of the shadow of Western dominance.

There is a transformative quality to the relationship. Grounded in realpolitik and structural realism, Russia and China have substantive common interests in achieving a balanced partnership and in rendering global governance more equitable. They face some common challenges. The emergence of a nuclear-armed Democratic People's Republic of Korea (DPRK) represents one of the greatest tests for the international community, and a matter of concern for both. Neither welcomed the emergence of an unstable nuclear power with ballistic missiles in their neighbourhood. The two agreed to UN resolutions intensifying sanctions, but Russia and China sought a 'dual freeze' option, whereby Pyongyang would impose a moratorium on nuclear and missile tests in exchange for a halt to US – South Korean military exercises.[80] However, they opposed talk of 'regime change', since this would almost certainly entail massive disruption and millions of refugees (Russia has an eleven-mile land frontier with North Korea), and both feared the prospect of a united Korea under American tutelage.

The 4 February 2022 Joint Statement, issued by the two leaders when they met at the opening of the Beijing Winter Olympics, demonstrated the high degree of normative convergence. The attempt by 'certain states' to impose their 'democratic standards' was condemned, accompanied by the assertion that China and Russia both have 'long-standing traditions of democracy', hence 'it is only up to the people of the country to decide whether their state is a democratic one'. The statement condemned 'further NATO enlargement' and called on the alliance to 'abandon its ideologised Cold War approaches'. China's support for Russia's stance against NATO enlargement was something new, and shaped Beijing's reaction to the war a few weeks later. This was accompanied by a resounding reaffirmation of the centrality of the UN Charter and the UDHR as 'fundamental principles, which all states must comply with and observe in deeds'. This was summed up as follows:

The sides underline that Russia and China, as world powers and permanent members of the United Nations Security Council, intend to firmly adhere to moral principles and accept their responsibility, strongly advocate the international system with the central coordinating role of the United Nations in international affairs, defend the world order based on international law, including the purposes and principles of the Charter of the United Nations, advance multipolarity and promote the democratization of international relations, together create an even more prospering, stable, and just world, jointly build international relations of a new type.

On regional issues, Beijing supported Russia's proposal 'to create long-term legally binding security guarantees in Europe', while re-affirming that 'Taiwan is an inalienable part of China' and denouncing 'any forms of independence for Taiwan'. Both countries were wary of trying to establish a bloc system of allies. As Richard Little notes, 'A military alliance between China and Russia would not enhance their level of security or shift the balance of power in their favour.'[81] However, as Cold War II intensifies, this may no longer be the case.

The fundamental principle was that 'No state can or should ensure its own security separately from the security of the rest of the world and at the expense of the security of other states' – something that Russia has been asserting since the end of the Cold War. The inter-state relations between Russia and China were defined as

superior to political and military alliances of the Cold War era. Friendship between the two states has no limits, there are no 'forbidden' areas of cooperation, strengthening of bilateral strategic cooperation is neither aimed against third countries nor affected by the changing international environment and circumstantial changes in third countries.[82]

Russia had long challenged US exceptionalist and hegemonic ambitions, and now it was joined by a China intent on asserting its status as a global power. The statement rejected the notion that the two countries were 'global autocracies' out to subvert Western liberal democracies and instead appealed for pluralism in an international system based on Charter principles. Order in international affairs could only be established on this basis. The alternative was disorder and permanent conflict.

The invasion of Ukraine twenty days later and the subsequent imposition of draconian sanctions placed the relationship under unprecedented strain. The ties had always been pragmatic and based on respective definitions of national self-interest, although the Joint Statement demonstrated just how close their normative alignment had become. As the war ground on and Russia failed to meet its immediate objectives, China was careful not to overstep the boundaries to incur secondary sanctions by the political West. Beijing offered Moscow diplomatic support and increased purchases of (discounted) oil and gas, but did not supply sophisticated weapons or advanced technology to replenish Russia's arsenal. Russia became a pariah state for the West and its allies, and hence its value as a partner for China was placed in question. There is much to keep the two countries aligned, but developments within the two countries as much as changes in international affairs will shape their relationship.[83]

RUSSIA TAKES ON THE WEST

With a relatively small and declining GDP, Russia took on the political West. NATO's European allies enjoy a combined GDP of $20.4 trillion, almost equal to that of the US. Russia's population in 2022 was just 147 million, whereas the European democracies number some 600 million, with combined armed forces of 1.26 million, compared to Russia's 900,000 active-duty troops (including the National Guard and other forces). Liberals had long argued that a substantive reform of political and economic governance was required to re-energise the economy, but that required a reassertion of the autonomy of the constitutional state accompanied by a reduction in international tension. In his Address to the Federal Assembly on 21 February 2023, Putin stressed Russia's resilience and promised that the Russian economy would remain open.[84] Sceptics were less sure, and in conditions of armed conflict and economic warfare, Russia has adopted elements of a mobilisation and autarchic model of development. This has allowed Russia to survive, but it threatens a return to a Soviet-style economy – and we know how that ended.

Neo-revisionism was always an unstable compromise, appealing to the norms of the Charter system but in practice undermining them. The 2022 invasion of Ukraine was an extreme instance, when perceived national interests trumped commitment to international norms. It was justified by appealing to Article 51 of the UN Charter and the right to self-defence, thus portraying the war as preventive. To the degree that the war was prompted by defence of the breakaway regions of Donetsk and Lugansk, Moscow had a point. However, given the horrific implications of armoured columns laying siege to cities, it can hardly be considered a just war (*jus ad bellum*), quite apart from the destructive way in which the fighting has been conducted (*jus in bello*). Russia argues it was pushed to the wall by the intransigence of the political West in refusing the balanced implementation of the core principles of the post-Cold War peace settlement, prioritising choice over the indivisibility of security. The door to diplomacy had not been entirely closed, but the continued arming of Ukraine, support for its anti-Russian positions and policies, and the possibility of an attack against the Donbass republics was perceived as a security threat of the highest order.

According to one estimate, since 1800 Russia has on average been invaded every thirty-three years.[85] This gave rise to an enduring security culture and an almost paranoid fear of external attack, which provoked domestic repression against potential 'fifth columnists'. However, after spending two decades stabilising Russia, the 2020 constitutional amendments undermined the foundations of constitutionalism amid intensified repression of the independent political opposition. The Russo-Ukraine war then threw the whole system into turmoil. The survival of the regime itself came on to the agenda. Whether deliberate or not, the punitive sanctions ultimately raised the question of regime change. The goal was not only to defeat Moscow's Ukraine policy but to damage the economy and society to permanently degrade Russia's military potential.

Putin insisted that Moscow would meet its goals in Ukraine, and although isolated from the West continued to build extensive global ties. The revised *Maritime Doctrine* published on 31 July 2022 outlined ambitious plans for a global navy, including a permanent presence in the Red Sea. Lavrov's multi-country tour of Africa a few weeks earlier demonstrated Russia's enduring international ambitions. These were reflected in the revised *Foreign Policy Doctrine*, approved in September. The new version focused on the idea of the Russian World (*Russkii mir*), an activist policy in defence of Russian-speakers abroad long advocated by Russian conservatives. Deploying the ill-defined concept of 'compatriot', although taken to refer to the 25 million ethnic Russians who found themselves abroad after 1991, the *Doctrine* asserted that 'The Russian Federation provides support to its compatriots living abroad in the fulfilment of their rights, to ensure the protection of their interests and the preservation of their Russian cultural identity.'[86]

The Putin era of the 'weak strongman' will not last for ever.[87] A Russia without Putin will be very different, but will a change of leadership fundamentally modify the security culture and grand strategy on which foreign policy has been based? If accompanied by thoroughgoing regime change or even state collapse, there is no guarantee that a new system will be more democratic. In crisis conditions, when the survival of the polity and of the state itself are at stake, it could well be more authoritarian. Putin in any case is likely to fight on to the bitter end. Even if he did leave office – either for health reasons or some elite coup or military putsch – then his successor would be faced with the same dilemmas. From the beginning, Putin has relied on opaque administrative methods and pedantic legalism, and over the years the regime's reliance on manipulation and coercion has increased. The autonomy of the constitutional state was commensurately diminished – after 2020 almost to vanishing point. Whatever comes next, the challenge of keeping the enormous state together, avoiding interethnic and confessional conflict and finding an appropriate place in the world endures.

8

EUROPE REDIVIDED

The way that one war ends shapes the next. This certainly applies to Europe after 1989, even if the war this time was a cold one. The Charter of Paris in 1990 spoke of the unification of the continent, but the transformation ultimately failed to create mechanisms to anchor the new peace order in institutions robust and capacious enough to satisfy all partners. No new political community was created from Lisbon to Vladivostok. Instead, the Atlantic power system expanded, and the transformation anticipated by Moscow was stillborn. The enlargement of NATO and the EU was couched in idealistic terms, but the power consequences of expansion were neglected.[1] The worthy principle of 'freedom of choice' was asserted over the equally relevant postulate of 'indivisibility of security'. The West European defence community scaled up to encompass the East, but in the absence of a robust overarching Euro-Asian security framework this generated conflict and ultimately war. Aspirations for a 'common European home' and for a 'Europe whole and free' were both disappointed, and instead traditional geopolitics returned. A new physical and ideological frontline divided the continent, reviving traditional patterns of confrontation. The earlier solution to the question of post-Cold War order became the new problem to be resolved.

EUROPE AS A POWER

The term 'Europe as a power' derives from French usage and is reinforced by the more recent idea of 'strategic autonomy' and even 'European sovereignty'. The tension remains between a more autonomous, and even 'geopolitical', Europe and the reality that in the European Union foreign and security policy remains the prerogative of member states. Charles de Gaulle was committed to the idea of the nation state, but he also appealed to the vision of a powerful and united continent acting as an independent force between the Soviet Union and the US. This is why he twice vetoed British entry, believing that the country would act as the American 'Trojan horse'. De Gaulle was also jealous of any country that could reduce French leadership, since he saw Europe acting as an 'Archimedes' lever' to restore France to the first rank of the great powers.[2] The Elysée Treaty in 1963 established a privileged partnership between France and Germany, which with varying intensity over the years acted as the 'motor' of European integration and a vector for French influence. This did not mean that France was ready to relinquish its power assets, above all its nuclear arsenal and its permanent seat on the UNSC, despite calls for their 'Europeanisation'. The concept of 'Europe as a power' provided France with a regional platform to enhance its global status.

Gaullism is one of the most coherent expressions of continental sovereign internationalism. In his famous speech of November 1959 in Strasbourg, de Gaulle spoke of a Europe 'from the Atlantic to the Urals', arguing that 'it is the whole of Europe, that would decide the destiny of the world'. He considered Atlanticism a project for Europe's subjugation and instead called for the continent to act as the third pole between the US and the Soviet Union (although he insisted, like Churchill, on calling the country 'Russia' rather than the USSR). He believed that Russia's place was in Europe. De Gaulle refused to accept the Cold War definition of the political West, which in his view subordinated Europe to American interests.[3] France was a founder member of the EEC in 1957, but de Gaulle resisted moves towards supranationalism and insisted that what in 1992 became the European Union should remain a 'union of nations' (*l'Europe des patries*) based on respect for national traditions. He was particularly critical of Anglo-Saxon claims to hegemony, and in March 1966 removed NATO headquarters from France, withdrew from its integrated military command, closed all NATO bases in the country and expelled all US forces.[4] Thirty years later, Gorbachev also delivered his common European home speech in Strasbourg, and this Gaullist conception of a larger pan-European identity, comprising a variety of states and social orders, is what Russia calls 'greater Europe' (*bol'shaya Evropa*), the idea that pan-continental Europe should become an independent global actor.[5]

There is still no answer as to how the West European version of this can be achieved. The US commitment to European integration was at its highest in the early postwar years, as part of the Cold War struggle against the Soviet Union, but as Europe recovered, policy became more equivocal. A united Europe would be rather less ready to submit to American political and economic leadership.[6] Repeated attempts to build an autonomous European defence community ran into the rock of British resistance, exaggerated French ambition and German concerns.[7] Nevertheless, a political and defence Europe remains one of the foundational aspirations of European integration. The treaty establishing the European Defence Community (EDC) was signed in May 1952 by the six 'inner' members of European integration (France, Italy, West Germany and Benelux – Belgium, the Netherlands and Luxembourg) with plans to create a European defence capacity. It was rejected by the French parliament in 1954 and never came into force. Instead, West Germany joined NATO in 1955 and the underpowered Western European Union was created. A renewed push for European defence autonomy has been under way since the end of the Cold War, and since 1999 the EU has its own Common Security and Defence Policy (CSDP). There have been numerous other initiatives to endow the idea of strategic autonomy with muscle, to which we shall return.

In 1989 it appeared that Europe would finally overcome its enduring divisions to devise a sustainable peace order. Europe's civilisational commonality would finally find adequate political expression and end the 'dark continent's' endemic civil wars.[8] The creation of the European Union at Maastricht in 1992 and its subsequent enlargement revived long-standing aspirations 'for an independent defence capability and a common foreign and security policy'.[9] The 'hour of Europe' appeared to have struck.[10] Reality rudely intervened as the wars of Yugoslav succession demonstrated Europe's strategic limitations and catapulted the US back into the management of European security. These wars pitted Russia against much of the West, while Ukraine became a 'wedge' that effectively divided the continent. Europe remained under the US defence umbrella, and despite much talk of strategic autonomy the EU remains firmly part of the Atlantic power system. The EU–NATO Joint Declaration of 10 January 2023 once again reiterated that the two organisations were part of a single security community.[11] In that community, the US continued to demand greater 'burden sharing' with its European partners, calling on them to devote more resources to defence and thus contribute more to NATO.

The US has been ambivalent to the point of hostility to the greater 'EU-isation' of European security, prompted by fears that the united front in relations with Russia would be breached.[12] There was genuine cause for concern as Europeans increasingly rejected the view that the continent could not manage its own security affairs.[13] The EU acted as a free-rider on US security guarantees and exploited the best of all worlds: defining itself as a normative power exercising *Moralpolitik* when it came to human rights and peace-building, but practising *Realpolitik* to advance its regional interests.[14] The US and the EU remain economic competitors and there are significant policy differences on a number of issues, including on relations with Iran and carbon trading. European powers and Brussels complain about the lack of consultation, an issue that came to a head over the creation of the AUKUS (Australia, UK and US) nuclear submarine deal in September 2021. Australia was to be supplied with nuclear-powered submarines, whose main purpose is to hunt, track and (in conflicts) destroy other nuclear-armed ballistic missile submarines, something that the diesel-electric ones originally contracted from France cannot do. Above all, AUKUS grants nuclear submarines logistics and basing rights in Australia, thus giving the Atlantic alliance a crucial vantage point in the Asia-Pacific region. The 4 February 2022 Sino-Russian Joint Statement explicitly condemned AUKUS as undermining 'objectives of security and sustainable development' in the Asia-Pacific region. The Trumpian disruption and the chaotic withdrawal from Afghanistan raised questions about the consistency and reliability of US security guarantees, while the failure to avert the Ukraine war and increased confrontation with China raised worrying questions about the wisdom of US policy. European interests do not necessarily coincide with those of the US.

Trump's disdain for allies made it easy for the EU, forcing the issue of strategic autonomy to the top of the agenda. By then the devastation of World War II had been overcome and the threat of Soviet land armies sweeping towards the Atlantic removed. Russia remained a looming threat, neither adequately integrated nor entirely hostile. Increased 'burden sharing' was an enduring mantra, and the Newport (Wales) NATO summit in September 2014 renewed the 2 per cent commitment to national spending on defence. By then the EU collectively outranked the US in population and GDP. Strategic autonomy was at the heart of the 2016 *EU Global Strategy* (EUGS).[15] The concept was open to a narrow interpretation, referring to the EU's ability to formulate a foreign and security policy of its own to assert its diplomatic weight in international affairs; but there is also a broader interpretation advancing Gaullist themes of pan-continental autonomy, a version that requires some form of rapprochement with Russia. Hence the concept was criticised in some East European states and even Germany as being anti-American, a perspective that could encourage the US to disengage from Europe.

The Trumpian disruption and the return of great-power politics reignited the debate over what Europe as a power actually means. Merkel declared that 'Europe must take its destiny into its own hands', and the European Council in December 2016 asserted that the Union must 'take greater responsibility for its own security'.[16] Following the tense Taormina (Sicily) G7 summit in May 2017, Merkel noted that 'The times in which we can count fully on others are somewhat over.'[17] The early days of Ursula von der Leyen's EU presidency from 2019 were replete with rhetoric about a more 'geopolitical' European

Commission and the EU's need to 'learn the language of power'. In fact, the challenge was rather different – to find a way of reconciling customary *Moralpolitik* with the new demands of *Realpolitik*. The EU could no longer have its cake and eat it. Atlantic-style hegemonic regionalism was reaching its natural limits, challenged from outside by Russia and China and facing unprecedented internal disarray. Josep Borrell, the High Representative for Foreign Affairs and Security Policy (the head of the European External Action Service, EEAS), made this explicit when he asserted that Europe must 'speak the language of power'.[18] In other words, 'Europe as a power' rose to the top of the agenda. However, there was no agreement on what form this should take. Later, Borrell proudly declared 'the awakening of geopolitical Europe'.[19] If this means a concern with 'territoriality', then the EU had always been geopolitical; but if it suggests more autonomous, stronger and harder power projection, then the EU still falls short.[20]

French president Emmanuel Macron naturally took the lead. In a landmark speech at the Sorbonne on 26 September 2017, he called for 'European sovereignty' with a common defence doctrine and budget and the capacity for strategic interventions. He also talked of food, technological, health and space sovereignty.[21] The Lisbon Treaty of 30 June 2009 granted the EU greater decision-making powers, but the tension between the inter-governmental character of most policy-making and the relatively limited range of supranational competencies was not overcome. European competencies remain restricted to some core activities – the customs union, competition policy, trade policy, monetary policy for euro-area states, and fisheries – in which Europe can be considered sovereign, but the budget still comprises no more than 2 per cent of total EU GDP. However, no other international organisation has such resources and competencies, and as a result of the pandemic the budget doubled. The Covid-19 recovery plan agreed in July 2020 was financed for the first time by European public debt of €750 billion raised on the bond market backed by the EU budget, disbursed through a mix of grants and loans.

Macron turned to the Gaullist tradition for inspiration, although inconsistently. Already during his 2017 presidential campaign he proclaimed his commitment to the 'Gaullo-Mitterrandist' approach to foreign policy, a term coined by Védrine. From very different political perspectives (one a neoliberal and the other a socialist), the two agreed that foreign policy should be based on three irreducible values: sovereignty, independence and strategic autonomy. Védrine condemned the way that President Nicolas Sarkozy and Prime Minister Lionel Jospin pursued what he called a 'neoconservative' foreign policy, based on close alignment with US policy, which led to the disastrous NATO intervention in Libya in 2011. Soon after assuming the presidency, Macron declared, 'I will bring to an end the form of neoconservatism that has been imported to France over the past 10 years.'[22] In 2019 Macron called for Russia to be invited to the G7 meeting in France, a move vetoed by Canada and the UK. In his landmark speech to ambassadors in August of that year, he argued that the corollary of the growing Atlantic divide was rapprochement with Russia. He declared, 'the European continent will never be stable, will never be secure, if we do not ease and clarify our relations with Russia'.[23] In 2020 he supported the reinstatement of Russia's full voting rights in the Council of Europe, suspended after the annexation of Crimea, and nominated Védrine to represent France on the commission established to consider NATO's future. Like de Gaulle, Macron believes that the US has too much power for its own good and argues that a more pluralistic system with countervailing forces would be beneficial for international affairs – and probably for the US as well. This is why he argued that 'If we [Europe] want to be seen and respected by China as an equal partner we need to organise ourselves.'[24] This was accompanied by renewed calls for UN reform.

Macron presented himself as the architect of a future Europe, but his appeal to the Gaullist pan-continental tradition sat uneasily with his commitment to deeper European integration. Even in the latter endeavour he was unable to win Germany over to his ideas, above all deeper integration in the eurozone. Ultimately, the next logical step for European integration was to resolve the fundamental problem of a common financial system that would divert the surpluses of the northern creditor states to the debtor states in the south, a gulf that had been exacerbated by the flaws in the creation of the eurozone as a monetary union without a common fiscal policy. This could well involve pan-European economic planning and redistributive policies. The Covid recovery fund took some steps in this direction, but foreign and defence policy still lacked autonomy. In a notorious intervention in *The Economist* in November 2019, Macron declared, 'What we are currently experiencing is the brain death of NATO.' Europe, he argued, could no longer rely on the US to defend NATO allies, and needed to start thinking of itself strategically as a geopolitical power, otherwise it would 'no longer be in control of [its] destiny'.[25]

Biden vowed to restore NATO, but Macron edged further towards some sort of Gaullist post-Atlanticism. In his Munich Security Conference speech in February 2021, he outlined a new transatlantic 'security architecture' for the twenty-first century. He envisaged an all-European defence community with adequate arms and resources to act independently. Europe had its own security issues and should not always rely on US participation or permission for military action on Europe's borders: 'We need more of Europe to deal with our neighbourhood. I think it is time for us to take much more of the burden for our own protection.'[26] On the eve of the NATO summit in June, Macron argued that the EU could not be expected automatically to side with the US in its growing rivalry with China, and thus demurred from Biden's attempt to rally a league of democracies to wage the conflict. He condemned the 'return to [the logic] of the Cold War', insisting that 'Europe is not simply an object or a territory for the distribution of influences. We are a subject of international geopolitics and we need to assert ourselves as such.'[27] To this end, in May 2022 he called for a 'European Political Community', a framework to foster cooperation between the EU and its neighbours.[28] The first meeting of the EPC on 6 October 2022 in Prague brought together the leaders of all European states, except Belarus and Russia.

The EPC was a very different body to that envisaged by Mitterrand when in December 1989 he called for a 'European confederation', encompassing Russia and offering an alternative to EU enlargement, an idea that aspirant EU members then and now rejected. Mitterrand considered German unification a threat to French leadership, and French pre-eminence was indeed shared with the larger Germany. A rough division of labour held, with Germany more focused on economic matters and France on security and diplomacy. In 2009, Sarkozy returned France to NATO's integrated military command, but at the same time pushed for a stronger European defence identity. This did not mean giving up its national armaments industry (the Rafale fighter, Leclerc tanks, aircraft carriers and frigates), and France remains one of the top arms exporters. The UK's withdrawal from the EU in 2020 restored the primacy of the Berlin – Paris axis, with the two continental states comprising over a third of the EU's population. The UK – EU Trade and Cooperation Agreement of 30 December 2020 did not cover foreign and security policy, hence London forged bilateral ties while stressing the importance of NATO. Various plans were advanced to coordinate foreign policy. The 'E3' framework, bringing together France, Germany and the UK, discussed issues like Syria and the South China Sea, and on this basis the French mooted the creation of a 'European Security Council'. The idea was controversial, acting outside of EU structures and excluding other states.[29]

The UK after Brexit continued to search for a post-imperial role, but its emphasis on the military aspect of Europe as a power only exacerbated the problem of creating a continental peace order. The idea of 'Global Britain' was vague, and only confirmed the pattern whereby rhetoric masked a deeper strategic failure to carve out a substantive forward-looking role for the country.[30] British identity was vested in Atlanticist ideas of European security and London looked for ways to demonstrate that it was still relevant, above all by recreating some sort of 'Anglosphere'.[31] The UK had always been one of the most 'sovereigntist' powers in the EU, and its withdrawal removed an impediment to greater continental integration, although it occurred at a time when there was no such appetite. Washington had always been ambivalent about whether it wanted Europe as a genuine partner in global affairs or whether it preferred an unequal alliance, and this uncertainty pervaded British policy. In the Ukraine war, the UK has restored elements of leadership at the head of the anti-Russian European powers, but has contributed nothing to a diplomatic solution.

POWER IN PRACTICE

Europe has unquestionably emerged as a power. Although beset by internal contradictions, the euro turned the EU into a monetary power as it became the world's second reserve currency and means of international settlements. It has long been a trade power, with a regulated market and body of law (competition policy, data protection and much more). Comprehensive trade agreements with South Korea, Canada and Japan expanded the EU's influence, while its official development assistance in Africa and elsewhere set global standards. The EU also takes the lead on environmental issues, aiming for carbon neutrality by 2050. Its values and standards provide a normative foundation for the exercise of power. The EU conducted over thirty missions within the framework of the CSDP, although most were small and engaged in peacekeeping. The European Defence Agency was established in 2004 to facilitate integration within the framework of the CSDP. Since 2018, this work has been reinforced by the Permanent Structured Cooperation (PESCO) framework. However, in diplomatic and security matters, the EU is part of the Atlantic power system, with twenty-one of its twenty-seven members also members of NATO (the exceptions are Austria, Cyprus, Ireland, Malta, Finland and Sweden, although Finland joined and Sweden applied as a result of the 2022 war). All are effectively under the umbrella of the American security guarantee, and therefore part of US hegemony. This does not mean that Europeans have not challenged US policies. The EU categorically rejected Trump's abrogation of the JCPOA (the nuclear deal) with Iran, pursued a more balanced policy in Palestine and with Israel, and in general opposed US unilateralism. Atlantic bonds have tightened as a result of the Ukraine war, with the European Commission no less active than Washington in devising punitive sanctions against Russia. A more disciplinary and militarised EU is in prospect, and in conditions of renewed cold war even more subordinate to US strategic priorities.[32]

When it comes to China, the EU and Beijing together created an alternative dispute mechanism when Washington blocked the WTO's system.[33] In March 2019, the *EU – China Strategic Outlook* declared that it would view China simultaneously as cooperation partner, economic competitor and 'systemic rival', while pursuing a flexible and pragmatic approach based on the EU's interests and values.[34] The EU refused to grant China the status of a market economy while tightening control over Chinese strategic investments in European industrial assets. By then, China had long been Germany's largest export market, and other countries welcomed Chinese technological and infrastructure investment. In December 2020, the EU and China unveiled their long-awaited Comprehensive Agreement on Investment (CAI), seven years in the making, opening up major new corporate opportunities. It was lauded as increasing market access, fair competition and sustainable development, although against the backdrop of rising concern about the security implications of Chinese investment in Europe. Just two days later, Biden made clear his approach: 'As we compete with China and hold China's government accountable for its abuses on trade, technology, human rights and other fronts, our position will be much stronger when we build coalitions of like-minded partners and allies.'[35] In May 2021, the European Parliament froze the ratification process, demanding the lifting of sanctions against its members. Beijing had overreacted when it imposed sanctions on MEPs, think tanks and academics in response to EU restrictive measures against two individuals and an organisation held responsible for human rights violations in Xinjiang. Administrative measures were applied to displace Huawei from its pre-eminent position in the European telecommunications market as the EU sought to achieve 'digital sovereignty'. Brussels was unsparing in its criticism of Chinese human rights practices in Hong Kong and Xinjiang.

As political relations deteriorated, in February 2021 China overtook the US as the EU's top trading partner. Europe became a battleground as the US sought to bolster European resolve as an ally. Despite early attempts to remain neutral and moderate the conflict, the EU gradually shifted closer to the US position, condemning

China not only for what it did but also for what it was. Europe brings much to the struggle. Its economic, technological and financial strength allows economic power to be converted into political leverage in a number of ways, including bargaining in trade negotiations. It is also exercised more directly, with the EU second only to the US in applying sanctions, accounting in 2020 for 110 (12.9 per cent) events out of 850, compared to America's 449 (52 per cent). The UN is the only legitimate source of international restrictions, but both the US and the EU, and to a lesser extent Russia and China, exercise sanctions regimes of their own. These include blocking sanctions (asset freezes), visa restrictions on individuals and sectoral curtailments.[36]

Military power remains a national competence, and overall is outsourced to NATO. As a result of Russia's war in Ukraine, Sweden and Finland dropped their neutral status. NATO itself was revived as the pre-eminent military body in Europe. Nevertheless, the EU continued to develop its options. The Saint-Malo agreement between France and the UK in 1998 called on the EU to develop autonomous defence capabilities but the creation of a European Defence Union was slow. Since 2007, the EU has had 'battlegroups' made up of troops from different member states, but they have never been used because of lack of agreement on their deployment. Most of the EU's three dozen operations conducted within the framework of the CSDP have focused on providing military training, conflict prevention and post-conflict stabilisation rather than combat operations.[37] The Common Foreign and Security Policy (CFSP) allows the EU to function as a coherent independent actor on certain issues, although the Maastricht Treaty enshrined the principle of unanimity. There is growing pressure for decisions in the European Council on CFSP issues to be taken by qualified majority voting (QMV), possibly complemented by a constructive abstention mechanism.

This was one of the issues discussed as the EU drafted its new security strategy. In the end, the *Strategic Compass* of March 2022 did little to improve the collective security of the Union. The document made no attempt to outline an overarching vision, unlike the 2016 *Global Strategy*, and instead noted that the EU is 'surrounded by instability and conflicts'. Russia was roundly condemned for 'grossly violating international law and the principles of the UN Charter and undermining European and global security and stability', whereas China once again was characterised as 'a partner for cooperation, an economic competitor and a systemic rival'. The document outlined a set of practical steps to strengthen EU security and defence policy by 2030. Four key areas were addressed: enhancing military capability; strengthening military and civilian operations; fostering resilience; and strengthening partnerships.[38]

Europe's emergence 'as a power' is inextricably connected to its relationship with the US. The question of America's strategic withdrawal from Europe has been on the cards since 1945. The rapid drawdown of US forces was partially reversed when the Washington Treaty creating NATO was signed in 1949. At the height of the Cold War, the US deployed over half a million troops but the number fell sharply after 1989. Deployments by early 2022 had crept back up to 67,000, 36,000 of whom were in Germany, and by 2023 reached 100,000. Under Obama, the US pivoted to Asia, but the Ukraine crisis once again returned US forces to a cold war posture. After Brexit the calculus within Europe also changed, and national 'sovereignty' was no longer automatically associated with autonomy from the EU. On the continent the belief that national power can be enhanced through European cooperation was revitalised.

Major impediments remain on the road to Europe becoming a power. These include the relatively limited range of EU competencies, with most civil, administrative, commercial and criminal law remaining national in character. There is also the enduring north–south divide. The 'New Hanseatic League', formed in 2018 and encompassing Denmark, Finland, Sweden, Estonia, Latvia, Lithuania, the Netherlands and Ireland, is reluctant to assume the financial burden of solidarity with the southern states. Nevertheless, if strategic autonomy is to mean anything, it requires greater coordination. From 2016, the EU allocated funds to enhance joint capability research and development work, a European Defence Fund was created with €7 billion for the period 2021–7, and the CSDP operations provided a limited military capacity, buttressed by national contributions when required (as in Mali and the Sahel region as a whole). However, as long as collective security remains NATO's responsibility, there will be a natural reluctance to devote greater resources to defence. The calculus changed as a result of the Russo-Ukrainian war, and as long as the US is willing to carry the burden of European defence, there is little incentive to break the transatlantic link.

FROM *OSTPOLITIK* TO CONSOLIDATED ATLANTICISM

Germany is the pre-eminent power in the EU and was forced to become a 'reluctant hegemon'. Germany took the lead through EU institutions in managing various crises, from the fate of the eurozone, to the Cyprus financial crisis in 2012–13, Greek debt and refugees, but kept military engagements to the minimum. Germany has traditionally acted as the favoured interlocutor between Russia and the West, leading some to believe that some sort of Moscow – Berlin axis should shape policy. Moscow never quite gave up hope that Germany would return 'to the role of *Mitteleuropäische* balancer of East and West', the tradition dating back to Germany's unification in 1870 and associated in particular with Bismarck.[39] In fact, the partnership goes back even further, with the Treaty of Kalisz in 1813 allying Russia and Prussia against Napoleon. In the Crimean War (1853–6), Prussia was the only great power that did not align against Russia. In turn, Moscow benevolently stood aside as Bismarck pursued the wars of German reunification, and then allied with the newly created German Empire. The failure to renew the treaty in 1890 set both countries on the path of destruction. Russia allied with France, while Germany chained itself to the failing Austro-Hungarian Empire.

In the modern era, *Ostpolitik* was forged in the early 1960s by the former SPD chancellor Willy Brandt and his close adviser Egon Bahr on the proposition of 'binding' (*Einbindung*) the Soviet Union, and later Russia, into European institutions and processes. Change in domestic and foreign policy could be achieved by ever closer relations (*Wandel durch Annäherung*) and 'transformation through trade' and economic exchanges (*Wandel durch Handel*). The idea was to create transnational networks of people and interlocking institutions

(*Verflechtung*). As former German chancellor Helmut Schmidt put it, 'Those who trade with each other do not shoot each other.' This is a version advanced by Thomas Friedman of the 'golden arches theory of conflict prevention', the idea that no two countries with McDonald's franchises have gone to war with each other.[40] What may have worked earlier does not apply today. Critics argued that trade only helped consolidate Russia as an 'authoritarian kleptocracy wrapped in neo-imperialist ideology'.[41]

The goodwill generated by Moscow's positive role in facilitating peaceful German unification has not entirely dissipated, reinforced by lingering sentiments of war guilt over the savagery committed by German forces on the Eastern Front. There is a broader view that peace and stability in the continent rely on friendly ties between Moscow and Berlin, although other powers view such amicable relations with suspicion.[42] Big business retained its commitment to the Russian market, but the German economy as a whole reoriented itself to the new markets of Eastern Europe and aligned with some of the region's anti-Russian sentiments. For long-time German chancellor Angela Merkel (2005–21), EU solidarity took priority over larger issues of pan-continental security. Merkel became the enforcer of post-2014 EU sanctions against Russia, ensuring their renewal every six months for the rest of her term in office. She insisted on Russia fulfilling the Minsk-2 agreement, which stipulated a special status for the breakaway Donbass republics and return of control over the state border to Ukraine, while failing to press Kiev to fulfil its side of the bargain.[43] She later admitted that her support for Minsk-2 had been a ruse to give Ukraine time to build up its armed forces.[44] For the new generation of politicians, notably the Greens and Free Democrats who made up Olaf Scholz's coalition following the end of the Merkel era in 2021, *Ostpolitik* sentiments were retrograde. For them, there was no scope for a peace order outside of the Atlantic framework. Trade and economic relations were important for both partners, but in 2022 they were ruptured with surprising ease.

Modern Germany is a child of the political West, and relations with Atlantic institutions will take priority over those with Moscow. Since the time of Konrad Adenauer, the country's first postwar chancellor,

Westbindung ('binding to the West') has been the heart of West German politics, focused on keeping America in Europe and resisting Gaullist temptations to find some sort of midpoint between Washington and Moscow. The Bahr view of 'change through rapprochement' and the even longer Bismarck great-power tradition that viewed amicable relations with Moscow as the predicate for peace in Europe were marginalised. As the German defence minister Annegret Kramp-Karrenbauer put it in October 2020, *Westbindung* 'positions us against a romantic fixation on Russia – and also against an illiberal corporative state that rejects parties and parliaments [China] ... Only America and Europe together can keep the West strong, defending it against the unmistakable Russian thirst for power and Chinese ambitions for global supremacy.'[45] Bloc unity was to be maintained at all costs, and this entailed suppressing deviant intrusions. Russian ideas were typically perceived as attempts to divide Europe and the US. Although Germany (and France) enjoyed some scope for policies of their own, they were constrained by ties of EU and NATO solidarity. European diplomatic initiatives lacked traction, hence the laudable attempts to avert the Russo-Ukrainian war proved futile. The result in Russia was growing alienation from Europe amid condemnation of its perceived hypocrisy (double standards).

Significant voices in Germany sought to maintain the policy of rapprochement. The party of the left, Die Linke, and the party of the right, Alliance for Germany (AfD), advocated the normalisation of relations. There was a solid social basis for such a policy. Identity discourse on Russia is torn between 'negative othering and the *Ostpolitik* narrative, which defines Russia as a partner'. The first Ukraine crisis did not destroy the *Ostpolitik* narrative, 'which is ready to resurface as soon as structural conditions change'.[46] Numerous polls reveal underlying support for good relations between Russia and Germany. The common view in German industrial circles was that 'US sanctions are no longer just about exerting political pressure but also about furthering their own economic interests'. This applied in particular to US attempts to shape European energy relations. Washington had long been hostile to Europe importing energy from Russia, and the 'gas bridge', as Thane Gustafson argues, was indeed used by the Soviet leadership under Brezhnev to fund the arms race against the West and the war in Afghanistan.[47] The Soviet Union was long gone, yet the hostility remained. As alternative pipelines were built, dependence on Ukraine as a transit country fell. Long-term hostility to Russian–West European energy projects was accompanied by plans to increase US LNG exports to Europe. Before the war, LNG was typically at least 50 per cent more expensive than pipeline gas and thus in purely market terms stood little chance of replacing Russian supplies, but its market share was growing. US pressure to halt the construction of the Nord Stream 2 gas pipeline reinforced perceptions of Europe's strategic subordination not only to US military but also commercial interests.[48] Moves to stop Nord Stream 2 intensified after the poisoning of Navalny in August 2020 and his subsequent hospitalisation in Berlin.

As the armed confrontation on Ukraine's borders from late 2021 intensified, Europe's dependence on Russian gas became politically untenable. Russia was accused of deliberately reducing gas flows as a lever of influence, amid a massive spike in energy prices provoked by a perfect storm of factors: rapid economic recovery after the pandemic, low wind speeds in summer 2021, low water levels affecting nuclear power generation, rising Asian demand (above all from China) as economies recovered, the closure of some European gas production facilities (including the Groningen supergiant field) and low storage. Pipeline gas is typically much cheaper than when sold on spot markets but it creates mutual dependency, and this was something that EU policy sought to reduce – prompted by Washington's concerns that gas dependency reduced Europe's willingness to confront Russia. By then the LNG market had rapidly expanded while the volumes of gas pumped through pipelines remained rela-tively constant. In 2020, for the first time more gas was shipped globally than delivered through pipelines.[49] When Russia invaded Ukraine it supplied 44 per cent of European gas supplies, but by October this had already fallen to 9 per cent and was due to be phased out entirely by the end of the year. With the sabotage of the Nord Stream pipelines in September 2022, it is unlikely that Russia will return as a major energy supplier to Western Europe any time soon.

Washington's hostility to gas trading with Russia fed into a persistent strain of anti-Americanism, from both left and right, but this was not enough to re-orient Germany towards a more articulated continentalism. Moscow's espousal of a greater Europe was viewed as not only dividing Germany from America, but as an attack on Germany's democratic transformation.[50] As the German *White Paper on Security Policy* put it, 'Our identity and the way we see security is influenced by the lessons we have learned from our history. They form part of our national identity and are enshrined in our constitution. At the same time, German identity is inseparably connected with European identity.' On that basis, security was about more than the absence of war and 'our ambition is also to improve the conditions of human coexistence in a sustainable manner and to protect and strengthen international human rights norms'.[51] The *White Paper* insisted that 'European security is indivisible', and excoriated Russia for

> openly calling the European peace order into question with its willingness to use force to advance its interests and to unilaterally redraw borders guaranteed under international law, as it has done in Crimea and eastern Ukraine. This has far-reaching implications for security in Europe and thus for the security of Germany.[52]

Moscow's assertion that it acted defensively was peremptorily dismissed. Moscow's strategic concerns may have been exaggerated, but diplomacy does not mean agreeing with the viewpoint of the other but accepting that viewpoint as legitimate (in this case, given added weight by Russia's perennial security concerns). Normative commitments trumped diplomacy and pragmatism.

Russian commentators are mistaken when they suggest that the European powers have simply succumbed to pressure from Washington. Germany is an example of a deep-seated European Atlanticism, and the tide had long turned against the maintenance of special ties with Russia. Merkel had no special sentiment about Germany's place as a mediator between Russia and Europe, and indeed her moralistic Protestant background made her a sharp critic of democratic backsliding. The days when Helmut Kohl and Gerhard Schroeder facilitated Russia's engagement with Western institutions were over. Pragmatic engagement remained but overall *Ostpolitik* pragmatism gave way to *Moralpolitik*. As Trenin observes, 'both Angela Merkel and Joachim Gauck [the German president] come from the Protestant milieu in the former GDR, where moralism traditionally occupied an important place'.[53] Germany gradually moved away from the shadow of the war and gratitude for the part played by Moscow in German unification, but 'normalisation' was thoroughly Atlanticist. On this altar, relations with Moscow were sacrificed.

The Russo-Ukrainian war put an end to *Ostpolitik* aspirations. In the days following the invasion, Merkel's successor, Olaf Scholz, not only halted the certification process of Nord Stream 2 but also announced wide-ranging sanctions on Russia, a permanent increase in German defence spending to reach the 2 per cent NATO threshold (up from 1.5 per cent) by 2024, accompanied by an immediate uplift of €100 billion. The country supplied offensive arms to Ukraine, a reversal of postwar policy that banned the export of military equipment to conflicting parties. He also pledged to phase out Russian energy supplies. At that time, Germany was dependent on Russia for 32 per cent of its natural gas, 34 per cent of its oil and 53 per cent of its hard coal. In his speech to the German parliament on 27 February, Scholz argued that 'The Russian invasion of Ukraine marks a turning point. It threatens our entire postwar order.'[54] He used the word *Zeitenwende* to mark the change of an era, an epochal rupture in the passage of time. He was less clear about what Germany's new foreign policy strategy would look like, even as the military dimension increased.

The Russo-Ukrainian war redefined the idea of European 'strategic autonomy' for a generation. The Europe shaped by the cold peace came to a brutal end, and the new Europe would be forged by the needs of renewed cold war: increased military spending, the loss of cheap energy resources, a devastated security environment, and reliance on Washington for strategic direction. The EU would 'build its security and defence strategy alongside NATO rather than separate from the Alliance'.[55] There would be intensified security cooperation between the EU and NATO and non-EU NATO allies.[56] The supreme act of Europe as a power was to fold itself into another power.

PART III
WAR AND INTERNATIONAL POLITICS

9
THE WORLD ON FIRE

In the nuclear age, cold wars are wars that no one dares fight. A sophisticated strategic arms control architecture was devised during Cold War I, creating channels of communication and fostering a modicum of trust. There were of course limitations, and one of the main criticisms of Barack Obama's Reset with Russia was that it was largely limited to arms control and failed to broaden into a rethinking of the relationship. Nevertheless, the arms control process is a crucial confidence-building instrument, and allows countries to monitor the activities of rivals. Deterrence has so far kept the nuclear peace, but probability theory suggests that the odds are shortening. This is why the International Campaign to Abolish Nuclear Weapons (ICAN), launched in 2007, seeks to fulfil earlier promises and put an end to the nuclear age in its entirety. The UN-sponsored Treaty on the Prohibition of Nuclear Weapons (TPNW) came into force in January 2021, and by September 2022 had been ratified by sixty-six nations. The treaty prohibits nations from developing, testing, producing, manufacturing, transferring, possessing, stockpiling, using or threatening to use nuclear weapons, or allowing nuclear weapons to be stationed on their territory.

In practice, the trend is the other way. In his Nobel Peace Prize speech of 5 April 2009, Obama promised to 'put an end to Cold War thinking' and 'reduce the role of nuclear weapons in our national security strategy'. Instead, two years later he launched the hugely expensive 'modernisation' of America's nuclear arsenal as the price to pay for the ratification of New START. As of 1 March 2021, Russia's nuclear arsenal comprised 517 deployed ICBMs, submarine-launched ballistic missiles (SLBMs) and strategic bombers with a total of 1,456 warheads, and the USA had 651 with 1,357 warheads.[1] China at that time had 290 deployed warheads but was rapidly increasing its arsenal and ultimately could match the US and Russia. The logic of deterrence remains, and today the US considers Russia a nuclear adversary and China a potential rival.[2] Arms control is the core of international security, but today the whole architecture is being dismantled. We are returning to the situation at the time of the Cuban missile crisis in October 1962.[3] Humanity dodged the bullet in the various crises of Cold War I, but it may not be so lucky second time round.

100 SECONDS TO MIDNIGHT

In 1991, the *Bulletin of the Atomic Scientists* set the Doomsday Clock to seventeen minutes to midnight. The clock had been tracking the nuclear peril since 1948, and now with peace on the horizon this was considered the most secure period since the onset of the Cold War. The peace was not to endure, and by 2018 the clock was set at two minutes, the closest to the Apocalypse it had ever been.[4] That was not the end, however, and by 2020 the clock was set at a frightening 100 seconds to midnight, reduced to 90 seconds in early 2023.[5] The Russo-Ukrainian war became an extended war of attrition accompanied by nuclear sabre-rattling.

The Ukraine conflict turned into a slow-motion Cuban missile crisis. The confrontation of October 1962 acted as a salutary warning, demonstrating 'how badly great powers can miscalculate when tensions are high and the stakes are great'.[6] The world came to the edge of nuclear conflict, and only adroit management by the Kennedy administration and no small dose of luck averted Armageddon. The Soviet Union withdrew its missiles from the island in return for a promise from Washington not to invade and to withdraw its Jupiter missiles from Turkey.[7] In addition, a telephone hotline was installed between Moscow and Washington, and the two sides informally accepted satellite reconnaissance. A Limited Test Ban Treaty was agreed in 1963 banning atmospheric tests, and in 1968 the Non-Proliferation Treaty (NPT) committed nuclear states not to help other states acquire nuclear weapons. Despite the commitments of the 190 signatories, since the treaty came into effect in 1970, four more countries have become nuclear powers (Israel, India, Pakistan and North Korea). Strategic Arms Limitation Talks (SALT) began in 1969 and produced an Interim Agreement in 1972 that for the first time restricted the number of permitted land- and sea-based ballistic missiles. In the same year, the ABM treaty banned most defences against long-range missiles. Rules governing deterrence and mutually assured destruction were now in place. Of the nine current nuclear powers, only two (India and China) are formally committed not to use nuclear weapons first.

The SALT I agreement of 1972 licensed a five-fold increase in Soviet and US nuclear warheads, although a cap was placed on delivery systems. By the time the SALT II treaty was signed in Vienna in June 1979, allowing an increase in strategic nuclear systems to some 12,000 warheads, the whole arms control process was subject to increased Congressional criticism on the grounds that it failed to increase security and allegedly gave the USSR unwarranted advantages.[8] SALT II was not ratified, and instead START was launched by Reagan, culminating in START I in 1991 and START II in 1993, greatly reducing strategic nuclear warheads. When the Soviet Union disintegrated in 1991 it possessed an astonishing 45,000 nuclear weapons.[9] In an act of strategic incompetence typical of the gerontocratic leadership, dominated by an ambitious military establishment, in 1977 the USSR began deploying a new intermediate-range missile, designated the SS-20 by NATO (RSD-10 Pioneer in Russian), targeting Western Europe. This changed the strategic balance, although the Soviet Union considered its move defensive. In response, the Carter administration deployed Pershing II and Tomahawk strike missiles, allowing a nuclear response to any Soviet attack limited to Europe and thus rendering the deterrent more credible to US allies. Western peace movements were revitalised, but with little effect.

Reagan in March 1983 was attracted to the Strategic Defense Initiative ('Star Wars') as a way of breaking the entire logic of deterrence and mutual destruction. It also made him receptive to Gorbachev's denuclearisation ideas. As Gorbachev launched perestroika, the US and the Soviet Union at the Geneva summit in November 1985 for the first time announced that 'A nuclear war cannot be won and must never be fought', the formula that was repeated on the eve of the Ukraine war.[10] This cooperative atmosphere produced the Intermediate-Range Nuclear Forces (INF) treaty in December 1987, prohibiting missiles with a range of 500 to 5,500 kilometres. For the first time, a whole class of missiles was removed from Europe. Gorbachev was 'one of the most committed arms reductionists to ever lead a nuclear country' and 'revolutionary when in the 1980s he called for the complete abolition of nuclear weapons'. His leadership opened the way for 85 per cent of US and Russian nuclear arsenals to be decommissioned by 2015. This demilitarisation is now being reversed, together with Gorbachev's principle that 'security starts with cooperation'.[11]

Attempts to manage nuclear issues continued into the post-Cold War era, marked by a rising reluctance by the nuclear powers to commit to deep controls and limits. As the continuer state, Russia assumed Soviet obligations as well as its nuclear arsenal. When the Soviet Union disintegrated there were over 1,900 strategic weapons in Ukraine and another 2,000 in Belarus and Kazakhstan. In May 1992 in Lisbon, the three committed to join the NPT. Ukraine's concerns about giving up the weapons stationed on its territory were assuaged by the Budapest Memorandum of December 1994.[12] Non-binding security assurances were offered by Russia, the UK and the US (joined later by China and France) to Belarus, Kazakhstan and Ukraine in return for their accession to the NPT as non-nuclear states. The former were prohibited from threatening or using military force against the latter except in self-defence or in conformity with the UN Charter. By 1996, the three had transferred their Soviet arsenals to Russia. The Comprehensive Test Ban Treaty (CTBT) outlaws the explosion of nuclear warheads and nuclear explosions for peaceful purposes in all environments (underground, underwater, in the atmosphere and in outer space). It was adopted by the UN on 24 September 1996, and by 2020 the agreement had been signed by 183 countries. It was ratified by Moscow in 2000, but on its twentieth anniversary it had still not come into effect because eight countries, including the US, had either not signed or ratified the document. The Republican Senate rejected the CTBT in 1999. The US later declared that it would not ratify the treaty, opening the door to the potential resumption of nuclear tests.

START I was signed on 31 July 1991 between Bush and Gorbachev, limiting deployed nuclear weapons on both sides to 6,000, and START II was signed by Clinton and Yeltsin on 3 January 1993. The Moscow Treaty of 2002 further reduced the arsenal to 2,200 apiece. With Obama installed as president in January 2009, his vice president, Biden, issued the call for a reset in relations with Russia. The fruits of that endeavour included the more ambitious New START, signed in Prague in April 2010 and coming into effect on 5 February 2011.[13] The treaty stipulated that, seven years after it had come into force, each party should have no more than a total of 700 deployed ICBMs, SLBMs and strategic bombers, as well as no more than 1,550 warheads on deployed ICBMs, deployed SLBMs and strategic bombers, and a total of 800 deployed and non-deployed ICBM launchers, SLBM launchers and strategic bombers. Crucially, although the treaty once again stressed the principle of the indivisibility of security, Russian concerns over missile defence were not addressed. This was the last major agreement limiting nuclear arms and its associated inspection regime. However, one of the conditions for it to be ratified by Congress was Obama's commitment to invest in the trillion-dollar nuclear modernisation programme mentioned earlier, accompanied by a prohibition on limiting missile defences. The duration of the treaty was ten years but was renewable for five years without renegotiation. Trump made Chinese participation a condition for renewal but Beijing, understandably, refused to participate. With fewer than 300 warheads, compared to the Russian stockpile of 6,370, America's 5,500, France's 300, the UK's 225 (planned to rise to 260), India and Pakistan with about 150 apiece, and Israel's 80, China is a relatively modest nuclear power, although it is rapidly increasing its arsenal. New START was the last remaining dialogue channel between Washington and Moscow on strategic arms, and thus served as a critical forum for strategic matters. Putin had long signalled willingness to extend its life, and on the eve of the treaty's expiry on 5 February 2021, the five-year extension without renegotiation was agreed by Biden.

Despite the war in Ukraine, the Biden administration has signalled its readiness to negotiate some sort of follow-on treaty when New START expires in 2026. However, in his address to the Federal Assembly on 21 February 2023, Putin announced that Russia was suspending its participation, having been accused by the US of not allowing the inspection regime to resume after the pandemic.[14] New START provides for eighteen on-site inspections annually. Putin also suggested that the US was planning to resume nuclear testing, in which case Russia would follow suit. This would jeopardise one of the last pillars of the arms control architecture, the CTBT, leaving only the Non-Proliferation Treaty. Putin mentioned the British and French nuclear arsenals, which had previously not figured in nuclear arms control negotiations. With the two countries committed to the war in Ukraine, it was clear that their assets were part of the Western arsenal and intended not just to defend their own countries. Only two states, the US and Soviet Union/Russia, have historically engaged in arms control, despite attempts to include China. This raises the fundamental question about when, if ever, China would be ready to engage, and how this would affect the whole conceptual basis of arms control as practised to date.

There were also agreements on chemical weapons. In 1991, Russia inherited the world's largest chemical weapons stockpile, comprising some 40,000 tonnes. In 1992, the UN General Assembly adopted the Chemical Weapons Convention (CWC), which entered into force in April 1997, to be monitored by the OPCW, established in that year. Russia ratified the CWC in December 1997 and committed to destroying its stock of chemical weapons. Financial problems delayed the start of the disposal programme to 2002, but with the financial assistance of the US, Germany and Italy, Russia formally announced on 27 September 2017 that it had liquidated its stockpile.

In the meantime, Russia worked with the US in 2013 to broker a deal whereby Syria destroyed its arsenal of chemical weapons, although this did not prevent later allegations that they had been used by Damascus against its enemies. The apparent use of a chemical weapon (the so-called Novichok A234) against Sergei Skripal (a former GRU agent exchanged in a spy swap in 2010) and his daughter Yulia in Salisbury on 4 March 2018 raised doubts whether Russia had indeed destroyed its stocks. These concerns increased following the poisoning of the oppositionist Alexei Navalny by a different strain of Novichok on 20 August 2020 in Tomsk.

Chemical agents of the Novichok group had never been part of the OPCW's list of 'controlled substances', in part because of concerns they could fall into the hands of terrorists, even though Vil Mirzayanov, one of their creators, had disclosed the formula in his 2008 book, *State Secrets: An Insider's Chronicle of the Russian Chemical Weapons Program*. It appears that a nerve agent from the Novichok group had been used to murder the prominent Russian banker Ivan Kivelidi in 1995. A leading chemical weapons researcher at the Shikhany laboratory, Leonid Rink, admitted that he had transferred at least nine ampoules (each one was enough to kill at least a hundred people) of the substance to criminals. Only in June 2002 was the Novichok group added to the list of controlled substances, but by then it was clear that some was circulating outside of state control. As a result of the early post-Cold War agreements, none of the great powers considers chemical weapons part of the strategic arsenal of deterrence. Growing tensions in the OPCW threaten to paralyse the organisation, jeopardising the viability of the CWC.[15]

THE END OF ARMS CONTROL

The fateful step on this road was taken when in December 2001 Washington announced its departure from the ABM treaty, and after the expiration of the notification period, in June 2002 the US formally left. The ABM treaty placed limits on long-range missile interceptors, and its unilateral abrogation opened the door to precisely what it had intended to prevent – an escalating strategic arms race.

Putin dates the new era of strategic arms competition to this period. Matters were further exacerbated by US ambitions to create a network of ballistic missile defences. From its inception, the BMD programme destabilised the arms control process. Since it was first announced in 1983 as the Strategic Defense Initiative, the US has spent over $300 billion on strategic missile defence programmes, with $20.3 billion out of the $740 billion 2021 defence budget devoted to the scheme. The goal was to protect the US by deploying missile interceptors and space weapons. Over the years, the programme registered more failures than successes, yet there appeared to be no way to stop the juggernaut.[16] This is a technocratic response to the genuine dilemma of security in the nuclear age. It is impossible to uninvent nuclear weapons, hence the MAD logic of deterrence. Arms control is designed to manage the associated risks. The deployment of BMD systems in Eastern Europe was perceived as a strategic and conventional threat. A month after the annexation of Crimea, on 17 April 2014 Putin argued that the action was designed to thwart Washington's plan to incorporate Ukraine and Crimea into an antiballistic deployment encircling Russia: 'This issue is no less, and probably even more important, than NATO's eastward expansion. Our decision on Crimea was partially prompted by this.'[17]

The Trump administration resolutely dismantled what was left of the Cold War arms control architecture. Washington accused Moscow of being in breach of the INF treaty by developing and testing a ground-launched cruise missile. It later became clear that the missile in question was the 9M729 (SSC-8, according to NATO classification), which NATO countries believed to be of intermediate range, although Moscow claimed that it was below the limit. On 2 February 2019, the US announced its withdrawal from the treaty, which became effective on 2 August, at which point Russia also withdrew – and thus the INF treaty became defunct. The optimistic Gorbachev-era strategic arms reductions came to a rather ignominious end. With the US deployment of the BMD system in Europe, Russia in any case had long chafed at the restrictions, which applied only to the former superpowers in Europe. Moscow argued that Russia was more exposed to such missiles from non-treaty states than the US, protected by two enormous oceans. The US also argued that the treaty was unbalanced and sought to get China involved.[18] Yet another brick fell from the arms control wall.

Russia pointed to the deployment of Aegis missile defence installations in Eastern Europe as potential INF treaty violations. Moscow argued that the Mk-41 vertical launchers can project not only interceptors but also Tomahawk cruise missiles. As noted, the first installation was built in Romania and the second in Poland and they are designed to intercept Iranian missiles. In fact, they are technically incapable of 'identifying attacking long-range ballistic missiles at long enough ranges to allow enough time for missile-defence interceptors to reach intercept points'. Instead, Moscow argues that with simple software modifications, the Aegis ashore system can launch nuclear-armed cruise missiles, although experts disagree whether this is the case.[19] In November 2020, the US conducted a test firing of an SM-3 interceptor, successfully hitting a target ICBM, confirming Russian fears that the Aegis system can shoot down Russian intermediate- and intercontinental-range missiles.[20]

Another falling brick was the end of the Open Skies agreement. At the Geneva summit with Khrushchev in July 1955, Eisenhower proposed an 'open skies' reconnaissance arrangement.[21] Moscow rejected the proposal, which encouraged the US to conduct aerial reconnaissance until the U-2 plane piloted by Gary Powers was shot down in May 1960, provoking a major crisis. With a positive peace order in prospect, the Open Skies treaty was signed in March 1992 and came into effect on 1 January 2002. The treaty allowed signatories to conduct unarmed aerial surveillance flights by member states over the territory of other participants. Over 1,500 such flights took place, mostly over Europe. Open Skies was intended to build trust among members, but by 2014 this had evaporated. The US accused Russia of selectively implementing its provisions, above all by banning flights over Kaliningrad, and violating some other provisions. Russia also accused the US of partially implementing the accord. Trump announced US withdrawal in May 2020 and the US formally left the agreement in November. European partners remained, but concern that the US would continue to receive data from NATO allies prompted Moscow in January 2021 to trigger the withdrawal procedure. After a review, the Biden administration in May confirmed that it would leave, and Moscow thereupon also formally left the treaty. The postwar era of arms control is over. Another appointment with Armageddon may get it started again, but by then it could be too late.

More down to earth, the US continued to deploy tactical weapons in Europe, a legacy of the Cold War when they were part of the 'flexible response' to a Soviet attack. These so-called 'battlefield' nuclear weapons were designed to offset the Soviet preponderance in conventional forces, but the US still deploys 230, of which 150 are in Europe (Belgium, Netherlands, Germany, Italy and Turkey). The B61 is a free-fall bomb delivered by non-stealthy fourth-generation fighters, vulnerable to anti-aircraft missiles.[22] They are part of the nuclear burden-sharing strategy, intended to signal that the US would be prepared to sacrifice New York to save Podgorica. This is part of the response to Russia's alleged 'escalate to de-escalate' nuclear strategy, the idea that Moscow would swiftly resort to nuclear weapons in any conflict to deter the opponent. Russia's 2,000 non-strategic or tactical nuclear weapons are understandably a matter of grave concern. It was feared that they could be used if Russia faced some existential threat, such as defeat in Ukraine. Even before the war, Germany in April 2020 announced that it would replace its ageing fleet of Tornado dual-capable aircraft (DCA) with ninety Eurofighter Typhoon and 45 US F-18 fighter aircraft, thirty of which would be certified to carry US nuclear weapons. With little fanfare and even less popular concern, Europe once again slid into an arms race.[23]

The Trump administration's *Nuclear Posture Review* of February 2018 reinforced the role of nuclear weapons in US national security. The document promised to accelerate nuclear modernisation, but disturbingly, it endorsed the use of such weapons to demonstrate American 'resolve', signalling a readiness to go over the edge in political disputes. The *Review* argued that the US needed a large and diverse arsenal to 'demonstrate resolve through positioning of forces, messaging, and flexible response options'. Nuclear bombers, it argued, were particularly suited to achieve these goals, hence 'Flights abroad display US capabilities and resolve, providing effective signalling for deterrence and assurance, including in times of tension.'[24] Although Russia is far outgunned in conventional terms, in strategic weaponry it is the West's equal. It, too, was no longer afraid to demonstrate 'resolve'. The 'escalation ladder' from the use of tactical nuclear weapons on the battlefield to a full-scale thermonuclear exchange is alarmingly short. In 1965, Herman Kahn (the purported model for the title character in Stanley Kubrick's film *Dr. Strangelove*) identified forty-four rungs on the ladder.[25] The first step is crucial. Once the taboo is broken, humanity could swiftly ascend the stairway to heaven.[26]

The US Space Force was established in December 2019 as the sixth branch of the US armed forces. The new body drew on the Air Force Space Command, set up in 1982. War in space is becoming a reality.[27] The Space Force's 'capstone doctrine' *Spacepower* of August 2020 warned of the danger of anti-satellite weapons, but it also envisaged offensive operations against US adversaries. Space was defined as 'a source and conduit of national power'. The document outlined seven areas in which the US would seek to dominate: 'orbital warfare, space electromagnetic warfare, space battle management, space access and sustainment, military intelligence and engineering/acquisitions'. A critical commentary noted that 'Plans for apocalyptic space weaponry are announced in the language of an accountancy firm'.[28] The US developed 'hit-to-kill' technology, the kinetic ability to strike ballistic missiles outside of the earth's atmosphere, further destabilising the foundations of deterrence.[29] Russia warned of the growing threat of an arms race in outer space, with the US and its allies embarking 'on a policy towards the use of the near-Earth space for combat operations (including offensive ones) and deployment of strike weapons systems'. Lavrov insisted that Russia remained committed to the non-discriminatory use and exploration of outer space for peaceful purposes. Closer to earth, he committed Russia to maintaining restraint in the missile sphere following the end of the INF treaty, promising not to deploy ground-based intermediate- and short-range missiles in any given region unless US-made missiles were deployed there.[30]

Meanwhile, the US continued the Obama-era modernisation of its nuclear forces. This included an estimated \$264 billion over its lifespan for a new ground-based strategic deterrent (GBSD) and associated warheads to replace the ageing Minuteman III missiles. Static ICBMs, of which the US has 400 in silos across the northern Midwest, are intrinsically destabilising since a leader has at most a few minutes to decide whether to respond to warnings of incoming missiles or risk losing them to a first-strike attack. There is a long history of false warnings, now accompanied by fears of cyberattacks. In September 2020, Northrop Grumman was awarded a \$13.3 billion uncontested contract for the engineering, manufacture and development phase of the GBSD, after Boeing pulled out of the tender. Work was continuing on modifying the W87-1 warhead to fit on the new missile. Attempts in Congress to assess whether the life of the Minuteman missiles could be extended to 2050 was blocked by vigorous defence industry lobbying.[31] As part of sixth-generation warfare, the Prompt Global Strike (PGS) programme was designed to allow the US to deliver a conventional precision-guided munition (PGM) almost anywhere globally. Moscow viewed this as particularly destabilising, fearing that its offensive and defensive strategic capabilities could be destroyed while remaining below the nuclear threshold. Russia's own hypersonic weapons were in part a response.

Russia undertook at least five major modernisations of its nuclear strike force, comprising new ICBMs, bombers, submarines, drones and tactical nuclear weapons.[32] There is considerable controversy over Russia's military doctrine, and in particular its nuclear strategy. The view that Russia operates an 'escalate to de-escalate' policy has been questioned.[33] Nevertheless, the possibility that there is such a strategy has prompted several responses. In addition to the deployment of tactical weapons, the 2018 US *Nuclear Posture Review* called for the restoration of nuclear dominance. Deterrence in principle requires a degree of ambiguity, but most experts agree that Russia does not have an escalation strategy.[34] Arms control provides strategic stability but cannot work if it is pursued at the expense of other actors.[35]

The strategic calculus is changing as a result of the development of hypersonic missiles and nuclear-powered underwater drones that can evade missile defences. The major powers have also tested intercept missiles that can destroy low earth orbit satellites (adding to the clutter of space junk in near-earth orbit). Putin's address to the Federal Assembly on 1 March 2018 was defiant:

> I want to tell all those who have fuelled the arms race over the last 15 years, sought to win unilateral advantages over Russia, and introduced unlawful sanctions aimed at containing our country's development – everything that you wanted to impede with your policies has already happened. You have failed to contain Russia.

Putin then unveiled several new Russian strategic weapons, including the Sarmat super-heavy ICBM and the Avangard hypersonic vehicle. He stressed that they had been developed in direct response to the US withdrawal from the ABM treaty. He reminded his audience that back in 2004 Russia had warned the US that it would respond in this way: 'No one listened to us then', Putin declared. 'So listen to us now.'[36]

The updated Russian *National Security Strategy* of 2 July 2021 warned that Moscow 'considers it legitimate to take symmetrical and asymmetric measures' to thwart and prevent 'unfriendly actions' by foreign states that 'threaten the sovereignty and territorial integrity of the Russian Federation'.[37] In his annual address to the Federal Assembly in April 2021, Putin announced the near-completion of the modernisation of Russia's nuclear triad. He announced the deployment of the Avangard hypersonic missile and the Peresvet combat laser system. The Sarmat ICBM would be commissioned imminently, while the number of combat air systems with Kinzhal hypersonic missiles and warships armed with precision hypersonic weapons was increasing. The Tsirkon (Zircon) hypersonic missile, flying at Mach 7, was almost ready to be deployed.[38] In addition, Russia was preparing to test a new Doomsday strategic weapon, the gigantic Poseidon nuclear-powered torpedo, capable of producing a radioactive tsunami to inundate coastal cities. There were also conventional weapon developments. The fifth-generation Su-57 multi-role fighter features stealth technology that provides a platform for variations, including the single-engine Su-75 (Checkmate) light tactical fighter. By then the US had developed the Northrop-Grumman B-21 Raider, the world's first sixth-generation bomber encompassing stealth, information advantage and open architecture. The Next Generation Air Dominance programme envisages the production of a sixth-generation fighter by the early 2030s.

The Fourth Industrial Revolution represents a revolution in military affairs. The development of hypersonic weapons and unmanned aerial vehicles (UAVs), together with precision-guided munitions, autonomous weapons, long-distance torpedoes and much more changes the character of warfare. It renders traditional battlefleets vulnerable to swift and complete destruction, and hence their utility in battle is potentially worse than useless. As US strategists put it, there are two types of naval vessels: submarines and targets. Meanwhile, cyber-enhanced informational warfare (CEIW) blurs the distinction between war and peace. While the practices underlying renewed cold war remain the same as those of the first, the technology has increased the risks of accidental conflict.[39] Former US secretary of defence William Perry and Tom Collina note that 'US nuclear policy is a disaster waiting to happen, and it could be only a matter of time until our luck runs out.' They argue that the Cold War has long been over and the US had thirty years to rethink its nuclear policy, but successive presidents since 1989 'failed to learn the correct lessons from the Cold War'. Every president 'sought to rearrange the deck chairs on the *Titanic*, but none set a new course away from the icebergs'. It was the US that brought the bomb into the world and then became the global leader in attempts to control it, but it should now 'once again take up the essential cause of nuclear disarmament'.[40]

In their view, the US for decades focused on the wrong threat, a first strike from Russia, when such an attack is extremely unlikely, while the greatest threat was blundering by accident into a nuclear war. Their core argument is that 'by preparing for the surprise first strike, we actually make the blunder more likely'. The 'launch on warning' strategy is inherently dangerous, and more so when accompanied by the enduring threat of false alarms, the escalating danger of cyberattacks and the persistent menace of unstable leaders. Instead of dealing with such issues, the US was committed to spending some $2 trillion to rebuild its nuclear arsenal 'as if the Cold War had never ended'. US security would be enhanced by shifting to a policy of second-strike retaliation, accompanied by phasing out the weapons that have to be used first and quickly, such as fixed-silo ICBMs. The submarine-based nuclear arsenal would be plenty enough to ensure that any attack would be countered, while removing the hair trigger response necessitated by the first-strike strategy. This would mean the end of presidential sole authority and the retirement of the 'football', what in Britain is called the 'suitcase', with the nuclear firing codes.

THE PERMANENT STORM

Nuclear apocalypse is a possibility, but climate change is a reality. The era of a habitable planet may be coming to an end. Unless serious mitigation measures are put in place, a global temperature increase of 3.5°C above pre-industrial levels is likely by the end of the century. This will be accompanied by the increased prevalence and intensity of heat waves accompanied by forest fires, floods and droughts. The icecaps will melt, glaciers recede into nothingness, deserts spread and sea levels rise. Coastal cities will drown, unless protected by massive engineering projects, and agriculture will become increasingly problematic and subject to unexpected and unpredictable seasonal extremes. The melting of permafrost releases methane, a deadlier greenhouse gas than carbon dioxide, and damages infrastructure across the polar regions. The climate emergency has become a permanent storm that will intensify unless action is taken. Instead, in the Russo-Ukraine conflict all sides weaponised energy security and climate action fell victim to the demands of war.

The UN has been at the centre of multilateral attempts to restrain greenhouse effects. The Intergovernmental Panel on Climate Change (IPCC) was established in 1988 in Geneva, and since then it has regularly published authoritative reports on the state of play. The 1992 UN Framework Convention on Climate Change committed state parties to reduce greenhouse gas emissions. The Kyoto Protocol of December 1997 set specific individual targets, and following a complicated ratification process entered into force in February 2005. By 2022, 196 states had signed up. The obligations were tightened at the Conference of Parties (CoP21) Paris meeting in December 2015, which set the goal of keeping global warming to 1.5°C above pre-industrial levels. Carbon dioxide concentration in the atmosphere had increased from the pre-industrial average of 280 parts per million to 383 ppm in 2019, with a reduction to 350 ppm considered essential if the 1.5°C target is to be met. By 2022, global warming reached 1.2°C, and will rise to more than 2.5°C by 2070 unless drastic action is taken.

The Paris Climate Agreement established Nationally Determined Contributions (NDCs) for every signatory state, reviewed on a five-year cycle. Because of the pandemic, the Conference of the Parties, CoP26, in Glasgow met a year late. For most observers, the November 2021 meeting was a profound disappointment. By then states had announced target dates for when they planned to become net-zero carbon. China and Russia declared that they would reach the goal by 2060 whereas India announced 2070 as its target date. The EU and the US were more ambitious, aiming to become carbon neutral by 2050. However, at the Glasgow CoP meeting, Russia followed the lead of the US, China and India to remove any commitment to 'phasing out coal' from the final agreement. Russia also failed to commit to the target of reducing methane emissions by 30 per cent by 2030 and instead advocated a 'smoother' (that is slower) transition. Russia was one of the 130 countries that pledged to halt deforestation by 2030, and relied on a forestry carbon offset strategy to meet its climate commitments.

Climate change has increased the strategic importance of the Arctic region and turned it into yet another military frontline. The Northeast Passage (known as the Northern Sea Route, NSR, in Russia) became a shortcut for shipping between Asia and Europe in the ever-longer ice-free summer months. The route had been reserved for Soviet shipping until it was opened to international traffic in 1991, and its importance was highlighted by the blockage of the Suez Canal for six days in March 2021. However, the shallow Arctic waters limit the size of ships that can transit. Russia's stringent (and expensive) transit rules, including advance notification and accompaniment by Russia's growing fleet of mega-class icebreakers, raised the divisive question whether passage should be regulated by rules pertaining to territorial waters or to international straits. If the latter, then UN Convention on the Law of the Sea (UNCLOS) regulations apply. Article 234 of the 1982 Convention grants coastal states the right of non-discriminatory control over shipping in ice-covered areas within the 200-mile exclusive economic zone, a principle that Russia is keen to defend. Russia has a special interest since it enjoys sovereignty over 53 per cent of the Arctic coastline, and its two million inhabitants comprise half of the total population of Arctic regions. As the melting ice facilitated the exploitation of the vast hydrocarbon resources in the Arctic Ocean, Russia laid claim to these resources as well as the right to regulate passage along the NSR. To defend its interests, it built up its military capabilities along the littoral.[41]

The Arctic has traditionally been considered a zone of peace but is gradually becoming militarised. Conflict is tempered by the Arctic Council, established in 1996 to provide a forum for the eight Arctic states (Canada, Denmark, Finland, Iceland, Norway, Russia, Sweden and the US). The Council works by consensus and is a good example of cooperative multilateralism. In May 2013, China became an observer member, along with India, Italy, Japan, Singapore and South Korea. Russia was reluctant to allow China to join, but later recognised China's claim to be a 'near-Arctic' state because of its shipping interests. UNCLOS grants states exclusive rights to exploit the seabed up to 200 nautical miles from their continental shelf, but they have to demonstrate the extent of the shelf. Russia, Canada and Denmark (Greenland) all sought to prove that the Lomonosov Ridge is an extension of their continental shelf. Russia went so far as to plant a flag on the seabed near the North Pole in August 2007 to reinforce its claim. Despite the heated rhetoric, all parties remain committed to resolve the issue within the framework of UNCLOS.

This collegial tone was disrupted when secretary of state Mike Pompeo attended the May 2019 meeting in Rovaniemi, Finland. He warned against Russia's growing military power in the region and pledged a strong American response. Fulfilling this pledge, the Pentagon published an Arctic strategy review in June 2019, re-established a Second Fleet for Atlantic and Arctic operations, and ramped up spending (with Canada) on upgrading the North American Aerospace Defense Command (NORAD), consisting of satellites, ground-based radar and air force bases located mostly in Alaska and the Canadian Arctic.[42] The Polar Security Cutter programme funds the construction of a new generation of icebreakers, and the US Coastguard leased two icebreakers for Arctic patrols. Washington regularly deploys warships to the region, while conducting increasingly elaborate military exercises with its allies accompanied by military flights across the region. The biennial Cold Response exercise in Norway's far north is held disturbingly close to Severomorsk, the home of Russia's Northern Fleet.

Cold War II affects 'shared spaces' – the oceans, the poles and even space. The 1967 Outer Space Treaty declares outer space and the celestial bodies the property of all of mankind. The US Artemis Accords aim to return humans to the moon for the first time since 1972, but also open the door to the commercial exploitation of space. This is made possible by the impressive development of space technologies by private US corporations. In 2020, Russia declined to take part in the construction of the Lunar Gateway, a space station that will orbit the moon. The head of Russia's space agency, Dmitry Rogozin, insisted that Russia would only participate if Roscosmos was placed on an equal footing with NASA, a rather unrealistic demand.[43] The days of Apollo – Soyuz cooperation in the mid-1970s were long gone. The US and the USSR worked together to create the International Space Station. Some of the old spirit was revived from 2011 when the US lost its capacity to lift astronauts into space, and the Soviet/Russian Soyuz rockets filled the gap. Later Russia threw in its lot with China, and in 2021 created the framework for an alliance for space development. Roscosmos announced that it would cooperate exclusively with China's equivalent, the China National Space Administration (CNSA), with the focus in the first instance on lunar exploration. Russia announced that it would be leaving the International Space Station 'after 2024', although no specific date has been set. It has plans to develop its own orbital launch complex, accompanied by nuclear-powered 'tugs' in space.

The Russo-Ukrainian war has subordinated climate change to immediate political and economic pressures. Energy supplies have been disrupted amid a worsening cost of living crisis and famine in parts of the Global South. Commitments to ban public investment in fossil fuel projects have been weakened, coal-burning power stations brought back online, while the scramble for scarce fossil fuel supplies has prompted a renewed wave of long-term investment. It is increasingly unlikely that climate change targets will be met. The planet is heading towards irreversible global warming.[44]

A WORLD ON EDGE

In March 2014, Putin placed Russia's nuclear forces on alert as the Ukraine crisis escalated over Crimea. In subsequent years there was relentless probing by both sides. On 21 August 2020, six nuclear-capable B-52H Stratofortress bombers flew from their home base in North Dakota via the UK to conduct intensive air operations over Europe, including along the Russian border. Each is capable of carrying eight AGM-86B nuclear-armed air-launched cruise missiles (ALCMs) in its bomb bay, as well as twelve ALCMs on external pylons. First entering service in 1952, the B-52 was designed to cross the Atlantic or Pacific to drop bombs on the Soviet Union, although it was later adapted to drop prodigious quantities of conventional bombs on Southeast Asia during the Vietnam War. In another provocative act, on 4 September three B-52s accompanied by Ukrainian fighter planes flew over the Black Sea near the coast of Crimea. Other B-52s conducted 'show-of-force' operations over the Barents Sea and Russia's Arctic coast, as well as the Sea of Okhotsk in Russia's far east.[45] Simulated bombing runs test Russian air defence capabilities and response times but represent a type of 'chicken' politics that is unlikely to end well. They are presented as 'reassuring allies', but the result is to provoke rivals.

Another close encounter of the most dangerous kind took place on 24 September 2020, when the USS *John S. McCain* guided missile destroyer entered the Russian-claimed Peter the Great Bay in the Sea of Japan to conduct a freedom-of-navigation operation, intended to challenge Russia's 'excessive maritime claims' that since 1957 declared full sovereign jurisdiction over the waters. The American ship was intercepted by the Russian anti-submarine destroyer *Admiral Vinogradov* and threatened with a ramming manoeuvre, forcing the US ship to change its course. The last such operation had taken place in 1987, but in yet another indication of the return to cold war, forays in the waters around Vladivostok resumed in December 2018.[46] The Russian response to the US plan announced in February 2021 to deploy four nuclear-capable B-1B bombers to Norway was to send two Tu-160 heavy bombers on a demonstrative sweep of Northern Europe, escorted for a time by a pair of MiG-31 interceptors. Russia has about 50 Tu-95, Tu-22M and Tu-160 bombers facing the West, on Cold War readiness alert levels. They, too, conducted provocative air patrols, testing Western air defences. The Russian exclave of Kaliningrad has become an armed camp, with S-300 and S-400 air defence missiles and Oniks anti-ship missiles and Iskander surface-to-surface missiles, as well as a fighter regiment with a dozen Su-27 fighters. Two B-52s in autumn 2020 conducted a mock attack on the region, probing the air defence reaction.[47] Simulated attacks are designed to observe defensive responses, but can go too far.

These encounters run the risk of inadvertent escalation. This was already the case when a Chinese fighter collided with a US Navy EP-3 off Hainan Island in 2001, provoking a diplomatic crisis. Trust levels decreased, rendering 'deconfliction' more tenuous. The term itself has changed its meaning, from advance coordination of military activities to responses to incidents. Force projection is intended to show that both sides mean business, but in times of high tension, 'resolve' could turn into conflict. The Baltic and Black Sea regions are particularly dangerous flashpoints, and Russian fighters repeatedly intercepted US Navy patrol aircraft in the Eastern Mediterranean and over Syria. NATO reported that in 2020 it intercepted Russian aircraft some 350 times over the Baltic, while the US Navy increasingly transited into the Black Sea. Deconfliction hotlines are far from enough to manage demonstrative manoeuvres along the whole line of confrontation in Europe, as well as across the South China Sea.[48] This is accompanied by increasingly ramified military exercises. The Able Archer war scare in autumn 1983 was triggered precisely by Soviet fears that a NATO offensive could start under its cover.[49]

Unlike in the time of the two great wars of the twentieth century, today there is not a genuinely revisionist state power looking to destroy the existing international system.[50] Russia's invasion of Ukraine was termed a 'special military operation' and presented as defensive and pre-emptive, reflecting the long-term erosion of the European security order, rather than driven by the explicit repudiation of Charter norms. The war has demonstrated just how precarious European security has become. In 1914, the catalyst was the assassination of Archduke Franz Ferdinand and his wife on 28 June in Sarajevo, which set the vast machinery of war into motion.[51] In 2022 the instruments were well oiled and sprang into action. The difference between a cold war and a world war should not be blurred, but the foothills of World War III certainly beckon.

10
WAR IN EUROPE

The former Soviet space was excluded from the post-Cold War settlement and became the enduring subject of contention.[1] The US de facto pursued a policy of containing Russia to prevent it reasserting its influence across the region. This was couched in terms of defending the sovereignty of the newly independent states, a worthy goal but one that was coloured by the underlying intent to prevent Russia re-emerging as a regional power. Spheres of influence were rejected as an archaic remnant of a bygone age, but in practice this meant the expansion of a single sphere of interest – the Western one. Countries were encouraged to forge deeper links with the political West, a policy that worked only too well as they sought to join NATO and the EU.[2] Moscow itself was uncertain about its relationship with what some called the 'near abroad', and in the early years focused on becoming a 'normal' state and winning acceptance as part of the 'civilised world'. A reaction set in later, provoked by the absence of a robust and inclusive European security order. Russia applied coercive diplomacy to impede the unmediated westward drift of its neighbours. Lacking a genuinely attractive alternative model, Russia failed to establish its own regional hegemonic order.[3] Instead, relations were marked by crises and distrust.[4] The impasse was complete.[5] The credibility of Russia's repeated proposals for a revision of the post-Cold War European security order was questioned, yet the need for some rethinking became all the more urgent.

THE UKRAINIAN IMPASSE

The Commonwealth of Independent States (CIS) was established in December 1991 to provide continuity as the Soviet Union disintegrated. It was designed to maintain some services, such as welfare and pension payments, and initially even a unified military command. It soon became clear that it would provide a framework not for integration but for the 'civilised divorce' of the former union states. Even Moscow was inconsistent in its commitment to integration, and was one of the first to establish a national currency. Finally, in the 2000s it began to create functional alternatives to the EU. Washington opposed Russia re-establishing what it called a 'sphere of influence' in the region, whereas Moscow insisted that it was entitled to a 'sphere of security'. The whole region, as Medvedev memorably put in in late August 2008, was considered a 'sphere of privileged interest'.[6] What this meant in practice was unclear.

Russia's resort to coercive diplomacy reflected the weakness of its position. It failed to devise an attractive model for hegemony, the creation of a system that its neighbours would actively want to join. In part this reflected the 'decolonising' dynamic at work, in which the various successor states sought to assert their national identity, traditions and autonomy, and this inevitably meant distancing themselves from the former imperial metropole. Some post-colonial states accept that hybridity is an essential characteristic of their condition, and on that basis embrace the multiplicity of identities, languages and cultures. Others seek to return to some form of pre-colonial purity, which entails expunging imperial impositions. In some cases this means the establishment of some sort of hierarchy of appropriateness, where the titular nationality enjoys certain privileges, but everywhere this is accompanied by contested histories and memory wars.

This applies with particular force to the post-Soviet region. The legatee of the Russian Empire, the Soviet Union, had always been a peculiar construction. It was established more as an empire of ideology than of hierarchical subordination to Moscow (although there was plenty of that), and its various 'affirmative action' policies, practised intensively in the 1920s but not entirely repudiated thereafter, led to a growing sense of grievance in Russia itself.[7] The view took hold that Russia had suffered under Soviet power as much as other nations.[8] The tension between Russia as victim and perpetrator was later incorporated into contrasting narratives, provoking increasingly bitter debate and attempts to manage the narrative. By the later Putin years there were increasingly heavy-handed attempts to impose an official version of history, focused above all on the Soviet victory in the struggle against Nazi Germany, suppressing the darker spots in Soviet and Russian history.

It was in Ukraine that the conflicting narratives were at their sharpest.[9] The second-largest country in Europe after Russia, with an estimated population of 41 million in 2021 (estimated, because the last and only national census had been taken in 2001), the struggle over the future of Europe assumed its most concentrated form here. Ukraine had long been contested territory. Its very name indicates a borderland, but it has also been a heartland. In 988, the Kievan Prince Volodymyr adopted Orthodox Christianity and for nearly 300 years the city was the centre of Rus' culture, although variously challenged by princes in Velikii Novgorod and Pskov. The Mongols destroyed Kiev in 1240, and the baton eventually passed to the Vladimir-Suzdal principality and ultimately to Moscow. What was to become Ukrainian territory was later contested by the Ottoman Turks, the Polish-Lithuanian Commonwealth, Hapsburg Austria and then Austria-Hungary, Poland and the Russian Empire. In conditions of division and occupation, like Poland after the third partition in 1795, the nation became the repository of identity rather than the state, a very different trajectory from the state-centric Russian tradition. The various attempts to create an independent state following the Russian Revolutions of 1917 were short-lived and bloody, until finally communist Ukraine became a founder member of the USSR in December 1922. As such, Ukraine, along with the other founder members, Belarus and Russia, agreed to the abolition of the Soviet Union in the Belovezh forest in December 1991.[10]

Independent Ukraine became a raucous democracy, with competitive elections and the regular turnover of leaders. It was also dominated by a particularly concentrated form of oligarchic capitalism, competing not only in business but also through media holdings and politics.[11] In Russia, the Yeltsin-era oligarchs had been tamed by Putin in July 2000, whereas in Ukraine's more open society they retained their influence. Despite its rich abundance of fertile land and natural resources, as well as developed industries inherited from the Soviet Union, Ukraine's economy failed to recover from the devastating transition disruptions in the 1990s. Its GDP in 2021 had still not returned to the level at independence in 1991, and Ukraine became the poorest country in Europe. The 1997 Russo-Ukrainian Treaty on Friendship, Cooperation and Partnership committed both parties to 'refrain from participation in or support of any actions capable of prejudicing the security of the other side'. Kiev adopted what was called a multivector foreign policy, looking both east and west, but this ultimately satisfied neither. Worse, Moscow came to believe that Ukraine was once again being used as a bridgehead against Russia, as it had been earlier by Poland and the Austro-Hungarian Empire and then by American strategic planners after the war when they supported Stepan Bandera's insurgency in Western Ukraine.

Russian concerns were amplified when the provocative strategy of keeping Russia and Ukraine separate was elaborated by Brzezinski. In his *The Grand Chessboard* he argued:

> Ukraine, a new and important space on the Eurasian chessboard, is a geopolitical pivot because its very existence as an independent country helps to transform Russia. Without Ukraine, Russia ceases to be a Eurasian empire. Russia without Ukraine can still strive for imperial status, but it would then become a predominantly Asian imperial state.[12]

With Ukraine, Russia would have access to resources and the Black Sea: 'Russia automatically again regains the wherewithal to become a powerful imperial state, spanning Europe and Asia.'[13] The argument (although not unchallenged) found a ready audience in Ukraine, where separation from Russia became part of the country's post-communist state-building strategy.[14] Already in 1992, Karaganov, at the time deputy head of the Institute of Europe, noted that 'Kiev is quite deliberately building up an enemy image of Russia. It aims at a relationship that we might describe as one of controlled tension. Kiev's propaganda campaign is truly massive.'[15] Moscow was unsure about the level of integration that it desired in post-Soviet Eurasia, but it certainly resented the Western strategy of keeping Russia and Ukraine apart.

Matters came to a head when the newly enlarged EU sought to draw its eastern neighbours into closer alignment. In May 2008, months before the Russo-Georgian War, Carl Bildt and Radek Sikorski, the foreign ministers of Sweden and Poland respectively, initiated the Eastern Partnership. Its more strident aspects were toned down by the European Commission, but the formal launch of EaP in May 2009 signalled a struggle for influence over the 'shared neighbourhood', the six countries lying between Russia and the EU: Belarus, Moldova, Ukraine, Armenia, Azerbaijan and Georgia.[16] Full membership was not imminent, but the countries were to be drawn into the EU's orbit through Association Agreements, each including a Deep and Comprehensive Free Trade Agreement (DCFTA). The AA with Ukraine also mandated 'convergence' on security issues, with integration into European security mechanisms (Articles 4 and 7). In the case of Ukraine, this potentially entailed the termination of the leasing arrangement with Russia of the Sevastopol naval base in Crimea. The twenty-year deal agreed in 1997 was due to expire in 2017 but in April 2010 it was extended for another twenty-five years to 2042.

The stage was set for an epic confrontation over what became known as the 'contested neighbourhood', the band of countries lying between the expanding Atlantic powers and Russia. There had been repeated conflicts in the 1990s, above all over energy transit issues, so it was hardly surprising that the unstable geopolitics of Russian – West relations came to a head over Ukraine. The vigorously pro-Western presidency of Viktor Yushchenko after the 2004 Orange Revolution proved unstable, and in 2010 his defeated opponent, Yanukovych, finally won the presidency in an election that was judged by the OSCE to be free and fair. The electoral geography reflected the 'cleft' character of the country, with the western regions, and in particular those that had only been incorporated into Ukraine by Stalin in 1945, clamouring for closer links with the West, whereas Yanukovych appealed to the Russophone sentiments of the Donbass and the south.

Yanukovych may have been 'pro-Russian', yet he resolutely pursued the AA with the EU, which he initialled in Brussels in March 2012. In August of that year a poll revealed that 32 per cent favoured association with the EU, while 42 per cent preferred Russia's Customs Union. By September 2013, the mood had shifted in favour of the EU (42 per cent), while a still substantial 37 per cent preferred a Customs Union deal with Russia.[17] Despite the divided views, Yanukovych was determined to pursue the EU deal, provoking Moscow to impose heavy-handed measures in summer 2013. The EU demanded the release of opposition politician Yulia Tymoshenko, from her seven-year jail term as a condition for signing the agreement. On 21 November, the Ukrainian parliament failed to agree to Tymoshenko's release, effectively putting the EU agreement on hold. Putin at the time offered Ukraine a financial loan of $15 billion, far exceeding anything offered by the EU. That day, Yanukovych desperately pleaded for three-way talks between Ukraine, Russia and the EU, a format that the EU had resolutely opposed since at least 2009, when at the EaP's inauguration Putin called for trilateral talks on modernising the Ukrainian gas pipeline system. His idea was to start a cooperative process that could soften the hard edges of potential confrontation in the region.

The logic of expansion inevitably encountered a defensive reaction by Russia, and the stage was set for a showdown. When Yanukovych baulked and on 21 November announced that he would postpone signing the AA, protesters gathered in Kiev's central square, the Maidan Nezalezhnosti (Independence Square). Galvanised by heavy-handed repression on 30 November, the demonstrations turned into a revolution. The US demonstratively supported the Maidan insurgency, and a leaked tape revealed how it took the lead in shaping a pro-Western government, overseen by Biden, even while the elected president was still in power.[18] An EU-brokered agreement signed on

21 February 2014 for pre-term elections and the withdrawal of security forces was repudiated by the Maidan that evening. Finding himself defenceless, Yanukovych the next day fled the city and soon after the country. George Friedman, the head of the authoritative Stratfor think tank, argued that this was 'the most blatant coup in history'. The historic US goal in his view was to ensure that no state could 'amass too much power in Europe', hence it twice prevented Germany from dominating the continent, and then blocked the USSR and Russia from 'strengthening their influence'. It was 'in the strategic interests of the United States to prevent Russia from becoming a hegemon. And it is in the strategic interests of Russia not to allow the United States to come to its borders.'[19] Moscow agreed, arguing that this was a Western-sponsored putsch against a legitimately elected leader whose cardinal sin was that he was considered 'pro-Russian' (despite his earlier commitment to EU integration).[20] Yanukovych's violent overthrow disrupted the domestic political balance and unleashed forces at home and abroad with devastating effects. The nationalist model of state-building (although at its best generous and tolerant) defeated and delegitimated more pluralist approaches.[21]

The immediate result was Moscow's intervention in Crimea. On 16 March, a Moscow-sponsored referendum demonstrated overwhelming support for reunification. Although the precise figures are disputed, independent opinion polls confirm the strong pro-reunification sentiment.[22] On 18 March, the territory was annexed. Putin's speech that day blamed the Western powers for the breakdown of the European system. He condemned them for ignoring international law, arguing that it was the height of hypocrisy and 'double standards' to accuse Russia of actions that simply replicated Western behaviour, including recognition of Kosovo's independence in February 2008. He referred to the ICJ judgment of 22 July 2010, which stated, 'General international law contains no prohibition on declarations of independence.' Second, Putin justified the annexation by the need to defend the 'Russian world' (*Russkii mir*). The term is vague, with unclear boundaries, but it appeals to the view that the Russian nation is broader than the Russian state, encompassing a community of *sootechvenniki* (compatriots). The concept was applied later by the insurgents in the Donbass who claimed a cultural affiliation with Russia.[23] Third, Putin generalised the crisis as an indication of the broader breakdown of global order:

> Like a mirror, the situation in Ukraine reflects what is going on and what has been happening in the world over the past several decades. After the dissolution of bipolarity on the planet, we no longer have stability. Key international institutions are not getting any stronger; on the contrary, in many cases, they are sadly degrading.

He stressed that enlargement 'meant that NATO's navy would be right there in this city of Russia's military glory [Sevastopol], and this would create not an illusory but a perfectly real threat to the whole of southern Russia'. Fourth, Putin insisted that he was a friend to Ukraine:

> I also want to address the people of Ukraine. I sincerely want you to understand us: we do not want to harm you in any way, or to hurt your national feelings. We have always respected the territorial integrity of the Ukrainian state, incidentally, unlike those who sacrificed Ukraine's unity for their political ambitions.[24]

He insisted that Ukrainians and Russians were one people, although at the time this did not mean that he thought they should be part of the same state.

By then the anti-Maidan insurgency had spread to the Donbass. The rebels believed that if Yanukovych had remained in power and the western parts of Ukraine had started an insurgency, then 'the West would have defended the people there'.[25] The goal initially was autonomy rather than separation, yet the launch of the so-called Anti-Terrorist Operation (ATO) by Kiev in April provoked a war in which by 2021 over 14,000 people had died. The Minsk-2 agreement of February 2015 provided the framework for the return of

Ukrainian sovereignty on condition of significant devolution. Faced by the implacable opposition of the militant nationalists empowered by the Maidan revolution, the Kiev authorities were unable to deliver. The Minsk Accords entailed a transformation of statehood and hence were understandably resented, yet Moscow was regularly sanctioned for not implementing the agreement. Minsk-2 was ultimately about the return of the republics to Ukrainian sovereignty, but as time passed this became increasingly difficult. Kiev cut off most contacts, water supplies, welfare payments and services to the population, who turned to Russia for support. By late 2021, some 750,000 had taken out Russian passports (out of a total population of some 2.3 million in the Donetsk People's Republic and 1.4 million in the Lugansk People's Republic), although most also retained Ukrainian citizenship. Signed under the pressure of military defeat, the Minsk Accords nevertheless offered a pathway 'towards a more democratic and pluralistic Ukraine that recognises and accepts its own political diversity'.[26]

It was in this spirit that Volodymyr Zelensky was elected with 73 per cent of the vote in April 2019 as the peace candidate. His early attempts to find some sort of solution within the framework of Minsk-2 were blocked by so-called anti-capitulation protests. Pathways to implementing Minsk-2 outlined at the meeting with Putin in Paris in December 2019 within the framework of the Normandy Format (France, Germany, Russia and Ukraine) were also blocked by anti-capitulationists, threatening him with a new Maidan.[27] Zelensky threw in his lot with the 'Galician' exclusive nationalist model of Ukrainian state-building.[28] The struggle was both 'geopolitical-civilisational' and 'Ukrainian domestic', and the combination of the two proved devastating.[29] Just as the 'Polish question' bedevilled European politics in the nineteenth century, the 'Ukraine question' will do the same in the twenty-first.

The constituency sensitive to Russophone concerns was dramatically reduced and the *Kulturkampf* against Russian cultural and political influence in post-Maidan Ukraine intensified. In his last days in office, the president elected in May 2014, Petro Poroshenko, introduced the law 'On ensuring the functioning of Ukrainian as the state language', imposing onerous restrictions on Russian and other languages. This and other 'derussianisation' measures were now introduced. Despite the loss of the strongly Russophone Crimea and Donbass, there was no overwhelming consensus about Ukraine joining NATO. The proportion increased from 34 per cent in March 2014 to just 54 per cent in November 2021, but a surprisingly high 21 per cent still supported joining the Customs Union with Russia, Belarus and Kazakhstan.[30]

The status of Ukraine is central to the security environment of the region and Europe as a whole. For those governed by a simple-minded geopolitical logic, it was the great 'prize', the view advanced by Brzezinski in his *The Grand Chessboard*.[31] Considered in those terms, Ukraine becomes a pawn to be won by external actors. Worse, the struggle over Ukraine mobilised and radicalised contending domestic forces that may otherwise have found a way to formalise the country's diversity and multiple foreign policy identities in its constitution.[32] The Ukraine conflict was always the single most likely cause of direct confrontation between Russia and the West. Although Minsk-2 stabilised the situation, as far as Kiev was concerned it did not provide a framework for a resolution of the Donbass problem. It was required to grant the region constitutionally guaranteed autonomy, which it feared would forever hold the rest of the country hostage and prevent NATO membership. The 'multivector' foreign policy until 2014 maintained a balance, but thereafter the country radically tilted to one side, destabilising the internal balance.[33] As confrontation turned into war, the US overreached and Russia over-reacted. All parties stumbled and 'everyone lost'.[34] Ukraine became an intractable conflict in the heart of Europe, a wedge that attested to the broader failure of the post-Cold War European security order.

EUROPEAN SECURITY AT STAKE

Cold War I was a global conflict, with numerous hot wars across the globe, but in Europe it became a static confrontation. NATO and the USSR respected the frontline established after the war, allowing the USSR to invade Hungary in 1956 and Czechoslovakia in 1968, while the status quo was defended in Berlin. By contrast, Cold War

II is a more dynamic contest, with NATO moving eastward, while Russia supported national populist movements within the political West and anti-hegemonic multilateral organisations in the world at large (see Chapter 12). The struggle was an unequal one, and Russia had a rather limited repertoire of instruments with which to counter the Atlantic powers. One of these was the normative appeal to Charter norms, international law and above all the principle of indivisibility of security enshrined in the Helsinki Final Act and subsequent declarations. Democratic internationalism was countered by sovereign internationalism, the right of states to manage their own affairs, a view widely supported in the Global South. In the end, Putin considered all of this inadequate, and launched the military attack on Ukraine. If the Russo-Georgian war of 2008 can be considered the first war to stop NATO enlargement, then the Russo-Ukrainian war of 2022 is the second.

Military strategists deal with possibilities, so the study of motivation and capabilities is crucial. The annexation of Crimea prompted debate: did it signal the beginning of Russian ambitions to restore its empire, with the Baltic republics next in line, or was it driven by a unique set of circumstances? Was Moscow simply responding to what it considered a coup in Kiev and the long-term advance of Western security institutions to its borders, or was it motivated by some sort of attempt to recreate the Russian Empire? If the latter, its ambition clearly exceeded its grasp. Moscow's power is markedly reduced compared to Cold War I. The independence of the fourteen non-Russian republics returned the country's western borders to approximately those of late Muscovy. Unlike the USSR, Russia no longer has a ring of allies, however restive, on its borders, with the partial exception of Belarus. The Soviet economy at its peak in the late 1970s amounted to half that of the US, and today the disparity is at least fivefold. The imbalance is even greater when the combined weight of the Atlantic alliance is taken into account. Russia retains nuclear parity with the US, and after 2008 its modernised armed forces turned Russia into a more credible protagonist. However, the gross imbalance in all but nuclear and diplomatic matters rendered the situation little more than a form of modified unipolarity: a powerful pole in the West countered by Moscow's semi-pole, bolstered by alignment with China. Despite the odds, Putin was ready to take on the political West.

The NATO summit in Newport, Wales, on 4–5 September 2014 responded to the changed European security situation. The 2 per cent defence spending target was reaffirmed and a 'Readiness Action Plan' adopted. This established 'spearhead' military bases in the front-line East European states and rapid reaction forces in Poland and the Baltic republics, with a fixed although not permanent deployment of brigade-strength forces. The deployments technically remained within the bounds of the NATO–Russia Founding Act, but its spirit was violated. The European Reassurance Initiative (ERI) was launched by Obama in June 2014 with a $1 billion budget for training and force rotation, but by 2017 the Pentagon envisaged a near-four-fold funding increase to $3.4 billion. US operations for NATO in Europe came under the umbrella of Operation Atlantic Resolve, including the deployment of rotating battalion groups and enhanced exercises for the 100,000 US troops (in all services) by then deployed on the continent. Post-9/11-style counter-insurgency strategies gave way to planning for great-power conflict.

Obama refused to authorise the transfer of lethal weapons to the Ukrainian armed forces for fear of escalating the confrontation, but the Trump administration reversed the policy in March 2018. Sales included Barrett sniper rifles and Javelin anti-tank missiles, which can destroy tanks and armoured vehicles apart from the T-90 and T-72B3M tanks equipped with the latest reactive armour and active defence systems. The changed strategic balance prompted specula-tion that Kiev would be tempted to launch an offensive to retake the separatist Donbass regions, and possibly Crimea. Russia in early 2021 gathered a major force on the border to deter such ideas, and the immediate threat of war ebbed. However, the delivery of offen-sive arms indicated that the US was now committed to building Ukraine's military power as part of a deepening proxy confrontation, destabilising what was left of European security. Although Ukraine demanded rapid entry into NATO, Washington understood that this was a 'red line' for Moscow that it prudently refused to cross.

NATO returned to its original mission of the hard containment of Russia. An 'iron curtain' once again divided Europe, this time running largely along Russia's border from Narva on the Baltic to Mariupol on the Sea of Azov. The cold peace gave way to renewed cold war, but as Valerii Gerasimov, the chief of the Russian General Staff, noted, it was becoming increasingly difficult to tell the difference between war and peace.[35] NATO reinforced its forces in the region and Russia responded in kind as part of the escalatory logic of a security dilemma. Moscow partially reversed the shift from the divisional to the brigade structure, one of the key elements of the post-2008 military reform. The brigade configuration signalled the end of a force posture shaped to fight a land war against NATO, and instead sought to create a mobile force prepared to engage in smaller conflicts. The intensifying confrontation with the political West saw a partial reversion to Soviet-era formations with the creation, inter alia, of the 1st Guards Tank Army and the 20th Combined Arms Army. The Western Military District was reinforced with an influx of modern weapons, including the S-400 Triumf anti-aircraft missile system, the new T-72B3M main battle tank and the BMP-3 infantry fighting vehicle.

The basic tenet of strategic thinking is that capability does not imply intent; but this is accompanied by the other core element of such thinking – preparation for any conceivable eventuality. This is why the dividing lines became increasingly fortified. The rotation of semi-permanent forces in Eastern Europe required bases, supply lines, the modernisation of airfields, the building of communications systems and the creation of a logistics and supply network reminiscent of those developed by Allied forces in the postwar years in West Germany. The scope and scale of military exercises increased. The 'Steadfast Defender' exercise between April and June 2021 mobilised 20,000 US troops as well as a 17,000-strong contingent from NATO allies and 'partners' like Ukraine. This was the largest military exercise of the twenty-first century. Later that summer, the naval Large-Scale Exercise brought together aircraft carriers, submarines, aircraft and various other vessels with 25,000 personnel across 17 time zones in both the Pacific and Atlantic oceans.

NATO's London summit of December 2019 commissioned a review to strengthen the alliance's political dimension in response to new challenges. The report congratulated itself on having 'defied innumerable predictions of its imminent demise' before wheeling round to proclaiming that it had 'responded with clarity, unity, and resolve to the threat posed by Russian aggression in the Euro-Atlantic region'. In sum, 'Today NATO stands as history's most successful alliance, encompassing nearly a billion people and half of global GDP across a space that stretches from the Pacific coast of North America to the Black Sea.'[36] The document reverted to classic Cold War language, arguing that Eastern enlargement 'represented both the closing of the geopolitical vacuum in Europe's East ... and the reincorporation of former captive nations into the democratic West'. Since 2014, NATO's Forward Presence, Readiness Action Plan and Readiness Initiative meant that NATO enjoyed a variety of tools 'not only for countering the Russian military threat but also for understanding, anticipating, and defending against terrorism and threats in the hybrid and cyber realms'. Discussion focused on how to achieve 'political cohesion and convergence' in light not only of the challenge from Russia but also from China. The new 'geopolitical competition' represented 'global challenges' against which the alliance needed to unite. This was a call to arms. Cold War II was becoming as deep and extensive as the first, and no less hard to end. Its dynamic character made it more dangerous than the first.

NATO forces in the Baltic and Poland acted as a 'tripwire' in the event of a Russian attack, but NATO's overall force posture suggested that the alliance considered such an assault extremely unlikely. Moscow enjoyed what military planners call 'escalation dominance', the ability to concentrate forces regionally very quickly. The disproportion in conventional forces would almost inevitably at some point entail recourse to nuclear weapons. This is why there were severe doubts whether NATO would come to the defence of Montenegro or North Macedonia, let alone allied but non-NATO states like Georgia or Ukraine. Nevertheless, Cold War fears revived. NATO had long been obsessed by the Fulda gap between the GDR border and Frankfurt, a lowland area through which it was feared Warsaw

Pact tanks would pour on their drive to the Atlantic. Now the so-called 'Suwałki Gap (Corridor)', the span of land between Belarus and Kaliningrad, was identified as the route that Russian forces would use to cut off the Baltic republics. The correlation of forces locally was overwhelmingly in Russia's favour, hence the deployment of NATO brigades in Poland and the Baltic to deter Moscow. Nevertheless, in almost any conceivable conventional military scenario, NATO would be unable to prevent Russia's occupation of the region.[37] The option of nuclear retaliation would arise, including NATO's tactical weapons and its new low-yield nuclear warheads placed on frontline submarine-launched ballistic missiles (SLBMs).[38]

SLIDE TO WAR

Cold war patterns were restored. The Atlantic powers supported what the Ukrainian analyst Mikhail Pogrebinsky calls the 'pro-Western authoritarian regime' in Kiev.[39] The regime in turn did what many states had done in Cold War I, internationalising domestic conflicts and exploiting tensions between the great powers.[40] Kiev hired a phalanx of public relations consultants in the West to consolidate the anti-Russian front. Emboldened by the Biden administration's tough line and his declining domestic popularity, Zelensky's decree of 24 March 2021 declared that retaking Crimea was now Ukraine's official policy. In his first telephone conversation with Zelensky on 2 April 2021, Biden 'affirmed the United States' unwavering support for Ukraine's sovereignty and territorial integrity in the face of Russia's ongoing aggression in the Donbass and Crimea'. The US defence secretary also used the term 'unwavering support' in a call with his Ukrainian counterpart at that time.[41] Zelensky redoubled efforts to accelerate Ukraine's accession to NATO, although in his visit to Kiev in May 2021 Blinken made clear that this was unlikely in the short term. Accession is precluded for states with unresolved territorial disputes, considered a major factor in Russia maintaining protracted conflicts in its neighbourhood. NATO was also hesitant about committing to Ukraine's defence and thereby risking war with Russia.

In increasingly uncompromising language, Russia challenged the right of the Atlantic powers to expand their security system to Russia's borders.[42] Moscow claimed to uphold the foundational principles of the Charter international system, and thus repudiated the alleged 'hijacking' of international norms and law by the so-called 'rules-based order'. The perceived 'great substitution' was not going to be allowed to stand. Speaking in Finland in July 2017, Putin condemned 'the transnational character of US legislation' and noted that he had long been speaking about the issue. He referenced his February 2007 Munich speech and reiterated the point: 'It is exactly as I said: This practice is unacceptable – it is destroying international relations and international law. We have never accepted it and will not accept it.'[43] In his annual address to the Federal Assembly in April 2021, Putin stressed that Russia really did 'not want to burn bridges' but warned that if 'someone mistakes our good intentions for indifference or weakness and intends to burn or even blow up these bridges, they must know that Russia's response will be asymmetrical, swift and tough'. Putin hoped that 'no one will think about crossing the "red line" with regard to Russia'.[44] In July, his essay 'On the Historical Unity of the Russians and Ukrainians' stressed that the two were one people and went further than before in questioning the viability of the Ukrainian state, although he did not deny the principle of Ukrainian state sovereignty.[45] Russia was moving towards revisionism and conflict.[46]

Both sides were locked in an escalatory cycle. On 1 September 2021, Zelensky visited the White House, the first such visit by a Ukrainian head of state, and the two countries signed a 'Joint Statement on US – Ukraine Strategic Partnership'. The document implacably depicted the struggle with Russia as one between democracy and autocracy, while lauding Ukraine's 'Euro-Atlantic aspirations'. The statement unequivocally asserted that 'Sovereign states have the right to make their own decisions and choose their own alliances', language that appeared designed to rile Moscow. Ukraine's intention to join NATO was confirmed, while Russia's 'aggression' was emphatically condemned. The US declared that it would never recognise 'Russia's purported annexation of Crimea', while looking for a diplomatic solution 'to the Russian-led conflict in eastern Ukraine' (with no mention of Minsk). The statement noted that the US had supplied Ukraine with $2.5 billion of security assistance, with $400 million in 2021 alone, and a new $60 million package included additional Stinger anti-armour and other systems 'to enable Ukraine to more effectively defend itself against Russian aggression'.[47] A more detailed but essentially similar ten-year 'US–Ukraine Charter on Strategic Partnership' was signed by the two foreign ministers on 10 November, emphasising enhanced 'defence and security cooperation', and updating the December 2008 document of the same name.[48] The intention may not have been to goad Russia, but it certainly had that effect. Moscow was incandescent, with Lavrov stating that relations had reached 'boiling point'.[49]

Later that month, Russia cut diplomatic ties with NATO after the bloc expelled eight diplomats, accused of espionage, from the Russian mission in Brussels. Against the background of military deployments adjacent to Ukraine, on 17 December Russia submitted two draft European security treaties, repeating some of the themes of Medvedev's proposal in 2008–9. One was addressed to the US and the other to NATO.[50] The documents contained three key demands: no further NATO enlargement, covering in the first instance Ukraine as well as Georgia; no deployment of weaponry or military forces on the border with Russia; and NATO's return to the force posture of May 1997, when the NATO–Russia Founding Act was signed. This would entail removing forces from the countries that had joined since then, including the multinational battlegroups from the Baltic republics and Poland. Subsidiary demands included the removal of Intermediate-range Nuclear Forces weapon systems from Europe and the end of meddling in Russia's internal affairs. The NATO document focused on the danger of military exercises, with three (1, 2 and 7) of its nine draft articles raising the issue. Article 1 called on NATO and Russia to 'exercise restraint in military planning and conducting exercises to reduce risks of eventual dangerous situations in accordance with their obligations under international law'.

The combination of military and diplomatic initiatives forced a substantive US – Russian dialogue on European security for the first time since the negotiations over German unification in 1990, which already represented a major Russian achievement. Putin had long signalled Russian dissatisfaction, dating at least from his Munich speech in 2007. For the first time in thirty years, Russia's security concerns were being discussed at the highest diplomatic levels, although that did not mean that they were being taken seriously. The White House, the State Department and NATO did little to test the degree to which Russia was prepared to be flexible over its maximalist demands. This provoked commentators 'to speculate that American intransigence was a deliberate ploy to goad the Russians into an Afghan-style quagmire'.[51] More likely, Washington for too long had inured itself against taking Russian concerns seriously, reflecting the increasingly 'hermetic' character of the political West. Secure in its achievements, why take the concerns of a 'spoiler' state seriously? Such views were amplified by the Russiagate scandal, the purported collusion between Trump and Putin in the 2016 US elections accompanied by hacking and social media interventions. The perception that Russia had tried to subvert American democracy ratcheted animosity to unprecedented levels. In these circumstances, it was hardly likely that Washington would be receptive to diplomatic off-ramps to the gathering storm. It is quite likely that US leaders did not even see the storm coming.

This was a crisis of the first order. Russia was effectively demanding veto rights in European security matters, something that had never been granted since the end of the Cold War. As far as the Western powers were concerned, there was nothing to discuss, since the fundamental principles of a Europe 'whole and free' had long been established. The US worked with European partners and NATO to expand its model of the post-Cold War peace order, and effectively suppressed alternatives. Critics argued that there was no need to revisit the Helsinki principles as developed in the Paris, Istanbul and Astana documents, hence rejected the idea of a Helsinki II conference, let alone a return to first principles such as a new iteration of Westphalian principles of state sovereignty. Disturbingly, the main dialogue was conducted between Washington and Moscow, with at most consultations with European powers (the EU was entirely marginalised), with the US leadership in effect positioning Ukraine as the frontline in conflict with Russia. This reeked of Yalta, where the fate of small states was decided by the great powers. This time Europe as a whole was diminished – or at least 'old Europe', the classic legacy powers of Germany, France and Italy. Most of the Eastern 'new Europe' equated negotiation with appeasement. They encouraged a hard line towards Moscow on the grounds that their experience of servitude gave them a unique insight into the enduring imperial features of Russian policy. This perspective increasingly shaped EU policy, and left little room for consideration of Russia's security concerns.

In presenting its draft security treaties, Moscow promised a 'military-technical' response if negotiations failed, but did not specify what form this would take. The Western response when it came on 26 January was disappointing, although hardly surprising. The demand of a written guarantee that Ukraine would not join NATO was rejected, insisting on 'the right of other states to choose or change security arrangements'. There was no immediate prospect of Ukraine joining in any case, so some sort of declaration about deferred membership (a decade or two was mooted) accompanied by neutrality could have defused the situation.[52] The NATO response offered general transparency and confidence-building measures, such as briefings on each other's military exercises, consultations, establishing a civilian hotline, and re-establishing respective missions in Brussels and Moscow, but these had been tried for three decades and had been found wanting. The US response insisted on maintaining the 'open door' policy on enlargement, but it was ready to discuss 'reciprocal commitments by both the United States and Russia to refrain from deploying offensive ground-based missile systems and permanent forces with a combat mission on the territory of Ukraine'. As for returning to the force status of 1997, Washington insisted their current deployment was 'limited, proportionate, and in full compliance with commitments under the NATO–Russia Founding Act'.[53]

Continuing dialogue was promised, although Russia needed to 'de-escalate' its forces on Ukraine's border. The US was ready to continue arms control discussions, including limits on the deployment of ballistic missiles and nuclear-equipped bombers. A new idea was a 'transparency mechanism' to verify the absence of Tomahawk missiles, capable of reaching Russian territory from the two NATO Aegis BMD sites in Romania and Poland, in return for which the US demanded access to two missile sites of its choice in Russia. The main difference with NATO's response was that the US acknowledged the concept of 'indivisibility of security', the principle that had been reiterated in the Astana Declaration in 2010. In sum, the US response offered limited concessions – arms control on medium-range weapons, confidence-building, transparency, and verification measures along the NATO–Russia borderlands. It was not as much as Moscow wanted, but it was more than the West had been willing to offer for a generation. The question of European security was once again on the agenda, something that Moscow had long been pushing for. The door to diplomacy was ajar if not open.

LAST CHANCE

This turned out not to be enough. After three decades of complaint, Moscow was looking for rather more. On 1 February, Putin noted that 'It's already clear now ... that fundamental Russian concerns were ignored.' Worse, he believed that the US strategy was to lure Russia into a conflict that would weaken its power, just as the Soviet invasion of Afghanistan had done a generation earlier:

> I still believe that the United States is not that concerned about Ukraine's security, though they may think about it on the sidelines. Its main goal is to contain Russia's development. This is the whole point. In this sense, Ukraine is simply a tool to reach this goal. This can be done in different ways: by drawing us into armed conflict, or compelling its allies in Europe to impose tough sanctions on us like the US is talking about today.

He outlined a scenario in which Ukraine was admitted to NATO and then tried to recapture Crimea: 'Let's imagine Ukraine is a NATO member and starts these military operations. Are we supposed to go to war with the NATO bloc? Has anyone given that any thought? Apparently not.'[54] Various ideas were advanced to defuse the situation, including a lengthy moratorium on Ukraine joining NATO, the provision of weapons for Ukraine to defend itself but accompanied by a pledge not to establish bases or deploy troops, missiles and other strike weapons on Ukrainian territory. Ukraine's official stance until December 2014 had been neutrality, and the idea was now resurrected. However, in one of his last acts as president, Poroshenko in February 2019 enshrined the aspiration to NATO membership in the Constitution of Ukraine, tightening the knot yet further. Above all, the prospect of resolving the Donbass conflict in the framework of the Minsk-2 Accords had faded.

A disappointed and uncompromising tone permeated the official Russian response of 17 February, handed to the US ambassador in Moscow, John Sullivan. The eleven-page document roundly criticised the US and detected 'no constructive answer' to Russia's key demands, including a guarantee of no further enlargement and a return to the force deployments of 1997. Amid a deepening confrontation on the Ukrainian border, the *comprehensive* character of the Russian proposals had been ignored. Certain 'convenient' topics had been chosen, which in turn had been 'twisted . . . to create advantages for the US and its allies'. The text stressed that there would be no 'invasion' of Ukraine, but reaffirmed the principle of the 'indivisibility of security'. The US insistence on NATO's 'open door' policy was characterised as running against the alliance's own principles, which at its foreign ministers' meeting in Copenhagen on 6–7 June 1991 had resolved 'not to gain one-sided advantage from the changing situation in Europe', not to 'threaten the legitimate interests' of other states or 'isolate' them, and not to 'draw new dividing lines in the continent'. The option of further diplomacy was retained, calling for joint work to develop a new 'security equation'. The document threatened that if Moscow failed to receive the requisite 'legally binding guarantees' it would react with 'military-technical means'.[55] The nature of these means was once again left unspecified. There was some room for negotiation, including over arms control and risk reduction, but Russia's main concerns had been left unaddressed.

The military campaign by Azerbaijan in the second Karabakh war in September–October 2020, supported by Israeli and Turkish drones and intelligence, recaptured the seven provinces lost to Armenia in the first war of 1992–4 as well as part of Nagorno-Karabakh proper. The operation served as an example of how lost territory can be retaken, just as Croatia had overrun Serbian secessionists in Krajina in August 1995 (Operation Storm). Ukraine purchased drones from Turkey and sought closer military relations. It was now feared that Ukraine would seek to regain its territory in the same way as Croatia and Azerbaijan had done. The massing of Ukrainian forces on the frontline with the Donbass republics could have been defensive, but the increase in ceasefire violations and recorded explosions from 16 February 2022, peaking on 19 February, when 2,026 artillery strikes were recorded, suggested that the conflict was entering a more dynamic phase.[56] On 19 February, the authorities in Donetsk ordered a mass evacuation, and 60,000 people fled to Russia. Some sort of 'Operation Storm' appeared to be in the offing.

Russia had engaged in coercive diplomacy for months, but it was not clear whether this would tip over into outright conflict.[57] The US intelligence services repeatedly warned Ukraine that an attack was imminent, but Zelensky downplayed the threat, hoping to avoid panic accompanied by a stop to financial aid. However, he did little to calm the situation, and indeed potentially escalated it. In his speech to the Munich Security Conference on 19 February, he warned that Ukraine could reconsider the Budapest Memorandum of December 1994, whereby it gave up the nuclear weapons deployed on its territory in exchange for security assurances. Zelensky argued that Ukraine ended up with 'neither weapons nor security', and implied that Kiev's non-nuclear status could be reversed if the country was threatened by Russia.[58]

THE RUSSO-UKRAINIAN WAR

In an emotional and tangled speech late at night on 21 February, Putin warned that Russia's enemies were using Ukraine as a platform to threaten the country's existence. He demonstratively recalled his conversation with Bill Clinton (probably in January 2001) about Russia's admission to NATO and the US leader's negative response, a rejection that 'left a mark on the Russian political consciousness'.[59] Putin argued that the delivery of offensive weapons would ultimately make Russia's defence impossible, and it was irrelevant whether that day arrived in one year or twenty.[60] On 23 February, Moscow recognised the independence of the Donetsk and Lugansk people's republics. The following day Russia declared the launch of a 'special military operation'. Putin delivered another emotional speech, reciting the usual litany of grievances, with NATO enlargement at the top followed by Kosovo, Iraq and Libya amid accusations of Western hypocrisy and bad faith. He warned of a direct threat to Russia: 'As NATO expands to the east, with every passing year, the situation for our country is getting worse and more dangerous.' He viewed the situation as existential:

And for our country, this is ultimately a matter of life and death, a matter of our historical future as a people. And this is not an exaggeration – it is true. This is a real threat not just to our interests, but to the very existence of our state, its sovereignty. This is the very red line that has been talked about many times. They crossed it.

He warned against 'genocide against the millions of people living [in the Donbass] who rely on Russia, only on us' by the 'extreme nationalists and neo-Nazis in the Ukrainian government'. 'Russia's clash with these forces is inevitable. It is only a matter of time: they are getting ready, they are waiting for the right time. Now they also claim to acquire nuclear weapons.' Putin ended with a warning: 'No matter who tries to stand in our way, or threatens our country or our people, they should know that Russia will respond immediately, and the consequences will be such as you have never seen in your entire history.'[61] The declared goal was the 'demilitarisation' and 'denazification' of Ukraine (the scope and terms of which were not defined), and a three-pronged invasion (with nine columns) was launched. Forces entered from Belarus in the north heading towards Kiev, from the east and the Donbass republics towards Kharkov and the parts of Donetsk and Lugansk regions administered by Ukraine, and from Crimea in the south. The North Crimea Canal, providing 85 per cent of Crimea's water, was unblocked, allowing supplies to flow for the first time since 2014. This was an act of 'preclusive imperialism', like the US invasion of Iraq in 2003, designed to avert what was perceived as a future threat.[62] The UN Charter (Article 51) allows states to act in self-defence, but preventive wars are another matter.

The war in Ukraine is the largest armed conflict in Europe since World War II. In the first weeks, Putin three times made veiled warnings about the potential of nuclear war in an attempt to localise the conflict. This did not deter the US and its allies from pouring weapons into Ukraine, including increasingly heavy and long-range artillery and howitzers, along with innumerable Javelins, Stingers, M142 HIMARS (High Mobility Artillery Rocket System) and other battlefield missiles. The conflict became a classic proxy war between the US and Russia, with both countries seeking to avoid direct armed confrontation. The US refused to impose a no-fly zone, whose enforcement would see NATO and Russian air forces fighting over the skies of Ukraine. Nevertheless, the risk of nuclear escalation is very real. Russian military doctrine allows the use of nuclear weapons in case of an existential threat to national territory. Defeat in conventional warfare could be construed as just such a threat, a risk made all the greater by the formal admission of Donetsk, Lugansk, Zaporozhye and Kherson regions into Russia in September 2022. Once committed, Putin is unlikely to retreat without some sort of tangible achievement, unless the regime in Moscow itself comes under threat. On the other side, the Biden administration repeatedly asserts that it will 'not fight the third world war in Ukraine', and although it has supplied copious quantities of offensive weapons, it seeks to avoid becoming a combatant in the field.[63]

Could the war have been averted? Would the simple statement 'Ukraine will never join NATO' have been enough? When the promise of ultimate NATO membership was issued to Ukraine and Georgia at the Bucharest NATO summit in 2008, deputy foreign minister Grigory Karasin warned that 'Ukraine's accession to NATO would cause a deep crisis in Russian – Ukrainian relations that would affect all of European security. Therefore, the West must also make a choice as to what kind of relationship with Russia is in its interests.'[64] His words were prophetic. Over the years, other factors came into play, including Moscow's turn towards a more assertive nationalism and domestic repression. The events of 2014 left numerous issues unresolved, including the status of Crimea, the Donbass question and scope for a diplomatic resolution of the conflict.

The intensifying European security dilemma culminated in war, but were there alternatives? Russia was serious when it proposed the two security treaties in December 2021, but neither side was ready to engage in serious diplomacy to test the other's readiness to compromise. Moscow issued increasingly urgent warnings in the form of declarations rather than detailed negotiating positions, while the Atlantic powers doubled down in defence of the open-door principle of NATO membership. The West admitted that Ukraine's membership was not likely in the coming decades, yet refused to accept some compromise formulation. There was little scope for diplomacy, since the deeper roots of the problem were not recognised, which lay in the failure since 1990 to create a mutually satisfactory pan-European security order. Instead, the Western powers were willing to put 'Ukraine's very existence in mortal danger to protect their [Ukraine's] right to join NATO'.[65] The neutrality option is not so unusual, with six EU member states in that category along with some 120 countries non-aligned globally. Neutrality would not have prevented Ukraine developing as a sovereign democratic state, yet the political West insisted on its version of the post-Cold War peace order. Russia's security concerns were effectively delegitimated. This does not justify the Russian invasion, although it helps explain it. The head of the US Joint Chiefs of Staff, General Mark Milley, warned that the war could last for years.[66]

11

CRISIS OF THE
INTERNATIONAL SYSTEM

Long before the war in Ukraine, little was left of positive peace. Instead, cold war returned, a period of entrenched confrontation accompanied by rhetorical condemnation of the opponent.[1] New practices of containment were devised.[2] However, there are sceptical voices who argue that the appropriation of the term 'cold war' is an abuse of history and misunderstands the realities of the present situation.[3] The Eurocentric character of cold war analogies obscures the transformations in international politics and changes in the global balance of power. The timescale can also be misleading, and instead of focusing on the post-Cold War or even postwar period, a longer historical view is required. The 500-year dominance of the civilisational West is being challenged as never before. A more immediate comparison is the late nineteenth- and early twentieth-century period of great-power confrontation, with the growing rivalry between the rising power of Germany and the relative decline of Great Britain. Even in conditions of a power shift, war is not inevitable. In his study of the power dynamics at the beginning and end of the Cold War, Shifrinson argues that dominant and rising powers can calibrate their relationship in a way that avoids war.[4]

The simplified application of historical parallels certainly impedes fresh thinking and leads to faulty analysis, obscuring the specific dynamics of the security dilemmas between the Western powers and the East, in particular with China.[5] However, it is clear that a new global conflict has emerged between contending representations of governance, competing models of global order and differing views of how international politics should be conducted. The US and its allies are intent on defending what they call a 'rules-based' international system, whereas a loose alignment of states argue that this disguises the dominance of the political West. For them a multiplex and multipolar representation of global affairs is more appropriate.[6] The political West has consolidated against Russia's invasion of Ukraine, accompanied by the mobilisation of a global anti-Russian coalition, yet parts of the non-West refused to get involved. There is resistance to the political West consolidating its dominance as a global West. The limits of the Cold War West have been exposed. It can no longer set the standards of civilisation, the global agenda and the behavioural norms in international affairs, as the civilisational West had done in the heyday of the age of imperialism. Cold War II is genuinely global but at the same time partial. Above all, the renewed conflict challenges the very foundations of the institutional framework established in 1945 for the conduct of international politics. The Charter international system is threatened as never before.

A PERILOUS WORLD

The tangle of alliances, the deep-rooted suspicions, the accumulation of grievances (real and imagined) and the struggle for status is today reminiscent of the period leading to World War I. There is a fundamental clash of narratives, with each side firm in their belief that they hold the high moral ground. Misperceptions lead to miscalculation, and it takes only a spark to set the tinder alight.[7] After a period of peace, the generation that suffered war passes away and memories of destruction and death fade. New generations seek to prove their worth, and how better to do this than by rituals of condemnation and spectacles of resolve. This is why Cold War II is more dangerous than the first. As Mearsheimer notes, because of the structural rivalry generated by the characteristics of international politics where there can only be one hegemon, 'proponents of engagement are whistling in the wind. Cold War II is already here, and when one compares the two cold wars, it becomes apparent that the US–Chinese rivalry is more likely to lead to a shooting war than the US–Soviet rivalry was'.[8]

The scholar Stephen F. Cohen identified five factors which make this confrontation more perilous than the first: after the Cuban missile crisis, a robust diplomatic framework regulated superpower relations, including a 'hotline' between the capitals, but today diplomacy is the frontline casualty in hostilities; the creation of a strategic arms architecture ensured continuing engagement, but today not much is left of this; the line of confrontation was far from Russia's borders, whereas today Russia's perimeter has become the new frontline, with numerous potential flashpoints, above all the 1,974-kilometre (1,226-mile) land border with Ukraine; the various proxy wars avoided direct confrontation, whereas today the two major powers have clashed in Syria and battle it out in Ukraine; and, finally, in the original Cold War the image of the enemy could be dismissed as propaganda or ideologically skin deep, whereas today the psychology is very different. The image of the enemy has sunk deep societal roots and can no longer be dismissed as an artificial elite project.[9] Cold war has become existential. Having survived the original postwar confrontation and averted a nuclear apocalypse, the complacent sentiment took hold that the nuclear bullet would again be dodged. This confidence is misplaced. The Charter system bans war as an instrument of policy, but the great powers have returned to aggressive militarism. In the end, Russia took the plunge and invaded Ukraine, undermining the postwar Charter international system and jeopardising the future of humanity.

The protagonists believed that preparing for war would not lead to war. This sense of invulnerability was fostered by studies suggesting that war is declining as a feature of relations between states.[10] In these accounts, the tamping down of domestic violence is accompanied by a range of factors that have an equivalent effect in international affairs. These include the balance of power, the deterrent effect of nuclear weapons, the enhanced destructiveness of conventional warfare, the pacifying effect of democracy, the mediating role of international institutions, and the conciliatory effect of economic interdependence. Evidence suggests that the 'democratic peace' applies only to the mature democracies of the postwar era, whereas earlier democracies fought each other regularly.[11] Peace is reinforced by what Gaddis calls the 'reconnaissance revolution', satellites that vigilantly monitor military movement by land, sea and air (although, significantly, not submarines). This gave rise to the 'long peace' in the latter stages of Cold War I, whose conditions were presumed still to apply.[12] This encouraged a degree of recklessness, assuming that achievements of the past would continue indefinitely into the future. Deterrence would continue to deter, and echoing Norman Angell's earlier arguments about economic interdependence, full-scale war, while not inconceivable, was improbable.[13] We know how that turned out in 1914. Not so long ago it was legitimate to ask, 'Where have all the soldiers gone?', but it soon became clear that this generation is not immune to the passions, mistakes and delusions that lead to war.[14]

Unresolved questions of the first cold war generated the second. In the internet age, the iron curtain is more permeable than earlier, yet it still represents a physical and psychological demarcation. In the South China Sea, the nine-dash line, indicating the maximum extent of Beijing's claims, is contested by the other littoral states, while the conflict over the status of Taiwan renders the country an Asian 'Ukraine', acting as the trigger for conflict in the region. North Korea's nuclear ambitions threaten its neighbours and increasingly the US mainland. Ukraine remained a simmering powder keg in Europe, liable to explode at any time. After 2014, the NATO allies poured in weaponry, trained the Ukrainian Armed Forces to NATO standards and interoperability, and built naval and military bases and installations. The army that Russia encountered in 2022 was unrecognisable from the demoralised, divided and poorly trained force of 2014. Rather less effort was devoted to diplomacy. The cyber, high-tech and space realms have become new vectors of conflict. The ramping up of military exercises on land and sea across the entire new 'iron curtain', including the placement of forces in Poland and American drone deployments in Ukraine and along the Crimean border, together with air and sea patrols, were primed for conflict. To use the analogy suggested earlier, the pistol was loaded but Putin was responsible for pulling the trigger.

History is always specific but broad patterns are repeated. In 1914, Germany's leaders believed that the country's rise was being stymied by the Atlantic powers, while in 1941 Japan felt the same about its Asian-Pacific ambitions. Today, China may be placed in that category, with commentators, as we have seen, identifying a 'Thucydides trap', comparable to Sparta's fears about the rise of Athens. This provoked a devastating war lasting ten years, forcing Athens to accept humiliating peace terms in 404 BC and weakening its long-term power. An alternative interpretation is that Chinese power has peaked, and faced with a demographic downturn, slowing economic growth and determined adversaries, the country faces inexorable decline – hence asserts itself at the moment of maximum power.[15] Mearsheimer argues that it is the structural characteristics of the international system that makes war between the US and China inevitable. America has to defend its hegemony, and that hegemony has to be challenged by China if it is to assert itself as a regional hegemon with global ambitions.[16] This rather deterministic approach is based on classic geopolitical concerns, drawn from Halford Mackinder, who in 1919 argued that whoever dominates the Eurasian heartland threatens to bid for global hegemony. This model is anachronistic and was devised before the onset of airpower, rockets and satellites. This view also discounts choice and agency. Structures certainly shape interactions over the long term, but premeditated wars begin when specific actors decide to take the offensive, and that is usually a function not only of capacity but also of perceptions and, above all, fears.

On this basis, Christopher Layne argues that 'the conditions that make [great-power war] possible still exist', noting the various tensions between the great powers, with the US and China 'on a collision course fuelled by the dynamics of a power transition and their competition for status and prestige'.[17] He discounts the various mitigating factors, above all the high level of economic interdependence between the two countries. Even these ties have begun to unravel in recent years. Nuclear deterrence in his view is further undermined by the creation of miniaturised low-yield nuclear warheads and highly accurate delivery systems that make a 'limited' nuclear war more tempting. At the same time, the liberal international order is less capable of maintaining peace because of the rise of populism and illiberal democracy accompanied by the erosion of domestic support. Before 1914, Britain and Germany were linked by innumerable social and economic ties, yet the British elite came to see Germany as an irredeemably bad actor. The struggle was as much about prestige as it was about power. As Layne puts it, 'Germany's goal was not necessarily to challenge the United Kingdom but to be acknowledged as its great-power equal.'[18] Today, China is in a comparable position, having gained the 'military and technological capabilities to wrest regional hegemony in East Asia away from the United States'.[19] Hence Pompeo depicted China as the new 'evil empire', an ideological challenge to the US, reminiscent of the demonisation of Germany and Japan earlier.

In keeping with the sovereign internationalist model, Layne argues that the US would be better advised

> to take ideology out of the equation and conduct its relationship with China as a traditional great-power rivalry, in which diplomacy aims to manage competition through compromise, conciliation, and the search for common ground. Ideological contests, on the other hand, are zero-sum in nature. If your rival is evil, compromise – indeed, negotiation itself – becomes appeasement.[20]

The same advice applies to the US relationship with Russia and other powers. This does not necessarily entail removing US security commitments to Taiwan or South Korea, but it does mean recognising limits to the universality of the current liberal order, moderating critical commentary on the character of China's political system, and above all renouncing the ambition of regime change. Crucially, however, Layne is pessimistic that the US is capable of taking such a step, since it 'would mean acknowledging the end of US primacy', making a hot war more likely. As he notes, unlike in the Cold War with the USSR, where spheres of influence were known and generally accepted, today there are stark disagreements about who should enjoy pre-eminence in the East and South China Seas and Taiwan.[21] Recognising China as a normal great power would mean ceding regional dominance to Beijing, and the same applies to Russia. This leaves out of account the framework provided by postwar Charter internationalism for more cooperative regional orders. ASEAN and its partners have tried to establish just such a cooperative order in the Asia-Pacific region.

The realist view that international politics is no more than the struggle for power and pre-eminence in an anarchic world of states is tempered by the liberal idea that an expansive hegemony moderates conflict for all those willing to join. Beijing advanced a third view, that the Charter international system provides a peaceful route for change. If this is correct, then the shift in the balance of global power does not necessarily entail conflict. The Chinese narrative that the US is 'experiencing a steady, irreversible structural decline' gave it confidence that time was on its side. However, the idea of 'a gradual, peaceful transition to an international order that accommodates Chinese leadership now seems far less likely to occur than it did just a few years ago'. In the US, this means that Trump's declaration that China was a strategic competitor was welcomed as a belated recognition of the threat.[22] If the realist view is correct, then the appropriate policy has to be pre-emptive to contain and even reverse China's rise. This only exacerbates the risk of conflict. Sanctions do not work against great powers, and only deepen antagonism and separation. There is no evidence that the cascade of sanctions changed Russian policy, although it is impossible to measure what may have happened in their absence. The same demonstrably applies to China.

IS THIS A COLD WAR?

A cold war is different from a normal adversarial relationship. Drawing on the experience of Cold War I, Robert Legvold identifies five distinctive characteristics. First, ideological division, with starkly different representations of the desirable political and economic order. Second, each side holds the other responsible for the conflict, with no scope for introspection or reflection about how one's own actions contribute to stoking division. Third, both sides assume that the conflict is driven not out of the interaction of two countries but from the character of the other side: 'The essence of the problem [is] the essence of the adversary.' The struggle becomes one not over interests but over purpose. Fourth, as a consequence, change can only come about if the other side in some way or other becomes something different, or at least is ready fundamentally to rethink its foreign policy. Finally, there is cooperation, but it can only be 'limited and transactional, not cumulative and transformative'.[23]

In our case, two conflicts are superimposed: the long-term shift in the balance of power away from the West towards the rising powers of Asia, Africa and Latin America; and entrenched cold war practices, regenerated as a result of the failure to transform European international relations at the end of Cold War I. In the US, the military-ideological complex forged in the original Cold War looked for 'dragons to slay' to justify its existence, while feeding the insatiable appetite of the Trumanite state. In Russia the old Soviet elite and security apparatus was reconstituted, driven now by geopolitical rather than ideological imperatives, although coloured by statist and civilisational concerns. China came late to the Cold War II party, but its leaders gradually came round to the view that the peaceful rise era had necessarily ended.

Like a game of chess, a cold war can play out in different ways. The rules remain the same, but the outcome depends on the skill and experience of the players. Cold War I was a rather static and defensive affair in Europe, whereas the second is more dynamic and more dangerous. The twenty years' crisis after 1919 ended in the greatest war in human history, and the twenty-five years of cold peace ended in another, rather more fragmented, Cold War. One axis of confrontation runs between Washington and Moscow, while the second divides Washington and Beijing. Cold wars by definition are on a knife edge, potentially escalating into military confrontation. Accidents and misjudgements can tip the balance. Christopher Clark notes that the bipolar stability of the Cold War 'made way for a more complex and unpredictable array of forces, including declining empires and rising powers – a condition that invites comparison with the Europe of 1914'.[24] With the exception of the Atlantic powers, the tight alliance system of the earlier period is absent, but a complex and dynamic relationship between blocs, alignments and affiliations shapes international politics.

The second Cold War differs from the earlier one just as World War II differs from the first. In both cases, the follow-on conflict was provoked by unresolved contradictions in the ending of the first. In our case, this took the form of a conflict between two representations of the appropriate peace order, precipitating a security dilemma and ultimately conflict. NATO's *Strategic Concept 2022* demonstrated how far the global strategic environment had deteriorated. Adopted by the Madrid summit in June 2022, the Preface asserted that NATO remains a 'bulwark of the rules-based international order', while Russia's 'war of aggression against Ukraine has shattered peace and gravely altered our security environment'. Russia was condemned as

the most significant and direct threat to Allies' security and to peace and stability in the Euro-Atlantic area. It seeks to establish spheres of influence and direct control through coercion, subversion, aggression and annexation. It uses conventional, cyber and hybrid means against us and our partners. Its coercive military posture, rhetoric and proven willingness to use force to pursue its political goals undermine the rules-based order (Article 8).

For the first time, similar language was also used about China, whose 'stated ambitions and coercive policies challenge our interests, security and values':

The PRC employs a broad range of political, economic and military tools to increase its global footprint and project power, while remaining opaque about its strategy, intentions and military build-up. The PRC's malicious hybrid and cyber operations and its confrontational rhetoric and disinformation target Allies and harm Alliance security. . . . The deepening strategic partnership between the People's Republic of China and the Russian

Federation and their mutually reinforcing attempts to undercut the rules-based order run counter to our values and interests (Article 13).[25]

The document claimed that 'NATO's enlargement has been a historic success' (Article 40), and thereby denied any responsibility for the breakdown of the European security order. This boosterish self-evaluation was hard to square with the renewed division of the continent and the brutal war being waged in Ukraine.

Cold War II is far more than a continuation of the first, although unresolved issues from the earlier period shape the renewed confrontation. The concept of 'cold war' describes a particular form of conflict with its own dynamics and regularities, appropriate to the nuclear age and the unparalleled destructiveness of conventional warfare. A cold war represents an enduring pattern of confrontation between a state or a set of states, accompanied by ideological differences, information campaigns and contrasting representations of how international politics should be conducted. Geopolitics and ideology are entwined in opposing poles of attraction or repulsion. Third-party states are drawn into the corresponding vortex, however much they may wish to stay out. Others exploit the antagonism for their own advantage – as they did in Cold War I.

The term 'cold war' is a metaphor, although it indicates a specific type of situation where conflict is endemic yet constrained. It is about managing rather than resolving conflict. However, as suggested earlier, not everyone is convinced that the current situation deserves to be so labelled.[26] Other approaches are deemed more appropriate, such as great-power conflict, balance of power politics, the rise of multipolarity, the contest between authoritarianism and democracy, or the rise of revisionism (defined as the attempt to change both the international system and the way that international politics are conducted). The original Cold War was about contrasting ideas about how society should be organised, and today this is replicated in terms of the struggle between democracies and autocracies. The struggle for status and primacy shapes geopolitical contestation, yet the condemnation of the moral failings of the other is part of the 'hybrid' character of all such conflicts. In the years before World War I, Germany was condemned for its militarism and imperial ambitions, although the socio-economic and aristocratic order of the main contenders (except France) were much the same.

Russia today is a capitalist society, although with a monopolistic and statist bent, while China is a market-oriented society within a communist state structure. The division between democracies and so-called autocracies is far from clear-cut since all states proclaim fidelity to the principles and norms of the Charter international system. Even in the heartlands of the political West there are major governance failings and the definition of the public good is intensely contested, while more authoritarian polities such as China and Singapore have delivered extraordinary improvements in social welfare and other public goods. Democratic internationalists insist that international politics is the continuation of domestic governance by other means, whereas defenders of sovereign internationalism condemn the flouting of Charter norms but argue that countries have to resolve their own problems. External 'nation-building' as often as not only exacerbates problems. The battle lines today are blurred, which liberals find disconcerting but realists accept as the normal state of affairs.

The ideological factor is important but does not determine whether a standard great-power conflict is a cold war. Washington today portrays the struggle as one between democracy and authoritarianism. If that is the central issue, then the US would be locked in cold war with any number of authoritarian states, many of which are in fact its allies. A characteristic feature of a cold war is the instrumental and selective application of the rules of one's own side to ensure maximum advantage over the adversary. Russia advanced its vision of conservative values to counter perceived liberal degradation and repudiation of traditional norms, although the whole endeavour was artificial and instrumental (although not of course to conservative enthusiasts). The values of Russian citizens in the main are indistinguishable from those of their Western counterparts. The main difference is greater tolerance for authoritarian practices promising stability, resulting from the repeated experience of societal collapse and political disintegration. This generated the fundamental paradox of the Putin system. The imposition of mechanical stability only intensified the 'Leninist trap' and undermined the development of more organic forms of sustainable stability.[27] The more intensely that society is pacified through stability politics, the less stable the system becomes.

Nuclear deterrence shapes cold war politics. Great-power relations since 1945 have been haunted by the nuclear threat. Direct confrontation has been avoided and, even as the proxy war over Ukraine intensified, Washington explicitly stated that one of its fundamental goals was to avoid starting World War III. The escalation ladder will remain unused unless one side perceives that it faces an immediate existential threat. The risk of nuclear apocalypse imposes an element of 'coldness' on all major interstate conflicts. The threat imposes a level of rationality in the conduct of international affairs that was often lacking in more heroic ages, in which martial virtues were lauded and the cleansing power of war exalted. However, this imposed rationality is constrained in cold war situations. As Legvold puts it, 'the miasma of Cold War destroys a capacity to assess accurately what is at stake and to rethink the narrow, stunted way security challenges, such as currently over Ukraine, are defined'.[28] The peace at the end of Cold War I promised mutual security, but new divisions undermined trust and confidence, and with it the whole edifice of arms control and conflict prevention. In a cold war the conflict assumes a starkly ideological and Manichean character, in which the enemy is demonised and there is minimal scope for constructive and enduring partnership. When peace is lost and security divided, total war is never more than a radar blip away.

Cold War II will not be a carbon copy of the first, with less accentuated bipolar features. The triangular character of Cold War II combines two interlocking cold wars – one US–Russia and the other US–China.[29] Each has its dynamic and logic, but the result is the return of twinned confrontation within the larger trend towards multipolarity. India, Indonesia, Nigeria and many more countries refuse to act as bit players in a show staged by others. There are profound ideological differences over how international affairs should be managed, with Russia and China opposed to the practices of substitution; and in domestic matters, the two countries insist on creating their own models of modernity – although critics with some justification argue that both represent a revolt against modernity, if the latter is defined as a critical, open-ended and reflexive approach to problems of development and political inclusion. Nevertheless, sceptics are not convinced that the notion of Cold War II describes the contemporary Sino-US relationship. Michael McFaul, who served as US ambassador to Russia between 2012 and 2014, argues that 'The cold war analogy distorts, more than illuminates, dynamics in US–China relations today'. He warns that those who seek a cold war confrontation with China 'underplay the costs and mistakes of the actual Cold War', while the 'many challenges from China's rise today have little in common with the Cold War, and therefore require creative strategic thinking, not simply dusting off the Cold War playbook'.[30] McFaul is undoubtedly right to warn against the unthinking revival of cold war confrontation and to warn against its costs. His argument is in keeping with those who argue that international affairs are reverting not to cold war but to great-power politics of the pre-1914 type.[31] Nonetheless, despite the reservations outlined above, the new global conflict can be deemed a second Cold War.

DIPLOMACY AND THE CHARTER SYSTEM

Diplomacy is about recognising pluralism and managing difference. Post-Cold War liberal anti-pluralism blurred this fundamental act of recognition. By proposing a universal set of norms and standards of domestic political behaviour, difference inevitably came to be viewed with suspicion and distrust. The pluralism of international society was thereby delegitimised. The CPC, for example, argues that its model of rule is in conformity with the country's millennia-long history and current developmental needs, yet the very foundations of its governance principles were questioned. James Der Derian argues that 'the purpose of diplomacy is to *mediate* estranged relations; anti-diplomacy's aim is to transcend *all* estranged relations'.[32] Democratic internationalism inevitably fosters 'anti-diplomacy', the suppression of difference and civilisational pluralism. The protagonist cannot be taken seriously since they flout the fundamental norms of liberal hegemony, and therefore concessions amount to appeasement. This Manichean division of the world provoked the 'ambassadorial war' between Russia and the West in which over 600 diplomats were expelled from host countries by late 2021. The former Russian foreign minister Igor Ivanov noted, 'We have never seen anything like this in the history of diplomacy.'[33]

Struggles over the legitimacy of the liberal order's claim to universality underlie the great-power conflicts of our time. This takes the specific form of questioning 'universalism' – the belief that the normative claims underlying liberal order are of universal validity and hence it was incumbent upon the power system in which these values were embedded to advance and defend these claims – the predicate for democratic internationalism and transdemocracy. This provoked some of the sharpest conflicts in the post-Cold War era. A telling example of this was the struggle over renewed membership of the forty-seven-member UNHRC in 2020. The US had withdrawn in 2018, condemning it as 'hypocritical and self-serving'. Fifteen countries were to be chosen for a three-year term, prompting the argument that China, Cuba, Russia, Saudi Arabia, Pakistan and Uzbekistan were 'unqualified' to serve because of their human rights record. The report was politically tendentious, although some of the criticisms were valid.[34] However, the point could easily be made that almost no country would escape censure, but the politicisation of UN procedures was worrying. Cold War tools were mobilised against sovereign internationalism.[35] The UN was shaped in 1945 to maintain balance between the world's then-great powers, while the inclusion of diverse cultures and ideologies strengthened its institutional foundations. The attempt later by a self-selected group of countries to become the arbiters of membership of UN agencies and institutions threatens to undermine the international system in its entirety. Post-Cold War universalism in practice meant the generalisation of a particular system as universal. This gave rise to the great substitution and undermined the integrity of the Charter international system.

A doubly destructive process is in train. The polarising consequences of the substitution undermines the efficacy of Charter institutionalism, but at the same time underfunding and the animus against the 'administrative state' has eroded the US ability to provide diplomatic leadership. Ronan Farrow laments the domestic substitution in which military-industrial agencies and their associated propagandists have taken the place of traditional statecraft, undermining America's vaunted leadership in peace-making.[36] Liberal institutionalists accept that international organisations on their own do little to change the behaviour of states, but when there is multilateral consensus and appropriate leadership, then institutions make a difference. Liberals suggest that international organisations shape the normative framework and behavioural expectations, and thus act with a degree of autonomy. By contrast, realists argue that states remain the foundational unit in a fundamentally anarchic international system. International institutions are effective to the degree that the great powers allow them to be. Multilateral institutions are most effective when they combine the power capacity and normative aspirations of their participants.

This explains why the UN and its specialised agencies have endured for so long. The Charter international system represents an equilibrium between state autonomy and multilateral governance. The balance changes over time and over different issues, but the principle remains. The US always chafed at the restrictions that the UN imposed on its freedom of action, leading to calls by some (for example, Alabama congressman Mike Rogers) for the US to withdraw entirely and not just from some of the UN's specialised agencies. However, as long as the US can mostly achieve its goals within the broad framework of the international system, it remains ready to accept the constraints. Breaches of the fundamental principles of the UN Charter and the UDHR are condemned in resolutions, but enforcement remains a matter of political discretion.

This applies to recalcitrant states as well as the hegemon. In the absence of the accustomed bipolarity and with the disappearance of the Soviet Union, the US was less willing to submit itself to external constraints. The temptation was to apply global rules in conformity with particular interests. This was apparent in the second Iraq War in 2003 and the radical extension of the provisions of Resolution 1973 of March 2011 imposing a no-fly zone in Libya. Trump's contempt for multilateral organisations and agreements represented a severe escalation, but it reflected a long-term dissatisfaction among part of the Washington elite. America ran the risk of becoming a 'rogue superpower'.[37] In the absence of a generally mandated world government, international institutions rely on great-power consensus to achieve their goals. Even this is contested. Hard-line offensive realists argue that multilateral institutions have almost no influence on the conduct of international politics.[38] Great powers like the US chafe at the curbs that multilateralism imposes on their freedom of action. As great-power confrontation and other challenges intensified, critiques of multilateralism and globalisation were amplified. Brzezinski as usual pithily summed up the response when he argued that the US 'must take the lead in realigning the global power architecture in such a way that the violence . . . can be contained without destroying the global order'.[39]

PARTING OF THE WAYS

The vulnerability of the Charter system is increasingly exposed. The UN in July 1998 hosted a diplomatic conference in Rome that established the International Criminal Court (the Rome Statute), the culmination of a long struggle dating back to the end of World War II but suspended during the Cold War. The civil conflict in Yugoslavia and the genocide of 800,000 Tutsis and moderate Hutus in Rwanda in 1994 revived the impetus to create an international mechanism to bring perpetrators to trial. In the first instance, ad hoc tribunals were created for the two cases. The International Criminal Tribunal for the Former Yugoslavia (ICTY) brought the 'butcher of Bosnia' Ratko Mladić – responsible for the massacre of 8,000 men and boys in Srebrenica in July 1995 – and his boss Radovan Karadžić to justice. The Rome Statute entered into force in 2002, granting the ICC the power to prosecute four offences: war crimes, crimes against humanity, genocide and the crime of aggression. By 2020, 123 countries had signed and ratified the document. Some of the major powers, however, did not, while Burundi withdrew in 2016, claiming that the ICC was excessively focused on African misdeeds, concerns also voiced by South Africa. Russia signed in 2000 but did not ratify, and in November 2016 withdrew following an ICC report that classified the Russian annexation of Crimea as an occupation.

Bill Clinton signed the document in 2000 but did not recommend its ratification until its alleged defects had been rectified. The main US objection was that the ICC could bypass American laws when indicting US soldiers, and in theory even senior US officials could be prosecuted. The US insisted that the ICC could not prosecute citizens of the US or its allies. A 2002 law prohibited US cooperation with the ICC, including investigations, extradition and financing. In June 2020 Trump signed an executive order creating a legal mechanism to impose sanctions against employees of large international organisations and related persons. This was in keeping with the right to declare a national emergency in connection with a particular threat to national security and foreign policy, as enshrined in the 1977 International Emergency Economic Powers Act. The trigger in this case was the ICC's 'Afghan dossier', which was approved by its Appeals Chamber in March 2020, allowing ICC prosecutors to investigate possible crimes in Afghanistan committed not only by the Taliban but also by US and allied forces.[40] Hitherto these international courts had focused on offences in the Global South, and the failure of the ICTY to investigate the possible breach of humanitarian law in the bombing of Serbia in 1999 was particularly egregious. Following the Russian invasion of Ukraine, the ICC announced that it would investigate whether Russia had committed war crimes and crimes against humanity. Neither Ukraine nor Russia are members of the ICC, but the ICC has the power to investigate alleged crimes on the territory of non-member states. In March 2023 the ICC issued an arrest warrant for Putin and his commissioner for children's rights, Maria Lvova-Belova, charging them with the 'war crime' of 'the unlawful deportation and transfer of Ukrainian children from occupied areas of Ukraine to the Russian Federation'.[41]

The tension between multilateralism and state sovereignty intensified. Trump made explicit what had long been American concerns about multilateralism. The attack on the ICC represented the thirty-first set of US sanctions. Previous ones had targeted individual countries (Iran, the DPRK, Russia, Belarus, Syria and others), or individuals associated with human rights abuses, terrorism, interference in US domestic affairs, information security and other issues), but this was the first time in which a body created to police the liberal international order was itself targeted. Sanctions could be imposed against anyone and their associates seeking to detain or prosecute American citizens without US consent. This, no doubt, is a sentiment shared by Putin and his colleagues.

Institutional innovation would not resolve the problem, since the necessary institutions such as the UN globally and the African Union, the OSCE and ASEAN regionally already exist to apply rules through international law, although not all actors play by the agreed rules. There is always a threefold tension between the rules, the interests of the actors and the scale of the challenges. Here at the margins, institutional innovation contributed to global manageability. The Group of Seven (G7) was created in 1975 as an informal forum of the leading industrial democracies (France, Germany, Italy, UK, US, Canada and Japan) to coordinate responses to the instability of the period provoked by Middle Eastern conflicts and the rise in oil prices, as well as the problems of economic growth as the postwar boom period, the *trente glorieuses*, came to a juddering halt. In 1997, Russia was granted membership to create the G8, but by 2012 Putin made it clear that he was no longer interested, and in 2014 Russia was effectively expelled. Following some fraught meetings in the Trump years, Biden used the Cornwall G7 summit in June 2021 to announce that America was back. Even so, the G7 represents only the Global North. The absence of representation from developing and emerging economies led to the call in 1999 for the creation of a Group of Twenty to strengthen the global financial architecture. Global crises require multilateral and representative solutions, and the need for a permanent forum for structured dialogue between advanced and emerging economies led to the creation of the G20.[42] The new body proved its worth, and the first G20 leaders' summit in 2008 adopted measures that helped avert a full-scale depression after the global financial crisis. Annual summits have become a prime steering mechanism for global affairs, accompanied by important side discussions.

The Trump administration undermined the international trading system based on rules while resorting to an increasingly ramified range of sanctions and trade wars. Multilateralism was then tested by the coronavirus pandemic. Despite earlier pandemics, lessons had not been learned and many of the major powers were found wanting. The long-standing American ambivalence about global governance was taken to a wholly new level, with the denigration of the UN, the World Health Organization and the WTO. This led to the marginalisation of the G20, and it was unable to repeat the coordinating role that it had assumed at the time of the global financial crisis. The US even withdrew funding and then in July 2020 announced its formal withdrawal from the 194-member WHO, reducing its budget by almost a quarter. The UN secretary general, António Guterres, in late March called for a worldwide ceasefire to give doctors space to save lives, and some militias in Cameroon, Thailand and the Philippines informally responded. However, disagreements between China and the US held up a UNSC resolution on Covid-19 for months, with the US objecting to any positive reference to the WHO in the text, and when, after three months, in June a resolution was agreed, all reference to the WHO was deleted. By that time 12 million people had been infected and 500,000 had died. By contrast, in 2014 the Security Council had passed a resolution on Ebola in one day. Guterres recognised the weakening role of multilateral institutions: 'Where there is power, there is no leadership, and where there is leadership, there is no power.' There was gridlock on all major issues, including the wars in Libya and Syria. Ghassan Salamé, a former UN special envoy for Libya, provided a broader analysis of what had gone wrong:

In the Cold War, the security council was blocked by the mutual veto. Nowadays we are blocked by the disintegration of the idea of collective security. It is not there in the council. We went in the 80s through a period of financial deregulation . . . what is called neoliberalism … We are now going through a period of deregulation of force. Now everybody who has the means to do something – and a lack of internal constraints, such as a parliament – has the means to act and there is no one to tell them 'you cannot do that'. Let's face it, it makes democracies weaker. Why do we not say that publicly?[43]

China became increasingly adept at assuming leadership roles in multilateral agencies and organisations. This was part of China's activist strategy launched in the 1990s to globalise its influence, as well as forging bodies that exclude the US.[44] China hosts the annual Boao Forum, which first met on Hainan Island in 2001, bringing together regional business leaders and government officials. Chinese citizens assumed important leadership positions in some major international bodies, including the World Bank and IMF, and by 2021 led four of the UN's fifteen specialised agencies: the Food and Agriculture Organization, the International Telecommunications Union, the UN Industrial Development Organization, and the International Civil Aviation Organization. Defenders of liberal hegemony were outraged by this trespass by an illiberal state, arguing that revisionist powers were subverting liberal order from within: 'In fact, the most transformative revisionists engage in rules-based revolutions.' They begin by calling for reform of existing institutions, but over time the 'salami slicing' of 'existing rules and norms can create significant weaknesses in international institutions that undermine the broader institutional order'.[45] The status quo powers correspondingly mobilised to oppose such appointments. According to Lavrov, 'the Americans have shown a tendency to privatise the secretariats of international organisations. They place their people in leading positions. To our great regret, they have influence over countries voting on personnel decisions. Americans are rushing round the world. What sovereign equality of states?'[46] The crisis of multilateralism prompted the creation of alternatives to Charter institutions in which the views of Russia and China were constitutionally entrenched.

As the Greater Eurasian powers and their allies moved into leadership positions in Charter institutions, the Atlantic powers also moved to create alternative structures, a tacit recognition that support for the UN Charter and international law was contingent. In 2018, James Lindsay of the Council on Foreign Relations called for a 'committee to save world order'. Later, the UK sponsored a putative 'club of democracies', consisting of the G7 plus South Korea, India and Australia (the D10). This reprised the Bush-cra idea of a 'league of democracies', designed explicitly to bypass the UN. There were also discussions about creating new bodies comprising only democracies to set standards for the internet, data flows and artificial intelligence. Fulfilling a campaign promise, Biden convened a Summit for Democracy in December 2021. There was considerable controversy over which countries would qualify to attend. In the end 110 were invited. These included some who had drifted towards authoritarianism, like Narendra Modi's India, Jair Bolsonaro's Brazil and Rodrigo Duterte's Philippines, while Singapore was snubbed. The Ukraine war offered an opportunity to restructure international politics. To preserve the collective unity engendered by the war, the idea of creating a G12 was mooted, bringing together the US and its allies to promote economic and security cooperation.[47]

The line between dictatorships and democracies is blurred, but the very idea of dividing the world in this way risks recasting 'America's own imagination of the world in terms of the old black-and-white Cold War paradigm of good against evil'.[48] Other powers were presented not just as rivals but as evil forces, making it harder for policy differences to be resolved through traditional methods of diplomatic engagement. Such a stark Manichean view was not shared by publics. A poll in 2021 by the aptly named Alliance of Democracies Foundation found that 44 per cent of respondents in fifty-three countries were concerned that the US threatened democracy, compared to 38 per cent for China and just 28 per cent for Russia.[49] Nevertheless, Biden argued that he would pursue two tiers of multilateralism – one with allies and the other with rivals.[50] A putative 'alliance of democracies' would represent provocative expression of the great substitution, but it would not thereby resolve the balance to be drawn 'between ideological aspirations and geopolitical necessities'.[51]

In the end, neither institutional innovation nor reform on their own can resolve the problem of rendering multilateral governance more effective. Realists recognise no problem, since for them the competitive pursuit of national interests is the natural state of affairs. Nevertheless, multilateral institutions are critical in managing global challenges. During the coronavirus pandemic, even a country as powerful as the US recognised that responding to the economic, health and social ramifications of the crisis could not be done in isolation. Various cooperative solutions were devised for coronavirus research, and production and distribution of vaccines. Trump preferred bilateral rather than multilateral solutions, yet the US donated $1.2 billion to GAVI, the alliance looking for a vaccine against Covid-19, and under Biden the US was an active participant in Covax, the UN-sponsored programme to distribute vaccines globally. The challenge of multilateralism is ultimately political rather than institutional. As a report by the Friedrich-Ebert-Stiftung put it, 'No regulatory mechanism exists that would bring big powers such as the US or Russia into compliance with the rules. Only an inclusive political process can ensure that big powers support rather than undermine a security order.' This is why they argued that 'A European security order should be built with Russia, not against it.'[52] They were right, but by then it was too late.

12
RISE OF THE POLITICAL EAST

The pre-eminence enjoyed by the political West at the end of the Cold War soon eroded.[1] At most the era of unipolarity and liberal hegemony lasted from 1989 to 2014, the quarter-century of the cold peace. In 1989 the Soviet Union effectively ended its resistance to US primacy (the end of Cold War I), while in 2014 Russia came into overt confrontation with the political West. This was followed in short order by the US opening a second front when it launched a trade war against China in 2018. The Asia-Pacific economies make up a growing proportion of global GDP, while China emerged as a peer competitor. This is an era of multiple centres accompanied by a shift in power from West to East, a process accelerated by the return of interstate war to Europe.[2] The days in which Western powers could claim a global 'sphere of influence' are over. The Ukraine war served to consolidate the political West and US primacy, but there were also perverse effects, especially on European self-identity.[3]

The contradiction between Charter universalism and the particularity of the 'rules-based order' was exposed. The new era of global rivalry reproduced cold war practices, with the character of international politics itself one of the defining issues. The political West portrayed the conflict as one between democracy and autocracy, but this was far from universally accepted and considered self-serving in large parts of the Global South. Supporters assert that the weakening of liberal hegemony and US leadership will herald an era of anarchy and disorder, whereas its critics suggest that sovereign inter-nationalism could inaugurate a more balanced and cooperative world order. The disruption generated by the changed correlation of forces, power transition and multipolarity does not necessarily entail conflict and war – but for this wise statecraft is required. The common challenges facing humanity, above all averting nuclear war and ameliorating climate change, require cooperative solutions. Negative peace solutions trend towards conflict, whereas 'peace as a process' can take the first steps towards a positive peace order. This is no arcane debate between scholars but a matter of life and death.

SANCTIONS AND EXTRA-TERRITORIALITY

The balance of power is one of the conditions for international law, but when the balance is disrupted and the very idea of such a balance deemed illegitimate, then international law and the system in which it is embedded lose credibility. Liberal hegemony's ambition to appropriate Charter internationalism was challenged by other powers, adding a jarring dimension to the return of great-power politics. The era of unipolar US dominance barely lasted three decades, and the chaotic retreat from Afghanistan and the war in Ukraine demonstrated the onset of epochal conflicts. The Western powers and their allies united in response to Russia's invasion and imposed unprecedented sanctions. The refusal of the Global South to sign up signalled that they did not consider Europe's wars theirs. The limits of the political West were exposed.

The world is becoming multipolar, but trade remains centred on the three major regions – the US, the EU and China. In financial matters the US remains the centre of a resolutely unipolar system, providing it with overwhelming power which it has weaponised in recent years. America's use of the world's financial infrastructure as a foreign policy tool reduced trust in US-led financial institutions, leading to dedollarisation and a potential crisis in Washington's ability to run extravagant debts. Fareed Zakaria notes that the US is the 'only country in the world to issue annual report cards on every other country's behaviour', as Washington became 'a bubble, smug and out of touch with the world outside'.[4] Under Obama, sanctions became the 'instrument of first resort', with economic warfare considered the alternative to armed force.[5] The US imposed sanctions on over thirty countries encompassing over a third of the world's population. The punitive and tutelary approach only intensified. For Russia the new era of sanctions began in December 2012 when the US Congress adopted the Magnitsky Act, imposing penalties on those allegedly involved in the death of the auditor Sergei Magnitsky. It took thirty-seven years to repeal the 1974 Jackson–Vanik amendment (tying the USSR's trade status to Jewish emigration), and on the very day that it was lifted the Magnitsky Act started a new cycle.

In March 2014, a series of escalating sanctions were adopted by the US, the EU and some allies in response to Russia's actions in Ukraine, which were drastically escalated when, on 17 July, Malaysia Airlines MH17 was brought down with the loss of all 298 passengers and crew on board. In 2016, the US adopted a Global Magnitsky Act allowing sanctions to be applied against individuals in any foreign jurisdiction responsible for egregious human rights violations, and some other countries adopted versions of their own. The principle of state sovereignty was subordinated to the imperative of punishing human rights abusers. The application of extra-territorial authority is unilateral and does not provide a judicial procedure for accused individuals to prove their innocence. In the dying days of his administration in December 2016, Obama expelled thirty-five Russian diplomats and confiscated some Russian diplomatic properties in response to the Russiagate allegations. Rather than the customary tit-for-tat response, Putin held fire in anticipation of changes in US policy by the new administration. In the event, instead of the hoped-for rapprochement, Trump imposed increasingly punitive measures against Russia.

Putin's 'cronies' became a convenient target, along with assorted oligarchs and genuine criminals. On 25 July 2017, the House of Representatives voted 419–3 and on 28 July the US Senate voted 98–2 to adopt new sanctions, officially called 'Countering America's Adversaries Through Sanctions Act' or CAATSA. The CAATSA sanctions limited the president's ability to ease or lift earlier ones.

Obama enacted sanctions through executive orders but they were now codified in statute and therefore cannot be rescinded by presidential decree.[6] The target was no longer alleged Russian crimes but the Russian corporate economy as a whole. This came on top of the cessation of most military-to-military contacts in the wake of the Ukraine crisis, with the exception of 'deconfliction' procedures in Syria. A reluctant Trump had no choice but to sign the measure on 2 August. CAATSA was a sprawling catch-all law, effectively 'expropriating' the management of foreign policy from the White House. It created a punitive dynamic with the potential to poison relations between Russia and the US for generations to come. The law extended sanctions to countries outside Russia (extra-territoriality) where US corporations or persons provided goods, services and technology for certain projects 'in which a Russian firm is involved', raising the concerns of European leaders and companies (especially those involved in building Nord Stream 2).[7] Congress feared that Trump would weaken or even reverse the Obama-era legislation, and hence closed ranks in a bipartisan manner against the president.[8] The adoption of CAATSA marked a watershed in Russo-US relations and global affairs in general.[9]

In April 2018, Trump imposed the most devastating targeted sanctions yet seen, in part in response to the Skripal affair and the later use of chemical weapons in Douma on the outskirts of Damascus. They targeted what the US claimed were individuals and companies that aided or benefited from what were considered the Kremlin's 'malign activities' around the world, including the alleged interference in the 2016 US presidential election, supplying weapons to Bashar al-Assad and subverting Western democracies. The US Treasury Department imposed sanctions on seven Russian oligarchs, twelve companies they either owned or controlled, and seventeen senior Kremlin officials. Those sanctioned could not do business in the US or gain access to financial markets. Oleg Deripaska, the head of one of the world's largest aluminium companies, Rusal, was targeted 'for having acted or purported to act for or on behalf of, directly or indirectly, a senior official of the Government of the Russian Federation'.[10] The disruption caused havoc in the aluminium market, forcing a partial reversal to allow Deripaska to divest himself of his majority interest in Rusal. The company, like some others, proved 'too big to sanction'.[11]

Prime Minister Medvedev condemned the April 2018 sanctions as 'outrageous and obnoxious' but stressed that they forced Russia to rethink its place in the world. In his view, the policy of containing Russia was part of the West's enduring strategy, and 'Our international partners will continue to pursue it regardless of how our country may be called. They did this with regard to the Russian Empire, and they did this many times with regard to the Soviet Union and Russia.' Russia would adapt and respond through import substitution and improvements to its own social institutions. The assumption was that 'sanctions will remain in place for a long time'.[12] This view was shared by the Russian public, with 43 per cent at that time believing that they would not be lifted in the next few years.[13] Putin himself noted that 'We are not surprised by any restrictions or sanctions: this does not frighten us and will never force us to abandon our independent, sovereign path of development.' And he went on to declare: 'I believe that either Russia will be sovereign, or it will not exist at all.'[14]

Russia imposed a range of counter-sanctions, including those of August 2014 (later extended) on food imports from sanctioning countries. In June 2018, Putin signed legislation allowing 'countermeasures against unfriendly actions' by the US and other foreign countries, effectively an upgrade of a December 2006 law providing for 'special economic measures'. The new law weakened earlier responses mooted by impassioned deputies in parliament, which would have damaged Russia more than the sanctions themselves.[15] The country's economy was reoriented to ensure greater resilience and autonomy. The role of the state in the economy was further increased, and import substitution intensified as self-reliance became the guiding principle.[16] The trend towards deglobalisation accelerated as reliance on domestic resources increased through localisation and import substitution to make the economy more resilient and insulated from external threats.[17] Sanctions acted as a form of ersatz war, entrenching the growing hostility between Russia and the West, a process that was later repeated vis-à-vis China. Beijing in turn sought to insulate itself from potential sanctions and the dominance of the dollar, further accelerating deglobalisation.

With Russiagate hanging over him, Trump bragged that 'there's never been a president as tough on Russia as I have been'.[18] Nevertheless, the draconian 2018 Defending Elections from Threats by Establishing Redlines Act (DETER) was put on hold, and the absence of any demonstrable Russian election interference activity that year lowered the pressure for action. Medvedev warned the US that 'If they introduce something like a ban on banking operations and currency trading, we will treat it as a declaration of economic war. And we'll have to respond to it accordingly – economically, politically, or in any other way, if required.' He added ominously, 'Our American friends should make no mistake about it.' He stressed that Russia has a long history of surviving economic sanctions, and never succumbed to pressure. He accused the US and its allies of employing sanctions to undercut global competition, notably by targeting Russian gas exports to Europe to allow US LNG to fill the market.[19] Russia has a limited arsenal of weapons with which to respond, and most measures – for example, banning the sale of rocket engines, titanium or uranium to the US – damage Russia more than the target. This was well understood, and explains why the country's military, informational and cyber responses were asymmetrical. Overall, the sanctions regime failed to act as a deterrent, and certainly did not prevent Russia from invading Ukraine in 2022. Advocates argue that they should have been even harsher, yet it is unlikely that the outcome would have been different.

Sanctions discredit the liberal order that they are designed to protect. The US is by far the global leader, responsible for 52 per cent (449 out of 850) sanction events between 5 January 2020 and 10 January 2021. China and Russia were minnows in the field, with China accounting for twelve events and Russia for sixteen. Remarkably, the UN accounted for only fifty-eight events, even though the UNSC is the only legitimate legal source of multilateral restrictive measures.[20] Most of the sanctions against Russia were associated with Ukraine, often imposed on individuals because of their alleged ties to the leadership and putative ability to influence policy. A new source of sanctions came from the 'Protecting Europe's Energy Security Act' (PEESA), adopted by Congress in 2019 as part of the 2020 National Defense Authorization Act and reinforced the following year.[21] The goal was to prevent the completion of Nord Stream 2, and thus was directed as much against Germany as Russia. Energy-related sanctions hark back to the Cold War days of the early Reagan period, when Europe resisted American pressure and provided the Soviet Union with the technology to complete large-bore pipelines. The European energy crisis from late 2021 was exacerbated by Russia's refusal to ramp up gas supplies, although contracted quantities were supplied. Russia sought new long-term contracts and regulatory approval of Nord Stream II. Russia's philosophy since the early 1970s had been to 'meet the contract at all costs', although its stoppages to Ukraine in early 2006 and again in early 2009 irreparably damaged its reputation for reliability. Ukraine simply diverted supplies destined for Europe for its own needs, leaving Europe in the cold. Russia intensified its long-term strategy of avoiding unreliable transit states.

The so-called Caesar sanctions on Syria in 2019 exacerbated an already grave humanitarian crisis, with rampant inflation, scarcity of goods and over 80 per cent of the population falling below the poverty line. These sanctions repeated those imposed on Iraq in the 1990s, which by some estimates led to at least half a million avoidable deaths, including thousands of children. The US ignored the appeal by the UN general secretary for a general suspension of sanctions during the pandemic. Sanctions against Iran were maintained, with restrictions on financial transactions making the purchase of foreign medicines almost impossible. Washington vetoed a $5 billion emergency loan Tehran requested from the IMF to buy equipment and medicines from abroad. Sanctions remained against Venezuela, threatening the programme that supplied food and medicines to some 24 million people. Following the Taliban takeover of Kabul in August 2021, Afghanistan's $7 billion of foreign currency reserves held in the US were effectively confiscated, although the country faced famine and a dire lack of funds to pay public employees. The sanctions imposed on Russia in response to the invasion of Ukraine are the most severe ever applied against a major country, and in effect have imposed a policy of collective responsibility. There has been little attempt made to mitigate their impact on the population at large. They target Russian energy, mineral, rare earth and other exports; the financial sector (impounding half of the $630 billion war chest held in the West that Putin had built up precisely to withstand such sanctions); and individuals allegedly associated with the war. The sanctions are not endorsed by the UN, and about forty countries have imposed restrictive measures of some sort. This has left the rest to take advantage of the new trading opportunities, particularly in energy.

America became 'addicted to sanctions', with one wave following another.[22] Between 2000 and 2021, the number of US-sanctioned individuals rose from 1,000 to 10,000, and new economic and other sanctions were imposed on more than 20 countries. Sanctions obviously work best when they offer an incentive to behave in a manner desired by the sanctioning power, but Cold War II is distinctive because ends have been typically decoupled from means. The means are more sanctions; but the end is not always defined. In the case of Ukraine, the goal was Russia's fulfilment of the Minsk Accords. After 2022 this was broadened to include a Russian withdrawal, in the first instance to the borders on the eve of the invasion, but more ambitiously encompassing a return to the 1991 borders. The latter would mean Russia giving up Crimea, annexed in March 2014, as well as the Donetsk and Lugansk people's republics and the Kherson and Zaporozhye regions, incorporated into Russia in September 2022. Now considered part of the national territory, it is hard to envisage Russia abandoning them unless it suffers a severe military defeat. Sanctions have become part of broader containment strategies applied against countries such as Cuba, Russia, Iran, North Korea and increasingly China. They are no longer connected to a designated cause with a specific outcome but have become part of an enduring war of attrition. They are designed to help the US 'trample its rivals' and 'accept US hegemony'.[23] Petro notes that the 'high' provided by sanctions soon wears off, and 'politicians become desperate for another fix.

Friends try to warn Americans that Washington's increasingly erratic behaviour is beginning to hurt them as well.'[24] Trump in August 2018 did suggest that sanctions on Russia could be lifted 'if they do something that would be good for us'.[25] This raised the intriguing question of how this 'good' could be measured, and how it would fit into the evolving dynamics of Cold War II.

Sanctions represent a type of 'foreign policy on the cheap', replacing diplomacy as the main instrument to achieve policy change. They are typically without domestic consequences, although those imposed on Russia in 2022 had devastating blowback effects, raising energy and some commodity prices to unprecedented levels. Sanctions are the functional equivalent of war, targeting civilian populations without any of the restrictive protocols regulating conventional warfare. The collective punishment imposed on Russia from 2022 reinforced regime narratives of a country under siege. Once imposed, sanctions are hard to lift. Congress and the White House compete to see who can be tougher, a symptom of the larger problem in which the UN's role as the main source of legitimate sanctions is eroded. The radicalised liberal hegemony substitutes for the UN and imposes sanction regimes of its own. They are overwhelmingly targeted against countries that challenge the US in one way or another. Sanctions are easy to impose but hard to rescind, and thus become part of the repertoire of 'forever wars'.[26] Imposed often in defence of human rights, there is little evidence that they improve conditions, and in some cases they provoke further repression.

TOWARDS A POST-WESTERN WORLD

International society today comprises over 200 states (193 of whom are members of the UN) and numerous international organisations and NGOs governed by the norms and practices enshrined in the UN Charter and subsequent protocols. The colonial era is long over, but today resistance is focused against the various practices of neo-colonialism – the subordination of the interests of smaller states to great powers and their exploitation by powerful economic actors. The political West's claim that it is the keeper of a special set of 'rules' is challenged by a growing coalition of anti-hegemonic states. Many of these rules coincide with those of the international system, indicating their common origin in Charter cosmopolitanism and liberal internationalism. However, the liberal order is also a power system, led by the US and the willing acquiescence of a group of like-minded states. Membership of that group is selective, with acceptance of American hegemony the entry price. This is where the problems begin, and countries such as Russia and China in the final analysis found the cost too high. The benefits would undoubtedly be bountiful, as the legacy powers in Europe and Japan discovered, but for civilisation states such as China, India and Russia, acquiescence was simply inconceivable.

A group of non-aligned states maintain their distance and try to avoid entanglement in great-power conflicts. The common denominator for non-Western states, usually described as the Global South, is anti-hegemonism. What this means in practice is the assertion of the autonomy of the Charter international system and its fundamental principle of sovereign internationalism. They demand that all states commit equally to Charter principles, including members of the rules-based order. As Cold War II intensified, the political West asserted that its principles, norms and interests took priority over the Charter system, because of the latter's susceptibility to unwarranted pressure from authoritarian states. US support for Charter multilateralism after 1945 was always contingent and selective, but now the politics of substitution became more overt. In turn, the counter-action of other powers also became more intense, rallying under the banner of 'anti-hegemonism'. The state system in the Global South has matured, and there could be no return to the so-called 'global majority' becoming instruments in the cold war struggles of others. The political West was losing its accustomed power.

Already in the 1990s, the Russian foreign minister, Primakov, argued that the world was becoming multipolar. At the time this was more of an aspiration than a reality, but it signalled incipient resistance to the global West's political agenda. He proposed a RIC (Russia, India and China) alignment to resist American dominance through a strategy of competitive coexistence, an idea that drew on

Khrushchev's idea of peaceful coexistence of the 1950s. This implicitly anti-Western stance failed to convince China and India, who doubted the seriousness of the idea and kept their distance. In keeping with the view that Sino-Russian friendship should not be directed against a third party, Beijing failed to respond.[27] In a move redolent with symbolism, as NATO started its bombing campaign against Serbia in March 1999, Primakov turned back his plane heading for Washington. The prospect of reconciling the two models of post-Cold War order receded, and the plane to Washington remains grounded. Meanwhile, multipolarity has become a reality, although far from uncontested.[28] This is the view that distinct models of world order do not necessarily have to come into conflict. In a 'multi-order' world there is room for a diversity of social orders and alignments.[29] In keeping with this idea, Amitav Acharya argues that the coming 'multiplex' world will remain connected economically but accompanied by political and cultural diversity.[30]

International politics reflects the changed balance of power, but the fundamentals of the international system endure. A leading Russian commentator, Fyodor Lukyanov, argues that Beijing intends to forge a 'group of countries that will resist the US, aimed at containing US activities and policies that are harmful to our two countries'.[31] A revitalised Russia and a vigorous China act as a counterweight to the US, confirming the onset of what Fareed Zakaria calls 'the post-American world'. Rising powers enter what he calls the 'Western order' but do so 'on their own terms – thus reshaping the system itself'.[32] This conceptual distinction provides a framework for what he identifies as the 'great project of the twenty-first century': for the US leadership 'to create a new system of international relations, one that produces genuine and effective global cooperation on the great common issues that plague us all'.[33] This is a powerful argument, but fails to distinguish between the overarching international system and the sub-orders that are contained within it. By sheer dint of its power and authority, the US will rightly assume a leadership role in international affairs, but its hegemony is most effective when it works through the institutions of the international system and diplomacy rather than through self-selecting groups of acolytes and supporters.

Zakaria acknowledges that with the exception of the politico-military level, the distribution of global power is shifting away from American dominance. This ushers in the post-American world: 'one defined and directed from many places and many people'.[34] Writing in 2009, he believed that this would not necessarily be an anti-American world, but one in which 'countries in all parts of the world are no longer objects or observers, but players in their own right. It is the birth of a truly global order.'[35] However, as Cold War II intensified, old hierarchies were reinforced and the anti-American element intensified. This was a far from linear process, and adroit and cooperative US leadership can restore US leadership on matters of common concern. Instead, the militarisation of great-power conflict jeopardised the green agenda and the shift to more sustainable economies. The struggle against climate change took a back seat to the struggle against geopolitical rivals. The primacy of the political West is undoubtedly eroding, exacerbated by failure to deal with domestic problems. The triumphal era of liberal hegemony is over. The consolidation of the political West against Russia in the Ukraine war will offer at best temporary relief. Defenders of the international system argue that the outcome of a post-American world is not necessarily chaos. This power shift is considered a second-order change since the fundamentals of the international system remain in place.

Anti-hegemonic sentiments remain disaggregated and inchoate, yet significant and growing. There is no longer a world communist movement to give expression, however compromised, to anti-imperialism. Hence the idea of some sort of 'arc of resistance' is misleading, just as the earlier idea of an 'axis of evil' had been false.[36] Russia, China, India, Iran, Syria, Venezuela and even Turkey agree on some issues, but there is no unified resistance movement. There is competition between the rising powers as much as there is within the political West. This has prompted the idea of a world increasingly out of control, described as 'no one's world'.[37] Russian commentators, by contrast, argue that genuine multipolarity is emerging, despite attempts by the US to recast international politics in terms of a world core (the West) interacting with a world periphery (the non-West).[38] In this model, the US represents the political West and China effectively speaks for the 'Third World', although it explicitly repudiates this neo-Maoist stance. More realistically, the tension between the political West and the greater Eurasian powers (China and Russia) is balanced by a relatively non-aligned Global South, refusing to become the arena for the proxy cold war conflicts or neo-colonial appendages to one or other power.

The outlines of a post-Western world are emerging, no longer tied to 'European' values but nevertheless based on Charter principles. The post-Cold War era of liberal hegemony can now be seen as a time of false universalism, disguising power ambitions in the rhetoric of democratic internationalism. If this view is correct, then the UN and other international institutions had been used when they advanced America's hegemonic goals, but otherwise discarded. If multipolarity is a reality, then the UN has the potential to become a genuine multilateral forum to shape world affairs. This does not imply world government, but the framework for great powers to conduct their business. In this model, China would share leadership and resume its position as a superpower, one that it had temporarily ceded to the European powers.[39] In practice, the opposite has taken place. The new configuration of international politics generated gridlock and recriminations in the UN Security Council, and exacerbated divisions. UN reform is perennially on the agenda, focused above all on adding new members onto the Security Council to represent Africa, Asia and Latin America, with India and Brazil the primary candidates. There is no consensus on the way forward. UN reform itself became yet another source of contention between the political West and the Eurasian powers.

Biden's *Interim National Security Strategic Guidance* in March 2021 recognised the problem, but the response only highlighted the enduring tension between autonomous multilateralism and US primacy. The document insisted that 'the United Nations and other international organizations, however imperfect, remain essential for advancing our interests . . . Across a range of crucial issues . . . effective global cooperation and institutional reform require America to resume a leadership role in multilateral organizations'. Following the turbulence of the Trump years, the terrain and scope of the competition was clear. As the *Guidance* put it: 'It is also critical that these institutions continue to reflect the universal values, aspirations, and norms that have underpinned the UN system since its founding 75 years ago, rather than an authoritarian agenda. In a world of deepening rivalry, we will not cede this vital terrain.'[40] This represented an important restatement of US commitment to the Charter system, both as a principle of association as well as the representation of a set of values, but in declaring that this was yet another arena for contestation, the autonomy of the Charter system was thereby diminished. The forceful assertion of democratic internationalism – the view that the ethical component in relations between states is of overriding importance – exacerbated the long-standing problem of double standards, where allies were treated more indulgently than opponents, but in certain respects ran counter to the pragmatic approach that had allowed the UN to be established in the first place. The sovereign equality proclaimed by the Yalta – Potsdam conferences was institutionalised in the UN Security Council, but now a higher order was advanced by the US and its allies. The open, rules-based and generally progressive model of liberal internationalism has been developing for some 200 years, but its more radical post-Cold War version destabilised its own achievements.[41] Diplomacy gave way to moral crusade.

The reassertion of liberal hegemony undermined sovereign internationalism, the fundamental principle that allows the Charter international system to function. Sovereign internationalism conducted within the constraints of the Charter system tempers the anarchy of the international state system, but by claiming certain tutelary rights over the system (the great substitution identified earlier), a disruptive dynamic was generated and anarchy intensified. It certainly made sense for the US, the dominant power since 1945, to assert that a hierarchy led by itself would provide hegemonic stability, but in conditions of developing bipolarity, if not fully fledged multipolarity, this only intensified Cold War II antagonisms. Realists argue that 'The global order is deteriorating before our eyes', caused by the 'relative decline of US power and the concomitant rise of China', which have 'eroded the partially-liberal rules-based system once dominated by the United States and its allies'. A possible outcome is 'a less prosperous and more dangerous world character-ized by an increasingly hostile United States and China, a remilitar-ized Europe, inward-oriented regional economic blocs, a digital realm divided along geopolitical lines, and the growing weaponiza-tion of economic relations for strategic ends'.

An alternative is a more benign order in which the US, China and other powers 'compete in some areas, cooperate in others, and observe new and more flexible rules of the road designed to preserve the main elements of an open world economy and prevent armed conflict'. There is even the possibility of a more benign outcome in which 'the leading powers actively work together to limit the effects of climate change, improve global health, reduce the threat of weapons of mass destruction, and jointly manage regional crises'.[42] The latter is precisely the positive peace order envisaged by the architects of the end of Cold War I. The earlier failure to achieve such an outcome suggests that the more negative scenario is the most likely. The 'European anarchy' that gave rise to World War I is now global.[43]

THE GLOBAL SOUTH FINDS ITS VOICE

The creation of non-Western associations and international organ-isations signals the emergence of what Oliver Stuenkel calls a 'post-Western' world.[44] Since the end of Cold War I the US has tried to forge an international politics (what Kissinger calls an international order) to suit its perceived interests. This prompted anti-hegemonic behaviour and counterbalancing. This is accompanied by selective and directed deglobalisation by regional alignments to dilute the dominance of the US financial system and to insulate economies from Western sanctions.[45] This is nested within the larger process of post-globalisation: the shortening of supply chains in response to the vulnerabilities exposed by the pandemic, the sustainability agenda in response to climate change, and the technological changes associated with the Fourth Industrial Revolution. Neoliberal state erosion gave way to the reshoring of production and industrial strategies.

With 'Sino-Russian relations . . . closer than they have been at any time in the past fifty years, giving them the chance to reshape the global order to their liking', Kissinger's worst nightmare was coming to pass.[46] His nightmare was better relations between Beijing and Moscow than either of them with Washington. Russia redoubled its efforts to engage with greater Asia, while China saw Eurasia as an essential part of its economic and also its political future. Parallel institutions of globalisation and regionalisation emerged as alternatives to those dominated by the political West (notably the IMF and World Bank), potentially serving as models for a more equitable and inclusive international society. They were post-Western to the degree that their reference point was no longer the political West, although they undoubtedly drew on the practices, culture and experience of the West over the past half-millennium. This marks an important turning point, not because it suggests that the historical West is in some way entering a terminal crisis, but that the era of unmitigated Western predominance is over. The old hierarchies are eroding and a less stigmatised and more self-confident post-Western world is emerging.[47] Status remains important, but its terms are no longer shaped by the preferences of the political West.[48] The existence of increasingly structured alternatives provides a framework for a fundamental restructuring of traditional patterns of international power. This is far more than a power shift; it is the global displacement of accustomed hierarchies.

The Non-Aligned Movement was rejuvenated, and building on its principles the Global South aligned with the Eurasian powers to demonstrate that the age of Western political and economic dominance was over. Russia and China are at the centre of a range of anti-hegemonic alignments, which systematically exclude the US. Sovereign internationalism entails a commitment to value pluralism and the coexistence of different regime types. It also tempers the nascent Cold War II bipolarity, allowing countries in the Global South to escape the emerging ideological and power confrontation. The leading 'post-Western' institutions include the Shanghai Cooperation Organisation (SCO) and BRICS, the alignment of Brazil, Russia, India, China and South Africa.[49] These are part of the broader post-Western architecture of non-alignment, encompassing the ASEAN Plus Three (APT), RCEP and the more specifically

China-centred bodies such as Belt and Road, the 16+1 in Europe, the AIIB, and the Forum on China–Africa Cooperation (FOCAC). Alternative financial institutions are at the heart of the new architecture, including China's Cross-Border Interbank Payment System, as noted, an alternative to the SWIFT payment system. They are part of the grand 'decoupling' between the Atlantic order and the post-Western powers. Half of global trade is still conducted in dollars, but dedollarisation has accelerated as countries seek to insulate themselves from sanctions. Since 2020, most trade between Russia and China has been conducted in roubles and yuan. A high degree of interdependence remains, but a global 'sorting' is taking place into rival camps.

Eurasia and the Global South come together in the BRICS alignment. The body has its roots in Primakov's idea of the RIC countries (Russia, India and China) countering the dominance of the Atlantic powers, and it was then generalised by Goldman Sachs analyst Jim O'Neill in 2001 to bring together what he saw as the five most promising emerging markets.[50] The first meeting of BRIC foreign ministers took place at the UN General Assembly in New York in September 2006, and the inaugural summit of leaders was hosted by Russia in Yekaterinburg in June 2009, and the following year South Africa joined. The grouping is just 'one element in the longer-term historical process by which a Western-dominated international society became global and as one stage in a longer-term revolt against Western dominance that has by no means ended'.[51] It encompasses five very different countries from across the world, each with their own vision of its purpose and rationale, although they unite in defence of sovereign development and non-alignment. Some may be closer to the liberal world order (South Africa), others at times sympathetic to the Trumpian disruption (Jair Bolsonaro in Brazil), others chart an independent course towards modernisation (India), while Russia sees the body as a vehicle for status and developmental goals. Russia and China endow BRICS with geopolitical and geo-economic heft and consider it a model of sovereign internationalism against the practices of substitution. Xi argued that 'BRICS members should firmly uphold multilateralism, safeguard the international order based on international law and the international system with the UN at its core'.[52] They also seek to 'democratise' global economic governance to make it fairer for non-Western states, and thereby revive elements of the 1970s UN-endorsed project for a New International Economic Order (NIEO). The goal initially was strictly focused on geo-economics, using BRICS to coordinate members' positions in the international economy, but over time Beijing began 'to see BRICS as a means of breaking through what it sees as the US' attempt to encircle the country and curb its development'.[53] BRICS is part of China's strategy to become a major world power and to rebalance international politics away from the predominance of the Atlantic system.

Since 2014, the BRICS Development Bank (now called the New Development Bank) helps fill the gap in infrastructure investment funding. Based in Shanghai, its first president came from India. Tension between India and China endures, even though trade ties between the two are the greatest of any BRICS members. Post-Western institutions are far from monolithic, and India has redoubled its efforts to decouple its economy from China's. India remains the leading candidate for a permanent Security Council seat and is committed to reform of the UN.[54] Since the Xiamen meeting in 2017, the BRICS+ format allows numerous other countries to attend. Over a dozen leaders from the Global South attended the 14th BRICS summit in June 2022, hosted virtually by China. The meeting issued the 'Beijing Declaration', asserting that all developing and least developed countries should have a say 'in global decision-making'. Defending multilateralism, the Declaration affirmed that international law and the UN Charter provides for 'an international system in which sovereign states cooperate to maintain peace and security, advance sustainable development, ensure the promotion and protection of democracy, human rights and fundamental freedoms for all'.[55] The principles resonated globally, provoking a rush to join, ranging from Argentina, Algeria, Saudi Arabia, UAE and Bahrain to Egypt and Indonesia.

Belt and Road signalled a new activism in Chinese foreign policy, 'one aimed at shaping China's external environment rather than merely adapting to it'.[56] It was also designed to solve the problem of Chinese domestic over-capacity, while transforming China from a regional to a global power. The programme was incorporated as part of the CPC's Constitution in October 2017. The focus in the first instance was Eurasia, and in particular Central Asia. Beijing assumed that this would be a relatively safe region to make its entry into world affairs. China's Eurasian strategy sought to make the country 'a leading power while avoiding the same security dilemmas and pitfalls that have accompanied other global power transitions in world history'.[57] It will take statecraft of a rare order to achieve these goals. Drawing on ancient Chinese philosophies, Yan Xuetong attributes 'international power transition to the greater capability to reform on the part of the leadership of a rising state than that of the dominant state'.[58] For him, leadership is the key variable, and thus he downplays Gilpin's focus on economic insufficiency or the imperial overstretch problem identified by Paul Kennedy as the primary factor in the decline of a hegemon.

The SCO mitigates some of the traditional security dilemmas in the greater Eurasian region. The 'Shanghai Five' was established in 1996 by Russia, China, Kazakhstan, Kyrgyzstan and Tajikistan, and at a summit in Shanghai in June 2001 it was reformatted as the Shanghai Cooperation Organisation. It was constituted as a regional multilateral mechanism for security and cooperation, joined by Uzbekistan as a founder member. The meeting adopted a charter and constitution and established a permanent secretariat. The SCO Charter pledges 'non-interference and non-alignment' and reaffirmed 'adherence to the goals and principles of the Charter of the United Nations', while seeking to establish 'a new political and economic order'. The June 2004 Tashkent summit expanded the SCO's activities, establishing a Regional Anti-Terrorist Structure (RATS) to deal with drug trafficking and transnational insurgencies, whose office relocated from Shanghai to Tashkent in 2005. In August of that year, Russia and China held their first joint military exercise. The SCO is envisioned as 'the prototype for the new international order envisioned by China', endowed with the ethos of what is dubbed the 'Shanghai spirit', encompassing 'mutual trust, mutual benefit, equality, consultation, respect for diverse civilisations and the pursuit of common development'.[59] The SCO provides a forum for dialogue between its member states and an instrument for political stability. The SCO is the model for multipolarity and the most developed institutional expression of greater Eurasia. Eurasia will no longer be the subject of colonisation but an agent of global self-expression. The Samarkand Declaration issued by the SCO summit in September 2022 condemned 'bloc, ideologised and confrontational approaches' while stressing that the SCO was not directed against other states or organisations but open to 'extensive cooperation with them in accordance with the purposes and principles of the UN Charter'.[60]

Originally established to combat the 'three evils' of terrorism, separatism and extremism, it later expanded its agenda of security cooperation, although it was far from becoming a substantive 'security community', where members reflexively turn to each other for security and dependable peace.[61] The SCO does not have binding collective security commitments, and it has not attempted to create mechanisms for preventive diplomacy or conflict resolution. In certain respects it is comparable to the OSCE, but in an environment where the guiding principle is sovereign internationalism it has thrived rather better. It certainly has no ambition to become an Eastern NATO. This role is taken up, although limited to post-Soviet Eurasia, by the Collective Security Treaty Organisation (CSTO), a Moscow-led military alliance comprising Russia, Armenia, Belarus, Kazakhstan, Kyrgyzstan and Tajikistan. However, the CSTO lacks NATO's ramified institutional development and Article 5 security guarantees (although a weaker Article 4 commitment exists). Chinese aspirations to turn the SCO into more of a multilateral economic cooperation body was blocked by its other members, including Russia, because of concerns over China's economic dominance. They preferred to rely on traditional forms of post-Soviet cooperation. Russia considered the SCO more of a political organisation than an instrument for economic integration, while the CSTO is its favoured instrument for regional security cooperation. Instead, China advanced its economic ambitions in other ways, including the AIIB, while BRI developed 'functionally complementary and mutually reinforcing' ties with the SCO. An SCO development bank has been proposed, to work closely with the BRICS New Development Bank and the Eurasian Development Bank.

Russia favoured SCO enlargement, supporting full membership for India and Pakistan while Iran's membership was initially conditional on the nuclear and sanctions issues being resolved. China was more hesitant, fearing that its influence would be diluted by the addition of another large regional power, especially one with which it had long had tense relations and with whom the border issue remains unresolved. Enlargement was also a matter of concern in Central Asia, with Uzbekistan in particular fearing being overshadowed by other regional powers. In the end, India and Pakistan joined as full members at the Astana summit in June 2017, and Iran in June 2023, overcoming objections from the Central Asian states faced with the return of the Taliban to power in Kabul. Three countries enjoy observer status (Afghanistan, Belarus and Mongolia) and nine are categorised as 'dialogue partners' (Turkey, Saudi Arabia, Egypt, Armenia, Azerbaijan, Cambodia, Nepal, Qatar and Sri Lanka), encompassing over half of the world's population. No fewer than eleven countries have expressed a desire to join, and Belarus has completed the necessary procedures. The SCO provides a forum for the resolution of conflicts between its members, but enlargement has imported some intractable issues. China's border dispute with India led to outright war in 1962, and the two faced off against each other in 2017 at Doklam, and in June 2020 there was a deadly clash in the Galwan valley on the Line of Actual Control (LAC) in the Himalayas. This posed a major challenge to Russia, which acted as a mediator between the two.

INDIA'S QUIET RISE

The original RIC triangle, as advanced by Primakov, was challenged by the rise of national populism in India and a more assertive approach in China. This tempted India to align more closely with the US to balance against Beijing, and Washington's Indo-Pacific strategy sought to capitalise on this. However, India, like Russia, tries to avoid being drawn too closely into the Sino-American confrontation, although neither could avoid it entirely.[62] India resisted US attempts to block the $5.2 billion mega-deal purchase of the Russian S-400 anti-missile system, considering it essential for its national security. The US, of course, was not keen for Russia to sell arms to anybody, and this became something of a test of wills. Russia stepped in to offer India co-production and technology transfer in the defence industries, thus encouraging the development of India's defence manufacturing. Total trade between India and Russia in 2019 stood at $11.6 billion, dwarfed by the $110 billion between Russia and China. In addition, India and Russia are engaged in joint military R&D and manufacturing, including the BrahMos missile and the licensed production of Sukhoi 30MK1 fighter jets, with plans for joint helicopter, rifle and frigate production. The two countries agree on multipolarity, but their views differ on regional issues and relations with the US and China.[63]

Russia's July 2021 *National Security Strategy* described relations with India as a 'special privileged strategic partnership'. Earlier that year the two countries announced the establishment of a '2+2' dialogue for the first time between their respective foreign and defence ministers. Lavrov reassured New Delhi that 'Russia has no plans to sign a military accord with China', and the two worked together on Covid-19 vaccine manufacturing and distribution programmes. Nevertheless, there were numerous points of tension.[64] On Afghanistan there were concerns that a nascent 'Russia–China–Pakistan axis' would exclude India from any influence over the country, a problem that became even more acute after the Taliban takeover in August 2021. Russia's defence sales to Pakistan are considered an irritant rather than a threat. On Iran the two sides were aligned, supporting the JCPOA and its revival, allowing India to exploit its investment in Iran's Chabahar port.

India supported the US notion of the 'Indo-Pacific', since it became a pillar of the new geopolitical narrative, but resists entrapment in the 'primacist' geography that the term implies.[65] In the Ukraine war India maintained a position of principled neutrality, abstaining in UN votes and refusing to impose sanctions. In practice,

India took advantage of deep discounts to increase oil purchases and sign long-term contracts. Despite the pressure from Washington, Russo-Indian ties remain strong. In September 2021, India took delivery of the first instalment of the S-400 air defence system. In one of Putin's rare trips abroad during the pandemic, a number of economic and defence agreements were signed during his brief visit in December 2021. Relations were once again described as a 'special and privileged strategic partnership', reminiscent of the strong Soviet–Indian ties, although New Delhi insisted that it would continue to maintain an independent foreign policy.[66] India took part in the Vostok joint military drills, although soon after at the Samarkand SCO summit in September 2022 Modi warned Putin that today is 'not an era of war'. Nevertheless, he reassured Putin about their 'unbreakable friendship'.[67]

In 2022, India overtook the UK to become the world's fifth-largest economy, and it is still growing fast. India maintains its traditional stance of neutrality and non-alignment.[68] Its model of international politics is 'cooperative pluralism', a synonym for sovereign internationalism.[69] This means the primacy of the UN and international law accompanied by a refusal to align unequivocally with either side in the emerging global Cold War. India retains friendly ties with Russia and is a member of BRICS and the SCO, but at the same time it is a member of the Quad. India has resisted US attempts to turn the Quad into a full alliance directed towards the containment of China. India also firmly disassociated itself from the AUKUS group, established to contain China. This spirit of independence is reflected in the revival of the RIC grouping, the three leading greater Eurasian powers meeting in a narrower format than the full BRICS. The February 2022 Sino-Russian Joint Statement was very much in keeping with Indian thinking on cooperative pluralism. This was manifested in plans for the 7,200-kilometre International North–South Transportation Corridor (INSTC), a network of ship, rail and road routes connecting Russia with India through Iran.

Despite US attempts to woo India, accompanied by the threat of the imposition of CAATSA sanctions, the partnership between

Russia and India endures. However, both sides understand that in a dynamic great-power environment, 'Countries have to forge one set of friends on one issue and another set on a second issue. India and Russia are mature enough to understand this dynamic.'[70] Indian foreign policy is still shaped by anti-colonial nationalism, as well as by the search for 'status in a hierarchical international system'. This is an 'identity-driven' approach, shaped by India's civilisation, large territory and population, growing economy and commitment to non-alignment, combining to reinforce the view that India is destined to be a great power.[71] It refuses to force the pace, and hence is a reticent great power.[72] Above all, the creation of a set of post-Western institutions suggests that international society is now delivering on the promises of the post-colonial era. The age of Western primacy is waning.

CONCLUSION

There is no escape from cold war. Whatever the outcome of current confrontations, one thing is certain: there will be costly and prolonged global conflicts along multiple dimensions. The dissolution of Soviet communism offered the prospect of a new security order in Europe and an era in which international law and norms would render peace more likely than conflict. The idea of a 'lost peace' does not imply that at some metaphysical level 1989–91 marked a rupture in the fabric of human destiny to overcome the tragic cycle of conflict, retribution and war. Nevertheless, some more substantive peace order was possible, a positive peace based on the achievements of the generations who had created and nurtured the Charter international system and the values on which it is based. This book does not appeal to some idealised vision of the universal harmony of interests, but it does ask some straightforward practical questions: did the end of the ideological divisions of the Cold War make possible some sort of enduring peace order; could the multilateral agencies (above all the UN) at the heart of the 1945 international system have come into their own, freed now from the Cold War overlay of bloc politics and ideological contestation; and was there an opportunity to manage great-power relations to ensure that peace and development took priority over conflict and hierarchy?

313

BACK TO BASICS

We now know that the answer to all three questions is in the negative. This book has provided a conceptual framework to explain the failure and traced the factors that led to the fleeting ideal of a positive peace giving way to renewed cold war. There is a fundamental unity to the entire period between 1945 and 2022. Within the framework of the Charter international system, various political orders contend and their fortunes wax and wane as the balance of power shifts (the old-style Soviet notion of the 'correlation of forces'). The competitive dynamic – of communism versus capitalism, democracies versus autocracies – endows the entire period with the characteristics of a negative peace, alleviated only briefly following the fall of the Berlin Wall. The logic of cold war is persistently reproduced, although great-power conflict is constrained by nuclear deterrence. In the end, more than any earlier crisis, the war in Ukraine threatened the very existence of the Charter international system. In previous confrontations the 1945 system provided a framework for conflict resolution, whereas in this case the system itself was at issue. Moscow and Beijing asserted that authoritarian states should have the same rights as democratic ones, whereas the 'alliance of democracies' discourse undermined the fundamental principle of sovereign equality.

Who won the Cold War and who lost the peace? Posing the question in terms of winners and losers is itself a form of defeat. The distinctive character of the late 1980s was not simply the end of the military confrontation that divided Europe and embroiled the superpowers in wars across the globe, but the view that a substantive peace order was possible. The sentiment is powerfully expressed by David Cornwell (better known as John le Carré) in his acceptance speech at the Olof Palme Prize ceremony on 30 January 2020:

When the cold war ended and the western world was still congratulating itself, Smiley felt betrayed, and so did I. And [Olof] Palme [the former Swedish prime minister] would have felt betrayed, if he had lived long enough. Where was the promised peace we had all been waiting for? Where was the Great

Vision? The reconciliation? The nuclear disarmament treaty that Palme had been tirelessly working for? Where was the Marshall Plan that would pull battered nations off their knees? And above all, where was the voice of hope and renewal?[1]

The absence of such voices is remarkable. Gorbachev continued to uphold the principles that had inspired perestroika and the end of the Cold War, but after 1991 he was a voice in the wilderness. Former dissidents in Eastern Europe very quickly turned into partisans of NATO enlargement and thereby lost the moral edge they had gained in their struggle against communist authoritarianism and their critiques of consumerist modernity and militarism. The political West basked in its apparent victory over communism, but this only intensified the contradictions that had provoked the Cold War in the first place. In the 1990s Russia plunged into crisis, and when it emerged it was unable to formulate a positive vision of a modernity of its own. In the East, China continued its spectacular rise, but when it was ready to defend sovereign internationalism and the autonomy of the postwar international system it failed to embed its national and geopolitical concerns in a universally inspirational manner. By contrast, the postwar US-led system enjoyed a universal appeal, although the contradiction remained between the inspirational language in which it was framed and the harsh realities of geopolitical ambition.

The various 'constitutional' documents of the post-Cold War I era sought to consolidate a positive peace order: the Charter of Paris and the Vienna, Istanbul and Astana declarations. Despite the prevalence of great-power confrontation, elements of a positive peace were generated by the systemic foundations of the post-Cold War order. Charter principles fostered some genuine achievements in the multilateral management of global affairs and in specific domains of culture, health and human rights. For a moment at the end of Cold War I it looked as if a new paradigm would allow the Charter system and its principles to flourish, and the competitiveness of international politics to be constrained. Deepening cooperative internationalism could combine the indivisibility of security with freedom of choice on the basis of common developmental goals. In the end 'old thinking' prevailed and traditional divisions returned.

The twenty-five years of the cold peace between 1989 and 2014 failed to resolve any of the fundamental problems of European security. Relations between Russia and the Atlantic powers were troubled from the outset, and soon set on a declining trajectory, although marked by moments when the cooperative spirit revived. For Russia, NATO enlargement represented not only a betrayal of the verbal assurances given at the time of German unification that the alliance would not move 'one inch to the east', but above all a provocation that only intensified the security dilemma that it was intended to avert. NATO was justified by the need to deal with the consequences of its own existence. The security dilemma intensified as the arms control architecture crumbled, and ballistic missile installations were built in Romania and Poland.

The circle could have been squared by the creation of some overarching pan-continental security structure, but US policy-makers resolutely opposed uncontrolled innovations. European pan-continentalism inevitably challenged the supremacy of US-led Atlanticism. Russia's slide into chaos in the 1990s and the brutal conduct of its Chechen wars, and then the dismantling of the liberal constitutional state from the 2000s, confirmed the need for liberal hegemony and US leadership. For the Atlantic powers, the enlargement of the zone of peace and security could only ultimately work to Moscow's benefit, avoiding a return to a cycle of conflicts between small states and the tensions between the great powers, which brought Europe to catastrophe in 1914 and which plagued the interwar years. By contrast, Russia considered the nineteenth-century Concert of Europe the golden age of diplomacy, inaugurating one of the most pacific periods in European history. It was also a founder member of the Charter international system, which created a mini-concert of powers in the form of the permanent members of the UNSC. Moscow's failure to commit consistently to one or another model – postwar multilateralism or the concert of great powers – generated confusion and distrust.

The Russo-Ukrainian war threatens the foundations of the postwar international system, but it also gives a new impetus to the political emergence of the Global South. The brinkmanship of the political West and Russia's immoderate ambitions have returned the scourge of war to Europe, demonstrating once again the Global North's inability to transcend its divisions. The Global South is mobilising the resources offered by Charter internationalism to challenge the political West's dominance. Anti-hegemonic alignments challenge the predominance of the old powers. This is accompanied by an irrevocable rupture between Russia and the political West, likely to endure as long as both are constituted in their present form. Russia's resources and future now lie in the global post-Western camp, challenging its identity as a European society. The Charter international system faces an even greater epochal challenge. The political West may be tempted to formalise the great substitution, throw off the constraints of Charter multilateralism and create a separate 'rules-based order' in some sort of 'Union of Democracies'. In the meantime, its hegemony is challenged, and the fate of the United Nations stands in the balance. Positive peace looks more unrealistic than ever.

FALSE HOPES

Gorbachev presented the end of the Cold War and the Soviet transformation as a moral victory for all of humanity and of the Charter international system. At the historic signing ceremony for the INF treaty in December 1987, Gorbachev outlined the choice facing humanity:

> Civilization has approached a dividing line, not so much between different systems and ideologies, but between common sense and mankind's feelings of self-preservation, on the one hand, and irresponsibility, national selfishness, prejudice – to put it briefly, old thinking – on the other. . . . What matters now is that we cannot let those opportunities pass, and must use them as fully as possible to build a safer and more democratic world, free from the trappings and the psychology of militarism.[2]

Lauded in the West for bringing the Cold War to a relatively peaceful end, his project was far broader than that. If his vision of East–West reconciliation and the transformation of international politics had prevailed, then the world today would be a very different place. Washington refused to allow the intellectual initiative to pass to Moscow, and instead advanced its own rather more partial vision of the post-Cold War peace order. Presenting the political West as the 'winner', the road lay open for Atlantic expansion and ultimately even the notion of a 'global NATO'. The Soviet collapse undermined the viability of Gorbachev's transformational agenda. Gorbachev's repudiation of Cold War practices was outflanked by Yeltsin's repudiation of the Soviet Union itself. The ground was cut from under Gorbachev, and for the rest of his life he became a lone voice. This does not mean that his ideas were discredited. The substance of what he had to say remains as relevant as when it was first voiced.

The positive peace order promised at the end of the Cold War was only partially institutionalised and remained declaratory. There was no post-Cold War peace conference, and instead two models of the new order contested. Both drew on the same normative well-spring, although emphasised different aspects – the freedom of choice versus the indivisibility of security. The difference of emphasis disguised the far more profound clash between different visions of the post-Cold War order. For Moscow it meant the reassertion of sovereign internationalism and ultimately multipolarity, a diversity of states and social systems united under the protection of the Charter international system. Instead, the Soviet collapse created a space in which the maximalist ambitions of neoconservatives and liberal internationalists thrived, including exceptionalist ideas about global primacy and the liberal transformation of the world.

Inevitably, it was post-communist Russia that found itself on the frontline. Moscow considered itself part of the winning coalition that had ended the Cold War, but the prestige gained by Gorbachev was not easily bequeathed to Yeltsin. Russia was recognised as the continuer state to the Soviet Union, assuming its obligations, privileges and treaty responsibilities, and at the same time it considered itself a great power, with the sovereign right to assess its own history and to judge its own pace of domestic transformation. Russia embarked on a perilous journey of transformation based on a triple repudiation:

against the geopolitics of cold war; against the structures of the Soviet Union; and against the ideology and 'totalitarian' practices of Leninist socialism. Russia assumed the troubled burden of the Soviet legacy, however much it tried to disassociate itself from it. This double role as victim and perpetrator fostered much misunderstanding and ambivalence, which endure to this day. Russia failed to build robust democratic institutions, which only deepened the gulf between Russia and the political West. This left Russia a disgruntled and increasingly hostile outsider to a peace order that it believed it had co-created.

A window of opportunity appeared to exist, prompting the fundamental question: could the undoubted triumph (if not 'victory') of the political West over the Soviet Union and its ideology have been institutionalised in a new form of benign internationalism regulated by Charter internationalism, allowing a more balanced and multilateral form of international politics to emerge? This multipolar form of sovereign internationalism would have removed the sting of 'defeat' from Russia and created a pathway for China's return as a global great power. The end of the 'American century' would never be easy, especially since a substantive body of opinion in the US denied that there was an end in sight anyway.[3] Nevertheless, the intensely conflictual character of twenty-first-century international politics was not pre-ordained.[4] Changes in international political economy also indicated that a new era of peace and development was on the cards. Advocates of globalisation in the early post-Cold War years argued that a post-national era had opened up because of technological and communications innovations. These were reinforced by the deep interdependence generated by enhanced trade and financial flows and global production and supply chains.[5] It was assumed that the swelling global middle class would generate pressure for constitutional and accountable government.

The peace was lost. Well before the Ukraine war in 2022, it was clear that there were fundamental problems in the European security order, reflecting larger dilemmas in international politics. Democratisation was perceived as an instrument to advance the interests of the political West, undermining its domestic legitimacy in Russia and elsewhere. Globalisation sharpened antagonisms and intensified contradictions at the local level. Problems of authoritarianism, under-development, illiberalism and societal fragmentation came to the fore. William Burns lamented that 'A more durable twenty-first-century European security architecture has eluded us in nearly three decades of fitful attempts to engage post-Cold War Russia.'[6] Why did so many agreements and declarations in favour of peace give way once again to conflict? As Burns puts it, despite the clear limits to America's ability to shape global politics, evident in relations with Yeltsin's Russia in the 1990s, 'there was still a presumption that Moscow had little alternative to accepting a subordinate, if grudging, role in Europe'. NATO expansion 'stayed on autopilot as a matter of US policy, long after its fundamental assumptions should have been reassessed. Commitments originally meant to reflect interests morphed into interests themselves.'[7] In other words, process took the place of substance, and principle trumped pragmatism. The consolidation of what was assumed to be an expansive peace order generated conflict that ultimately destroyed the peace.

The history that putatively ended in 1989 did not simply resume in 2014. Issues that rekindled confrontation in 2014 predate the fall of communism and reach back even beyond 1945 and World War II. Questions of national identity and national interest, great-power competition, status concerns and the balance of power are enduring themes of the modern state system and of the earlier dynastic and imperial polities. Conflicts and wars have accompanied human history from the earliest days. The myth of the end of history and the reign of peace has also been an enduring and alluring vision, typically accompanied by war and vicissitudes. This explains why the concept of revolution became so popular in the twentieth century, offering the prospect of transcending class conflict and war between nations. The attraction of communism had drastically faded by the end of the twentieth century, as it became clear that it simply reproduced old conflicts in new forms. The idea of revolution as a fundamental turning point in human affairs gave way to a more traditional understanding of 'revolution' as another turn of the wheel of human history, where the cycle of rise, maturity and decline of civilisations and states is as old as humanity itself.

Each turn of the wheel contains novel elements, thus marking each cycle with characteristics of its own. Since 1945, international politics has been conducted in the shadow of nuclear weapons but today technological changes and the development of hypersonic and space weapons transform the strategic environment, but not the patterns of history in which they are embedded. The return of China to global status is part of a much larger cycle, and the gradual reassertion of India marks no less of a potentially irreversible shift towards multipolarity. In brute economic terms, China's power equals that of the US, but its character as a 'peer competitor' is not clear – is the challenge to US primacy as a superpower or to the way of life of the Atlantic powers as a whole?[8] There is much consternation about the return of great-power politics, but in certain respects this had never gone away. The existence of 200 sovereign states today is a novel feature, each with its own claims in international politics. Cold War I was accompanied by decolonisation and the establishment of the contemporary state system. In some cases these states were able to take on and defeat great powers, as with Algeria in the 1950s and Vietnam in the 1970s, a pattern that continues to this day. The humiliating retreat of the US and its NATO allies from Afghanistan in August 2021 is a stark reminder of the limits of democratic internationalism and its associated nation-building aspirations.

Gaddis talked in terms of a 'long peace', covering most of the original Cold War. However, we now know (to use the title of his analysis of the conflict) that 1989 marked only a temporary pause in the multidimensional conflict that we call 'cold war'. The enduring tension between the Charter international system, generating a network of institutions and norms, and the sub-orders within it was not transcended, and in fact intensified. The Soviet order, claiming to represent a revolutionary alternative to Western modernity, proved to be an inept challenger, although no less dangerous for that. Its disappearance left the field open for the US-led liberal international order. Enjoying a quarter-century of unipolar dominance, the ambitions of what now became liberal hegemony knew no bounds. American leadership undoubtedly has an important role to play, but it works best within the terms of the original postwar settlement:

leadership embedded in robust multilateralism, but now engaging not only with allies (as required during the Cold War) but also through new forms of engagement with potential adversaries. The US remains a separable but essential part of the international system.

By 2014, the era of unparalleled dominance had ended, but no new forms of interaction had been devised. Russia drew a red line in Ukraine, while China cast off the 'hide and bide' strategy to assert its new authority. Russia and China aligned in defence of the international system that they co-created, and thus the struggle today is about interpretations of how that system will work and whether the liberal powers will enjoy special tutelary privileges. The long-term trend is for power to shift to the Asia-Pacific region accompanied by the re-emergence of China as a major power, and therefore resistance to hegemony and dominion will intensify. The resulting struggle will shape the twenty-first century. India, Brazil, Japan, Indonesia, Mexico, Vietnam and many other powers are gaining in self-confidence and strive for greater autonomy and responsibility. They are finding their voice, and the language they speak is sovereign internationalism.

PATHWAYS TO PEACE

Amid these enduring and novel global processes, are there viable pathways to peace? Amid a plethora of proposals and plans, one thing is clear – there can be no going back to the past for models of the future.[9] While the Charter international system remains the institutional bedrock, it allows a multiplicity of combinations in international politics. Numerous schemes have been advanced to overcome the security dilemma in Europe and Asia. One idea is to reconstitute some sort of 'concert of powers'. Putin stressed that the permanent members of the UNSC bore a special responsibility, and he repeatedly called for a summit of the five mature nuclear states. This was not revisionism since the proposal was in keeping with the principles of sovereign internationalism. He stressed that 'We have consistently advocated the preservation and strengthening of the key role of the United Nations in international affairs', including in the settlement of regional conflicts.[10] This is true, but a return to a formal concert of powers, while offering the prospect of some 'grand bargain' to resolve pressing strategic issues, would only accentuate the anachronistic character of the Security Council's permanent membership. The 1945 arrangement integrated the leading powers as an operative mechanism into the international system, and any separation as some sort of world government would challenge the efficacy and legitimacy of the Charter system as a whole.

A persistent theme is the need for US restraint to allow the 'normalisation' of US foreign policy. This entails a new type of security order 'that the United States doesn't pretend to police – limiting, not intensifying, great power conflict'.[11] This would include the revival of arms control, new conventional force agreements, and global cooperation on climate change and pandemics. It is assumed that this would lead to a more rational and responsive grand strategy, one less driven by the urge to expand. As for Europe, Michael O'Hanlon argues, 'by promising eventual membership yet with no timetable and no interim security guarantees to those nations, we have managed to paint a giant bullseye on the backs of Ukrainian and Georgian friends'. Instead,

> It is time to envision a new security architecture for eastern Europe. The core concept should be one of permanent non-alignment for countries of eastern Europe. Ideally, the zone would include Finland and Sweden; Ukraine and Moldova and Belarus; Georgia, Armenia and Azerbaijan; and finally Cyprus plus Serbia. Under such a new construct, these non-aligned countries' existing security affiliations with NATO and/or Russia could be continued, but formal security commitments would not be extended or expanded by Brussels or Moscow.[12]

Such notions return us to the debates of the 1990s, but those times are gone and, with the war in Ukraine, irrevocably lost. There is general agreement that a 'Yalta II' grand bargain would be an inappropriate way to resolve the conflict, with the great powers once again dividing up spheres of interest. Peace is always about compromise, and in the nuclear age total peace, like total war, is inconceivable.

Kennedy ended his American University speech in 1963 with an exhortation that remains as valid now as it was then: 'We must do our part to build a world of peace, where the weak are safe and the strong are just. We are not helpless before that task or hopeless for its success. Confident and unafraid, we must labour on towards a strategy of peace.'[13]

New ideas are required, and that has been the purpose of this book. More accurately, it is perhaps not so much new ideas as new ways of thinking about old problems that are required. A 'gestalt switch' in this context would mean acknowledging the almost incomprehensible complexity of international politics while recognising that pathways to peace can be found within the framework of the current international system. Above all, the idea of peace as a process means recognition of the legitimate interests of others. This is not abstract utopianism of the sort that was current in the interwar years, or even founded on a belief in a fundamental 'harmony of interests'. Instead, competitive relations can be managed within the bounds of diplomacy and common interests. The return of great-power politics is typically viewed through the prism of an *adversarial* balance of power, encompassing power transition theories and zero-sum relationships. However, some sort of equilibrium can be found in international politics through the practices of an *associational* balance of power, a concept with deep roots in antiquity. This was the idea behind the various international systems since the 1713 Utrecht settlement, based on the view that 'no state could be allowed to expand to the point where it threatened the independence of the other states of Europe, and so there needed to be a distribution of power that ensured that no state could overwhelm the system'.[14] The 1945 settlement, however, was dual: the Charter international system incorporated the idea of an associational balance of power in its workings, above all in the Security Council (charter liberalism); but at the same time, it proposed a set of normative principles that transcended classical postulates about the balance of power, spheres of interest and hierarchy. This settlement in turn was flanked by liberal internationalism and its military component, which provided a multilateral format for American power. At the end of Cold War I, liberal internationalism radicalised to become liberal hegemony, representing the triumph of liberal anti-pluralism, thus revoking the settlement that had made the Charter international system possible in the first place. Liberal hegemony repudiates the very notion of a balance of power, and with it the specific institutional format for the representation of the interests of other powers. This usurpation and disruption provoked the return of war in Europe and threatened conflict in Asia.

Equilibria are always fragile and susceptible to disordering. The US remained committed to its European and global alliance system after Cold War I to avoid a return to the type of international politics that provoked the two great wars of the twentieth century. However, we are once again faced with a policy failure of the first order, since the world has once again slipped into confrontations of the sort that provoked the earlier wars. The US deployed its undoubted supremacy to suppress the resurgence of balance of power politics and thus to keep the peace. American hyperpower thereby – wittingly or unwittingly – reincorporated practices of containment that characterised Cold War I. De facto, the US practised an adversarial approach to the balance of power, part of whose strategy was to deny the very premise of a balance of power in international politics. Democratic internationalism assumed that this could become permanent only when all other states conformed to the model of domestic relations drawn from the repertoire of Western liberal democracies. This approach transcended even the idea of an associational balance of power. The terrain for traditional diplomacy and international politics was thereby constricted.

It is now apparent that the original Cold War was not much more than the preamble to a far more substantial, and dangerous, era of contestation. Contrasting models of global order shaped international politics in the post-1945 era, and now contest for predominance. They do so within the framework of an international system based on sovereign nation states competing in an anarchical system for status and benefit, but constrained by the norms and institutions of that system. The parallel order established at the same time was by historical standards unique and genuinely revolutionary. The

US-sponsored liberal world order was always expansive, but after 1989 claimed a universal status that in the end proved damaging to its viability by blurring the distinction between system and order. Charter internationalism was challenged by US hegemony. The intensified emphasis on human rights, while normatively engaging, was accompanied by deterioration in competent statecraft, leading to ill-considered and hubristic interventions. These were not only inept but also costly failures. The 'great substitution', in which a particular order claims to be synonymous with the larger system in which it is embedded, relieved the sub-order of the constraints and moral imperatives of the Charter system in which it operated. An operative software program assumed the characteristics of the hardware system, blurring the fundamental distinction that allowed the system to operate, threatening the system in its entirety.

The tension between the two aspects of postwar international politics was exposed. On the one hand, the postwar settlement sought to 'constitutionalise' international relations, assuming that anarchy could be tamed through institutions, law and norms, enshrining thereby the (relative) equality of states. On the other hand, this constitutional order could not be trusted to operate autonomously and instead the US sponsored its own dual system, the agencies of liberal internationalism (which mostly reinforced the sovereign internationalism of the international system) and the security apparatus devised to fight the Cold War. This equilibrium was sustained as long as the Soviet Union generated constraints, but after 1989 this balance was disrupted. As Hans Morgenthau noted, the Cold War was fought as a crusade and interpreted as a struggle between good and evil. After the Cold War this nationalistic universalism was radicalised to become a struggle to bring 'the true political religion to the rest of the world'. In the absence of a balance of power, international law was subordinated to power and purpose.[15] Hierarchy was abolished in theory but rearticulated in the form of normative universalism.

All states couch their interests in terms of compliance with universal norms and principles, and the contesting states today do so no less than in the past. The earlier struggle between capitalism and revolutionary socialism is exhausted, but new lines of division have emerged. Great-power confrontation is back, but the ideological and normative element is crucial. This book depicted the struggle in terms of contestation between models of globalism as well as between ideologies of civilisation. The 'great substitution' left little scope for anything outside, but it is precisely these 'outsiders' that withdrew their consent to the hegemony of the US-led liberal order. However, while resisting hegemony in all its forms, the anti-hegemonic alignment and non-aligned states are not thereby relieved of responsibility towards the norms of the international system. In short, the struggle today is to achieve effective forms of sovereign internationalism in which the diversity of civilisations, developmental paths and social orders is recognised within the framework of Charter governance. This includes responsibility for the maintenance of standards of human dignity that are intrinsic to the system, although this encompasses differing interpretations of the common good. Some prioritise human rights, others social rights, development and national cohesion, while others focus on identity politics, but the system is flexible enough to encompass them all. When Utopia is presented as a single model, it soon turns into its opposite.

The proximate cause of renewed cold war was the failure to create some sort of enduring and inclusive structure of European security. The Atlantic powers did not set out deliberately to humiliate and marginalise the country, but there was no place for Russia in the new order. The slide into Cold War II thus became a tragedy in the classical sense, in which people of good intent become the victims of their own fate. It cannot be explained by sinister motives on either side (although there was no shortage of that), but by the larger institutional and ideational framework of the post-Cold War world.[16] For offensive realists, the structurally anarchic character of international relations predisposes states to contest for power and survival, while the dominant power seeks to maintain its primacy through the practices of hegemonic internationalism. By contrast, liberals focus on the domestic character of a regime, and through democratic internationalism seek to extend the peace that is generated by the modern state at home into the global arena. This book suggests that the two approaches can be combined through substantive commitment to

Charter principles and above all respect for the two aspects of sovereign internationalism: non-interference combined with cooperative internationalism.

Tragedy in the Greek sense is far more than a regrettable occurrence but emerges from the wilful blindness of humans who make choices that give offence to others, provoking the desire for revenge, thus launching a tragic cycle of misdeed and retribution. In Greek tragedy, genuine dialogue is considered a way of achieving empathy for the views of others, opening the way to reconciliation through *catharsis*. Instead, as Petro puts it, 'tragedy results when, by trying to correct an injustice, we unwittingly perpetuate it'.[17] This can be applied to the cold peace as a whole, where the primacy of a particular view of the world was advanced as a universal model. The view that a particular combination of ideas and institutions, derived from a specific cultural and geopolitical context, would apply to countries at dissimilar stages of development and with very different histories and cultures inevitably provoked resistance. The resisting states were only revisionist to the extent that they challenged liberal hegemony; but they were conservative in their defence of the autonomy of the international system and sovereign internationalism. This does not mean giving up on progressive programmes for peace, development and international cooperation. As Richard Ned Lebow puts it in his study of the tragic in politics, postwar realists 'rejected as naïve and dangerous . . . far-reaching proposals for transformations of domestic or international orders, but still believed that the world might be made a better place through incremental changes, instituted through consensus by people who had an enlightened sense of self-interest'.[18]

The international system is more than an artefact of the balance of power or the dominance of liberal order. Changes in the relative balance do not thereby undermine the system. The Charter international system was co-created in 1945, but after 1989 the great substitution blurred the lines between the system and its dominant sub-order. But order is not simply 'an artefact of concentrations of power' – its rules and institutions have a more enduring quality. There has been a complex relationship between American hegemony and the international system.[19] The challenge today is to ensure that the international order governed by relations between states is integrated into the order generated by Charter internationalism. For that to occur, hegemonic ambitions and substitutions have to give way to the equitability generated by sovereign internationalism. The alternative is the breakdown of the Charter international system. If that happens, then we are literally in uncharted waters.

ENDNOTES

INTRODUCTION

1. George Orwell, 'You and the Atomic Bomb', *Tribune*, 19 October 1945, https://www.orwellfoundation.com/the-orwell-foundation/orwell/essays-and-other-works/you-and-the-atom-bomb/.
2. Gerry Simpson, 'Two Liberalisms', *European Journal of International Law*, 12/3, 2001, pp. 539, 560.
3. G. John Ikenberry, *A World Safe for Democracy: Liberal Internationalism and the Crisis of Global Order* (New Haven, CT and London, Yale University Press, 2020).
4. As defined by Antonio Gramsci. See Perry Anderson, *The H-Word: The Peripeteia of Hegemony* (London, Verso, 2017) and James Martin, *Hegemony* (Cambridge, Polity, 2022).
5. Robert D. Kaplan, *The Tragic Mind: Fear, Fate, and the Burden of Power* (New Haven, CT and London, Yale University Press, 2023), p. xiv. He devotes a chapter to 'The Battle of Good against Good', pp. 1–16.
6. Max Weber, 'Politics as a Vocation', in H.H. Gerth and C. Wright Mills, *From Max Weber: Essays in Sociology* (New York, Oxford University Press, 1946), pp. 77–128.
7. Institute for Economics and Peace, *Positive Peace Report 2022*, https://www.economicsandpeace.org/wp-content/uploads/2022/01/PPR-2022-web-1.pdf, p. 2.
8. President John F. Kennedy, 'Commencement Address at American University', 10 June 1963, https://www.jfklibrary.org/archives/other-resources/john-f-kennedy-speeches/american-university-19630610.

1: THE PROMISE OF PEACE

1. Christopher Clark, 'A Rock of Order', review of Wolfram Siemann, trans. Diane Steuer, *Metternich: Strategist and Visionary* (Cambridge, MA, Harvard University Press, 2019), in *London Review of Books*, 8 October 2020, pp. 5–7, at p. 5.

2. E.H. Carr, *The Twenty Years' Crisis, 1919–1939: An Introduction to the Study of International Relations*, reissued with a new introduction and additional material by Michael Cox (London, Palgrave, 2001 [1939]).
3. Discussed in Richard Sakwa, '"New Cold War" or Twenty Years' Crisis?: Russia and International Politics', *International Affairs*, 84/2, March 2008, pp. 241–67.
4. Edward Hallett Carr, *Conditions of Peace* (New York, Macmillan, 1943).
5. G. John Ikenberry, *After Victory: Institutions, Strategic Restraint, and the Rebuilding of Order after Major Wars* (Princeton, NJ, Princeton University Press, 2001).
6. The designation 'Charter international system' draws on the notion of charter liberalism outlined by Simpson, 'Two Liberalisms', and Anne L. Clunan, 'Russia and the Liberal World Order', *Ethics & International Affairs*, 32/1, 2018, pp. 45–59, although the term is in broader usage.
7. Thomas A. Bailey, *Woodrow Wilson and the Lost Peace* (New York, Macmillan, 1944).
8. Ikenberry, *World Safe for Democracy*, p. 140.
9. *The Atlantic Charter*, 14 August 1941, http://www.nato.int/cps/en/natolive/official_texts_16912.htm.
10. Henry Kissinger, *World Order: Reflections on the Character of Nations and the Course of History* (London, Allen Lane, 2014), p. 271.
11. *Convention on the Prevention and Punishment of the Crime of Genocide*, adopted 9 December 1948, entered into force after ratification 12 January 1951, https://www.un.org/en/genocideprevention/documents/atrocity-crimes/Doc.1_Convention%20on%20the%20Prevention%20and%20Punishment%20of%20the%20Crime%20of%20Genocide.pdf.
12. John Charvet and Elisa Kaczynska-Nay, *The Liberal Project and Human Rights: The Theory and Practice of a New World Order* (Cambridge, Cambridge University Press, 2008), pp. 81–109.
13. Cf. David Held, *Democracy and the Global Order: From the Modern State to Cosmopolitan Governance* (Cambridge, Polity, 1995).
14. John Lewis Gaddis, *The Cold War* (London, Penguin, 2005), p. ix.
15. Gaddis, *Cold War*, p. 11.
16. Gaddis, *Cold War*, p. 18.
17. Geoffrey Roberts, *Stalin's Wars: From World War to Cold War, 1939–1953* (New Haven, CT and London, Yale University Press, 2008).
18. For analysis, see Melvyn Leffler, *A Preponderance of Power: National Security, the Truman Administration, and the Cold War* (Stanford, CA, Stanford University Press, 1992); Melvyn Leffler (ed.), *Origins of the Cold War: An International History* (London, Routledge, 2005).
19. David Mayers, *America and the Postwar World: Remaking International Society, 1945–1956* (London, Routledge, 2018).
20. Stephen Wertheim, *Tomorrow the World: The Birth of US Global Supremacy* (Cambridge, MA, Belknap Press, 2020), p. 1.
21. George F. Kennan [X], 'The Sources of Soviet Conduct', *Foreign Affairs*, 25, July 1947, p. 575.
22. Alan Cafruny, Vassilis K. Fouskas, William D.E. Mallinson and Andrey Voynitsky, 'Ukraine, Multipolarity and the Crisis of Grand Strategies', *Journal of Balkan and Near Eastern Studies*, published online 14 June 2022 (emphasis in original).

23. John A. Thompson, 'The Appeal of "America First"', in Robert Jervis et al. (eds), *Chaos in the Liberal Order* (New York, Columbia University Press, 2018), p. 155.

24. Daniel Deudney and G. John Ikenberry, 'The Nature and Sources of Liberal International Order', *Review of International Studies*, 25/2, 1999, pp. 179–96.

25. Odd Arne Westad, *The Global Cold War: Third World Interventions and the Making of Our Times* (Cambridge, Cambridge University Press, 2007).

26. *The North Atlantic Treaty*, Washington DC, 4 April 1949, https://www.nato.int/ cps/en/natolive/official_texts_17120.htm/cps/en/natolive/official_ texts_17120.htm.

27. Glenn Diesen describes this as 'interdemocratic', the effective fusion of democratic instruments, in his *EU and NATO Relations with Russia: After the Collapse of the Soviet Union* (London, Routledge, 2016).

28. John Ruggie, 'International Regimes, Transactions, and Change: Embedded Liberalism in the Postwar Economic Order', *International Organization*, 36/2, 1982, pp. 379–415.

29. Marc Trachtenberg, *A Constructed Peace: The Making of the European Settlement, 1945–1963* (Princeton, NJ, Princeton University Press, 1999).

30. A.J. Williams, *Failed Imagination?: The Anglo-American New World Order from Wilson to Bush*, 2nd edn (Manchester, Manchester University Press, 2007).

31. Available at https://www.nationalarchives.gov.uk.

32. For a detailed analysis, see Michael Cotey Morgan, *The Final Act: The Helsinki Accords and the Transformation of the Cold War* (Princeton, NJ, Princeton University Press, 2018).

33. Conference on Security and Cooperation in Europe, *Final Act*, 1 August 1975, https://www.osce.org/files/f/documents/5/c/39501.pdf.

34. Samuel Moyn, *The Last Utopia: Human Rights in History* (Cambridge, MA, Belknap Press, 2012), p. 150.

35. This was later formulated by the Princeton Project in terms of a project for 'liberal world order' and a global 'Concert of Democracies'. If the UN could not be reformed, then an alternative forum should be created to authorise collective action. G. John Ikenberry and Anne-Marie Slaughter, *Forging a World of Liberty Under Law: US National Strategy Security in the Twenty-First Century* (Princeton, NJ, Woodrow Wilson School of Public and International Affairs, 2006).

36. Fred Halliday, *The Making of the Second Cold War* (London, Verso, 1983).

37. For commentary on how the US began its support for the mujahideen as early as 3 July 1979, when Carter signed the first directive for secret aid to anti-regime forces, see Joe Lauria, 'What a US Trap for Russia Might Look Like', *Consortium News*, 4 February 2022, https://consortiumnews.com/2022/02/04/ what-a-us-trap-for-russia-in-ukraine-might-look-like/.

38. The participation of East German forces was cancelled at the last moment.

39. Mikhail Gorbachev, *Perestroika: New Thinking for Our Country and the World* (London, Collins, 1987).

40. Vendulka Kubálková and A.A. Cruickshank, *Thinking about Soviet 'New Thinking'* (Berkeley, CA, University of California Press, 1989).

41. Robert D. English, *Russia and the Idea of the West: Gorbachev, Intellectuals and the End of the Cold War* (New York, Columbia University Press, 2000).

42. Notably, Vladimir Lomeiko and Anatoly Gromyko, *New Thinking in the Nuclear Age* (Moscow, 1984) (in Russian). I am grateful to Alexei Gromyko (Anatoly's son) for pointing out the importance of this book in the evolution of the NPT. For a study of the role of the *institutchiki* in bringing an end to the Cold War, see Nick Bisley, *The End of the Cold War and the Causes of the Soviet Collapse* (Basingstoke, Palgrave, 2004).

43. Anatoly Chernyaev, *My Six Years with Gorbachev: Notes from a Diary* (Philadelphia, PA, University of Pennsylvania Press, 2000), p. 51.

44. Vladislav Zubok, *A Failed Empire: The Soviet Union in the Cold War from Stalin to Gorbachev* (Chapel Hill, NC, University of North Carolina Press, 2007), p. 344.

45. Francis Fukuyama, 'The End of History', *National Interest*, 16, Summer 1989, pp. 3–17; Francis Fukuyama, *The End of History and the Last Man* (New York, Free Press, 1992). The idea of perpetual peace is from Immanuel Kant, 'Perpetual Peace: A Philosophical Sketch', in *Kant: Political Writings*, ed. Hans Reiss, 2nd enlarged edn (Cambridge, Cambridge University Press, 1991), pp. 93–130.

46. Andrei Sakharov, *Progress, Coexistence and Intellectual Freedom* (New York, W.W. Norton, 1970).

47. 'Gorbachev's Speech to the UN', 7 December 1988, *AP News*, https://apnews.com/article/1abea48aacda1a9dd520c380a8bc6be6.

48. The charge was led by Yevgeny Primakov, who served as foreign minister from January 1996 to September 1998, and then as prime minister to May 1999.

49. Vividly described in his memoir: Andrei Kozyrev, *The Firebird: A Memoir. The Elusive Fate of Russian Democracy* (Pittsburgh, PA, University of Pittsburgh Press, 2019).

50. Dwight D. Eisenhower, 'Chance for Peace Speech', 16 April 1953, https://www.presidency.ucsb.edu/documents/address-the-chance-for-peace-delivered-before-the-american-society-newspaper-editors.

51. Michael J. Glennon, *National Security and Double Government* (Oxford, Oxford University Press, 2015).

52. Dwight D. Eisenhower, 'Military-Industrial Complex Speech', 17 January 1961, https://avalon.law.yale.edu/20th_century/eisenhower001.asp.

53. There is a large literature to suggest that this did indeed happen. See, for example, James McCartney with Molly Sinclair McCartney, *America's War Machine: Vested Interests, Endless Conflicts* (New York, Thomas Dunne Books, 2015).

54. Kennedy, '1963 Commencement'.

55. L. Fletcher Prouty, *The CIA, Vietnam and the Plot to Assassinate John F. Kennedy* (New York, Skyhorse Publishing, 2011).

2: TIME OF GREAT HOPES

1. Archie Brown, *The Human Factor: Gorbachev, Reagan, and Thatcher and the End of the Cold War* (Oxford, Oxford University Press, 1996). The role of Reagan's secretary of state, George Shultz, should be stressed. He faced down those opposed to constructive engagement with Gorbachev's reforms, including anti-Soviet hardliners in the administration such as CIA director William

Casey, CIA deputy director Robert Gates, secretary of defence Caspar Weinberger and assistant secretary of defence Richard Perle. See Philip Taubman, *In the Nation's Service: The Life and Times of George P. Shultz* (Stanford, Stanford University Press, 2023).

2. 'Joint Soviet–United States Statement on the Summit Meeting in Geneva', 21 November 1985, https://www.reaganlibrary.gov/archives/speech/joint-soviet-united-states-statement-summit-meeting-geneva.

3. Ian Clark, *The Post-Cold War Order: The Spoils of Peace* (Oxford, Oxford University Press, 2001), p. 133.

4. '"Europe as a Common Home": Address Given by Mikhail Gorbachev to the Council of Europe', Strasbourg, 6 July 1989, https://chnm.gmu.edu/1989/archive/files/gorbachev-speech-7-6-89_e3ccb87237.pdf.

5. Deborah Welch Larson and Alexei Shevchenko, 'Shortcut to Greatness: The New Thinking and the Revolution in Soviet Foreign Policy', *International Organization*, 57/1, 2003, pp. 77–109. See also Deborah Welch Larson and Alexei Shevchenko, 'Russia Says No: Power, Status, and Emotions in Foreign Policy', *Communist and Post-Communist Studies*, 47/3–4, 2014, pp. 269–79 and Deborah Welch Larson and Alexei Shevchenko, *Quest for Status: Chinese and Russian Foreign Policy* (New Haven, CT and London, Yale University Press, 2019).

6. See, for example, S.N. Eisenstadt, 'Multiple Modernities', *Daedalus*, 129/1, Winter 2000, pp. 1–29.

7. 'Excerpts from Gorbachev's Speech', *New York Times*, 29 July 1986, https://www.nytimes.com/1986/07/29/world/excerpts-from-gorbachev-s-speech.html.

8. Isabella M. Weber, *How China Escaped Shock Therapy: The Market Reform Debate* (London and New York, Routledge, 2021).

9. George Bush and Brent Scowcroft, *A World Transformed* (New York, Knopf, 1998), pp. 42–3.

10. William J. Burns, *The Back Channel: American Diplomacy in a Disordered World* (London, Hurst & Company, 2021), p. 50.

11. Richard Sakwa, 'The End of the Revolution: Mimetic Theory, Axiological Violence, and the Possibility of Dialogical Transcendence', *Telos*, No. 185, December 2018, pp. 35–66.

12. Bush and Scowcroft, *World Transformed*, p. 133.

13. 'The Gorbachev Challenge', *Time Magazine*, 132/5, 19 December 1988. The cover stated: 'Gorbachev's Newest Peace Offensive Challenges the U.S. to Respond'.

14. For analysis, see Wolfgang Streeck, 'The EU after Ukraine', *American Affairs*, 20 May 2022, https://americanaffairsjournal.org/2022/05/the-eu-after-ukraine/.

15. George H.W. Bush, 'A Europe Whole and Free: Remarks to the Citizens in Mainz', 31 May 1989, http://usa.usembassy.de/etexts/ga6-890531.htm.

16. Reflected in the transcript of the discussions, 'The Malta Summit and US–Soviet Relations: Testing the Waters Amidst Stormy Seas. New Insights from American Archives', no date, http://www.wilsoncenter.org/publication/the-malta-summit-and-us-soviet-relations-testing-the-waters-amidst-stormy-seas.

17. Bush and Scowcroft, *World Transformed*, pp. 163–7.

18. William H. Hill, *No Place for Russia: European Security Institutions since 1989* (New York, Columbia University Press, 2018), p. 39. See also Robert Service, *The End of the Cold War* (London, Pan, 2016), pp. 416–26.

19. Analysed by Raymond L. Garthoff, *The Great Transition: American–Soviet Relations and the End of the Cold War* (Washington DC, Brookings Institution Press, 1994).

20. George H.W. Bush, 'Address Before a Joint Session of the Congress on the Persian Gulf Crisis and the Federal Budget Deficit', 11 September 1990, http://www.presidency.ucsb.edu/ws/?pid=18820.

21. Fareed Zakaria, *The Post-American World* (New York, Norton, 2009), p. 35.

22. These are detailed in Svetlana Savranskaya and Tom Blanton, 'NATO Expansion: What Gorbachev Heard', National Security Archive, George Washington University, 12 December 2017, https://nsarchive.gwu.edu, from where the quotations are taken.

23. See Mary Elise Sarotte, *1989: The Struggle to Create Post-Cold War Europe* (Princeton, NJ, Princeton University Press, 2009); Mary Elise Sarotte, 'Perpetuating US Pre-eminence: the 1990 Deals to "Bribe the Soviets Out" and Move NATO In', *International Security*, 35/1, 2010, pp. 110–37; Mary Elise Sarotte, 'A Broken Promise? What the West Really Told Moscow about NATO Expansion', *Foreign Affairs*, 93/5, Sep/Oct 2014, pp. 90–7.

24. As stated by Burns, *Back Channel*, p. 55.

25. Mary Elise Sarotte, *Not One Inch: America, Russia and the Making of Post-Cold War Stalemate* (New Haven, CT and London, Yale University Press, 2022).

26. As argued by Joshua R. Itzkowitz Shifrinson, 'Put it in Writing: How the West Broke its Promises to Moscow', *Foreign Affairs*, 29 October 2014, www.foreignaffairs.com/articles/united-states/2014-10-29/put-it-writing/articles/united-states/2014-10-29/put-it-writing.

27. As Hill notes, 'rivers of ink' have been spilled over what precisely was promised and there is still no consensus on the issue: *No Place for Russia*, p. 45. For a review of the issue and the decision to enlarge, see Angela Stent, *Putin's World: Russia against the West and with the Rest* (New York, Twelve, 2019), pp. 113–21.

28. Joshua R. Itzkowitz Shifrinson, 'Deal or No Deal?: The End of the Cold War and the U.S. Offer to Limit NATO Expansion', *International Security*, 40/4, 2016, p. 11. Shifrinson argues that the spirit of the 'deal' was violated, and he is right.

29. This is the view of Fyodor Lukyanov in an interview with Vladimir Pozner, Meduza, 26 January 2022, https://www.1tv.ru/shows/pozner/vypuski/gost-fedor-lukyanov-pozner-vypusk-ot-24-01-2022.

30. Mike Eckel, 'Did the West Promise Moscow that NATO Would Not Expand?', RFE/RL Russia Report, 19 May 2021, https://www.rferl.org/a/nato-expansion-russia-mislead/31263602.html.

31. 'The Malta Summit: Transcript of the Bush–Gorbachev News Conference at Malta', 3 December 1989, *New York Times*, 4 December 1989, p. A12, https://www.nytimes.com/1989/12/04/world/the-malta-summit-transcript-of-the-bush-gorbachev-news-conference-in-malta.html.

32. *The London Declaration on a Transformed North Atlantic Alliance*, 6 July 1990, https://www.cvce.eu/en/obj/the_london_declaration_on_a_transformed_north_atlantic_alliance_6_july_1990-en-9c5fa86b-12a0-4f59-ad90-e69503ef6036.html.

33. Mary Kaldor, *New & Old Wars: Organized Violence in a Global Era*, 3rd edn (Cambridge, Polity, 2012).
34. *Charter of Paris for a New Europe* (Paris, CSCE, 1990), https://www.oscepa. org/documents/all-documents/documents-1/historical-documents-1/673-1990-charter-of-paris-for-a-new-europe/file.
35. Clark, *Post-Cold War Order*, Preface and *passim*.
36. Michael Wines, 'Bush and Yeltsin Declare Formal End to Cold War: Agree to Exchange Visits', *New York Times*, 2 February 1992, p. 1; see also Kozyrev, *Firebird*, p. 4.
37. George H.W. Bush, 'State of the Union Address', 28 January 1992, https://www.nytimes.com/1992/01/29/us/state-union-transcript-president-bush-s-address-state-union.html.
38. Zbigniew Brzezinski, *The Grand Chessboard: American Primacy and Its Geostrategic Imperatives* (New York, Basic Books, 1997), p. 100.

3: HOW THE PEACE WAS LOST

1. John J. Mearsheimer, 'Bound to Fail: The Rise and Fall of the Liberal International Order', *International Security*, 43/4, Spring 2019, pp. 7–50.
2. G. John Ikenberry, *Liberal Leviathan: The Origins, Crisis, and Transformation of the American World Order* (Princeton, NJ, Princeton University Press, 2011), p. 70.
3. Seth Connell, 'Flashback: Time Magazine Brags about US Interfering in Russian Election', *Federalist Papers*, 17 July 2017, https://thefederalistpapers. org/us/time-magazine-interfered-russia.
4. Stephen Kotkin, 'The Cold War Never Ended: Ukraine, the China Challenge, and the Revival of the West', *Foreign Affairs*, 101/3, May/June 2022, p. 67. See also his 'Russia's Perpetual Geopolitics: Putin Returns to the Historical Pattern', *Foreign Affairs*, 95/3, May/June 2016, pp. 2–9.
5. William C. Wohlforth and Vladislav Zubok, 'An Abiding Antagonism: Realism, Idealism, and the Mirage of Western–Russian Partnership after the Cold War', *International Politics*, 54/4, 2017, pp. 405–19.
6. Jack F. Matlock, *Super-Power Illusions: How Myths and False Ideologies Led America Astray – and How to Return to Reality* (New Haven, CT and London, Yale University Press, 2010), p. xi.
7. Ikenberry, *World Safe for Democracy*, p. 257. For a more extensive version of the argument, see G. John Ikenberry, 'The End of Liberal International Order?', *International Affairs*, 94/1, 2018, pp. 7–23.
8. Richard Sakwa, 'The Perils of Democratism', *Polis: Political Studies*, No. 2, 2023, pp. 88–102.
9. Charles Krauthammer, 'The Unipolar Moment', *Foreign Affairs*, 70/1, Winter 1990/1, pp. 23–33.
10. David P. Calleo, *Follies of Power: America's Unipolar Fantasy* (Cambridge, Cambridge University Press, 2009), p. 4.
11. Charles Krauthammer, 'The Unipolar Moment Revisited', *National Interest*, 70, Winter 2002/3, p. 17.
12. As predicted by Christopher Layne, 'The Unipolar Illusion: Why Great Powers Will Arise', *International Security*, 17/4, Spring 1993, pp. 5–51; and for

later analysis, his 'The Unipolar Illusion Revisited: The Coming End of the United States' Unipolar Moment', *International Security*, 31/2, 2006, pp. 7–41.

13. Calleo, *Follies of Power*, p. 4.
14. Krauthammer, 'Unipolar Moment', p. 25.
15. Krauthammer, 'Unipolar Moment', p. 29.
16. Krauthammer, 'Unipolar Moment', p. 32.
17. Krauthammer, 'Unipolar Moment Revisited', p. 7.
18. 'To Paris, US Looks Like a "Hyperpower"', *New York Times*, 5 February 1999, https://www.nytimes.com/1999/02/05/news/to-paris-us-looks-like-a-hyper-power.html.
19. Krauthammer, 'Unipolar Moment Revisited', p. 10.
20. David Rieff, *At the Point of a Gun: Democratic Dreams and Armed Intervention* (New York, Simon & Schuster, 2005).
21. Krauthammer, 'Unipolar Moment Revisited', p. 12.
22. Krauthammer, 'Unipolar Moment Revisited', p. 13.
23. Krauthammer, 'Unipolar Moment Revisited', p. 14.
24. Krauthammer, 'Unipolar Moment Revisited', p. 17.
25. Slavoj Žižek, *Iraq: The Borrowed Kettle* (London, Verso, 2004), pp. 5–6.
26. Timothy J. Lynch, *In the Shadow of the Cold War: American Foreign Policy from George Bush Sr. to Donald Trump* (Cambridge, Cambridge University Press, 2020), p. 9.
27. Lynch, *Shadow of the Cold War*, p. 83.
28. Clark, *Post-Cold War Order*, pp. 4, 7.
29. Bush and Scowcroft, *World Transformed*, p. 12.
30. Branko Marcetic, 'Ignoring Gorbachev's Warnings', *Current Affairs*, 7 September 2022, https://www.currentaffairs.org/2022/09/ignoring-gorbachevs-warnings. The article provides a compendium of references in which Gorbachev condemns the exaggerated ambitions of US foreign policy and NATO enlargement.
31. Hill, *No Place for Russia*, pp. 60, 65.
32. Kenneth N. Waltz, 'The Emerging Structure of International Politics', *International Security*, 18/2, 1993, pp. 75–6; idem., 'Structural Realism after the Cold War', *International Security*, 25/1, Summer 2000, p. 19.
33. Hill, *No Place for Russia*, p. 3.
34. Richard Sakwa, 'The Cold Peace: Russo-Western Relations as a Mimetic Cold War', *Cambridge Review of International Affairs*, 26/1, 2013, pp. 203–24.
35. Kozyrev, *Firebird*, p. 63.
36. Kozyrev, *Firebird*, p. 136.
37. Kozyrev, *Firebird*, p. 93.
38. Kozyrev, *Firebird*, p. 123.
39. Sergei A. Karaganov, *Russia: The New Foreign Policy and Security Agenda* (London, Centre for Defence Studies, No. 12, June 1992), p. 8.
40. Kozyrev, *Firebird*, p. 130.
41. Evgeny Primakov, *A World Challenged* (Washington DC, Brookings Institution Press, 2004).
42. Edward Lozansky, 'The Roots of US–Russia Crisis that Could Lead Us to WWIII', *Washington Times*, 28 October 2020, https://www.washingtontimes.com/news/2020/oct/28/roots-us-russia-crisis-could-lead-us-wwiii-can-doo/.

43. For an excoriating critique, see Stephen F. Cohen, *Failed Crusade: America and the Tragedy of Post-Communist Russia* (New York, W.W. Norton, 2000).

44. Gulnaz Sharafutdinova, *The Red Mirror: Putin's Leadership and Russia's Insecure Identity* (Oxford, Oxford University Press, 2020).

45. James M. Goldgeier, *Not Whether but When: The US Decision to Enlarge NATO* (Washington DC, Brookings Institution Press, 1999). See also James M. Goldgeier and Michael McFaul, *Power and Purpose: US Policy toward Russia after the Cold War* (Washington DC, Brookings Institution Press, 2003).

46. The view of retired Colonel-General Leonid Ivashov, interviewed by Yevgeny Senshin, 'One Year Ago, I Warned that Invading Ukraine Will Hurt Russia', Republic.ru, 9 February 2023, MEMRI *Special Dispatch* No. 10489, 14 February 2023, https://www.memri.org/reports/retired-russian-colonel-general-ivashov-one-year-ago-i-warned-invading-ukraine-will-hurt.

47. Kozyrev, *Firebird*, p. 192.

48. Kozyrev, *Firebird*, p. 193.

49. Kozyrev, *Firebird*, p. 197.

50. Quoted by Kozyrev, *Firebird*, p. 200.

51. Kozyrev, *Firebird*, p. 201.

52. Kozyrev, *Firebird*, p. 205.

53. Kozyrev, *Firebird*, p. 201.

54. The speech is summarised by Kozyrev, *Firebird*, p. 283. For his view, see Andrei Kozyrev, 'Partnership or Cold Peace?', *Foreign Policy*, No. 99, Summer 1995, pp. 3–14.

55. Kozyrev, *Firebird*, p. 271.

56. Burns, *Back Channel*, p. 108.

57. Brzezinski, *Grand Chessboard*, p. 101.

58. Zbigniew Brzezinski, 'A Plan for Europe', *Foreign Affairs*, 74/1, Jan/Feb 1995, p. 35.

59. Burns, *Back Channel*, p. 92.

60. Burns, *Back Channel*, p. 105.

61. Burns, *Back Channel*, p. 107.

62. William J. Perry, 'How the US Lost Russia – and How We Can Restore Relations', *Outrider*, 5 September 2022, https://outrider.org/nuclear-weapons/articles/how-us-lost-russia-and-how-we-can-restore-relations.

63. Jeff Gerth and Tim Weiner, 'Arms Makers See Bonanza in Selling NATO Expansion', *New York Times*, 29 June 1997, https://www.nytimes.com/1997/06/29/world/arms-makers-see-bonanza-in-selling-nato-expansion.html.

64. Burns, *Back Channel*, p. 109.

65. Burns, *Back Channel*, p. 110.

66. Federico Fubini, 'Sergey Karaganov: We Are at War with the West. The European Security Order is Illegitimate', *Corriere della Sera*, 8 April 2022, https://www.corriere.it/economia/aziende/22_aprile_08/we-are-at-war-with-the-west-the-european-security-order-is-illegitimate-c6b9fa5a-b6b7-11ec-b39d-8a197cc9b19a.shtml.

67. Mary Elise Sarotte, 'Containment beyond the Cold War: How Washington Lost the Post-Soviet Peace', *Foreign Affairs*, 100/6, Nov/Dec 2021, p. 23.

68. Brzezinski, *Grand Chessboard*, p. 201.

69. Brzezinski, *Grand Chessboard*, p. 213.

4: THE ROAD TO WAR

1. Sergei Kortunov, 'Is the Cold War Really Over?', *International Affairs* (Moscow), 44/5, 1998, pp. 141–54; summarised by Paul Goble, 'Cold War Continued', *The New Presence*, March 1999, p. 6.
2. From *The Independent*, 21 March 1991, p. 11, in Paul D'Anieri, *Ukraine and Russia: From Civilized Divorce to Uncivil War* (Cambridge, Cambridge University Press, 2019), p. 59.
3. Savranskaya and Blanton, 'NATO Expansion'.
4. Mikhail Gorbachev, 'I Am Against All Walls', *Russia beyond the Headlines*, 16 October 2014, https://www.rbth.com/international/2014/10/16/mikhail_gorbachev_i_am_against_all_walls_40673.html.
5. George F. Kennan, 'A Fateful Error', *New York Times*, 5 February 1997, p. A23.
6. 'Former Policy-Makers Voice Concern over NATO Expansion', *Global Beat*, 26 June 1997. The letter and commentary can be found at https://www.armscontrol.org/act/1997-06/arms-control-today/opposition-nato-expansion.
7. Michael MccGwire, 'NATO Expansion: "A Policy Error of Historic Importance"', *Review of International Studies*, 24/1, 1998, pp. 23–42; reprinted in *International Affairs*, 84/6, November 2008, pp. 1282–301.
8. Rajan Menon, 'The Strategic Blunder that Led to Today's Conflict in Ukraine', *The Nation*, 10 February 2022, https://www.thenation.com/article/world/nato-clinton-ukraine-russia/.
9. Thomas Friedman, 'Foreign Affairs; Now a Word from X', *New York Times*, 2 May 1998.
10. Marcetic, 'Ignoring Gorbachev's Warnings'.
11. Marcetic, 'Ignoring Gorbachev's Warnings'.
12. *Founding Act on Mutual Relations, Cooperation and Security Between NATO and the Russian Federation*, 27 May 1997, https://www.nato.int/cps/su/natohq/official_texts_25468.htm.
13. Samantha Power, *A Problem from Hell: America and the Age of Genocide* (New York, Basic Books, 2002).
14. Philip Cunliffe, *The New Twenty Years' Crisis: A Critique of International Relations, 1999–2019* (Montreal, McGill-Queen's University Press, 2020), p. 48.
15. Lynch, *Shadow of the Cold War*, p. 92.
16. David Ignatius, 'Who Robbed Russia?', *Washington Post*, op-ed, 25 August 1999.
17. 'Text of Yeltsin Statement after Start of Bombing', *Reuters*, 24 March 1999, in Johnson's Russia List, No. 3109, 25 March 1999, http://www.russialist.org/archives/3109.html.
18. Hill, *No Place for Russia*, p. 169.
19. Information from one of the leading participants, who prefers to remain anonymous.
20. OSCE, *Istanbul Document 1999*, https://www.osce.org/files/f/documents/6/5/39569.pdf.
21. OSCE, *Astana Commemorative Declaration: Towards a Security Community*, December 2010, https://www.osce.org/files/f/documents/b/6/74985.pdf.
22. Russian Foreign Ministry, 'Foreign Minister Sergey Lavrov's Answer to a Media Question', 27 January 2022, https://www.rusemb.org.uk/fnapr/7060.

23. Eckel, 'Did the West Promise Moscow'.

24. Burns, *Back Channel*, p. 233. He had earlier warned that 'Ukraine remained the reddest of red lines for Putin', p. 222.

25. Burns, *Back Channel*, p. 237.

26. Burns, *Back Channel*, p. 238.

27. Olexiy Haran and Mariia Zolkina, 'The Demise of Ukraine's "Eurasian Vector" and the Rise of Pro-NATO Sentiment', PONARS Eurasia Policy Memo No. 458, 16 February 2017, https://www.ponarseurasia.org/the-demise-of-ukraine-s-eurasian-vector-and-the-rise-of-pro-nato-sentiment/.

28. Burns, *Back Channel*, p. 239.

29. From the WikiLeaks US cables published in 2010, Clinton Fernandes, *What Uncle Sam Wants: US Foreign Policy Objectives in Australia and Beyond* (London, Palgrave Macmillan, 2019), p. 62. Burns later develops these points in his memoir, *The Back Channel*.

30. Strobe Talbott, *The Russia Hand: A Memoir of Presidential Diplomacy* (New York, Random House, 2003).

31. Noam Chomsky, *World Orders Old and New* (New York, Columbia University Press, 1994).

32. Cf. Ikenberry, *World Safe for Democracy*, p. 181.

33. Bill Clinton, 'I Tried to Put Russia on Another Path', *Atlantic*, 7 April 2022, https://www.theatlantic.com/ideas/archive/2022/04/bill-clinton-nato-expansion-ukraine/629499/.

34. Hill, *No Place for Russia*, p. 116.

35. John H. Herz, 'Idealist Internationalism and the Security Dilemma', *World Politics*, 2/2, January 1950, p. 157.

36. Christopher Clark, *The Sleepwalkers: How Europe Went to War in 1914* (London, Penguin, 2013), p. 333.

37. Clark, *Sleepwalkers*, p. 350.

38. On the practice of the security dilemma, see Robert Jervis, *Perception and Misperception in International Politics* (Princeton, NJ, Princeton University Press, 1976).

39. Hill, *No Place for Russia*, p. 169.

40. Hill, *No Place for Russia*, p. 193.

41. Yascha Mounk, 'Democracy on the Defense: Turning Back the Authoritarian Tide', *Foreign Affairs*, 100/2, March/April 2021, p. 168.

42. Madeleine Albright on NBC's *Today* show on 19 February 1998.

43. Angela Stent, *The Limits of Partnership: US–Russian Relations in the Twenty-First Century* (Princeton, NJ, Princeton University Press, 2014), pp. 49–81.

44. Lynch, *Shadow of the Cold War*, p. 73.

45. Anatol Lieven, 'How the "Global War on Terror" Failed Afghanistan', *National Interest*, 1 January 2022, https://nationalinterest.org/feature/how-%E2%80%98global-war-terror%E2%80%99-failed-afghanistan-198735.

46. Burns, *Back Channel*, p. 197.

47. Burns, *Back Channel*, p. 213.

48. 'Russian President Vladimir Putin's Speech at the 2007 Munich Conference on Security Policy', Kremlin.ru, 10 February 2007, http://en.kremlin.ru/text/appears/2007/02/118109.shtml.

49. NATO, *Brussels Summit Communiqué*, 14 June 2021, paras 43, 44, https://www.nato.int/cps/en/natohq/news_185000.htm.

50. Ben Aris, 'It's Time for a New Pan-European Security Treaty', *Intellinews*, 9 April 2021, https://www.intellinews.com/moscow-blog-it-s-time-for-a-new-pan-european-security-treaty-207608/.
51. Dmitry Medvedev, 'Speech at Meeting with German Political, Parliamentary and Civic Leaders', Berlin, 5 January 2008, https://www.europarl.europa.eu/meetdocs/2004_2009/documents/dv/d_ru_20080617_04_/D_RU_20080617_04_en.pdf.
52. 'Medvedev Address at the World Policy Forum', Evian, 8 October 2008, cited by Bobo Lo, 'Medvedev and the New European Security Architecture', Centre for European Reform (CER), July 2009, https://www.cer.eu/sites/default/files/publications/attachments/pdf/2011/pbrief_medvedev_july09-741.pdf, p. 4.
53. President of Russia, 'Draft of the European Security Treaty', 29 November 2009, http://en.kremlin.ru/events/president/news/6152.
54. For full discussion, see Hill, *No Place for Russia*, pp. 290–6.
55. The White House, 'Remarks by Vice President Biden at 45th Munich Conference on Security Policy', 7 February 2009, https://obamawhitehouse.archives.gov/the-press-office/remarks-vice-president-biden-45th-munich-conference-security-policy.
56. For an overview, see Stent, *Limits of Partnership*, pp. 211–34.
57. NATO, *Strategic Concept: Active Engagement, Modern Defence*, adopted by Lisbon summit, 19–20 November 2010, https://www.nato.int/nato_static_fl2014/assets/pdf/pdf_publications/20120214_strategic-concept-2010-eng.pdf, p. 10.
58. NATO, *Strategic Concept*, p. 29.
59. NATO, *Strategic Concept*, p. 25.
60. Hill, *No Place for Russia*, p. 311.
61. C-Span, 'Bush Saw Putin's Soul', 17 June 2001, https://www.c-span.org/video/?c4718091/user-clip-bush-putins-soul.
62. 'US Vice President Biden Says Putin Has No Soul', *Reuters*, 21 July 2014, https://www.reuters.com/article/us-usa-russia-biden-idUSKBN-0FQ1CU20140721.
63. Richard Sakwa, *Putin Redux: Power and Contradiction in Contemporary Russia* (London and New York, Routledge, 2014).
64. Thomas Rid, *Active Measures: The Secret History of Disinformation and Political Warfare* (London, Profile Books, 2020).
65. Michael McFaul, 'Putin, Putinism, and the Domestic Determinants of Russian Foreign Policy', *International Security*, 45/2, Fall 2020, pp. 95–139.
66. Eloquently articulated by John J. Mearsheimer, 'Why the Ukraine Crisis is the West's Fault: The Liberal Delusions that Provoked Putin', *Foreign Affairs*, 93/5, Sep/Oct 2014, pp. 77–89.
67. For a detailed analysis, see Derek Averre, *Russian Strategy in the Middle East and North Africa* (Manchester, Manchester University Press, 2024).

5: AMERICA BETWEEN LEADERSHIP AND PRIMACY

1. Debated in Jacob Heilbrunn, 'What is the Purpose of American Foreign Policy?', *National Interest*, 20 December 2020, https://nationalinterest.org/feature/what-purpose-american-foreign-policy-174848.

2. The argument of Wertheim, *Tomorrow the World*. See also Ikenberry, *World Safe for Democracy*, pp. 177–211.
3. The term was coined by Henry Luce in 1941, when the new model of hegemonic internationalism was being forged. Henry R. Luce, 'The American Century', *Life*, 17 February 1941, pp. 61–5.
4. Zakaria, *Post-American World*.
5. Available at https://www.jhwolfanger.com/uploads/2/3/1/1/23113918/primary_source_john_q_adams_fourth_july_address.pdf (emphasis in original).
6. Pippa Norris and Ronald Inglehart, *Cultural Backlash: Trump, Brexit, and Authoritarian Populism* (Cambridge, Cambridge University Press, 2019).
7. Stanley Hoffmann, *Primacy or World Order: American Foreign Policy since the Cold War* (New York, McGraw-Hill, 1978).
8. The classic case is made by Barry Posen, *Restraint: A New Foundation for US Grand Strategy* (Ithaca, NY, Cornell University Press, 2014).
9. Christopher Layne, *The Peace of Illusions: American Grand Strategy from 1940 to the Present* (Ithaca, NY, Cornell University Press, 2006).
10. Joseph S. Nye, *Soft Power: The Means to Success in World Politics* (New York, Public Affairs, 2004).
11. Stephen G. Brooks and William Wohlforth, *America Abroad: Why the Sole Superpower Should Not Pull Back from the World* (New York, Oxford University Press, 2018).
12. Bush and Scowcroft, *World Transformed*, p. 564.
13. Bush and Scowcroft, *World Transformed*, pp. 565–6.
14. John Mueller, *The Stupidity of War: American Foreign Policy and the Case for Complacency* (Cambridge, Cambridge University Press, 2021).
15. George Kennan, 'Morality and Foreign Policy', *Foreign Affairs*, 64, 1985/6, p. 212.
16. David Hendrickson, *Republic in Peril: American Empire and the Liberal Tradition* (Oxford, Oxford University Press, 2017). For discussion, see Patrick Lawrence, 'David Hendrickson: We Need a "New Internationalism"', *The Nation*, 2 November 2018, https://www.thenation.com/article/david-hendrickson-foreign-policy-interview/.
17. The rationality of the administration is defended by Lynch, *Shadow of the Cold War*, pp. 103–61.
18. Kaplan, *Tragic Mind*, p. 97.
19. Kaplan, *Tragic Mind*, p. xiii.
20. *The National Security Strategy of the USA*, 17 September 2002, https://2009-2017.state.gov/documents/organization/63562.pdf.
21. Quoted by Blake Hounshell, 'Russia's Splendid Little War', *Foreign Policy*, 12 August 2008, https://foreignpolicy.com/2008/08/12/russias-splendid-little-war/.
22. Ron Suskind, 'Faith, Certainty and the Presidency of George W. Bush', *New York Times Magazine*, 17 October 2004, https://www.nytimes.com/2004/10/17/magazine/faith-certainty-and-the-presidency-of-george-w-bush.html.
23. As enunciated by H.R. McMaster, 'The Retrenchment Syndrome: A Response to "Come Home America"', *Foreign Affairs*, 99/4, July/Aug 2020, pp. 183–6.
24. Robert Kagan, 'A Superpower, Like It or Not: Why Americans Must Accept Their Global Role', *Foreign Affairs*, 100/2, March/April 2021, pp. 28–39. See

also his 'The Price of Hegemony: Can America Learn to Use Its Power?',
Foreign Affairs, 101/3, May/June 2022, pp. 10–19.

25. Robert Kagan, *The Jungle Grows Back: America and Our Imperiled World* (New York, Vintage, 2018).

26. Glennon, *National Security and Double Government*.

27. Stephen M. Walt devotes an instructive chapter to 'defining the "blob"' in *The Hell of Good Intentions: America's Foreign Policy Elite and the Decline of US Primacy* (New York, Farrar, Straus and Giroux, 2019), pp. 91–136.

28. Hunter DeRensis, 'The Blob Strikes Back', *National Interest*, 23 October 2019, https://nationalinterest.org/feature/blob-strikes-back-90476.

29. For her views, see Jeane Kirkpatrick, 'A Normal Country in a Normal Time', *National Interest*, Fall 1990. For her overall perspective, see *Making War to Keep Peace* (New York, Regan Books, 2007).

30. An argument developed by Anatol Lieven and John Hulsman, 'Ethical Realism and Contemporary Challenges', *American Foreign Policy Interests*, 28, 2006, pp. 413–20.

31. There are substantive critiques from the anti-militarist and peace movement left, and from traditional conservatives on the right, but their ability to shift the consensus has been limited.

32. Patrick Porter, *The False Promise of Liberal Order: Nostalgia, Delusion and the Rise of Trump* (Cambridge, Polity Press, 2020), p. 21.

33. For details, see Noam Chomsky and Vijay Prashad, 'Cuba Is Not a State-Sponsor of Terrorism', *CounterPunch*, 14 February 2023, https://www.counter punch.org/2023/02/14/cuba-is-not-a-state-sponsor-of-terrorism/.

34. Michael McFaul, *Advancing Democracy Abroad: Why We Should and How We Can* (New York, Rowman & Littlefield, 2009).

35. Kit Klarenberg, 'US Regime-Change Agency NED Admits Its Role in the Strife in Belarus', RT.com, 21 May 2021, https://www.rt.com/russia/524296-western-meddling-belarus-power-change/.

36. David Ignatius, 'Innocence Abroad: The New World of Spyless Coups', *Washington Post*, 22 September 1991, https://www.washingtonpost.com/archive/opinions/1991/09/22/innocence-abroad-the-new-world-of-spyless-coups/92bb989a-de6e-4bb8-99b9-462c76b59a16/.

37. Kit Klarenberg, 'Anatomy of a Coup: The NED in Ukraine', *The Scrum*, 26 May 2022, https://thescrum.substack.com/p/anatomy-of-a-coup. See also Alec Luhn, 'National Endowment for Democracy is First "Undesirable" NGO Banned in Russia', *Guardian*, 28 July 2015, https://www.theguardian.com/world/2015/jul/28/national-endowment-for-democracy-banned-russia.

38. Michael McFaul, 'Cold War Lessons and Fallacies for US–China Relations Today', *Washington Quarterly*, 43/4, 2020, p. 16.

39. For analysis, see James Headley, 'Challenging the EU's Claims to Moral Authority: Russian Talk of "Double Standards"', *Asia Europe Journal*, 13/3, 2015, pp. 297–307.

40. Glenn Diesen, 'The EU, Russia and the Manichean Trap', *Cambridge Review of International Affairs*, 30/2–3, 2017, pp. 177–94.

41. Alexander Cooley and Daniel Nexon, *Exit from Hegemony: The Unravelling of the American Global Order* (New York, Oxford University Press, 2020).

42. Walter Russell Mead, 'The End of the Wilsonian Era: Why Liberal Internationalism Failed', *Foreign Affairs*, 100/1, Jan/Feb 2021, pp. 123–37.

43. Michael Anton, 'The Trump Doctrine', *Foreign Policy*, 20 April 2019, https://foreignpolicy.com/2019/04/20/the-trump-doctrine-big-think-america-first-nationalism/.
44. Aaron Ettinger, 'Principled Realism and Populist Sovereignty in Trump's Foreign Policy', *Cambridge Review of International Affairs*, 33/3, 2020, pp. 410–31.
45. Burns, *Back Channel*, p. 9.
46. Jonathan Kirshner, 'Gone But Not Forgotten: Trump's Long Shadow and the End of American Credibility', *Foreign Affairs*, 100/2, March/April 2021, p. 22.
47. G. John Ikenberry, 'The Rise of China and the Future of the West: Can the Liberal System Survive?', *Foreign Affairs*, 87/1, Jan/Feb 2008, pp. 33–4.
48. Steve Chan, 'Challenging the Liberal Order: The US Hegemon as a Revisionist Power', *International Affairs*, 97/5, 2021, pp. 1335–52.
49. Peter Baker, '"Use That Word!": Trump Embraces the "Nationalist" Label', *New York Times*, 23 October 2018, https://www.nytimes.com/2018/10/23/us/politics/nationalist-president-trump.html.
50. H.R. McMaster, national security adviser, and Gary Cohn, director of the National Economic Council, 'America First Does Not Mean America Alone', *Wall Street Journal*, 30 May 2017, https://www.wsj.com/articles/america-first-doesnt-mean-america-alone-1496187426.
51. Randall L. Schweller, 'Why Trump Now', in Jervis et al. (eds), *Chaos in the Liberal Order*, p. 23.
52. Schweller, 'Why Trump Now', p. 25.
53. Christopher Layne, 'From Preponderance to Offshore Balancing: America's Future Grand Strategy', *International Security*, 22/1, Summer 1997, pp. 86–124.
54. Lauren Wolfe, 'Trump's Insidious Reason for Leaving the UN Human Rights Council', *Atlantic*, 20 June 2018, https://www.theatlantic.com/international/archive/2018/06/trump-haley-un-human-rights-israel-venezuela-withdrawal/563246/.
55. Outlined in Hillary Rodham Clinton, *Hard Choices: A Memoir* (New York, Simon & Schuster, 2014).
56. 'Trump: NATO Is Obsolete and Expensive, "Doesn't Have the Right Countries in It for Terrorism"', interview on ABC's *This Week*, 27 March 2016, http://www.realclearpolitics.com/video/2016/03/27/trump_europe_is_not_safe_lots_of_the_free_world_has_become_weak.html.
57. David E. Sanger and Maggie Haberman, 'Donald Trump Sets Conditions for Defending NATO Allies against Attack', *New York Times*, 20 July 2016, https://www.nytimes.com/2016/07/21/us/politics/donald-trump-issues.html?_r=0.
58. 'Transcript: Donald Trump's Foreign Policy Speech', *New York Times*, 27 April 2016, https://www.nytimes.com/2016/04/28/us/politics/transcript-trump-foreign-policy.html?_r=0.
59. Richard Sakwa, *Deception: Russiagate and the New Cold War* (Lanham, MD, Lexington Books, 2022).
60. *National Security Strategy of the United States*, December 2017, https://www.whitehouse.gov/wp-content/uploads/2017/12/NSS-Final-12-18-2017-0905.pdf, p. 25.
61. 'Donald Trump Delivers a Speech on National Security Policy', 18 December 2017, https://factba.se/transcript/donald-trump-speech-national-security-december-18-2017.

62. Julian Borger, 'Trump Says US Could Use Nuclear Weapons against Conventional Attacks', *Guardian*, 19 December 2017, p. 16.
63. Figures given by Putin in his annual press conference on 14 December 2017.
64. 'Washington's New Security Strategy Has "Imperial Nature" – Kremlin', 19 December 2017, https://www.rt.com/news/413625-us-security-strategy-peskov/.
65. '"Abandon Cold War Mentality": China Hits Back at Trump's "Selfish" National Strategy', 19 December 2017, https://www.rt.com/news/413630-china-us-national-security-strategy/.
66. *Summary of the 2018 National Defense Strategy: Sharpening the American Military's Competitive Edge*, Department of Defense, 2018, https://dod.defense.gov/Portals/1/Documents/pubs/2018-National-Defense-Strategy-Summary.pdf, p. 1.
67. *Summary of the 2018 National Defense Strategy*, p. 2.
68. *Summary of the 2018 National Defense Strategy*, p. 3.
69. Secretary of Defense, *Nuclear Posture Review*, February 2018, https://www.defense.gov/News/SpecialReports/2018NuclearPostureReview.aspx, p. 1.
70. *Nuclear Posture Review*, February 2018, p. 2.
71. *Nuclear Posture Review*, February 2018, p. 7.
72. Joseph R. Biden, Jr and Michael Carpenter, 'How to Stand Up to the Kremlin', *Foreign Affairs*, 97/1, Jan/Feb 2018, pp. 44–57.
73. Joseph R. Biden Jr, 'Why America Must Lead Again: Rescuing US Foreign Policy after Trump', *Foreign Affairs*, 99/2, March/April 2020, p. 71.
74. Samantha Power, 'The Can-Do Power: America's Advantage and Biden's Chance', *Foreign Affairs*, 100/1, Jan/Feb 2021, pp. 10–24.
75. Biden, 'Why America Must Lead Again', p. 73.
76. Biden, 'Why America Must Lead Again', p. 75.
77. Jessica T. Mathews, 'Present at the Re-creation? US Foreign Policy Must Be Remade, Not Restored', *Foreign Affairs*, 100/2, March/April 2021, p. 12.
78. Mathews, 'Present at the Re-creation?', p. 14.
79. Mathews, 'Present at the Re-creation?', p. 15.
80. Dimitri K. Simes, 'Getting Serious about Russia', *National Interest*, 25 February 2021, https://nationalinterest.org/feature/getting-serious-about-russia-178832.
81. M.K. Bhadrakumar, 'Biden Has Adult Conversations with China, Russia on Iran', *Asia Times*, 18 February 2021, https://asiatimes.com/2021/02/biden-has-adult-conversations-with-china-russia-on-iran/.
82. 'Remarks by President Biden on America's Place in the World', State Department, 4 February 2021, https://www.whitehouse.gov/briefing-room/speeches-remarks/2021/02/04/remarks-by-president-biden-on-americas-place-in-the-world/.
83. Willis L. Krumholz, 'Biden's "America is Back" Speech Misunderstands How Overstretched America Is Abroad', *National Interest*, 16 February 2021, https://nationalinterest.org/blog/skeptics/biden%E2%80%99s-%E2%80%98america-back%E2%80%99-speech-misunderstands-how-overstretched-america-abroad-178269.
84. 'Remarks by President Biden at the 2021 Virtual Munich Security Conference', 19 February 2021, https://www.whitehouse.gov/briefing-room/speeches-remarks/2021/02/19/remarks-by-president-biden-at-the-2021-virtual-munich-security-conference/.

85. White House, *Interim National Security Strategic Guidance*, March 2021, https://www.whitehouse.gov/wp-content/uploads/2021/03/NSC-1v2.pdf.

86. Joe Gould and Megan Eckstein, 'Russia, First in the Headlines, Is Pentagon's No. 2 Challenge', *Defense News*, 29 March 2022, https://www.defensenews.com/pentagon/2022/03/29/russia-first-in-the-headlines-is-pentagons-no-2-challenge/.

87. Matthew Kroenig, 'Washington Must Prepare for War with Both Russia and China: Pivoting to Asia and Forgetting about Europe Is Not an Option', *Foreign Policy*, 18 February 2022, https://foreignpolicy.com/2022/02/18/us-russia-china-war-nato-quadrilateral-security-dialogue/. For elaboration, see his *The Return of Great Power Rivalry: Democracy versus Autocracy from the Ancient World to the US and China* (New York, Oxford University Press, 2020).

88. 'President of Iran Addressed Members of the State Duma', 20 January 2022, http://duma.gov.ru/en/news/53251/.

89. Hamidreza Azizi and Hanna Notte, 'Where Are Russia's Red Lines on Iran's Nuclear Brinkmanship?', Carnegie Moscow Center, 19 February 2021, https://carnegie.ru/commentary/83915.

90. 'US Announces $125 Million Aid Package for Ukraine, Condemns Russia', Warsaw Institute, 19 April 2021, https://warsawinstitute.org/us-announces-125-million-aid-package-ukraine-condemns-russia/.

91. Andriy Zagorodnyuk, Alina Frolova, Hans Petter Midtunn and Oleksii Pavliuchyk, 'Is Ukraine's Reformed Military Ready to Repel a New Russian Invasion?', Ukraine Alert, Atlantic Council, 23 December 2021, https://www.atlanticcouncil.org/blogs/ukrainealert/is-ukraines-reformed-military-ready-to-repel-a-new-russian-invasion/.

92. Office of the Director of National Intelligence, 'Foreign Threats to the 2020 US Federal Elections: Intelligence Community Assessment', 10 March 2021, https://www.dni.gov/files/ODNI/documents/assessments/ICA-declass-16MAR21.pdf.

93. James W. Carden and Patrick Lawrence, 'Our Cold, Two-Front War: We're Already Losing This One', *The Scrum*, 21 March 2021, https://thescrum.substack.com/p/our-cold-two-front-war.

94. David P. Goldman, 'Biden's Firing Squad Stands in a Circle', *Asia Times*, 22 March 2021, https://asiatimes.com/2021/03/bidens-firing-squad-stands-in-a-circle/.

95. Nikkei Asia, 'How It Happened: Transcript of the US–China Opening Remarks in Alaska', 19 March 2021, https://asia.nikkei.com/Politics/International-relations/US-China-tensions/How-it-happened-Transcript-of-the-US-China-opening-remarks-in-Alaska.

96. Patrick Lawrence, '(In)competence', *The Scrum*, 26 March 2021, https://thescrum.substack.com/p/incompetence.

97. Yan Xuetong, 'Becoming Strong: The New Chinese Foreign Policy', *Foreign Affairs*, 100/4, July/Aug 2021, p. 40.

98. 'Foreign Minister Sergey Lavrov's Opening Remarks During Talks with Foreign Minister of the People's Republic of China Wang Yi', Guilin, 23 March 2021, https://www.mid.ru/en/foreign_policy/news/-/asset_publisher/cKNonkJE02Bw/content/id/4647593.

99. AP, 'China, Russia Officials Meet in Show of Unity against EU, US', 23 March 2021, https://apnews.com/article/joe-biden-europe-beijing-wang-yi-coronavirus-pandemic-b8797b405a609945eef3a8dade8b12e1.

100. 'Foreign Minister Sergey Lavrov's Remarks and Answers to Media Questions Following Talks with Foreign Minister of China Wang Yi', Guilin, 23 March 2021, https://www.mid.ru/en/foreign_policy/news/-/asset_publisher/cKNonkJE02Bw/content/id/4647898.

101. For analysis, see Tom Casier, 'Russia's Energy Leverage over the EU: Myth or Reality?', *Perspectives on European Politics and Society*, 12/4, 2011, pp. 493–508; Tom Casier, 'Great Game or Great Confusion?: The Geopolitical Understanding of EU–Russia Energy Relations', *Geopolitics*, 21/4, 2016, pp. 763–78.

102. Stephen Kinzer, 'Europe Is Rebelling against American Power', *Boston Globe*, 16 March 2021, https://www.bostonglobe.com.

103. The veteran and respected reporter Seymour Hersh argues that the US was responsible, working with the Norwegians: 'How America Took Out the Nord Stream Pipeline', 8 February 2023, https://seymourhersh.substack.com/p/how-america-took-out-the-nord-stream.

104. US National Intelligence Council, *Global Trends 2040: A More Contested World*, March 2021, https://www.dni.gov/files/ODNI/documents/assessments/GlobalTrends_2040.pdf, p. 1.

105. US NIC, *Global Trends 2040*, p. 98.

106. US NIC, *Global Trends 2040*, p. 95.

107. Department of Defense, 'Biden Approves Global Posture Review Recommendations', 29 November 2021, https://www.defense.gov/News/News-Stories/Article/Article/2856053/biden-approves-global-posture-review-recommendations/.

108. Quoted by Angela Stent, 'Trump's Russia Legacy and Biden's Response', *Survival*, 63/4, 2021, p. 72.

109. 'Ryabkov: Rossiya mozhet pereiti k politike aktivnogo sderzhivaniya SShA', Radio Sputnik, 17 February 2021, https://radiosputnik.ria.ru/20210217/ryabkov-1597805761.html.

110. Konstantin Khudoley, 'Russia and the USA: In Search of a New Model of Relations', Valdai Discussion Club, 25 May 2021, https://valdaiclub.com/a/highlights/russia-and-the-usa-in-search-of-a-new-model/.

111. David J. Kramer, 'Is Biden Going Soft on Putin?', *Kyiv Post*, 24 May 2021, https://www.kyivpost.com/article/opinion/op-ed/david-j-kramer-is-biden-going-soft-on-putin.html.

112. Garry Kasparov, 'Has Biden Lost His Nerve with Putin?', *Wall Street Journal*, 1 June 2021, https://www.wsj.com./articles/has-biden-lost-his-nerve-with-putin-11622566741?page=1.

113. Andrew J. Bacevich, *The Age of Illusions: How America Squandered Its Cold War Victory* (New York, Metropolitan Books, 2020).

6: GLOBAL CHINA

1. Jonathan E. Hillman, *The Emperor's New Road: China and the Project of the Century* (New Haven, CT and London, Yale University Press, 2020).

2. Robert Gilpin, *War and Change in World Politics* (Cambridge, Cambridge University Press, 1981). See also Paul Kennedy, *The Rise and Fall of the Great Powers: Economic Change and Military Conflict from 1500 to 2000* (London, Unwin Hyman, 1988). In confirmation of the argument, as early as 2009

Fareed Zakaria identified alarm among neoconservatives and the Pentagon 'about the Chinese threat, speaking of it largely in military terms'; Zakaria, *Post-American World*, p. 126.

3. For earlier anticipations, see John Thornton, 'Long Time Coming: The Prospects for Democracy in China', *Foreign Affairs*, 87/1, Jan/Feb 2008, pp. 2–22.

4. Gordon G. Chang notoriously long asserted this: *The Coming Collapse of China* (New York, Random House, 2001).

5. Yu Jie, 'China's Communist Century: An Ongoing Balancing Act', *The World Today*, 4 June 2021, https://www.chathamhouse.org/publications/the-world-today/2021-06/chinas-communist-century-ongoing-balancing-act.

6. Tom Phillips, 'Xi Pledges Brilliant New Era as He Becomes Most Powerful Chinese Leader since Mao', *Guardian*, 25 October 2017, p. 17.

7. 'Xi Jinping's Report at 19th CPC National Congress', 18 October 2017, http://www.xinhuanet.com.

8. Giovanni Arrighi, *Adam Smith in Beijing: Lineages of the Twenty-First Century* (London, Verso, 2009).

9. Nye famously argued that ultimately only the US enjoys soft power, in the way that he defined it at that point: Joseph S. Nye, 'What China and Russia Don't Get about Soft Power', *Foreign Policy*, 29 April 2013, http://foreignpolicy.com.

10. Yana Leksyutina, 'Chinese Transfer: From Soft to Discursive Power', Valdai International Club, 15 February 2023, https://valdaiclub.com/a/highlights/chinese-transfer-from-soft-to-discursive-power/.

11. Clive Hamilton, *Silent Invasion: China's Influence in Australia* (London, Hardie Grant Books, 2018); Clive Hamilton and Mareike Ohlberg, *Hidden Hand: Exposing How the Chinese Communist Party Is Reshaping the World* (London, Oneworld Publications, 2021).

12. Directorate of Intelligence, 'A Comparison of the US and Soviet Economies: Evaluating the Performance of the Soviet System', *CIA Historical Review Program*, October 1985, https://www.cia.gov/library/readingroom/docs/DOC_0000497165.pdf.

13. James B. Stewart, 'Why Russia Can't Afford Another Cold War', *New York Times*, 8 March 2014, https://www.nytimes.com/2014/03/08/business/why-russia-cant-afford-another-cold-war.html.

14. Zhang Weiwei, *The China Horizon: Glory and Dream of a Civilizational State* (Hackensack, NJ, World Century Publishing Corporation, 2016), p. 13.

15. Ikenberry, 'Rise of China', p. 23.

16. The report of the Office of the UN High Commissioner for Human Rights, prepared by the Commissioner Michelle Bachelet and published on her last day in office, 31 August 2022, sums up the charges of systematic and wide-scale human rights abuses: https://news.un.org/en/story/2022/08/1125932.

17. Helena Kennedy, 'China Cannot Stop Me from Speaking Out', *Guardian Opinion*, 27 March 2021, p. 4.

18. Elizabeth C. Economy, *The Third Revolution: Xi Jinping and the New Chinese State* (New York, Oxford University Press, 2018), p. 4.

19. Elizabeth C. Economy, *The World According to China* (Cambridge, Polity, 2021).

20. As argued by Rush Doshi, *The Long Game: China's Grand Strategy to Displace American Order* (New York, Oxford University Press, 2021).

21. Elizabeth Economy, 'Xi Jinping's New World Order: Can China Remake the International System?', *Foreign Affairs*, 101/1, Jan/Feb 2022, pp. 52–67.
22. Rana Mitter, 'Xi Jinping Has Rewritten China's History, but Even He Can't Predict Its Global Future', *Guardian*, 14 November 2021, https://www.theguardian.com/commentisfree/2021/nov/14/xi-jinping-has-rewritten-chinas-history-but-even-he-cant-predict-its-global-future.
23. Ikenberry, 'Rise of China', p. 37.
24. Economy, *Third Revolution*, p. 189.
25. For analysis of the concept, see Christopher Coker, *The Rise of the Civilizational State* (Cambridge, Polity, 2019).
26. Zhang, *China Horizon*, p. xiii.
27. Daniel A. Bell, *The China Model: Political Meritocracy and the Limits of Democracy* (Princeton, NJ, Princeton University Press, 2015).
28. Zhang, *China Horizon*, p. 43.
29. Zhang, *China Horizon*, pp. 47, 46.
30. Zhang, *China Horizon*, p. 78.
31. Zhang, *China Horizon*, pp. 89, 145.
32. Zhang, *China Horizon*, p. 107.
33. Zhang, *China Horizon*, p. 137.
34. Kishore Mahbubani, *Has China Won? The Chinese Challenge to American Primacy* (New York, Public Affairs, 2020), p. 2.
35. Mahbubani, *Has China Won?*, p. 4.
36. Mahbubani, *Has China Won?*, p. 7 (emphasis in original).
37. Mahbubani, *Has China Won?*, p. 21.
38. Mahbubani, *Has China Won?*, p. 33.
39. Mahbubani, *Has China Won?*, p. 35.
40. Mahbubani, *Has China Won?*, p. 42.
41. Mahbubani, *Has China Won?*, p. 57, quoting Martin Wolf, 'How We Lost America to Greed and Envy', *Financial Times*, 17 July 2018.
42. Mahbubani, *Has China Won?*, p. 253.
43. Mahbubani, *Has China Won?*, p. 254.
44. Martin Jacques, *When China Rules the World: The End of the Western World and the Birth of a New Global Order*, 2nd edn (London, Penguin, 2012), p. 16.
45. The argument made by Shmuel N. Eisenstadt, *Multiple Modernities* (Piscataway, NJ, Transaction Publishers, 2002).
46. Jacques, *When China Rules the World*, p. 579.
47. Shmuel N. Eisenstadt, *Japanese Civilization: A Comparative View* (Chicago, University of Chicago Press, 1996).
48. Samuel P. Huntington, 'The Clash of Civilizations?', *Foreign Affairs*, 72/3, Summer 1993, pp. 23–49; Samuel P. Huntington, *The Clash of Civilizations and the Remaking of World Order* (New York, Simon & Schuster, 1996).
49. Economy, *Third Revolution*, p. 222.
50. Andrew Hurrell, 'Beyond the BRICS: Power, Pluralism, and the Future of Global Order', *Ethics & International Affairs*, 32/1, 2018, p. 93.
51. Shiping Tang, 'China and the Future International Order(s)', *Ethics and International Affairs*, 32/1, 2018, p. 34.
52. 'Full Text of Xi Jinping Keynote at the World Economic Forum', Davos, 17 January 2017, https://america.cgtn.com/2017/01/17/full-text-of-xi-jinping-keynote-at-the-world-economic-forum.

53. For an examination of the dynamics, see Jessica Chen Weiss and Jeremy L. Wallace, 'Domestic Politics, China's Rise, and the Future of the Liberal International Order', *International Organization*, 75, Spring 2021, pp. 635–64.

54. Jacques, *When China Rules the World*, p. 12.

55. Yong Deng, *China's Struggle for Status: The Realignment of International Relations* (Cambridge, Cambridge University Press, 2008), p. 6.

56. Yong, *China's Struggle for Status*, p. 5.

57. Yong, *China's Struggle for Status*, p. 121.

58. 'Full Text of Chinese President Xi Jinping's Speech at Opening Ceremony of 2018 FOCAC Beijing Summit', 3 September 2018, http://www.xinhuanet.com/english/2018-09/03/c_137441987.htm.

59. 'Wang Yi Delivers a Speech at the 56th Munich Security Conference', 15 February 2020, https://www.mfa.gov.cn/ce/ceus//eng/zgyw/t1746135.htm.

60. Theresa Fallon, 'The New Silk Road: Xi Jinping's Grand Strategy for Eurasia', *American Foreign Policy Interests*, 37, 2015, pp. 140–7.

61. Alexander Cooley, *New Silk Route or Developmental Cul-de-Sac?*, PONARS Eurasia, PONARS Eurasian Policy Memo No. 372, July 2015.

62. Council on Foreign Relations, *China's Belt and Road: Implications for the United States*, March 2021, https://www.cfr.org/report/chinas-belt-and-road-implications-for-the-united-states/, pp. 4–5.

63. A point made by Hans Kribbe, *The Strongmen: European Encounters with Sovereign Power* (Newcastle, Agenda Publishing, 2020), p. 157.

64. Quoted by Kribbe, *The Strongmen*, p. 157.

65. Cf. Bruno Maçães, *Belt and Road: A Chinese World Order* (London, Hurst, 2018), p. 5, who argues that the BRI 'is the Chinese plan to build a new world order replacing the US-led international system'.

66. Lee Jones and Shahar Hameiri, *Debunking the Myth of 'Debt-Trap Diplomacy': How Recipient Countries Shape China's Belt and Road Initiative*, Chatham House Research Paper, August 2020, https://www.chathamhouse.org/2020/08/debunking-myth-debt-trap-diplomacy.

67. Economy, *Third Revolution*, p. 119.

68. Zbigniew Brzezinski, 'The Group of Two that Could Change the World', *Financial Times*, 13 January 2009, https://www.ft.com/content/d99369b8-e178-11dd-afao-0000779fd2ac.

69. Hillary Clinton, 'America's Pacific Century', *Foreign Policy*, 11 October 2011, http://foreignpolicy.com/2011/10/11/americas-pacific-century/.

70. Zhang, *China Horizon*, pp. 25–6.

71. Vasily Kashin and Alexander Lukin, 'China's Approach to Relations with the United States: The Military Aspect', in *Russia: Arms Control, Disarmament and International Security*, SIPRI Yearbook Supplement (Moscow, IMEMO, 2021), p. 16.

72. Kashin and Lukin, 'China's Approach to Relations with the United States', p. 17.

73. Fu Ying, *Seeing the World* (Beijing, 2019), p. iii.

74. Julian Borger, 'The Challenge of China', *Guardian*, 10 June 2021, p. 23.

75. Ministry of Foreign Affairs, 'US Hegemony and Its Perils', 20 February 2023, https://www.fmprc.gov.cn/mfa_eng/wjbxw/202302/t20230220_11027664.html.

76. For the long-term effects, see Adam Tooze, *Crashed: How a Decade of Financial Crises Changed the World* (London, Penguin, 2019).

77. Graham Allison, *Destined for War: Can America and China Avoid Thucydides's Trap?* (London, Scribe, 2018).

78. Rafael Behr, 'Joe Biden's G7 Mission: Recruit Allies for the Next Cold War', *Guardian Review*, 9 June 2021, p. 3.

79. John J. Mearsheimer, *The Tragedy of Great Power Politics*, updated edn (New York, W.W. Norton, 2014, originally published 2001), p. xi.

80. The argument was elaborated in John J. Mearsheimer and Stephen M. Walt, 'The Case for Offshore Balancing', *Foreign Affairs*, 95/4, July/Aug 2016, pp. 70–83.

81. John J. Mearsheimer, *The Great Delusion: Liberal Dreams and International Realities* (New Haven, CT and London, Yale University Press, 2018).

82. Mearsheimer, 'Bound to Fail'.

83. 'Read Trump's Speech to the UN General Assembly', *Vox*, 25 September 2018, https://www.vox.com/2018/9/25/17901082/trump-un-2018-speech-full-text.

84. John Haltiwanger, 'Trump Accuses China of Attempting to Meddle in the Midterms, Tells World Leaders "They Do Not Want Me or Us to Win"', *Business Insider UK*, 26 September 2018, http://uk.businessinsider.com/trump-accuses-china-of-attempted-meddling-in-2018-midterms-2018-9?r=US&IR=T.

85. 'Vice President Mike Pence's Remarks on the Administration's Policy towards China', Hudson Institute, 4 October 2018, https://www.hudson.org/events/1610-vice-president-mike-pence-s-remarks-on-the-administration-s-policy-towards-china102018.

86. James Walker, 'China – Not Russia – Elected Trump', *National Interest*, 27 August 2018, https://nationalinterest.org/feature/china—not-russia—elected-trump-29877.

87. Walker, 'China – Not Russia – Elected Trump'.

88. Lily Kuo and Julian Borger, 'Tension Rises as US Closes Chinese Consulate in Houston', *Guardian*, 23 July 2020, p. 27.

89. Examined in *NATO and the Asia-Pacific*, NATO Association of Canada, Fall 2020, https://natoassociation.ca/wp-content/uploads/2020/12/NAOC-Fall-2020-Issue.pdf.

90. 'Indo-Pacific Strategy of the United States', February 2022, https://www.whitehouse.gov/wp-content/uploads/2022/02/U.S.-Indo-Pacific-Strategy.pdf.

91. Fareed Zakaria, 'The New China Scare: Why America Shouldn't Panic about Its Latest Challenger', *Foreign Affairs*, 99/1, Jan/Feb 2020, pp. 52–69.

92. Anatol Lieven, 'Euro Tour Notes for Biden: "Listen" on China, Don't Tell', *Responsible Statecraft*, 9 June 2021, https://responsiblestatecraft.org/2021/06/09/euro-tour-notes-for-biden-listen-on-china-dont-tell/.

93. Vasily Kashin and Ivan Timofeev, 'US–China Relations: Moving towards a New Cold War?', Valdai Discussion Club Report, January 2021, p. 3.

94. White House, *United States Strategic Approach to the People's Republic of China*, May 2020, https://china.usembassy-china.org.cn/wp-content/uploads/sites/252/U.S.-Strategic-Approach-to-The-Peoples-Republic-of-China-Report-5.24v1.pdf.

95. Michael R. Pompeo, 'Communist China and the Free World's Future', speech at the Nixon Center, California, 23 July 2020, https://2017-2021.state.gov/communist-china-and-the-free-worlds-future-2/index.html.

96. Michael R. Pompeo, 'Announcing the Expansion of the Clean Network to Safeguard America's Assets', press statement, State Department, 5 August 2020, https://www.state.gov/announcing-the-expansion-of-the-clean-network-to-safeguard-americas-assets/.

97. Motoko Rich, 'Pompeo's Message in Japan: Countering China Is Worth Meeting Face to Face', *New York Times*, 6 October 2020, https://www.nytimes.com/2020/10/06/world/asia/pompeo-japan.html.

98. Janan Ganesh, 'America's Eerie Lack of Debate about China', *Financial Times*, 15 July 2020, https://www.ft.com/content/9b7e64c9-c7c4-47b7-b038-f728bfd23e28.

99. C. Fred Bergsten, *The United States vs. China: The Quest for Global Economic Leadership* (Cambridge, Polity, 2022).

100. Aaron L. Friedberg, *Getting China Wrong* (Cambridge, Polity, 2022).

101. Andrey Kortunov, 'US Will Remain a Difficult Partner', RIAC, 20 July 2020, https://russiancouncil.ru/en/analytics-and-comments/analytics/us-will-remain-a-difficult-partner/.

102. Alexander Lukin, 'Why China Won't Break with Russia over Ukraine', *National Interest*, 28 March 2022, https://nationalinterest.org/feature/why-china-won%E2%80%99t-break-russia-over-ukraine-201495.

103. Vincent Ni, 'China's Evolving Stance on the War in Ukraine Reflects a Deepening Distrust of the West', *Guardian*, 7 June 2022, p. 21.

104. Nathaniel Sher, 'Why Isn't China Going All Out to Help Russia in Ukraine?', *Responsible Statecraft*, 4 April 2022, https://responsiblestatecraft.org/2022/04/04/why-isnt-china-going-all-out-to-help-russia-in-ukraine/.

105. Lukin, 'Why China Won't Break with Russia over Ukraine'.

106. Laura Zhou, 'US Has "Lost Its Mind, Morals and Credibility", China's Foreign Minister Tells Russian Counterpart', *South China Morning Post*, 18 July 2020, https://www.scmp.com/news/china/diplomacy/article/3093762/us-has-lost-its-mind-morals-and-credibility-chinas-foreign.

107. Kevin Rudd, *The Avoidable War: The Dangers of a Catastrophic Conflict between the US and Xi Jinping's China* (London, Public Affairs, 2022).

7: THE RUSSIA QUESTION

1. For more extended analysis, see Richard Sakwa, *Russia against the Rest: The Post-Cold War Crisis of World Order* (Cambridge, Cambridge University Press, 2017).

2. Adrian Pabst, *Liberal World Order and Its Critics: Civilisational States and Cultural Commonwealths* (London, Routledge, 2018). See also Elena Chebankova and Piotr Dutkiewicz (eds), *Civilizations and World Order* (London, Routledge, 2021).

3. Eugene Rumer and Richard Sokolsky, *Grand Illusions: The Impact of Misperceptions about Russia on US Policy* (Washington DC, CEIP, 2021), p. 8.

4. 'Press Conference with President Obama and Prime Minister Rutte of the Netherlands', The Hague, 25 March 2014, https://obamawhitehouse.archives.gov/the-press-office/2014/03/25/press-conference-president-obama-and-prime-minister-rutte-netherlands.

5. Kathryn E. Stoner, *Russia Resurrected: Its Power and Purpose in a New Global Order* (New York, Oxford University Press, 2021), pp. 246–56.

6. Stoner, *Russia Resurrected*, p. 237.
7. The Atlantic Council is the most resolute exponent of this view. For example, Daniel Fried and Adrian Karatnycky, 'A New Sanctions Strategy to Contain Putin's Russia', *Foreign Policy*, 4 May 2021, https://foreignpolicy.com/2021/05/04/sanctions-contain-russia-putin-west-us-eu-uk-europe-weaken-economy/.
8. Andrea Kendall-Taylor and David Shullman, 'China and Russia's Dangerous Convergence', *Foreign Affairs*, 3 May 2021, https://www.foreignaffairs.com/articles/china/2021-05-03/china-and-russias-dangerous-convergence.
9. Manjari Chatterjee Miller, *Why Nations Rise: Narratives and the Path to Great Power* (Oxford, Oxford University Press, 2021), p. 145.
10. Lyle J. Goldstein, 'Threat Inflation, Russian Military Weakness, and the Resulting Nuclear Paradox', Costs of War, Watson Institute, Brown University, 15 September 2022, https://watson.brown.edu/costsofwar/files/cow/imce/papers/Threat%20Inflation%20and%20Russian%20Military%20Weakness_Goldstein_CostsofWar-2.pdf.
11. Jozef Hrabina, 'The Year of Crises: How 2020 Will Reshape the Structure of International Relations', *Russia in Global Affairs*, 1, Jan–March 2021, p. 185.
12. Hill, *No Place for Russia*, p. 249.
13. Hill, *No Place for Russia*, p. 258.
14. Hill, *No Place for Russia*, p. 255.
15. Johannes Sochor, *Russia and the Right to Self-Determination in the Post-Soviet Space* (Oxford, Oxford University Press, 2021).
16. Maria Shagina, 'How Disastrous Would Disconnection from SWIFT Be for Russia?', Carnegie Moscow Center, 28 May 2021, https://carnegie.ru/commentary/84634.
17. Jake Cordell, 'Should Russian Banks Be Scared of SWIFT Disconnection?', *Moscow Times*, 22 April 2021, https://www.themoscowtimes.com/2021/04/22/should-russian-banks-be-scared-of-swift-disconnection-a73644.
18. 'Russia and China to Bolster Financial Security Systems', 26 March 2021, https://www.rt.com/russia/519287-financial-security-payments-system/.
19. Simon Saradzhyan and Nabi Abdullaev, 'Measuring National Power: Is Putin's Russia in Decline?', *Europe-Asia Studies*, 73/2, March 2021, p. 315.
20. Richard Sakwa, 'Russian Neo-revisionism', *Russian Politics*, 4/1, 2019, pp. 1–21.
21. Richard Sakwa, 'The Dual State in Russia', *Post-Soviet Affairs*, 26/3, July–Sep 2010, pp. 185–206.
22. Doug Bandow, 'How Biden Can (and Should) Cooperate with Putin', *American Conservative*, 27 May 2021, https://www.theamericanconservative.com.
23. Daniel Treisman, 'Putin Unbound: How Repression at Home Presaged Belligerence Abroad', *Foreign Affairs*, 101/3, May/June 2022, pp. 40–53.
24. Sergey Lavrov, 'Remarks at the General Debate of the 77th UN General Assembly', 24 September 2022, https://mid.ru/en/foreign_policy/news/1831211/.
25. Fyodor Lukyanov, 'The Time to Be By Yourself', *Russia in Global Affairs*, 15 March 2021, https://eng.globalaffairs.ru/articles/time-to-be-by-yourself/.
26. Clark, *Post-Cold War Order*, p. 241.

27. An argument made by a range of authors in Tuomas Forsberg, 'Status Conflicts between Russia and the West: Perceptions and Emotional Biases', *Communist and Post-Communist Studies*, 46/3, 2014, p. 334.

28. Deborah Welch Larson and Andrei Shevchenko, 'Status Seekers: Chinese and Russian Responses to US Primacy', *International Security*, 34/4, 2010, p. 93.

29. Gordon M. Hahn, 'Putin 5.0: Tea Leaves', *Russian and Eurasian Politics*, 1 June 2018, https://gordonhahn.com/2018/06/01/putin-5-0-tea-leaves/.

30. Brzezinski, *Grand Chessboard*, pp. 50, 51.

31. Andrei P. Tsygankov, *Russia's Foreign Policy: Change and Continuity in National Identity*, 6th edn (Lanham, MD, Rowman & Littlefield, 2022).

32. Zbigniew Brzezinski, *The Choice: Global Domination or Global Leadership* (New York, Basic Books, 2004), p. 102.

33. Brzezinski, *The Choice*, pp. 85, 103 and *passim*.

34. Andrei Makine, 'To Stop This War [in Ukraine], We Must Understand the Background that Made It Possible', Simone Weil Centre, *Landmarks*, 27 March 2022, https://simoneweilcenter.org/publications/2022/3/27/andrei-makine-to-stop-this-war-we-must-understand-the-background-that-made-it-possible.

35. Bruce Russett and Allan C. Stam, 'Courting Disaster: NATO vs. Russia and China', in Bruce Russett, *Hegemony and Democracy* (London, Routledge, 2011), p. 110. For a perceptive early critique of enlargement, see J.L. Black, *Russia Faces NATO Expansion: Bearing Gifts or Bearing Arms?* (Lanham, MD, Rowman & Littlefield, 2000).

36. Valerie A. Pacer, *Russian Foreign Policy under Dmitry Medvedev* (London, Routledge, 2016).

37. Dmitri Trenin, *Novyi balans sil: Rossiya v poiskakh vneshnepoliticheskogo ravnovesiya* (Moscow, Al'pina, 2021).

38. Brzezinski, *Grand Chessboard*, p. 55.

39. See Charles Clover, *Black Wind, White Snow: The Rise of Russia's New Nationalism*, new edn (New Haven, CT and London, Yale University Press, 2022).

40. Analysed by Mark Bassin, *The Gumilev Mystique* (Ithaca, NY, Cornell University Press, 2016).

41. Alexander Dugin, 'Russia and China as the Vanguard of Multipolarity', 5 February 2022, https://www.geopolitica.ru/en/article/russia-and-china-vanguard-multipolarity.

42. Mikhail Zygar', *All the Kremlin's Men: Inside the Court of Vladimir Putin* (New York, Public Affairs, 2016), p. 300.

43. I. Egorov, '"Kto upravlyaet khaosom" – SShA pytayutsya odolet' krisiz za schet drugikh, razrushaya tselye strany – intervyu s nikolaem Patrushevym', *Rossiiskaya gazeta*, 15 October 2014.

44. Zygar', *All the Kremlin's Men*, p. 343.

45. Vladimir Putin, 'Address to the Federal Assembly', 12 December 2012, http://eng.kremlin.ru/news/4739.

46. Vladimir Putin, 'Meeting of the Valdai Discussion Club', 19 September 2013, http://eng.kremlin.ru.

47. For a broad analysis, see Andrei P. Tsygankov, 'Crafting the State-Civilization', *Problems of Post-Communism*, 63/3, 2016, pp. 146–58.

48. Vadim Tsymburskii, 'Ostrov Rossiya: Perspektivy Rossiiskoi Geopolitika', *Polis*, No. 5, 1993, pp. 11–17.

49. Vladislav Surkov, 'The Loneliness of the Half Breed', *Russia in Global Affairs*, 28 May 2018, https://eng.globalaffairs.ru/articles/the-loneliness-of-the-half-breed/.
50. Henry Kissinger, *Diplomacy* (New York, Simon & Schuster, 1995), pp. 817–18.
51. Brzezinski, *Grand Chessboard*, pp. xiii–xiv.
52. Owen Matthews, 'Revealed: Putin's Covert War on Western Decadence', *Spectator*, October 2016.
53. 'Strategiya natsional'noi bezopasnosti Rossiiskoi Federatsii', *Rossiiskaya gazeta*, 31 December 2015, http://rg.ru/2015/12/31/nac-bezopasnost-site-dok.html.
54. Barry Buzan, Ole Waever and Jaap de Wilde, *Security: A New Framework for Analysis* (Boulder, CO, Lynne Rienner Publishers, 1998). For the Russian case, see Edwin Bacon and Bettina Renz with Julian Cooper, *Securitising Russia: The Domestic Politics of Putin* (Manchester, Manchester University Press, 2006).
55. Bernhard Stahl, Robin Lucke and Anne Felfeli, 'Comeback of the Transatlantic Security Community? Comparative Securitisation in the Crimea Crisis', *East European Politics*, 32/4, 2016, p. 539.
56. *National Security Strategy of the USA*, February 2015, https://obamawhitehouse.archives.gov/sites/default/files/docs/2015_national_security_strategy_2.pdf.
57. *The Foreign Policy Concept of the Russian Federation*, 30 November 2016, https://www.voltairenet.org/article202038.html.
58. Vladimir Putin, 'Presidential Address to the Federal Assembly', 15 January 2020, http://en.kremlin.ru/events/president/news/62582.
59. Vladimir Putin, 'Meeting of the Valdai Discussion Club', 22 October 2020, http://en.kremlin.ru/events/president/news/64261.
60. Putin, 'Valdai Discussion Club', 22 October 2020.
61. 'Ukaz Prezidenta RF ot 2 iyulya 2021g. N 400 "Strategii Natsional'noi Bezopasnosti Rossiiskoi Federatsii"', http://www.kremlin.ru/acts/bank/47046.
62. Analysed by Andrei P. Tsygankov, 'The Revisionist Moment: Russia, Trump, and Global Transition', *Problems of Post-Communism*, 68/6, 2021, pp. 457–67. For his more elaborated argument, see Andrei P. Tsygankov, *Russian Realism: Defending 'Derzhava' in International Relations* (London and New York, Routledge, 2022).
63. Sergei Karaganov, 'Mirovoi shtorm i russkii kurazh', *Russia in Global Affairs*, 28 October 2020, https://globalaffairs.ru/articles/mirovoj-shtorm-i-russkij-kurazh/.
64. This is the argument of Michael McFaul, *From Cold War to Hot Peace: The Inside Story of Russia and America* (London, Allen Lane, 2018).
65. Jennifer Anderson, *The Limits of Sino-Russian Strategic Partnership*, Adelphi Paper 315, 1997, p. 14.
66. The issue examined by Alexander Lukin, 'Have We Passed the Peak of Sino-Russian Rapprochement?', *Washington Quarterly*, 44/3, 2021, pp. 155–73.
67. 'Xi Tells Russian Media He Cherishes Deep Friendship with Putin', *Global Times*, 5 June 2019, https://www.globaltimes.cn/content/1153186.shtml.
68. M.K. Bhadrakumar, 'Russia and China Cementing an Enduring Alliance', *Asia Times*, 11 October 2020, https://asiatimes.com/2020/10/russia-and-china-cementing-an-enduring-alliance/.
69. Igor Denisov and Alexander Lukin, 'Russia's China Policy: Growing Asymmetries and Hedging Options', *Russian Politics*, 6, 2021, pp. 531–50.

70. Yan Xuetong, *Leadership and the Rise of Great Powers* (Princeton, NJ, Princeton University Press, 2019), p. 65.
71. Fu Ying, 'Are China and Russia Partnering to Create an Axis?', in Fu Ying, *Seeing the World*, pp. 235–6.
72. See Marcin Kaczmarski, 'Russia–China Closer Relationship, but Not an Alliance Yet', *Russian Analytical Digest*, No. 265, 19 March 2021, pp. 2–4.
73. Graham Allison, 'Opportunity for Diplomacy', *National Interest*, 4 February 2022, https://nationalinterest.org.
74. Economy, *Third Revolution*, p. 214.
75. Vita Spivak, 'What Does China's Latest Five-Year Plan Mean for Russia?', Carnegie Moscow Center, 19 March 2021, https://carnegie.ru/commentary/84121.
76. Allison, 'Opportunity for Diplomacy'.
77. Leonid Kovachich, 'Who Will Get a Slice of Russia's 5G Pie?', Carnegie Moscow Center, 27 December 2021, https://carnegiemoscow.org/commentary/86092.
78. Dimitri Alexander Simes, 'Huawei's Highway to Success Goes through Russia', *National Interest*, 7 March 2021, https://nationalinterest.org/feature/huawei%E2%80%99s-highway-success-goes-through-russia-179338.
79. Larisa Smirnova, 'The Real Meaning of Xi Jinping's Visit to Moscow', *Russia Direct*, 15 May 2015, http://www.russia-direct.org/analysis/real-meaning-xi-jinpings-visit-moscow.
80. Artyom Lukin, 'The North Korea Nuclear Problem and the US–China–Russia Strategic Triangle', *Russian Analytical Digest*, No. 209, 24 October 2017, pp. 2–5.
81. Richard Little, *The Balance of Power in International Relations: Metaphors, Myths and Models* (Cambridge, Cambridge University Press, 2007), p. 285.
82. 'Joint Statement of the Russian Federation and the People's Republic of China on the International Relations Entering a New Era and the Global Sustainable Development', 4 February 2022, http://en.kremlin.ru/supplement/5770.
83. Bobo Lo, 'Turning Point? Putin, Xi, and the Russian Invasion of Ukraine', Lowy Institute Analysis, May 2022, https://www.lowyinstitute.org/publications/turning-point-putin-xi-and-russian-invasion-ukraine.
84. Vladimir Putin, 'Presidential Address to Federal Assembly', 21 February 2023, http://en.kremlin.ru/events/president/news/70565.
85. John R. Deni, 'Would a Russian Coup Solve Anything?', *Wall Street Journal*, 14 March 2022, https://www.wsj.com/articles/would-a-russian-coup-solve-anything-vladimir-putin-authoritarian-regimes-ukraine-invasion-overthrown-11647195873.
86. 'Putin Approves New Foreign Policy Doctrine Based on "Russian World"', *Reuters*, 5 September 2022, https://www.reuters.com/world/putin-approves-new-foreign-policy-doctrine-based-russian-world-2022-09-05/.
87. Timothy Frye, *Weak Strongman: The Limits of Power in Putin's Russia* (Princeton, NJ, Princeton University Press, 2021).

8: EUROPE REDIVIDED

1. Kevork K. Oksanian, 'Carr Goes East: Reconsidering Power and Inequality in a Post-Liberal Eurasia', *European Politics and Society*, 20/2, 2019, pp. 172–89.

2. Maxime Lefebvre, *Europe as a Power, European Sovereignty and Strategic Autonomy*, Fondation Robert Schuman, Policy Paper No. 582, 2 February 2021, p. 1.
3. Éric Anceau, 'De Gaulle and Europe', *Encyclopédie pour une histoire nouvelle de l'Europe* [online], 22 June 2020, https://ehne.fr/en/node/12243.
4. R.T. Howard, *Power and Glory: France's Secret Wars with Britain and America, 1945–2016* (London, Biteback, 2016).
5. Alexei A. Gromyko and V.P. Fëdorova (eds), *Bol'shaya Evropa: Idei, real'nost', perspektivy* (Moscow, Ves' mir, 2014).
6. Klaus Larres, *Uncertain Allies: Nixon, Kissinger, and the Threat of a United Europe* (New Haven, CT and London, Yale University Press, 2022).
7. Jolyon Howorth, *Security and Defence Policy in the European Union* (Basingstoke, Palgrave, 2014).
8. Mark Mazower, *Dark Continent: Europe's Twentieth Century* (New York, Knopf, 1999).
9. Hill, *No Place for Russia*, p. 51.
10. The term used in 1991 by Jacques Poos, President of the European Council.
11. 'EU–NATO Joint Declaration', 10 January 2023, https://www.consilium.europa.eu/en/policies/defence-security/eu-nato-cooperation/#2023.
12. Jolyon Howorth, 'European Defence Policy between Dependence and Autonomy: A Challenge of Sisyphean Dimensions', *British Journal of Politics and International Relations*, published online 6 January 2017.
13. Most cogently, significantly, by an American, Stephen M. Walt, 'Exactly How Helpless Is Europe?', *Foreign Policy*, 21 May 2021, https://foreignpolicy.com/2021/05/21/exactly-how-helpless-is-europe/.
14. Amitav Acharya, *The End of American World Order*, 2nd edn (Cambridge, Polity, 2018), p. 119.
15. *Shared Vision, Common Action: A Stronger Europe. A Global Strategy for the European Union's Foreign and Security Policy*, June 2016, https://europa.eu/globalstrategy/sites/globalstrategy/files/about/eugs_review_web_4.pdf.
16. Lefebvre, *Europe as a Power*, pp. 4–5.
17. Speech in Munich on 28 May, reported in *Financial Times*, 29 May 2017.
18. Lefebvre, *Europe as a Power*, pp. 4–5.
19. Josep Borrell, 'Europe in the Interregnum: Our Geopolitical Awakening after Ukraine', EEAS, 24 March 2022, https://www.eeas.europa.eu/eeas/europe-interregnum-our-geopolitical-awakening-after-ukraine_en.
20. Richard Youngs, 'The Awakening of Geopolitical Europe?', Carnegie Europe, 28 July 2022, https://carnegieeurope.eu/2022/07/28/awakening-of-geopolitical-europe-pub-87580.
21. 'President Macron Gives Speech on New Initiative for Europe', 26 September 2017, https://www.elysee.fr/emmanuel-macron/2017/09/26/president-macron-gives-speech-on-new-initiative-for-europe.en.
22. Robert Zaretsky, 'Macron Is Going Full De Gaulle', *Foreign Policy*, 11 February 2019, https://foreignpolicy.com/2019/02/11/macron-is-going-full-de-gaulle/.
23. Emmanuel Macron, 'Ambassadors Conference – Speech by M. Emmanuel Macron, President of the Republic', Paris, 27 August 2019, https://lv.ambafrance.org/Ambassadors-conference-Speech-by-M-Emmanuel-Macron-President-of-the-Republic. Video of the speech available on YouTube.

24. Patrick Wintour, '"Anything Goes": First Syria, then Covid-19. Is Global Cooperation Dead?', *Guardian*, 23 July 2020, p. 30.
25. 'Emmanuel Macron Warns Europe: NATO Is Becoming Brain Dead', *The Economist*, 7 November 2019, https://www.economist.com/europe/2019/11/07/emmanuel-macron-warns-europe-nato-is-becoming-brain-dead.
26. Kevin Baron, 'Biden Wants to Restore NATO, Macron Is Looking to Move On', *Defence One*, 19 February 2021, https://www.defenseone.com/ideas/2021/02/biden-wants-restore-nato-macron-looking-move/172189/.
27. Ido Vock, 'Why Tensions Remain between Joe Biden and Emmanuel Macron', *New Statesman*, 12 June 2021, https://www.newstatesman.com/world/g7/2021/06/why-tensions-remain-between-joe-biden-and-emmanuel-macron-despite-their-warm-body.
28. For analysis, see Michael Emerson, 'Will the European Political Community Actually Be Useful?', CEPS Explainer, 2022–03, https://www.ceps.eu/ceps-publications/will-the-european-political-community-actually-be-useful/.
29. Luigi Scazzieri, 'Foreign Policy Cooperation: Brexit's Missing Link', CER, 1 February 2021, https://www.cer.eu/publications/archive/bulletin-article/2021/foreign-policy-co-operation-brexits-missing-link.
30. Already in the mid-1990s, Brzezinski unsentimentally argued that 'Great Britain is not a geostrategic player. It has fewer major options. It entertains no ambitious vision of Europe's future, and its relative decline has also reduced its capacity to play the traditional role of European balancer'. *Grand Chessboard*, p. 42.
31. Reflected in *Global Britain in a Competitive Age: The Integrated Review of Security, Defence, Development and Foreign Policy*, HM Government, March 2021.
32. An argument made by Heikki Patomäki in his presentation 'Brexit and Disintegrative Tendencies Affecting the EU', at the EuroMemo conference, London, 2–3 September 2022.
33. Rosa Balfour and Lizza Bomassi, 'EU and China Seal a Deal behind Biden's Back', Chatham House, 5 February 2021, https://www.chathamhouse.org/publications/the-world-today/2021-02/eu-and-china-seal-deal-behind-bidens-back.
34. European Commission, *EU–China: A Strategic Outlook*, 12 March 2019, https://ec.europa.eu/info/publications/eu-china-strategic-outlook-commission-contribution-european-council-21-22-march-2019_en, p. 1.
35. Brian Cloughley, 'Biden, China and Russia', *Strategic Culture*, 5 January 2021, https://www.strategic-culture.org/news/2021/01/05/biden-china-and-russia/.
36. Ivan Timofeev, 'The EU as a Significant Initiator of Sanctions', Valdai Discussion Club, 15 February 2021, https://valdaiclub.com/a/highlights/the-eu-as-a-significant-initiator-of-sanctions/.
37. Luigi Scazzieri, 'Could EU-Endorsed "Coalitions of the Willing" Strengthen EU Security Policy?', CER, 9 February 2022, https://www.cer.eu/insights/could-eu-endorsed-coalitions-willing.
38. *Strategic Compass for Security and Defence*, adopted by the Council of the European Union 21 March 2022, https://eeas.europa.eu/doc/document/ST-7371-2022-INIT/en/pdf.
39. Sten Rynning, 'The False Promise of Continental Concert: Russia, the West and the Necessary Balance of Power', *International Affairs*, 91/3, 2015, p. 545.

40. Thomas L. Friedman, *The Lexus and the Olive Tree: Understanding Globalization* (New York, Farrar, Straus and Giroux, 1999).
41. Jan-Werner Müller, 'Germany Inc', *London Review of Books*, 26 May 2022, p. 19.
42. Artin DerSimonian, 'Europe Needs a Stable Russian–German Relationship', *National Interest*, 12 September 2022, https://nationalinterest.org/feature/europe-needs-stable-russian-german-relationship-204696, provides historical context.
43. A point made by Sergei Lavrov, 'Interview with Russian and Foreign Media', 12 November 2020, https://www.mid.ru/en/en/press_service/minister_speeches/-/asset_publisher/7OvQR5KJWVmR/content/id/4429844.
44. Tina Hildebrandt and Giovanni di Lorenzo, 'Angela Merkel: "Hatten Sie gedacht, ich komme mit Pferdeschwanz?"', *Zeit Online*, 7 December 2022, https://www.zeit.de/2022/51/angela-merkel-russland-fluechtlingskrise-bundeskanzler.
45. Annegret Kramp-Karrenbauer, 'Speech by Federal Minister of Defence', 23 October 2020, https://nato.diplo.de/blob/2409698/75266e6a100b6e35895f43 1c3ae66c6d/20201023-rede-akk-medienpreis-data.pdf.
46. Marco Siddi, 'An Evolving Other: German National Identity and Constructions of Russia', *Politics*, 38/1, 2018, p. 38.
47. Thane Gustafson, *The Bridge: Natural Gas in a Redivided Europe* (Cambridge, MA, Harvard University Press, 2020).
48. Pierre Rimbert, 'How to Sabotage a Pipeline', *Le Monde Diplomatique*, May 2021, https://mondediplo.com/2021/05/09pipelines.
49. Daniel Gross, 'A (E)U-Turn from Nord Stream 2 towards a European Strategic Gas Reserve', CEPS Policy Brief, No. 2022–02, January 2022, https://sep.luiss. it/brief/2022/01/26/d-gros-eu-turn-nord-stream-2-towards-european-strategic-gas-reserve, p. 2.
50. For a stimulating discussion, see James Hawes, 'What Britain Needs to Understand about the Profound and Ancient Divisions in Germany', *New Statesman*, 19 September 2017, https://www.newstatesman.com/world/europe/2017/09/what-britain-needs-understand-about-profound-and-ancient-divisions-germany.
51. *White Paper on German Security Policy and the Future of the Bundeswehr* (Berlin, Federal Government, July 2016), https://issat.dcaf.ch/download/111704/2027268/2016%20White%20Paper.pdf, p. 22.
52. *White Paper on German Security Policy*, p. 31.
53. Dmitri Trenin, 'The End of Consensus: What Does Europe Want from Russia?', Carnegie Moscow Center, 15 December 2014, http://carnegie-moscow.org/eurasiaoutlook/?fa=57511.
54. 'German Chancellor Olaf Scholz Announces Paradigm Change in Response to Ukraine Invasion', 27 February 2022, https://www.dw.com/en/german-chancellor-olaf-scholz-announces-paradigm-change-in-response-to-ukraine-invasion/a-60932652.
55. Iren Marinova, 'Europe's Security and Defence Hour Is Here, and the Longevity of the European Union Depends on it', European Leadership Network, 31 March 2022, https://www.europeanleadershipnetwork.org/commentary/europes-security-and-defence-hour-is-here-and-the-longevity-of-the-european-union-depends-on-it/.

56. Luigi Scazzieri, 'Russia's Assault on Ukraine and European Security', CER, 30 March 2022, https://www.cer.org.uk/publications/archive/bulletin-article/2022/russias-assault-ukraine-and-european-security.

9: THE WORLD ON FIRE

1. 'Russian Foreign Ministry Releases Data on Russia, US Weapons under New Start Deal', *Sputnik*, 24 May 2021.

2. The context and dynamics are explored by Paul Rogers, *Losing Control: Global Security in the Twenty-First Century*, 4th edn (London, Pluto Press, 2021).

3. For a thoughtful and informative analysis, see Rodric Braithwaite, *Armageddon and Paranoia: The Nuclear Confrontation* (London, Profile Books, 2017).

4. 'It is Now 2 Minutes to Midnight', *Bulletin of the Atomic Scientists*, 2018, https://thebulletin.org/sites/default/files/2018%20Doomsday%20Clock%20Statement.pdf.

5. 'A Time of Unprecedented Danger: It Is 90 Seconds to Midnight', 24 January 2023, https://thebulletin.org/doomsday-clock/current-time/.

6. Gaddis, *Cold War*, p. 75.

7. Serhii Plokhy, *Nuclear Folly: A History of the Cuban Missile Crisis* (New York, W.W. Norton, 2021).

8. Gaddis, *Cold War*, p. 202.

9. Peter Huessy, 'Entangled America: Why Another International Nuclear Arms Race Has Begun', *National Interest*, 22 August 2021, https://nationalinterest.org/feature/entangled-america-why-another-international-nuclear-arms-race-has-begun-192136.

10. 'Joint Soviet–United States Statement on the Summit Meeting in Geneva', 21 November 1985, https://www.reaganlibrary.gov/archives/speech/joint-soviet-united-states-statement-summit-meeting-geneva.

11. Katrina vanden Heuvel, 'Here's What Leaders Facing Global Crises Can Learn from Mikhail Gorbachev', *Washington Post*, 23 February 2021, https://www.washingtonpost.com.

12. In Ukraine, the nuclear question became bound up with territorial issues and the status of the Black Sea Fleet stationed in Sevastopol. See Kozyrev, *Firebird*, pp. 77–8.

13. Bryan Bender, 'Leaked Document: Putin Lobbied Trump on Arms Control', *Politico*, 7 August 2018, https://www.politico.com/story/2018/08/07/putin-trump-arms-control-russia-724718.

14. For analysis, see Scott Ritter, 'Arms Control or Ukraine?', *Consortium News*, 22 February 2023, https://consortiumnews.com/2023/02/22/scott-ritter-arms-control-or-ukraine/.

15. Hanna Notte, 'Chemical Weapons Impasse Reflects Russia's Broader Conflict with the West', Carnegie Moscow Center, 16 December 2021, https://carnegiemoscow.org/commentary/86015.

16. Subrata Ghoshroy, 'Why Does Missile Defense Still Enjoy Bipartisan Support in Congress?', *Bulletin of the Atomic Scientists*, 24 September 2020, https://thebulletin.org/2020/09/why-does-missile-defense-still-enjoy-bipartisan-support-in-congress/.

17. 'Direct Line with Vladimir Putin', 17 April 2014, http://www.en.kremlin.ru/events/president/news/20796.

18. Moritz Pieper, 'Strategic Stability beyond New START', *Russian Analytical Digest*, No. 260, 20 December 2020, pp. 2–7.
19. Theodore A. Postol, 'Is Russia Solely to Blame for Violations of the INF Treaty?', *The Nation*, 17 January 2019, https://www.thenation.com/article/russia-inf-nuclear-treaty-aegis/.
20. Scott Ritter, 'US' Successful ICBM Intercept Test Brings Us Closer to Nuclear War and Proves Moscow's Concerns Were Well Grounded', 17 November 2020, https://www.rt.com/op-ed/507015-icbm-intercept-aegis-russia/.
21. Gaddis, *Cold War*, pp. 72–3; John Lewis Gaddis, *We Now Know: Rethinking Cold War History* (Oxford, Oxford University Press, 1997), p. 245.
22. Zack Brown, 'Why America Should Bring Home Its Nuclear Weapons', *National Interest*, 2 October 2020, https://nationalinterest.org/blog/skeptics/why-america-should-bring-home-its-nuclear-weapons-170055.
23. Oliver Meier, 'Debating the Withdrawal of US Nuclear Weapons from Europe: What Germany Expects from Russia', *Vestnik of Saint Petersburg University: International Relations*, 14/1, 2021, pp. 82–96.
24. *Nuclear Posture Review*, February 2018.
25. Herman Kahn, *On Escalation: Metaphors and Scenarios* (London, Routledge, 1965, reissued 2009).
26. For analysis, see Michael Fitzsimmons, 'The False Allure of Escalation Dominance', *War on the Rocks*, 16 November 2017, https://warontherocks.com/2017/11/false-allure-escalation-dominance/.
27. Bleddyn Bowen, *War in Space: Strategy, Spacepower, Geopolitics* (Edinburgh, Edinburgh University Press, 2020).
28. Tom Stevenson, 'Where Are the Space Arks?', *London Review of Books*, 4 March 2021, pp. 25–8, at p. 25.
29. Ankit Panda, 'A New US Missile Defense Test May Have Increased the Risk of Nuclear War', Carnegie Endowment for International Peace, 19 November 2020, https://carnegieendowment.org/2020/11/19/new-u.s.-missile-defense-test-may-have-increased-risk-of-nuclear-war-pub-83273.
30. Russian Foreign Affairs Ministry, 'Address by Sergei Lavrov', 24 February 2021, https://www.mid.ru/en/press_service/minister_speeches.
31. Julian Borger, 'US Democrats Call for $1bn Transfer from Missile Fund to Tackle Pandemic Threat', *Guardian*, 27 March 2021, p. 43.
32. Lyle J. Goldstein, 'The Shadow of a New Cold War Hangs over Europe', *National Interest*, 30 March 2021, https://nationalinterest.org/blog/skeptics/shadow-new-cold-war-hangs-over-europe-181559.
33. For a convincing negative assessment of the idea, see Olga Oliker, 'Russia's Nuclear Doctrine: What We Know, What We Don't, and What That Means', Washington DC, CSIS, 5 May 2016, https://www.csis.org/analysis/russia%E2%80%99s-nuclear-doctrine.
34. Pieper, 'Strategic Stability beyond New START', p. 4.
35. Liana Fix and Ulrich Kühn, 'Strategic Stability in the 21st Century', *Russian Analytical Digest*, No. 260, 20 December 2020, pp. 7–11.
36. Vladimir Putin, 'Presidential Address to the Federal Assembly', 1 March 2018, http://www.en.kremlin.ru/events/president/news/56957.
37. *Strategiya natsional'noi bezopasnosti Rossiiskoi Federatsii*, 2 July 2021, http://static.kremlin.ru/media/events/files/ru/QZw6hSk5z9gWq0plD1Zzm R5cER0g5tZC.pdf.

38. Vladimir Putin, 'Presidential Address to the Federal Assembly', 21 April 2021, http://en.kremlin.ru/events/president/news/65418.
39. For analysis of cyber and communication warfare, see Richard Sakwa, *The Russia Scare: Fake News and Genuine Threat* (London, Routledge, 2022), pp. 133–65.
40. William J. Perry and Tom Z. Collina, 'The Atomic Titanic: An Excerpt from "The Button"', *Bulletin of the Atomic Scientists*, 19 June 2020, https://thebulletin.org/2020/06/the-atomic-titanic-an-excerpt-from-the-button/. The book is William J. Perry and Tom Z. Collina, *The Button: The New Nuclear Arms Race and Presidential Power from Truman to Trump* (Dallas, TX, BenBella Books, 2020).
41. Mathieu Boulègue, *The Militarization of Russian Polar Politics*, Chatham House Research Paper, Russia and Eurasia Programme, June 2022, https://www.chathamhouse.org/2022/06/militarization-russian-polar-politics.
42. Vipal Monga and Paul Viera, 'Cold War-Era Defence System to Get Upgrade to Counter Russia, China', *Wall Street Journal*, 27 February 2021, https://www.wsj.comarticles/cold-war-era-defense-system-to-get-upgrade-to-counter-russia-china-11614438048.
43. Natalia Azarova, 'In the New Space Race, Will Russia and China Triumph over America?', Carnegie Moscow Center, 28 December 2021, https://carnegiemoscow.org/commentary/86094.
44. See Anatol Lieven, *Climate Change and the Nation State* (London, Penguin Books, 2021); and Eugene Linden, *Fire and Flood* (London, Allen Lane, 2022).
45. For more detail, see Michael T. Klare, 'The Nuclearization of American Diplomacy', *CounterPunch*, 12 October 2020, https://www.counterpunch.org/2020/10/12/the-nuclearization-of-american-diplomacy/.
46. Artyom Lukin, 'US–Russia Naval Game of Chicken off Vladivostok Is More Dangerous than It Seems', 25 November 2020, https://www.rt.com/op-ed/507781-us-russia-navy-cold-war/.
47. David Axe, 'The US Air Force's Norwegian Bomber Jaunt Has Got the Russians All Worked Up', *Forbes*, 18 February 2021, https://www.forbes.com/sites/davidaxe/2021/02/18/the-us-air-forces-norwegian-bomber-jaunt-has-got-the-russian-air-force-all-worked-up/?sh=112fc4377480.
48. Ralph Clem, 'Risky Encounters with Russia: Time to Talk about Real Deconfliction', *War on the Rocks*, 18 February 2021, https://warontherocks.com/2021/02/risky-encounters-with-russia-time-to-talk-about-real-deconfliction/.
49. Nate Jones, *Able Archer 83: The Secret History of the NATO Exercise that Almost Triggered Nuclear War* (New York, The New Press, 2016).
50. For analysis of this proposition, see Andrej Krickovic, 'Revisionism Revisited: Developing a Typology for Classifying Russia and Other Revisionist Powers', *International Politics*, published online 27 June 2021.
51. T.G. Otte, *July Crisis: The World's Descent into War, Summer 1914* (Cambridge, Cambridge University Press, 2014).

10: WAR IN EUROPE

1. For details and data on the developing conflict, see Richard Sakwa, *Frontline Ukraine: Crisis in the Borderlands*, revised edn 2017 (London, Bloomsbury Academic, reprinted 2022).

2. Samuel Charap, 'How to Break the Cycle of Conflict with Russia', *Foreign Affairs*, 7 February 2022, https://www.foreignaffairs.com/articles/russia-fsu/2022-02-07.

3. Michael O. Slobodchikoff, *Building Hegemonic Order Russia's Way: Order, Stability, and Predictability in the Post-Soviet Space* (Lanham, MD, Lexington Books, 2014).

4. Richard Sakwa, 'The Ukraine Syndrome and Europe: Between Norms and Space', *Soviet and Post-Soviet Review*, No. 44, 2017, pp. 9–31.

5. Richard Sakwa, 'No Exit: Logic and Rationality in the Ukraine Crisis', in Peter W. Schulze and Winfried Veit (eds), *Ukraine in the Crosshairs of Geopolitical Power Play* (Frankfurt and New York, Campus Verlag, 2020), pp. 101–28.

6. Dmitry Medvedev, 'Interv'yu Dmitriya Medvedeva telekanalam "Rossiya", Pervomu, NTV', Sochi, 31 August 2008, http://www.kremlin.ru/text/appears/2008/08/205991.shtml.

7. Terry Martin, *The Affirmative Action Empire: Nations and Nationalism in the Soviet Union, 1923–1939* (Ithaca, NY, Cornell University Press, 2001).

8. Yitzhak Brudny, *Reinventing Russia: Russian Nationalism and the Soviet State, 1953–1991* (Cambridge, MA, Harvard University Press, 2000).

9. See Nicolai N. Petro, *The Tragedy of Ukraine: What Classical Greek Tragedy Can Teach Us about Conflict Resolution* (Berlin, De Gruyter, 2022).

10. For good histories, see Serhii Plokhy, *The Gates of Europe: A History of Ukraine* (London, Penguin, 2015); Orest Subtelny, *Ukraine: A History*, 4th edn (Toronto, University of Toronto Press, 2009); Andrew Wilson, *The Ukrainians: The Story of How a People Became a Nation*, 5th edn (New Haven, CT and London, Yale University Press, 2022); and Serhy Yekelchyk, *Ukraine: Birth of a Modern Nation* (Oxford, Oxford University Press, 2007).

11. Yuliya Yurchenko, *Ukraine and the Empire of Capital: From Marketisation to Armed Conflict* (London, Pluto Press, 2018).

12. Brzezinski, *Grand Chessboard*, p. 46, and the point is repeated on p. 113.

13. Brzezinski, *Grand Chessboard*, p. 46.

14. For the logic of antagonism and the ensuing security dilemma, see D'Anieri, *Ukraine and Russia*.

15. Karaganov, *Russia*, p. 11.

16. Nathaniel Copsey and Karolina Pomorska, 'The Influence of Newer Member States in the European Union: The Case of Poland and the Eastern Partnership', *Europe-Asia Studies*, 66/3, May 2014, pp. 421–43.

17. International Republican Institute, *Public Opinion Survey Residents of Ukraine, 27 August – 9 September 2013*, https://www.iri.org.

18. 'Ukraine Crisis: Transcript of Leaked Nuland–Pyatt Call', *BBC News*, 7 February 2014, https://www.bbc.co.uk/news/world-europe-26079957.

19. Elena Chernenko and Alexander Gabuev, '"Interesy RF i SShA v otnoshenii Ukrainy nesovmestimy drug s drugom"', *Kommersant*, 19 December 2014, translated by Paul Grenier, 'In Ukraine, U.S Interests Are Incompatible with the Interests of the Russian Federation' Stratfor Chief George Friedman on the Roots of the Ukraine Crisis', January 2015, http://us-russia.org/2902-in-ukraine-us-interests-are-incompatible-with-the-interests-of-the-russian-federation-stratfor-chief-george-friedman-on-the-roots-of-the-ukraine-crisis.html.

20. For a contrary view, see Andrew Wilson, *Ukraine Crisis: What it Means for the West* (New Haven, CT and London, Yale University Press, 2014).
21. Nicolai N. Petro, 'Bringing Ukraine Back into Focus', Carnegie Council, 19 August 2015, https://www.carnegiecouncil.org/publications/articles_papers_reports/742.
22. Analysed by Gerard Toal, *Near Abroad: Putin, the West and the Contest over Ukraine and the Caucasus* (Oxford, Oxford University Press, 2017).
23. Marlene Laruelle, *The 'Russian World': Russia's Soft Power and Geopolitical Imagination* (Washington DC, Center on Global Interests, May 2015).
24. Vladimir Putin, 'Address by the President of the Russian Federation', 18 March 2014, http://en.kremlin.ru/events/president/news/20603.
25. A quotation from the rebel leader 'Prince', in Anna Matveeva, *Through Times of Trouble: Conflict in Southeastern Ukraine Explained from Within* (Lanham, MD, Lexington Books, 2017), p. 100.
26. Volodymyr Ishchenko, 'Ukrainians Are Far from Unified on NATO', *Truthout*, 28 December 2021, https://truthout.org/articles/ukrainians-are-far-from-unified-on-nato-let-them-decide-for-themselves/.
27. Serhiy Rudenko, *Zelensky: A Biography* (Cambridge, Polity, 2022), p. 49.
28. Analysed by Petro, *Tragedy of Ukraine*, pp. 36–89, 90, 103, 241.
29. Gordon Hahn, *Ukraine over the Edge: Russia, the West and the 'New Cold War'* (Jefferson, NC, McFarland Books, 2017).
30. International Republican Institute, 'IRI Ukraine Poll Shows Support for EU/NATO Membership, Concerns over Economy and Vaccines for Covid-19', 17 December 2021, https://www.iri.org/resource/iri-ukraine-poll-shows-support-eunato-membership-concerns-over-economy-and-vaccines-covid.
31. The basic argument was first adumbrated in Brzezinski's 'The Premature Partnership', *Foreign Affairs*, 73/2, March/April 1994, pp. 67–82.
32. These are explored by a number of essays in J.L. Black and Michael Johns (eds), *The Return of the Cold War: Ukraine, the West and Russia* (London, Routledge, 2016).
33. For a concise and informative analysis, see Ramon Marks, 'Russia Alone Did Not Destabilize Ukraine', *National Interest*, 19 December 2021, https://nationalinterest.org/feature/russia-alone-did-not-destabilize-ukraine-198065.
34. Samuel Charap and Timothy Colton, *Everyone Loses: The Ukraine Crisis and the Ruinous Contest for Post-Soviet Eurasia* (London, Routledge/Adelphi, 2016).
35. Valerii Gerasimov, 'Mir na granyakh voiny', *Voenno-promyshlennyi kur'er*, 10, 15 March 2017.
36. *NATO 2030: United for a New Era*, 25 November 2020, https://www.nato.int/nato_static_fl2014/assets/pdf/2020/12/pdf/201201-Reflection-Group-Final-Report-Uni.pdf.
37. Notably, the RAND report by David Shlapak and Michael Johnson, *Reinforcing Deterrence on NATO's Eastern Flank*, 2016, https://www.rand.org/content/dam/rand/pubs/research_reports/RR1200/RR1253/RAND_RR1253.pdf.
38. Scott Ritter, 'How Polish Wargame Where It Loses to Russia Could Become a Self-Fulfilling Prophecy', 23 February 2021, https://www.rt.com/op-ed/516389-poland-wargame-russia-nato-war/.
39. Mikhail Pogrebinsky, 'Why Zelensky's Ukraine Is Becoming Increasingly Autocratic', *National Interest*, 6 April 2021, https://nationalinterest.org/

feature/why-zelensky%E2%80%99s-ukraine-becoming-increasingly-auto-cratic-182124.

40. Ted Galen Carpenter, 'Why Ukraine Is a Dangerous and Unworthy Ally', *National Interest*, 28 June 2021, https://nationalinterest.org/blog/skeptics/why-ukraine-dangerous-and-unworthy-ally-188742.

41. Gary Leupp, 'Biden to Ukraine: "Unwavering Support for Euro-Atlantic Aspirations"', *CounterPunch*, 7 April 2021, https://www.counterpunch.org/2021/04/07/biden-to-ukraine-unwavering-support-for-euro-atlantic-aspirations/.

42. Anatol Lieven, 'Russia Has Been Warning about Ukraine for Decades: The West Should Have Listened', *Time*, 25 January 2022, https://time.com/6141806/russia-ukraine-threats/.

43. 'Joint News Conference with President of Finland Sauli Niinisto', 27 July 2017, http://en.kremlin.ru/events/president/news/55175.

44. Vladimir Putin, 'Presidential Address to the Federal Assembly', 21 April 2021, http://en.kremlin.ru/events/president/news/65418.

45. Vladimir Putin, 'On the Historical Unity of Russians and Ukrainians', 12 July 2021, http://en.kremlin.ru/events/president/news/66181.

46. As argued by Mearsheimer, 'Why the Ukraine Crisis is the West's Fault'.

47. White House, 'Joint Statement on the US–Ukraine Strategic Partnership', 1 September 2021, https://www.whitehouse.gov/briefing-room/statements-releases/2021/09/01/joint-statement-on-the-u-s-ukraine-strategic-partnership/.

48. State Department, 'US–Ukraine Charter on Strategic Partnership', 10 November 2021, https://www.state.gov/u-s-ukraine-charter-on-strategic-partnership/#:~:text=The%20United%20States%20and%20Ukraine%20endorse%20the%202021%20Strategic%20Defense,such%20as%20Black%20Sea%20security%2C.

49. David Sacks, 'The State Department Failed to Prevent the War. Will It Now Prevent the Peace?', *American Conservative*, 8 April 2022, https://www.theamericanconservative.com/articles/the-state-department-failed-to-prevent-the-war-will-it-now-prevent-the-peace/.

50. Russian Foreign Affairs Ministry, 'Treaty between the United States of America and the Russian Federation on Security Guarantees', 17 December 2021, https://mid.ru/ru/foreign_policy/rso/nato/1790818/?lang=en; 'Agreement on Measures to Ensure the Security of the Russian Federation and Member States of the North Atlantic Treaty Organisation', 17 December 2021, https://mid.ru/ru/foreign_policy/rso/nato/1790803/?lang=en&clear_cache=Y. The actual date of the documents is 15 December.

51. Sacks, 'The State Department Failed to Prevent the War'.

52. The dilemmas of neutrality are explored by Roy Allison, 'Russia, Ukraine and State Survival through Neutrality', *International Affairs*, 98/6, 2022, pp. 1849–72.

53. Hibai Arbide Aza and Miguel González, 'US Offered Disarmament Measures to Russia in Exchange for De-escalation of Military Threat in Ukraine', *El País*, 2 February 2022, https://english.elpais.com/usa/2022-02-02/us-offers-disarmament-measures-to-russia-in-exchange-for-a-deescalation-of-military-threat-in-ukraine.html.

54. 'News Conference Following Russian–Hungarian Talks', 1 February 2022, http://en.kremlin.ru/events/president/news/67690.

55. MID RF, 'O peredache pis'mennoi reaktsii na otvet amerikanskoi storony po garantiyam bezopasnosti' ['Transfer of Written Reaction to American Response to Security Guarantees'], 17 February 2022.

56. OSCE, Special Monitoring Mission to Ukraine, *Daily Report*, 42/2022, 23 February 2022, 2022-02-23 Daily Report_ENG.pdf.

57. James Siebens, 'Is Russia's Invasion a Case of Coercive Diplomacy Gone Wrong?', *War on the Rocks*, 31 March 2022, https://warontherocks.com/2022/03/is-russias-invasion-a-case-of-coercive-diplomacy-gone-wrong/.

58. 'Zelensky's Full Speech at Munich Security Conference', *Kyiv Independent*, 19 February 2022, https://kyivindependent.com/national/zelenskys-full-speech-at-munich-security-conference/.

59. Fyodor Lukyanov, 'Old Thinking for Our Country and the World', *Russia in Global Affairs*, 13 April 2022, https://eng.globalaffairs.ru/articles/old-thinking/.

60. Vladimir Putin, 'Address by the President of the Russian Federation', 21 February 2022, http://en.kremlin.ru/events/president/transcripts/67828.

61. Vladimir Putin, 'Address by the President of the Russian Federation', 24 February 2022, http://en.kremlin.ru/events/president/transcripts/67843.

62. Hal Gardner, 'Washington and Kyiv versus Moscow', *Other News*, 23 May 2022, https://www.other-news.info/washington-and-kyiv-versus-moscow/.

63. Analysed by Graham Allison, 'Putin's Doomsday Threat: How to Prevent a Repeat of the Cuban Missile Crisis in Ukraine', *Foreign Affairs*, 5 April 2022, https://www.foreignaffairs.com/articles/ukraine/2022-04-05/putins-doomsday-threat.

64. Richard Chetwode, '"Ukraine Will Never Join NATO". Five Simple Words We Refused to Say', *Intellinews*, 14 March 2022, https://intellinews.com/comment-ukraine-will-never-join-nato-five-simple-words-we-refused-to-say-are-we-now-about-to-double-down-on-our-mistake-237885/?source=ukraine.

65. Chetwode, '"Ukraine Will Never Join NATO"'.

66. Patrick J. Buchanan, 'No One Wins if Ukraine Becomes a Long War', *American Conservative*, 9 April 2022, https://www.theamericanconservative.com/buchanan/no-one-wins-if-ukraine-becomes-a-long-war/.

11: CRISIS OF THE INTERNATIONAL SYSTEM

1. Robert Legvold, *Return to Cold War* (Cambridge, Polity, 2016).

2. Michael Mandelbaum, 'The New Containment: Handling Russia, China and Iran', *Foreign Affairs*, 98/2, March/April 2019, pp. 123–31.

3. Andrew Monaghan, *A 'New Cold War'? Abusing History, Misunderstanding Russia* Chatham House Research Paper, London, May 2015.

4. Joshua Shifrinson, *Rising Titans, Falling Giants: How Great Powers Exploit Power Shifts* (Ithaca, NY, Cornell University Press, 2018).

5. Andrew Monaghan, *Dealing with the Russians* (Cambridge, Polity, 2019).

6. Michael T. Klare, 'With Russia at War in Ukraine, America Is Back (and Never Left)', *Le Monde Diplomatique*, March 2022, https://mondediplo.com.

7. Analysed by Stephen S. Roach, *Accidental Conflict: America, China and the Clash of False Narratives* (New Haven, CT and London, Yale University Press,

2022), who identifies an escalation in Ukraine and Taiwan as the likely sparks today.

8. John J. Mearsheimer, 'The Inevitable Rivalry', *Foreign Affairs*, 100/6, Nov/Dec 2021, p. 54.

9. Stephen F. Cohen, *War with Russia: From Putin and Ukraine to Trump and Russiagate* (New York, Hot Books, 2018).

10. The classic statement is Steven Pinker, *The Better Angels of Our Nature: Why Violence Has Declined* (New York, Viking Books, 2011). See also Joshua S. Goldstein, *Winning the War on War: The Decline of Armed Conflict Worldwide* (London, Plume, 2012); Michael Mandelbaum, *The Rise and Fall of Peace on Earth* (Oxford, Oxford University Press, 2019); and Michael Mousseau, 'The End of War: How a Robust Marketplace and Liberal Hegemony Are Leading to Perpetual World Peace', *International Security*, 44/1, 2019, pp. 160–96; and for an earlier account, John E. Mueller, *Retreat from Doomsday: The Obsolescence of Major War* (New York, Basic Books, 1989).

11. Sebastian Rosato, 'The Flawed Logic of Democratic Peace Theory', *American Political Science Review*, 97/4, November 2003, pp. 585–602.

12. John Lewis Gaddis, *The Long Peace: Inquiries into the History of the Cold War* (Oxford, Oxford University Press, 1989).

13. Norman Angell, *The Great Illusion: A Study of the Relation of Military Power to National Advantage* (San Francisco, CA, Bottom of the Hill Publishing, [1910] 2012).

14. James J. Sheehan, *Where Have All the Soldiers Gone? The Transformation of Modern Europe* (New York, Mariner Books, 2009).

15. Hal Brands and Michael Beckley, 'China Is a Declining Power – and That's the Problem', *Foreign Policy*, 24 September 2021, https://foreignpolicy.com/2021/09/24/china-great-power-united-states/.

16. Mearsheimer, *Tragedy of Great Power Politics*, pp. 360–411.

17. Christopher Layne, 'Coming Storms: The Return of Great-Power War', *Foreign Affairs*, 99/6, Nov/Dec 2020, p. 42.

18. Layne, 'Coming Storms', p. 44.

19. Layne, 'Coming Storms', p. 45.

20. Layne, 'Coming Storms', p. 46.

21. Layne, 'Coming Storms', p. 47.

22. Kevin Rudd, 'Short of War: How to Keep US–Chinese Confrontation from Ending in Calamity', *Foreign Affairs*, 100/2, March/April 2001, pp. 64, 69.

23. Robert Legvold, 'Ending the New Cold War with Russia', *National Interest*, 2 February 2022, https://nationalinterest.org/feature/ending-new-cold-war-russia-199997.

24. Clark, *Sleepwalkers*, pp. xxv–xxvi.

25. *NATO 2022: Strategic Concept*, adopted by the Madrid summit, 29–30 June 2022, https://www.nato.int/strategic-concept.

26. Andrei Tsygankov, for example, rejects the metaphor and instead stresses the ongoing global power shift accompanied by patterns of great-power conflict and cooperation: *Russia and America: The Asymmetric Rivalry* (Cambridge, Polity, 2019), Chapter 1.

27. Richard Sakwa, *The Putin Paradox* (London and New York, I.B. Tauris, 2020).

28. Legvold, 'Ending the New Cold War with Russia'.

29. Robert Legvold, 'Two Cold Wars in a New Bipolar World', *National Interest*, 4 September 2022, https://nationalinterest.org./feature/two-cold-wars-new-bipolar-world-204553.

30. McFaul, 'Cold War Lessons', p. 8.

31. Mark Kramer, 'US–Russian Relations and the "New Cold War" Metaphor', *Ponars Eurasia*, No. 547, Winter 2018, http://www.ponarseurasia.org/memo/us-russian-relations-and-new-cold-war-metaphor.

32. James Der Derian, *On Diplomacy: A Genealogy of Western Estrangement* (Oxford, Blackwell, 1987), p. 135 (emphasis in original).

33. Igor Ivanov, 'Time for Diplomacy', RIAC, 13 May 2021, https://russian-council.ru/en/analytics-and-comments/analytics/time-for-diplomacy/.

34. UN Watch, Human Rights Foundation and Raoul Wallenberg Centre for Human Rights, *Evaluation of UNHRC Candidates for 2021–23*, 5 October 2020,https://unwatch.org/wp-content/uploads/2020/10/Evaluation-of-2021-23-UNHRC-Candidates-1.pdf.

35. For the debate, see Simpson, 'Two Liberalisms', pp. 549–56.

36. Ronan Farrow, *War on Peace: The Decline of American Influence* (London, William Collins, 2021).

37. Michael Beckley, 'Rogue Superpower: Why This Could Be an Illiberal American Century', *Foreign Affairs*, 99/6, Nov/Dec 2020, pp. 73–87.

38. John J. Mearsheimer, 'The False Promise of International Institutions', *International Security*, 19/3, 1994/5, pp. 5–49.

39. Zbigniew Brzezinski, 'Toward a Global Realignment', *American Interest*, 11/6, 17 April 2016, http://www.the-american-interest.com/2016/04/17/toward-a-global-realignment/.

40. Ivan Timofeev, 'USA vs. the International Criminal Court', Valdai Discussion Club, 17 June 2020, https://valdaiclub.com/a/highlights/usa-vs-the-international-criminal-court/.

41. Statement by Prosecutor Karim A.A. Khan KC, ICC, 17 March 2023, https://www.icc-cpi.int/news/statement-prosecutor-karim-khan-kc-issuance-arrest-warrants-against-president-vladimir-putin.

42. Hosse Almutairi, 'G20, G7 and Covid-19: An Opportunity for Cooperation', *ISPI Online*, 10 June 2020, https://www.ispionline.it/en/pubblicazione/g20-g7-and-covid-19-opportunity-cooperation-26454.

43. Wintour, '"Anything Goes"'.

44. For details on institutions and the underlying strategy, see Miller, *Why Nations Rise*, pp. 98–118.

45. Stacie Goddard, 'The Outsiders', *Foreign Affairs*, 101/3, May/June 2022, p. 35.

46. Russian Foreign Affairs Ministry, 'Foreign Minister Sergey Lavrov's Remarks and Answers to Questions', Yevgeny Primakov School, 23 May 2022, https://www.mid.ru/en/press_service/minister_speeches/1814502/.

47. Ivo. H. Daalder and James M. Lindsay, 'Last Best Hope: The West's Final Chance to Build a Better World Order', *Foreign Affairs*, 101/4, July/Aug 2022, pp. 120, 121 and 125.

48. Anatol Lieven, 'Why Biden's "Summit for Democracy" Is a Bad Idea', *Responsible Statecraft*, 24 May 2021, https://responsiblestatecraft.org/2021/05/24/why-bidens-summit-for-democracy-is-a-bad-idea/.

49. Patrick Wintour, 'US Seen as Bigger Threat to Democracy than Russia or China, Global Poll Finds', *Guardian*, 5 May 2021, https://www.theguardian.com/world/2021/may/05/us-threat-democracy-russia-china-global-poll.

50. Wintour, ' "Anything Goes" '.
51. Thomas Graham, 'Can the United States Build an Alliance of Democracies?', Valdai Discussion Club, 19 May 2021, https://valdaiclub.com/a/highlights/can-the-us-build-an-alliance-of-democracies/.
52. Alexandra Dienes, Reinhard Krumm and Simon Weiss, 'Europeans Today Are Much Less Belligerent than in 1914 or 1939', *Takeaways*, FES Regional Office for Cooperation and Peace in Europe, June 2020, p. 5.

12: RISE OF THE POLITICAL EAST

1. The point is made by Zbigniew Brzezinski, *Strategic Vision: America and the Crisis of Global Power* (New York, Basic Books, 2012), p. 7.
2. Already in 1989–91, when the political West was rejoicing in the 'end of history', Janet Abu-Lughod predicted not only the end of Western hegemony but also the return to elements of the early fourteenth-century international system, with multiple power centres, *Before European Hegemony: The World System AD 1250–1350* (Oxford, Oxford University Press, 1991).
3. For a sceptical perspective, see Gordon Adams, 'We Don't Write the Rules Anymore', *Responsible Statecraft*, 14 May 2022, https://responsiblestatecraft.org/2022/05/14/lessons-from-the-1990s-must-inform-post-ukraine-war-us-policy/.
4. Zakaria, *Post-American World*, p. 47.
5. For a historical analysis, see Nicholas Mulder, *The Economic Weapon: The Rise of Sanctions as a Tool of Modern War* (New Haven, CT and London, Yale University Press, 2022).
6. Obama imposed executive sanctions on 6 March and 18 December 2014, 1 April 2015, and 26 July and 29 December 2016.
7. Wolfgang Ischinger, 'Why Europeans Oppose the Russia Sanctions Bill', *Wall Street Journal*, 17 July 2016, https://www.wsj.com/articles/why-europeans-oppose-the-russia-sanctions-bill-1500232733.
8. Mikhail Alexseev, 'Why Trump's Bid to Improve US–Russian Relations Backfired', Ponars Eurasia, February 2018, http://www.ponarseurasia.org/memo/why-trumps-bid-improve-us-russian-relations-backfired-congress.
9. See Konstantin Khudoley, 'Russia and the US: The Way Forward', *Russia in Global Affairs*, No. 4, 2017, http://eng.globalaffairs.ru/number/Russia-and-the-US-The-Way-Forward-19263.
10. Sabra Ayres, 'Russia Feeling the Financial Bite of US Sanctions', *Los Angeles Times*, 10 April 2018, p. A3.
11. Jeanne Whalen and John Hudson, 'Too Big to Sanction? US Struggles with Punishing Large Russian Businesses', *Washington Post*, 26 August 2018.
12. 'Excerpts from Dmitry Medvedev's Interview with Vesti and Subbotu Programme', 28 April 2018, http://government.ru/en/news/32506/.
13. 'Over 40% of Russians Believe Western Sanctions Likely to Remain for Years', Sputnik, 29 April 2018, https://sputniknews.com/russia/201804291064013398-sanctions-lift-poll/.
14. Vladimir Putin, 'Interview with China Media Group', 5 June 2018, http://en.kremlin.ru/events/president/news/57684.

15. Ivan Timofeev, 'Fighting Sanctions: From Legislation to Strategy', Valdai Club, 18 June 2018, http://valdaiclub.com/a/highlights/fighting-sanctions-strategy/.

16. See Richard Connolly, *Russia's Response to Sanctions: How Western Economic Statecraft is Reshaping Political Economy in Russia* (Cambridge, Cambridge University Press, 2018).

17. Richard Connolly, *Russia's Responses to Sanctions: How Western Sanctions Reshaped Political Economy in Russia*, Valdai Paper No. 94, November 2018, http://valdaiclub.com/a/valdai-papers/russia-s-response-to-sanctions-how-western-sanctio/.

18. Quoted by Fyodor Lukyanov, 'Trump May Be Leaving, but Russia Sanctions Will Stay', Carnegie Moscow Center, 20 November 2020, https://carnegie.ru/commentary/83282.

19. 'US Curbs on Russian Banks Would Be an Act of Economic War – PM Medvedev', *Reuters*, 10 August 2018, https://www.reuters.com/article/uk-usa-russia-sanctions-moscow-reaction-idUKKBN1KV0FM.

20. Ivan Timofeev, *Sanctions against Russia: A Look into 2021*, Moscow, RIAC Report No. 65, 2021, https://russiancouncil.ru/en/activity/publications/sanctions-against-russia-a-look-into-2021/, p. 7.

21. Timofeev, *Sanctions against Russia*, p. 13.

22. Nicolai N. Petro, 'America Is Addicted to Sanctions', *National Interest*, 16 August 2018, https://nationalinterest.org/blog/skeptics/america-addicted-sanctions-28952.

23. Andrei Tsygankov, 'Sanctions Serve to Maintain US Global Hegemony', Valdai Discussion Club, 16 August 2018, http://valdaiclub.com/a/highlights/sanctions-serve-to-maintain-the-us-global-hegemony/.

24. Petro, 'America Is Addicted to Sanctions'.

25. Steve Holland, Jeff Mason and James Oliphant, 'Exclusive: Trump Vows "No Concessions" with Turkey over Detained US Pastor', *Reuters*, 20 August 2018, https://www.reuters.com/article/us-usa-trump-exclusive/exclusive-trump-vows-no-concessions-with-turkey-over-detained-u-s-pastor-idUSKCN1L5223.

26. Krishen Mehta, 'Sanctions and Forever Wars', US Committee on US–Russia Accord, 4 May 2021, https://usrussiaaccord.com/acura-viewpoint-sanctions-and-forever-wars-by-krishen-mehta/.

27. Yong, *China's Struggle for Status*, p. 143.

28. Stephen G. Brooks and William C. Wohlforth, 'The Myth of Multipolarity: American Power's Staying Power', *Foreign Affairs*, 18 April 2023, https://www.foreignaffairs.com/united-states/china-multipolarity-myth.

29. For a later theoretical analysis, see Trine Flockhart, 'The Coming Multi-Order World', *Contemporary Security Policy*, 37/1, 2016, pp. 3–30.

30. Amitav Acharya, 'After Liberal Hegemony: The Advent of a Multiplex World Order', *Ethics & International Affairs*, 31/3, 2017, pp. 271–85.

31. Fyodor Lukyanov, the influential editor of *Russia in Global Affairs*, quoted by Fred Weir, 'Worse than the Cold War? US–Russia Relations Hit New Low', *Christian Science Monitor*, 20 April 2021, https://www.csmonitor.com.

32. Zakaria, *Post-American World*, p. 36.

33. Zakaria, *Post-American World*, p. xxx.

34. Zakaria, *Post-American World*, p. 3.

35. Zakaria, *Post-American World*, p. 36.
36. The speechwriter David Frum inserted the term 'axis of evil' to describe Iran, Iraq and North Korea into Bush's January 2002 State of the Union address. The argument is developed by Richard Perle and David Frum, *An End to Evil* (New York, Random House, 2003).
37. Charles Kupchan, *No One's World: The West, the Rising Rest and the Coming Global Turn* (Oxford, Oxford University Press, 2012).
38. Andrey Kortunov, 'Consolidation of the West: Opportunities and Limits', RIAC, 31 May 2022, https://russiancouncil.ru/en/analytics-and-comments/analytics/consolidation-of-the-west-opportunities-and-limits/.
39. Michael Schuman, *Superpower Interrupted: The Chinese History of the World* (New York, Public Affairs, 2020).
40. *Interim National Security Strategic Guidance*, p. 13.
41. Cf. Ikenberry, *World Safe for Democracy*.
42. Stephen M. Walt and Dani Rodrik, 'How to Build a Better Order', *Foreign Affairs*, 101/5, Sep/Oct 2022, pp. 142–55.
43. G. Lowes Dickinson, *The European Anarchy*, first published in 1916 (London, Routledge Revivals, 2015).
44. Oliver Stuenkel, *Post-Western World: How Emerging Powers Are Remaking Global Order* (Cambridge, Polity, 2016).
45. Lorenzo Kamel, 'Has the Russo-Ukraine War Really Changed the Global Order?', *National Interest*, 14 April 2022, https://nationalinterest.org/blog/buzz/has-russo-ukraine-war-really-changed-global-order-201835.
46. Mathew Burrows and Robert A. Manning, *Kissinger's Nightmare: How an Inverted US–China–Russia May Be a Game-Changer*, Valdai Paper No. 33, Moscow, November 2015, p. 3.
47. Ayşe Zarakol, *Hierarchies in World Politics* (Cambridge, Cambridge University Press, 2017).
48. Ayşe Zarakol, *After Defeat: How the East Learned to Live with the West* (Cambridge, Cambridge University Press, 2011).
49. Oliver Stuenkel, *The BRICS and the Future of Global Order* (London and Lanham, MD, Lexington Books, 2015).
50. Jim O'Neill, *Building Better Global Economic BRICs*, Goldman Sachs Global Economics Paper No. 66, New York, November 2001, http://www.goldmansachs.com/our-thinking/archive/archive-pdfs/build-better-brics.pdf. The idea was further developed in a paper by Dominic Wilson and Roopa Purushothaman, *Dreaming with the BRICs: The Path to 2050*, Goldman Sachs Global Economics Paper No. 99, New York, October 2003, http://avikdgreat.tripod.com/InterestingReads/BRIC_GoldmanSachs.pdf.
51. Hurrell, 'Beyond the BRICS', p. 92.
52. Alexander Lukin and Fan Xuesong, 'What Is BRICS for China?', *Strategic Analysis*, 43/6, 2019, p. 621.
53. Lukin and Fan, 'What Is BRICS for China?', p. 623.
54. Nivedita Das Kundu, 'BRICS@15: India to Chair 13th BRICS Summit', Valdai Club, 9 April 2021, https://valdaiclub.com/a/highlights/brics-15-india-to-chair-13th-brics-summit/.
55. 'Full Text of the 14th BRICS Summit Beijing Declaration', 24 June 2022, http://www.china.org.cn/world/2022-06/24/content_78288365.htm.
56. Maçães, *Belt and Road*, p. 15.

57. Xiang Lanxin, 'Impact of the US–China Conflict on Greater Eurasia: A New Cold War is Looming?', Valdai Discussion Club, 12 October 2020, https://valdaiclub.com/a/highlights/impact-of-the-us-china-conflict-on-greater-eurasia/.

58. Yan Xuetong, *Leadership*, p. xiv.

59. Zhao Huasheng, 'Modern Approaches of China to the Shanghai Cooperation Organization', Valdai Club, 12 April 2022, https://valdaiclub.com/a/highlights/modern-approaches-of-china-to-the-sco/.

60. 'Samarkand Declaration of the Council of Heads of State of Shanghai Cooperation Organization', 16 September 2022, https://www.mea.gov.in/bilateral-documents.htm?dtl/35724/Samarkand_Declaration_of_the_Council_of_Heads_of_State_of_Shanghai_Cooperation_Organization.

61. Karl Deutsch et al., *Political Community and the North Atlantic Area: International Organization in the Light of Historical Experience* (Princeton, NJ, Princeton University Press, 1957).

62. Brian G. Carlson, 'Russia and the China–India Rivalry', *Russian Analytical Digest*, No. 265, 19 March 2021, pp. 8–11.

63. Sumanth Samsani, 'The Way Forward for India–Russia Relations', *Asia Times*, 21 May 2021, https://asiatimes.com/2021/05/the-way-forward-for-india-russia-relations/.

64. Analysed by Rajan Menon and Eugene Rumer, *Russia and India: A New Chapter* (Washington DC, Carnegie Endowment for International Peace, September 2022), https://carnegieendowment.org/2022/09/20/russia-and-india-new-chapter-pub-87958.

65. Sarang Shidore, 'India Tilts towards Russia in Ukraine Fight at UN', *Responsible Statecraft*, 3 February 2022, https://responsiblestatecraft.org/2022/02/03/india-tilts-towards-russia-in-ukraine-fight-at-the-un/.

66. For a good analysis, see Rajeswari Pillai Rajagopalan, 'Why Did Russian President Putin Visit India?', Observer Research Foundation, 15 December 2021, https://www.orfonline.org/research/why-did-russian-president-putin-visit-india/.

67. Patryk Kugiel, 'What Modi and Putin's "Unbreakable Friendship" Means for the EU', *EUobserver*, 3 October 2022, https://euobserver.com/opinion/156193.

68. For an elaboration of the philosophy underpinning India's foreign policy, see S. Jaishankar (India's foreign minister), *The India Way: Strategies for an Uncertain World* (Gurugram, HarperCollins, 2020).

69. The term used by Indian prime minister Manmohan Singh in 2004.

70. Sreeram Chaulia, 'India–Russia Friendship Is Too Pragmatic for US and China to Ruin It', 11 April 2021, https://www.rt.com/op-ed/520751-russia-india-pragmatic-friendship/.

71. Deepa M. Ollapally, 'India and the International Order: Accommodation and Adjustment', *Ethics & International Affairs*, 32/1, 2018, p. 62.

72. Miller, *Why Nations Rise*, pp. 119–41.

CONCLUSION

1. 'John le Carré on Brexit: "It's Breaking My Heart"', *Guardian*, 1 February 2020, https://www.theguardian.com/books/2020/feb/01/john-le-carre-breaking-heart-brexit.

2. Quoted by George Shultz, *Turmoil and Triumph: My Years as Secretary of State* (Hoboken, NJ, Prentice Hall, 1993). The relevant section is available at https://www.margaretthatcher.org/document/110622.

3. Analysed by Joseph S. Nye, *Is the American Century Over?* (Cambridge, Polity, 2015).

4. Adam Tooze, 'Is This the End of the American Century?', *London Review of Books*, 4 April 2019, pp. 3–7.

5. For a maximalist interpretation, see David Held, Anthony McGrew, David Goldblatt and Jonathan Perraton, *Global Transformations: Politics, Economics and Culture* (Cambridge, Polity, 1999). For a more sceptical view, see Joseph Stiglitz, *Globalization and Its Discontents* (London, Penguin, 2002).

6. Burns, *Back Channel*, p. 403.

7. Burns, *Back Channel*, p. 413.

8. See Paolo Urio, *America and the China Threat: From the End of History to the End of Empire* (Atlanta, GA, Clarity Press, 2022).

9. Acharya, *End of American World Order*, p. 133, who outlines some scenarios, including his model of a multiplex world, pp. 139–43.

10. Vladimir Putin, 'Presidential Address to the Federal Assembly', 21 April 2021, http://en.kremlin.ru/events/president/news/65418.

11. Katrina vanden Heuvel, 'How to Avoid a New Cold War and Focus on What America Really Needs', *Washington Post*, 15 March 2022, https://www.washingtonpost.com/opinions/2022/03/15/how-to-avoid-new-cold-war/.

12. Michael O'Hanlon, 'To Face Russia and Vladimir Putin, Joe Biden Needs a Smart Strategy', Brookings, 28 May 2021, https://www.brookings.edu/blog/order-from-chaos/2021/05/28/to-face-russia-and-vladimir-putin-joe-biden-needs-a-smart-strategy/. O'Hanlon is the author of *The Art of War in an Age of Peace: US Grand Strategy and Resolute Restraint* (New Haven, CT and London, Yale University Press, 2021), arguing that the US needs a more focused and restrained foreign policy.

13. Kennedy, '1963 Commencement'.

14. Little, *Balance of Power*, p. 67.

15. Hans J. Morgenthau, *Politics among Nations: The Struggle for Power and Peace*, 5th edn (New York, Alfred A. Knopf, 1973), pp. 108, 274.

16. For a broad discussion, see Adrian Pabst, *Postliberal Politics: The Coming Era of Renewal* (Cambridge, Polity, 2021).

17. Nicolai N. Petro's talk on the subject can be found on YouTube at https://lnkd.in/dGT_kCh, discussed in his 'Looking beyond the Current Tragedy in Ukraine', *American Committee for US–Russia Accord*, 9 April 2021, https://usrussiaaccord.com/nicolai-n-petro-looking-beyond-the-current-tragedy-in-ukraine/. For his analysis of Ukrainian history through the prism of tragedy, see Petro, *The Tragedy of Ukraine*.

18. Richard Ned Lebow, *The Tragic Vision of Politics: Ethics, Interests and Orders* (Cambridge, Cambridge University Press), p. xi.

19. Ikenberry, G. John, 'Why the Liberal World Order Will Survive', *Ethics & International Affairs*, 32/1, 2018, p. 20.

BIBLIOGRAPHY OF MAJOR
WORKS CITED

Abu-Lughod, Janet L., *Before European Hegemony: The World System AD 1250–1350* (Oxford, Oxford University Press, 1991)

Acharya, Amitav, 'After Liberal Hegemony: The Advent of a Multiplex World Order', *Ethics & International Affairs*, 31/3, 2017, pp. 271–85

—, *The End of American World Order*, 2nd edn (Cambridge, Polity, 2018)

Allison, Graham, *Destined for War: Can America and China Escape Thucydides's Trap?* (London, Scribe, 2018)

Allison, Roy, 'Russia, Ukraine and State Survival through Neutrality', *International Affairs*, 98/6, 2022, pp. 1849–72

Anderson, Jennifer, *The Limits of Sino-Russian Strategic Partnership*, Adelphi Paper 315, 1997

Anderson, Perry, *The H-Word: The Peripeteia of Hegemony* (London, Verso, 2017)

Angell, Norman, *The Great Illusion: A Study of the Relation of Military Power to National Advantage* (San Francisco, CA, Bottom of the Hill Publishing, [1910] 2012)

Averre, Derek, *Russian Strategy in the Middle East and North Africa* (Manchester, Manchester University Press, 2024)

Bacevich, Andrew J., *The Age of Illusions: How America Squandered Its Cold War Victory* (New York, Metropolitan Books, 2020)

Bacon, Edwin, and Bettina Renz with Julian Cooper, *Securitising Russia: The Domestic Politics of Putin* (Manchester, Manchester University Press, 2006)

Bailey, Thomas A., *Woodrow Wilson and the Lost Peace* (New York, Macmillan, 1944)

Bassin, Mark, *The Gumilev Mystique* (Ithaca, NY, Cornell University Press, 2016)

Beckley, Michael, 'Rogue Superpower: Why This Could Be an Illiberal American Century', *Foreign Affairs*, 99/6, Nov/Dec 2020, pp. 73–87

Bell, Daniel A., *The China Model: Political Meritocracy and the Limits of Democracy* (Princeton, NJ, Princeton University Press, 2015)

Bergsten, C. Fred, *The United States vs. China: The Quest for Global Economic Leadership* (Cambridge, Polity, 2022)

Biden, Jr, Joseph R., 'Why America Must Lead Again: Rescuing US Foreign Policy after Trump', *Foreign Affairs*, 99/2, March/April 2020, pp. 64–76

Biden, Jr, Joseph R., and Michael Carpenter, 'How to Stand Up to the Kremlin', *Foreign Affairs*, 97/1, Jan/Feb 2018, pp. 44–57

Black, J.L., *Russia Faces NATO Expansion: Bearing Gifts or Bearing Arms?* (Lanham, MD, Rowman & Littlefield, 2000)

Black, J.L., and Michael Johns (eds), *The Return of the Cold War: Ukraine, the West and Russia* (London, Routledge, 2016)

Bowen, Bleddyn, *War in Space: Strategy, Spacepower, Geopolitics* (Edinburgh, Edinburgh University Press, 2020)

Braithwaite, Rodric, *Armageddon and Paranoia: The Nuclear Confrontation* (London, Profile Books, 2017)

Brands, Hal, and Michael Beckley, 'China Is a Declining Power – and That's the Problem', *Foreign Policy*, 24 September 2021, https://foreignpolicy.com

Brands, Hal, and John Lewis Gaddis, 'The New Cold War: America, China, and the Echoes of History', *Foreign Affairs*, 100/6, Nov/Dec 2021, pp. 10–20

Brooks, Stephen G., and William Wohlforth, *America Abroad: Why the Sole Superpower Should Not Pull Back from the World* (New York, Oxford University Press, 2018)

—, 'The Myth of Multipolarity: American Power's Staying Power', *Foreign Affairs*, May/June 2023, https://www.foreignaffairs.com/united-states/china-multipolarity-myth

Brown, Archie, *The Human Factor: Gorbachev, Reagan, and Thatcher and the End of the Cold War* (Oxford, Oxford University Press, 2020)

Brudny, Yitzhak, *Reinventing Russia: Russian Nationalism and the Soviet State, 1953–1991* (Cambridge, MA, Harvard University Press, 2000)

Brzezinski, Zbigniew, *The Choice: Global Domination or Global Leadership* (New York, Basic Books, 2004)

—, *The Grand Chessboard: American Primacy and Its Geostrategic Imperatives* (New York, Basic Books, 1997)

—, 'A Plan for Europe', *Foreign Affairs*, 74/1, Jan/Feb 1995, pp. 26–42

—, 'The Premature Partnership', *Foreign Affairs*, 73/2, March/April 1994, pp. 67–82

—, *Strategic Vision: America and the Crisis of Global Power* (New York, Basic Books, 2012)

—, 'Toward a Global Realignment', *American Interest*, 11/6, 17 April 2016, http://www.the-american-interest.com

Burns, William J., *The Back Channel: American Diplomacy in a Disordered World* (London, Hurst & Company, 2021)

Burrows, Mathew, and Robert A. Manning, *Kissinger's Nightmare: How an Inverted US–China–Russia May Be a Game-Changer* Valdai Paper No. 33, Moscow, November 2015

Bush, George, and Brent Scowcroft, *A World Transformed* (New York, Knopf, 1998)

Buzan, Barry, Ole Waever and Jaap de Wilde, *Security: A New Framework for Analysis* (Boulder, CO, Lynne Rienner Publishers, 1998)

Cafruny, Alan, Vassilis K. Fouskas, William D.E. Mallinson and Andrey Voynitsky, 'Ukraine, Multipolarity and the Crisis of Grand Strategies', *Journal of Balkan and Near Eastern Studies*, published online 14 June 2022

Calleo, David P., *Follies of Power: America's Unipolar Fantasy* (Cambridge, Cambridge University Press, 2009)

Carlson, Brian G., 'Russia and the China–India Rivalry', *Russian Analytical Digest*, No. 265, 19 March 2021, pp. 8–11

Carr, Edward Hallett, *Conditions of Peace* (New York, Macmillan, 1943)

—, *The Twenty Years' Crisis, 1919–1939: An Introduction to the Study of International Relations*, reissued with a new introduction and additional material by Michael Cox (London, Palgrave, [1939] 2001.

Casier, Tom, 'Great Game or Great Confusion?: The Geopolitical Understanding of EU–Russia Energy Relations', *Geopolitics*, 21/4, 2016, pp. 763–78

—, 'Russia's Energy Leverage over the EU: Myth or Reality?', *Perspectives on European Politics and Society*, 12/4, 2011, pp. 493–508

Chan, Steve, 'Challenging the Liberal Order: The US Hegemon as a Revisionist Power', *International Affairs*, 97/5, 2021, pp. 1335–52

Chang, Gordon G., *The Coming Collapse of China* (New York, Random House, 2001)

Charap, Samuel, and Timothy Colton, *Everyone Loses: The Ukraine Crisis and the Ruinous Contest for Post-Soviet Eurasia* (London, Routledge/Adelphi, 2016)

Charvet, John, and Elisa Kaczynska-Nay, *The Liberal Project and Human Rights: The Theory and Practice of a New World Order* (Cambridge, Cambridge University Press, 2008)

Chebankova, Elena and Piotr Dutkiewicz (eds), *Civilizations and World Order* (London, Routledge, 2021)

Chernyaev, Anatoly, *My Six Years with Gorbachev: Notes from a Diary* (Philadelphia, PA, University of Pennsylvania Press, 2000)

Clark, Christopher, *The Sleepwalkers: How Europe Went to War in 1914* (London, Penguin, 2013)

Clark, Ian, *The Post-Cold War Order: The Spoils of Peace* (Oxford, Oxford University Press, 2001)

Clinton, Bill, 'I Tried to Put Russia on Another Path', *The Atlantic*, 7 April 2022, https://www.theatlantic.com

Clinton, Hillary, 'America's Pacific Century', *Foreign Policy*, 11 October 2011, http://foreignpolicy.com

Clinton, Hillary Rodham, *Hard Choices: A Memoir* (New York, Simon & Schuster, 2014)

Clover, Charles, *Black Wind, White Snow: The Rise of Russia's New Nationalism*, new edn (New Haven, CT and London, Yale University Press, 2022)

Clunan, Anne L., 'Russia and the Liberal World Order', *Ethics & International Affairs*, 32/1, 2018, pp. 45–59

Cohen, Stephen F., *Failed Crusade: America and the Tragedy of Post-Communist Russia* (New York, W.W. Norton, 2000)

—, *War with Russia: From Putin and Ukraine to Trump and Russiagate* (New York, Hot Books, 2018)

Coker, Christopher, *The Rise of the Civilizational State* (Cambridge, Polity, 2019)

Connolly, Richard, *Russia's Response to Sanctions: How Western Economic Statecraft Is Reshaping Political Economy in Russia* (Cambridge, Cambridge University Press, 2018)

Cooley, Alexander, and Daniel Nexon, *Exit from Hegemony: The Unravelling of the American Global Order* (New York, Oxford University Press, 2020)

Copsey, Nathaniel, and Karolina Pomorska, 'The Influence of Newer Member States in the European Union: The Case of Poland and the Eastern Partnership', *Europe-Asia Studies*, 66/3, May 2014, pp. 421–43

Cunliffe, Philip, *The New Twenty Years' Crisis: A Critique of International Relations, 1999–2019* (Montreal, McGill-Queen's University Press, 2020)

Daalder, Ivo H., and James M. Lindsay, 'Last Best Hope: The West's Final Chance to Build a Better World Order', *Foreign Affairs*, 101/4, July/Aug 2022, pp. 120, 121 and 125

D'Anieri, Paul, *Ukraine and Russia: From Civilized Divorce to Uncivil War* (Cambridge, Cambridge University Press, 2019)

Denisov, Igor, and Alexander Lukin, 'Russia's China Policy: Growing Asymmetries and Hedging Options', *Russian Politics*, 6, 2021, pp. 531–50

Der Derian, James, *On Diplomacy: A Genealogy of Western Estrangement* (Oxford, Blackwell, 1987)

Deudney, Daniel, and G. John Ikenberry, 'The Nature and Sources of Liberal International Order', *Review of International Studies*, 25/2, 1999, pp. 179–96

Deutsch, Karl et al., *Political Community and the North Atlantic Area: International Organization in the Light of Historical Experience* (Princeton, NJ, Princeton University Press, 1957)

Dickinson, G. Lowes, *The European Anarchy*, first published in 1916 (London, Routledge Revivals, 2015)

Dienes, Alexandra, Reinhard Krumm and Simon Weiss, 'Europeans Today Are Much Less Belligerent than in 1914 or 1939', *Takeaways*, FES Regional Office for Cooperation and Peace in Europe, June 2020

Diesen, Glenn, *EU and NATO Relations with Russia: After the Collapse of the Soviet Union* (London, Routledge, 2016)

—, 'The EU, Russia and the Manichean Trap', *Cambridge Review of International Affairs*, 30/2–3, 2017, pp. 177–94

Doshi, Rush, *The Long Game: China's Grand Strategy to Displace American Order* (New York, Oxford University Press, 2021)

Dower, John W., *Embracing Defeat: Japan in the Wake of World War II* (New York, Norton, 2000)

Economy, Elizabeth C., *The Third Revolution: Xi Jinping and the New Chinese State* (New York, Oxford University Press, 2018)

—, *The World According to China* (Cambridge, Polity, 2021)

—, 'Xi Jinping's New World Order: Can China Remake the International System?', *Foreign Affairs*, 101/1, Jan/Feb 2022, pp. 52–67

Eisenhower, Dwight D., 'Chance for Peace Speech', 16 April 1953, https://www.presidency.ucsb.edu/documents/address-the-chance-for-peace-delivered-before-the-american-society-newspaper-editors

—, 'Military-Industrial Complex Speech', 17 January 1961, https://avalon.law.yale.edu

Eisenstadt, Shmuel N., *Japanese Civilization: A Comparative View* (Chicago, University of Chicago Press, 1996)

—, 'Multiple Modernities', *Daedalus*, 129/1, Winter 2000, pp. 1–29

—, *Multiple Modernities* (Piscataway, NJ, Transaction Publishers, 2002)

English, Robert D., *Russia and the Idea of the West: Gorbachev, Intellectuals and the End of the Cold War* (New York, Columbia University Press, 2000)

Ettinger, Aaron, 'Principled Realism and Populist Sovereignty in Trump's Foreign Policy', *Cambridge Review of International Affairs*, 33/3, 2020, pp. 410–31

Fallon, Theresa, 'The New Silk Road: Xi Jinping's Grand Strategy for Eurasia', *American Foreign Policy Interests*, 37, 2015, pp. 140–7

Farrow, Ronan, *War on Peace: The Decline of American Influence* (London, William Collins, 2021)

Fernandes, Clinton, *What Uncle Sam Wants: US Foreign Policy Objectives in Australia and Beyond* (London, Palgrave Macmillan, 2019)

Fix, Liana, and Ulrich Kühn, 'Strategic Stability in the 21st Century', *Russian Analytical Digest*, No. 260, 20 December 2020, pp. 7–11

Flockhart, Trine, 'The Coming Multi-Order World', *Contemporary Security Policy*, 37/1, 2016, pp. 3–30

Friedberg, Aaron L., *Getting China Wrong* (Cambridge, Polity, 2022)

Friedman, Thomas L., *The Lexus and the Olive Tree: Understanding Globalization* (New York, Farrar, Straus and Giroux, 1999)

Frye, Timothy, *Weak Strongman: The Limits of Power in Putin's Russia* (Princeton, NJ, Princeton University Press, 2021)

Fu Ying, *Seeing the World* (Beijing, 2019)

Fukuyama, Francis, 'The End of History', *National Interest*, 16, Summer 1989, pp. 3–17

—, *The End of History and the Last Man* (New York, Free Press, 1992)

Gaddis, John Lewis, *The Cold War* (London, Penguin, 2005)

—, *The Long Peace: Inquiries into the History of the Cold War* (Oxford, Oxford University Press, 1989)

—, *We Now Know: Rethinking Cold War History* (Oxford, Oxford University Press, 1997)

Garthoff, Raymond L., *The Great Transition: American–Soviet Relations and the End of the Cold War* (Washington DC, Brookings Institution Press, 1994)

Gerasimov, Valerii, 'Mir na granyakh voiny', *Voenno-promyshlennyi kur'er*, 10, 15 March 2017

Gilpin, Robert, *War and Change in World Politics* (Cambridge, Cambridge University Press, 1981)

Glennon, Michael J., *National Security and Double Government* (Oxford, Oxford University Press, 2015)

Global Britain in a Competitive Age: The Integrated Review of Security, Defence, Development and Foreign Policy, HM Government, March 2021

Goddard, Stacie, 'The Outsiders', *Foreign Affairs*, 101/3, May/June 2022, pp. 28–39

Goldgeier, James M., *Not Whether but When: The US Decision to Enlarge NATO* (Washington DC, Brookings Institution Press, 1999)

Goldgeier, James M., and Michael McFaul, *Power and Purpose: US Policy toward Russia after the Cold War* (Washington DC, Brookings Institution Press, 2003)

Goldstein, Joshua S., *Winning the War on War: The Decline of Armed Conflict Worldwide* (London, Plume, 2012)

Goldstein, Lyle J., 'Threat Inflation, Russian Military Weakness, and the Resulting Nuclear Paradox', Costs of War, Watson Institute, Brown University, 15 September 2022, https://watson.brown.edu/costsofwar/files/cow/imce/papers/Threat%20Inflation%20and%20Russian%20Military%20Weakness_Goldstein_CostsofWar-2.pdf

Gorbachev, Mikhail, *Perestroika: New Thinking for Our Country and the World* (London, Collins, 1987)

Gromyko, Alexei A., and V.P. Fëdorova (eds), *Bol'shaya Evropa: Idei, real'nost', perspektivy* (Moscow, Ves' mir, 2014)

Gustafson, Thane, *The Bridge: Natural Gas in a Redivided Europe* (Cambridge, MA, Harvard University Press, 2020)

Hahn, Gordon, *Ukraine over the Edge: Russia, the West and the 'New Cold War'* (Jefferson, NC, McFarland Books, 2017)

Halliday, Fred, *The Making of the Second Cold War* (London, Verso, 1983)

Hamilton, Clive, *Silent Invasion: China's Influence in Australia* (London, Hardie Grant Books, 2018)

Hamilton, Clive, and Mareike Ohlberg, *Hidden Hand: Exposing How the Chinese Communist Party Is Reshaping the World* (London, Oneworld Publications, 2021)

Headley, James, 'Challenging the EU's Claims to Moral Authority: Russian Talk of "Double Standards"', *Asia Europe Journal*, 13/3, 2015, pp. 297–307

Held, David, *Democracy and the Global Order: From the Modern State to Cosmopolitan Governance* (Cambridge, Polity, 1995)

Held, David, Anthony McGrew, David Goldblatt and Jonathan Perraton, *Global Transformations: Politics, Economics and Culture* (Cambridge, Polity, 1999)

Hendrickson, David, *Republic in Peril: American Empire and the Liberal Tradition* (Oxford, Oxford University Press, 2017)

Herz, John H., 'Idealist Internationalism and the Security Dilemma', *World Politics*, 2/2, January 1950, pp. 157–80

Hill, William H., *No Place for Russia: European Security Institutions since 1989* (New York, Columbia University Press, 2018)

Hillman, Jonathan E., *The Emperor's New Road: China and the Project of the Century* (New Haven, CT and London, Yale University Press, 2020)

Hoffmann, Stanley, *Primacy or World Order: American Foreign Policy since the Cold War* (New York, McGraw-Hill, 1978)

Howard, R.T., *Power and Glory: France's Secret Wars with Britain and America, 1945–2016* (London, Biteback, 2016)

Howorth, Jolyon, 'European Defence Policy between Dependence and Autonomy: A Challenge of Sisyphean Dimensions', *British Journal of Politics and International Relations*, 19/1, 2017, pp. 13–28

—, *Security and Defence Policy in the European Union* (Basingstoke, Palgrave, 2014)

Hrabina, Jozef, 'The Year of Crises: How 2020 Will Reshape the Structure of International Relations', *Russia in Global Affairs*, 1, Jan/March 2021, pp. 174–99

Huntington, Samuel P., 'The Clash of Civilizations?', *Foreign Affairs*, 72/3, Summer 1993, pp. 23–49

—, *The Clash of Civilizations and the Remaking of World Order* (New York, Simon & Schuster, 1996)

Hurrell, Andrew, 'Beyond the BRICS: Power, Pluralism, and the Future of Global Order', *Ethics & International Affairs*, 32/1, 2018, pp. 89–101

Ikenberry, G. John, *After Victory: Institutions, Strategic Restraint, and the Rebuilding of Order after Major Wars* (Princeton, NJ, Princeton University Press, 2001)

—, 'The End of Liberal International Order?', *International Affairs*, 94/1, 2018, pp. 7–23

—, *Liberal Leviathan: The Origins, Crisis, and Transformation of the American World Order* (Princeton, NJ, Princeton University Press, 2011)

—, 'The Rise of China and the Future of the West: Can the Liberal System Survive?', *Foreign Affairs*, 87/1, Jan/Feb 2008, pp. 23–37

—, 'Why the Liberal World Order Will Survive', *Ethics & International Affairs*, 32/1, 2018, pp. 17–29

—, *A World Safe for Democracy: Liberal Internationalism and the Crisis of Global Order* (New Haven, CT and London, Yale University Press, 2020)

Ikenberry, G. John, and Anne-Marie Slaughter, *Forging a World of Liberty under Law: US National Security in the Twenty-First Century* (Princeton, NJ, Woodrow Wilson School of Public and International Affairs, 2006)

Ishchenko, Volodymyr, 'Ukrainians Are Far from Unified on NATO', *Truthout*, 28 December 2021, https://truthout.org/articles/ukrainians-are-far-from-unified-on-nato-let-them-decide-for-themselves/

Jacques, Martin, *When China Rules the World: The End of the Western World and the Birth of a New Global Order*, 2nd edn (London, Penguin, 2012)

Jaishankar, S., *The India Way: Strategies for an Uncertain World* (Gurugram, HarperCollins, 2020)

Jervis, Robert, *Perception and Misperception in International Politics* (Princeton, NJ, Princeton University Press, 1976)

Jervis, Robert, Francis J. Gavin, Joshua Rovner and Diane N. Labrosse (eds), *Chaos in the Liberal Order: The Trump Presidency and International Politics in the Twenty-First Century* (New York, Columbia University Press, 2018)

Jones, Nate, *Able Archer 83: The Secret History of the NATO Exercise that Almost Triggered Nuclear War* (New York, The New Press, 2016)

Kaczmarski, Marcin, 'Russia–China: Ever Closer Relationship, but Not an Alliance Yet', *Russian Analytical Digest*, No. 265, 19 March 2021, pp. 2–4

Kagan, Robert, *The Jungle Grows Back: America and Our Imperiled World* (New York, Vintage, 2018)

—, 'The Price of Hegemony: Can America Learn to Use Its Power?', *Foreign Affairs*, 101/3, May/June 2022, pp. 10–19

—, 'A Superpower, Like It or Not: Why Americans Must Accept Their Global Role', *Foreign Affairs*, 100/2, March/April 2021, pp. 28–39

Kahn, Herman, *On Escalation: Metaphors and Scenarios* (London, Routledge, 1965, reissued 2009)

Kaldor, Mary, *New and Old Wars: Organized Violence in a Global Era*, 3rd edn (Cambridge, Polity, 2012)

Kant, Immanuel, 'Perpetual Peace: A Philosophical Sketch', in *Kant: Political Writings*, ed. Hans Reiss, 2nd enlarged edn (Cambridge, Cambridge University Press, 1991), pp. 93–130

Kaplan, Robert D., *The Tragic Mind: Fear, Fate, and the Burden of Power* (New Haven, CT and London, Yale University Press, 2023)

Karaganov, Sergei A., *Russia: The New Foreign Policy and Security Agenda* (London, Centre for Defence Studies, No. 12, June 1992), p. 8

Kashin, Vasily, and Alexander Lukin, 'China's Approach to Relations with the United States: The Military Aspect', in *Russia: Arms Control, Disarmament and International Security*, SIPRI Yearbook Supplement (Moscow, IMEMO, 2021), pp. 13–33

Kashin, Vasily, and Ivan Timofeev, 'US–China Relations: Moving towards a New Cold War?', Valdai Discussion Club Report, January 2021

Kennan, George F. [X], 'The Sources of Soviet Conduct', *Foreign Affairs*, 25, July 1947

Kennan, George, 'Morality and Foreign Policy', *Foreign Affairs*, 64, 1985/6, pp. 205–18

Kennedy, John F., '1963 Commencement', American University, 10 June 1963, https://www.jfklibrary.org/archives/other-resources/john-f-kennedy-speeches/american-university-19630610

Kennedy, Paul, *The Rise and Fall of the Great Powers: Economic Change and Military Conflict from 1500 to 2000* (London, Unwin Hyman, 1988)

Kirkpatrick, Jeane, *Making War to Keep Peace* (New York, Regan Books, 2007)

Kirshner, Jonathan, 'Gone but Not Forgotten: Trump's Long Shadow and the End of American Credibility', *Foreign Affairs*, 100/2, March/April 2021, pp. 18–26

Kissinger, Henry, *Diplomacy* (New York, Simon & Schuster, 1995)

—, *World Order: Reflections on the Character of Nations and the Course of History* (London, Allen Lane, 2014)

Kortunov, Sergei, 'Is the Cold War Really Over?', *International Affairs* (Moscow), 44/5, 1998, pp. 141–54

Kotkin, Stephen, 'The Cold War Never Ended: Ukraine, the China Challenge, and the Revival of the West', *Foreign Affairs*, 101/3, May/June 2022, pp. 64–78

—, 'Russia's Perpetual Geopolitics: Putin Returns to the Historical Pattern', *Foreign Affairs*, 95/3, May/June 2016, pp. 2–9

Kozyrev, Andrei, *The Firebird: A Memoir. The Elusive Fate of Russian Democracy* (Pittsburgh, PA, University of Pittsburgh Press, 2019)

—, 'Partnership or Cold Peace?', *Foreign Policy*, No. 99, Summer 1995, pp. 3–14

Kramer, Mark, 'US–Russian Relations and the "New Cold War" Metaphor', *Ponars Eurasia*, No. 547, Winter 2018, http://www.ponarseurasia.org/memo/us-russian-relations-and-new-cold-war-metaphor

Krauthammer, Charles, 'The Unipolar Moment', *Foreign Affairs*, 70/1, 1990/1, pp. 23–33

—, 'The Unipolar Moment Revisited', *National Interest*, 70, Winter 2002/3, pp. 5–17

Kribbe, Hans, *The Strongmen: European Encounters with Sovereign Power* (Newcastle, Agenda Publishing, 2020)

Krickovic, Andrej, 'Revisionism Revisited: Developing a Typology for Classifying Russia and Other Revisionist Powers', *International Politics*, 59, 2022, pp. 616–39

Kroenig, Matthew, *The Return of Great Power Rivalry: Democracy versus Autocracy from the Ancient World to the US and China* (New York, Oxford University Press, 2020)

Kubálková, Vendulka, and A.A. Cruickshank, *Thinking about Soviet 'New Thinking'* (Berkeley, CA, University of California Press, 1989)

Kupchan, Charles, *No One's World: The West, the Rising Rest and the Coming Global Turn* (Oxford, Oxford University Press, 2012)

Laclau, Ernesto, *On Populist Reason* (London, Verso, 2007)

Larres, Klaus, *Uncertain Allies: Nixon, Kissinger, and the Threat of a United Europe* (New Haven, CT and London, Yale University Press, 2022)

Larson, Deborah Welch, and Alexei Shevchenko, *Quest for Status: Chinese and Russian Foreign Policy* (New Haven, CT and London, Yale University Press, 2019)

—, 'Russia Says No: Power, Status, and Emotions in Foreign Policy', *Communist and Post-Communist Studies*, 47/3–4, 2014, pp. 269–79

—, 'Shortcut to Greatness: The New Thinking and the Revolution in Soviet Foreign Policy', *International Organization*, 57/1, 2003, pp. 77–109

—, 'Status Seekers: Chinese and Russian Responses to US Primacy', *International Security*, 34/4, 2010, pp. 63–95

Laruelle, Marlene, *The 'Russian World': Russia's Soft Power and Geopolitical Imagination* (Washington DC, Center on Global Interests, May 2015)

Layne, Christopher, 'Coming Storms: The Return of Great-Power War', *Foreign Affairs*, 99/6, Nov/Dec 2020, pp. 42–8

—, 'From Preponderance to Offshore Balancing: America's Future Grand Strategy', *International Security*, 22/1, Summer 1997, pp. 86–124

—, *The Peace of Illusions: American Grand Strategy from 1940 to the Present* (Ithaca, NY, Cornell University Press, 2006)

—, 'The Unipolar Illusion: Why Great Powers Will Arise', *International Security*, 17/4, Spring 1993, pp. 5–51

—, 'The Unipolar Illusion Revisited: The Coming End of the United States' Unipolar Moment', *International Security*, 31/2, 2006, pp. 7–41

Lebow, Richard Ned, *The Tragic Vision of Politics: Ethics, Interests and Orders* (Cambridge, Cambridge University Press, 2003)

Lefebvre, Maxime, *Europe as a Power, European Sovereignty and Strategic Autonomy*, Fondation Robert Schuman, Policy Paper No. 582, 2 February 2021

Leffler, Melvyn (ed.), *Origins of the Cold War: An International History* (London, Routledge, 2005)

—, *A Preponderance of Power: National Security, The Truman Administration, and the Cold War* (Stanford, CA, Stanford University Press, 1992)

Legvold, Robert, *Return to Cold War* (Cambridge, Polity, 2016)

Lieven, Anatol, *Climate Change and the Nation State* (London, Penguin Books, 2021)

—, 'Russia Has Been Warning about Ukraine for Decades: The West Should Have Listened', *Time*, 25 January 2022, https://time.com

Lieven, Anatol, and John Hulsman, 'Ethical Realism and Contemporary Challenges', *American Foreign Policy Interests*, 28, 2006, pp. 413–20

Lind, Jennifer, and William C. Wohlforth, 'The Future of the Liberal Order is Conservative', *Foreign Affairs*, 98/2, March/April 2019, pp. 70–80

Linden, Eugene, *Fire and Flood* (London, Allen Lane, 2022)

Little, Richard, *The Balance of Power in International Relations: Metaphors, Myths and Models* (Cambridge, Cambridge University Press, 2007)

Lo, Bobo, 'Medvedev and the New European Security Architecture', Centre for European Reform, July 2009, https://www.cer.eu

—, 'Turning Point? Putin, Xi, and the Russian Invasion of Ukraine', Lowy Institute Analysis, May 2022, https://www.lowyinstitute.org

Luce, Henry R., 'The American Century', *Life*, 17 February 1941, pp. 61–5

Lukin, Alexander, 'Have We Passed the Peak of Sino-Russian Rapprochement?', *Washington Quarterly*, 44/3, 2021, pp. 155–73

Lukin, Alexander, and Fan Xuesong, 'What is BRICS for China?', *Strategic Analysis*, 43/6, 2019, pp. 620–31

Lynch, Timothy J., *In the Shadow of the Cold War: American Foreign Policy from George Bush Sr. to Donald Trump* (Cambridge, Cambridge University Press, 2020)

Maçães, Bruno, *Belt and Road: A Chinese World Order* (London, Hurst, 2018)

McCartney, James, with Molly Sinclair McCartney, *America's War Machine: Vested Interests, Endless Conflicts* (New York, Thomas Dunne Books, 2015)

McFaul, Michael, *Advancing Democracy Abroad: Why We Should and How We Can* (New York, Rowman & Littlefield, 2009)

—, 'Cold War Lessons and Fallacies for US–China Relations Today', *Washington Quarterly*, 43/4, 2020, pp. 7–39

—, *From Cold War to Hot Peace: The Inside Story of Russia and America* (London, Allen Lane, 2018)

—, 'Putin, Putinism, and the Domestic Determinants of Russian Foreign Policy', *International Security*, 45/2, Fall 2020, pp. 95–139

MccGwire, Michael, 'NATO Expansion: "A Policy Error of Historic Importance"', *Review of International Studies*, 24/1, 1998, pp. 23–42; reprinted in *International Affairs*, 84/6, November 2008, pp. 1282–301

McMaster, H.R., 'The Retrenchment Syndrome: A Response to "Come Home America"', *Foreign Affairs*, 99/4, July/Aug 2020, pp. 183–6

MacMillan, Margaret, *The War that Ended Peace: How Europe Abandoned Peace for the First World War* (London, Profile Books, 2014)

Macron, Emmanuel, 'Ambassadors Conference – Speech by M. Emmanuel Macron, President of the Republic', Paris, 27 August 2019, https://lv.ambafrance.org. Video of the speech available on YouTube.

Mahbubani, Kishore, *Has China Won? The Chinese Challenge to American Primacy* (New York, Public Affairs, 2020)

Mandelbaum, Michael, 'The New Containment: Handling Russia, China and Iran', *Foreign Affairs*, 98/2, March/April 2019, pp. 123–31

—, *The Rise and Fall of Peace on Earth* (Oxford, Oxford University Press, 2019)

Marcetic, Branko, 'Ignoring Gorbachev's Warnings', *Current Affairs*, 7 September 2022, https://www.currentaffairs.org

Martin, James, *Hegemony* (Cambridge, Polity, 2022)

Martin, Terry, *The Affirmative Action Empire: Nations and Nationalism in the Soviet Union, 1923–1939* (Ithaca, NY, Cornell University Press, 2001)

Mathews, Jessica T., 'Present at the Re-creation? US Foreign Policy Must Be Remade, Not Restored', *Foreign Affairs*, 100/2, March/April 2021, pp. 10–16

Matlock, Jack F., *Super-Power Illusions: How Myths and False Ideologies Led America Astray – and How to Return to Reality* (New Haven, CT and London, Yale University Press, 2010)

Matveeva, Anna, *Through Times of Trouble: Conflict in Southeastern Ukraine Explained from Within* (Lanham, MD, Lexington Books, 2017)

Mayers, David, *America and the Postwar World: Remaking International Society, 1945–1956* (London, Routledge, 2018)

Mazower, Mark, *Dark Continent: Europe's Twentieth Century* (New York, Knopf, 1999)

Mead, Walter Russell, 'The End of the Wilsonian Era: Why Liberal Internationalism Failed', *Foreign Affairs*, 100/1, Jan/Feb 2021, pp. 123–37

Mearsheimer, John J., 'Bound to Fail: The Rise and Fall of the Liberal International Order', *International Security*, 43/4, Spring 2019, pp. 7–50

—, 'The False Promise of International Institutions', *International Security*, 19/3, 1994/5, pp. 5–49

—, *The Great Delusion: Liberal Dreams and International Realities* (New Haven, CT and London, Yale University Press, 2018)

—, 'The Inevitable Rivalry', *Foreign Affairs*, 100/6, Nov/Dec 2021, pp. 48–58

—, *The Tragedy of Great Power Politics*, updated edn (New York, W.W. Norton, 2014, originally published 2001)

—, 'Why the Ukraine Crisis is the West's Fault: The Liberal Delusions that Provoked Putin', *Foreign Affairs*, 93/5, Sep/Oct 2014, pp. 77–89

Mearsheimer, John J., and Stephen M. Walt, 'The Case for Offshore Balancing', *Foreign Affairs*, 95/4, July/Aug 2016, pp. 70–83

Meier, Oliver, 'Debating the Withdrawal of US Nuclear Weapons from Europe: What Germany Expects from Russia', *Vestnik of Saint Petersburg University: International Relations*, 14/1, 2021, pp. 82–96

Menon, Rajan, and Eugene Rumer, *Russia and India: A New Chapter* (Washington DC, Carnegie Endowment for International Peace, September 2022), https://carnegieendowment.org/2022/09/20/russia-and-india-new-chapter-pub-87958

Miller, Manjari Chatterjee, *Why Nations Rise: Narratives and the Path to Great Power* (Oxford, Oxford University Press, 2021)

Monaghan, Andrew, *Dealing with the Russians* (Cambridge, Polity, 2019)

—, *A 'New Cold War'? Abusing History, Misunderstanding Russia* Chatham House Research Paper, London, May 2015

Morgan, Michael Cotey, *The Final Act: The Helsinki Accords and the Transformation of the Cold War* (Princeton, NJ, Princeton University Press, 2018)

Morgenthau, Hans J., *Politics among Nations: The Struggle for Power and Peace*, 5th edn (New York, Alfred A. Knopf, 1973)

Mounk, Yascha, 'Democracy on the Defense: Turning Back the Authoritarian Tide', *Foreign Affairs*, 100/2, March/April 2021, pp. 163–73

Mousseau, Michael, 'The End of War: How a Robust Marketplace and Liberal Hegemony Are Leading to Perpetual World Peace', *International Security*, 44/1, 2019, pp. 160–96

Moyn, Samuel, *The Last Utopia: Human Rights in History* (Cambridge, MA, Belknap Press, 2012)

Mueller, John, *Retreat from Doomsday: The Obsolescence of Major War* (New York, Basic Books, 1989)

—, *The Stupidity of War: American Foreign Policy and the Case for Complacency* (Cambridge, Cambridge University Press, 2021)

Mulder, Nicholas, *The Economic Weapon: The Rise of Sanctions as a Tool of Modern War* (New Haven, CT and London, Yale University Press, 2022)

NATO, *NATO 2030: United for a New Era*, 25 November 2020, https://www.nato.int/nato_static_fl2014/assets/pdf/2020/12/pdf/201201-Reflection-Group-Final-Report-Uni.pdf

—, *Strategic Concept: Active Engagement, Modern Defence*, adopted by Lisbon summit, 19–20 November 2010, https://www.nato.int/nato_static_fl2014/assets/pdf/pdf_publications/20120214_strategic-concept-2010-eng.pdf

Norris, Pippa, and Ronald Inglehart, *Cultural Backlash: Trump, Brexit, and Authoritarian Populism* (Cambridge, Cambridge University Press, 2019)

Nye, Joseph S., *Is the American Century Over?* (Cambridge, Polity, 2015)

—, *Soft Power: The Means to Success in World Politics* (New York, Public Affairs, 2004)

Office of the Director of National Intelligence, 'Foreign Threats to the 2020 US Federal Elections: Intelligence Community Assessment', 10 March 2021, https://www.dni.gov

O'Hanlon, Michael, *The Art of War in an Age of Peace: US Grand Strategy and Resolute Restraint* (New Haven, CT and London, Yale University Press, 2021)

Oksanian, Kevork K., 'Carr Goes East: Reconsidering Power and Inequality in a Post-Liberal Eurasia', *European Politics and Society*, 20/2, 2019, pp. 172–89

Oliker, Olga, 'Russia's Nuclear Doctrine: What We Know, What We Don't, and What That Means', Washington DC, CSIS, 5 May 2016, https://www.csis.org

Ollapally, Deepa M., 'India and the International Order: Accommodation and Adjustment', *Ethics & International Affairs*, 32/1, 2018, pp. 61–74

Otte, T.G., *July Crisis: The World's Descent into War, Summer 1914* (Cambridge, Cambridge University Press, 2014)

Pabst, Adrian, *Liberal World Order and Its Critics: Civilisational States and Cultural Commonwealths* (London, Routledge, 2018)

—, *Postliberal Politics: The Coming Era of Renewal* (Cambridge, Polity, 2021)

Pacer, Valerie A., *Russian Foreign Policy under Dmitry Medvedev* (London, Routledge, 2015)

Perle, Richard, and David Frum, *An End to Evil* (New York, Random House, 2003)

Perry, William J., and Tom Z. Collina, *The Button: The New Nuclear Arms Race and Presidential Power from Truman to Trump* (Dallas, TX, BenBella Books, 2020)

Petro, Nicolai N., *The Tragedy of Ukraine: What Classical Greek Tragedy Can Teach Us about Conflict Resolution* (Berlin, De Gruyter, 2022)

Pieper, Moritz, 'Strategic Stability beyond New START', *Russian Analytical Digest*, No. 260, 20 December 2020, pp. 2–7

Pinker, Steven, *The Better Angels of Our Nature: Why Violence Has Declined* (New York, Viking Books, 2011)

Plokhy, Serhii, *The Gates of Europe: A History of Ukraine* (London, Penguin, 2015)

—, *Nuclear Folly: A History of the Cuban Missile Crisis* (New York, W.W. Norton, 2021)

Pompeo, Michael R., 'Communist China and the Free World's Future', Nixon Centre, Yorba Linda, California, 23 July 2020, https://2017-2021.state.gov/communist-china-and-the-free-worlds-future-2/index.html

Porter, Patrick, *The False Promise of Liberal Order: Nostalgia, Delusion and the Rise of Trump* (Cambridge, Polity Press, 2020)

Posen, Barry, *Restraint: A New Foundation for US Grand Strategy* (Ithaca, NY, Cornell University Press, 2014)

Power, Samantha, 'The Can-Do Power: America's Advantage and Biden's Chance', *Foreign Affairs*, 100/1, Jan/Feb 2021, pp. 10–24

—, *A Problem from Hell: America and the Age of Genocide* (New York, Basic Books, 2002)

Primakov, Evgeny, *A World Challenged* (Washington DC, Brookings Institution Press, 2004)

Prouty, L. Fletcher, *The CIA, Vietnam and the Plot to Assassinate John F. Kennedy* (New York, Skyhorse Publishing, 2011)

Rid, Thomas, *Active Measures: The Secret History of Disinformation and Political Warfare* (London, Profile Books, 2020)

Rieff, David, *At the Point of a Gun: Democratic Dreams and Armed Intervention* (New York, Simon & Schuster, 2005)

Roach, Stephen S., *Accidental Conflict: America, China and the Clash of False Narratives* (New Haven, CT and London, Yale University Press, 2022)

Roberts, Geoffrey, *Stalin's Wars: From World War to Cold War, 1939–1953* (New Haven, CT and London, Yale University Press, 2008)

Rogers, Paul, *Losing Control: Global Security in the Twenty-First Century*, 4th edn (London, Pluto Press, 2021)

Rosato, Sebastian, 'The Flawed Logic of Democratic Peace Theory', *American Political Science Review*, 97/4, November 2003, pp. 585–602

Rudd, Kevin, *The Avoidable War: The Dangers of a Catastrophic Conflict between the US and Xi Jinping's China* (London, Public Affairs, 2022)

—, 'Short of War: How to Keep US–Chinese Confrontation from Ending in Calamity', *Foreign Affairs*, 100/2, March/April 2001, pp. 58–72

Rudenko, Serhiy, *Zelensky: A Biography* (Cambridge, Polity, 2022)

Ruggie, John, 'International Regimes, Transactions, and Change: Embedded Liberalism in the Postwar Economic Order', *International Organization*, 36/2, 1982, pp. 379–415

Rumer, Eugene, and Richard Sokolsky, *Grand Illusions: The Impact of Misperceptions About Russia on US Policy* (Washington DC, CEIP, 2021)

Russett, Bruce, *Hegemony and Democracy* (London, Routledge, 2011)

Rynning, Sten, 'The False Promise of Continental Concert: Russia, the West and the Necessary Balance of Power', *International Affairs*, 91/3, 2015, pp. 539–52

Ryzhkov, Vladimir, 'From "Greater Europe" to Confrontation: Is a "Common European Home" Still Possible?', *Russian Politics*, 6/4, 2021, pp. 551–71

Sakharov, Andrei, *Progress, Coexistence and Intellectual Freedom* (New York, W.W. Norton, 1970)

Sakwa, Richard, 'The Cold Peace: Russo-Western Relations as a Mimetic Cold War', *Cambridge Review of International Affairs*, 26/1, 2013, pp. 203–24

—, *Deception: Russiagate and the New Cold War* (Lanham, MD, Lexington Books, 2022)

—, 'The Dual State in Russia', *Post-Soviet Affairs*, 26/3, July–September 2010, pp. 185–206

—, 'The End of the Revolution: Mimetic Theory, Axiological Violence, and the Possibility of Dialogical Transcendence', *Telos*, No. 185, December 2018, pp. 35–66

—, *Frontline Ukraine: Crisis in the Borderlands*, revised edn 2017 (London, Bloomsbury Academic, reprinted 2022)

—, '"New Cold War" or Twenty Years' Crisis?: Russia and International Politics', *International Affairs*, 84/2, March 2008, pp. 241–67

—, 'No Exit: Logic and Rationality in the Ukraine Crisis', in Peter W. Schulze and Winfried Veit (eds), *Ukraine in the Crosshairs of Geopolitical Power Play* (Frankfurt and New York, Campus Verlag, 2020), pp. 101–28

—, 'The Perils of Democratism', *Polis: Political Studies*, No. 2, 2023, pp. 88–102

—, *The Putin Paradox* (London and New York, I.B. Tauris, 2020)

—, *Putin Redux: Power and Contradiction in Contemporary Russia* (London and New York, Routledge, 2014)

—, *Russia against the Rest: The Post-Cold War Crisis of World Order* (Cambridge, Cambridge University Press, 2017)

—, *The Russia Scare: Fake News and Genuine Threat* (London, Routledge, 2022)

—, 'Russian Neo-Revisionism', *Russian Politics*, 4/1, 2019, pp. 1–21

—, 'The Ukraine Syndrome and Europe: Between Norms and Space', *Soviet and Post-Soviet Review*, No. 44, 2017, pp. 9–31

Saradzhyan, Simon, and Nabi Abdullaev, 'Measuring National Power: Is Putin's Russia in Decline?', *Europe-Asia Studies*, 73/2, March 2021, pp. 291–317

Sarotte, Mary Elise, *1989: The Struggle to Create Post-Cold War Europe* (Princeton, NJ, Princeton University Press, 2009)

—, 'A Broken Promise? What the West Really Told Moscow about NATO Expansion', *Foreign Affairs*, 93/5, Sep/Oct 2014, pp. 90–7

—, 'Containment beyond the Cold War: How Washington Lost the Post-Soviet Peace', *Foreign Affairs*, 100/6, Nov/Dec 2021, pp. 22–35

—, *Not One Inch: America, Russia and the Making of Post-Cold War Stalemate* (New Haven, CT and London, Yale University Press, 2022)

—, 'Perpetuating US Pre-eminence: The 1990 Deals to "Bribe the Soviets Out" and Move Nato In', *International Security*, 35/1, 2010, pp. 110–37

Savranskaya, Svetlana, and Tom Blanton, 'NATO Expansion: What Gorbachev Heard', National Security Archive, George Washington University, 12 December 2017, https://nsarchive.gwu.edu

Schuman, Michael, *Superpower Interrupted: The Chinese History of the World* (New York, Public Affairs, 2020)

Sharafutdinova, Gulnaz, *The Red Mirror: Putin's Leadership and Russia's Insecure Identity* (Oxford, Oxford University Press, 2020)

Sheehan, James J., *Where Have All the Soldiers Gone? The Transformation of Modern Europe* (New York, Mariner Books, 2009)

Shifrinson, Joshua R. Itzkowitz, 'Deal or No Deal?: The End of the Cold War and the U.S. Offer to Limit NATO Expansion', *International Security*, 40/4, 2016, pp. 7–44

—, 'Put It in Writing: How the West Broke Its Promises to Moscow', *Foreign Affairs*, 29 October 2014, www.foreignaffairs.com/articles/united-states/2014-10-29/put-it-writing

—, *Rising Titans, Falling Giants: How Great Powers Exploit Power Shifts* (Ithaca, NY, Cornell University Press, 2018)

Siddi, Marco, 'An Evolving Other: German National Identity and Constructions of Russia', *Politics*, 38/1, 2018, pp. 35–50

Simpson, Gerry, 'Two Liberalisms', *European Journal of International Law*, 12/3, 2001, pp. 537–71

Slobodchikoff, Michael O., *Building Hegemonic Order Russia's Way: Order, Stability, and Predictability in the Post-Soviet Space* (Lanham, MD, Lexington Books, 2014)

Sochor, Johannes, *Russia and the Right to Self-Determination in the Post-Soviet Space* (Oxford, Oxford University Press, 2021)

Stent, Angela, *The Limits of Partnership: US–Russian Relations in the Twenty-First Century* (Princeton, NJ, Princeton University Press, 2014)

—, *Putin's World: Russia against the west and with the Rest* (New York, Twelve, 2019)

—, 'Trump's Russia Legacy and Biden's Response', *Survival*, 63/4, 2021, pp. 55–80

Stiglitz, Joseph, *Globalization and its Discontents* (London, Penguin, 2002)

Stoner, Kathryn E., *Russia Resurrected: Its Power and Purpose in a New Global Order* (New York, Oxford University Press, 2021)

Strategic Compass for Security and Defence, adopted by the Council of the European Union 21 March 2022, https://eeas.europa.eu

Streeck, Wolfgang, 'The EU after Ukraine', *American Affairs*, 20 May 2022, https://americanaffairsjournal.org

Stuenkel, Oliver, *The BRICS and the Future of Global Order* (London and Lanham, MD, Lexington Books, 2015)

—, *Post-Western World: How Emerging Powers Are Remaking Global Order* (Cambridge, Polity, 2016)

Subtelny, Orest, *Ukraine: A History*, 4th edn (Toronto, University of Toronto Press, 2009)

Surkov, Vladislav, 'The Loneliness of the Half Breed', *Russia in Global Affairs*, 28 May 2018, https://eng.globalaffairs.ru

Tang, Shiping, 'China and the Future International Order(s)', *Ethics and International Affairs*, 32/1, 2018, pp. 31–43

Taubman, Philip, *In the Nation's Service: The Life and Times of George P. Shultz* (Stanford, Stanford University Press, 2023)

Thornton, John, 'Long Time Coming: The Prospects for Democracy in China', *Foreign Affairs*, 87/1, Jan/Feb 2008, pp. 2–22

Timofeev, Ivan, 'Sanctions against Russia: A Look into 2021', Moscow, RIAC Report No. 65, 2021, p. 7, https://russiancouncil.ru

Toal, Gerard, *Near Abroad: Putin, the West and the Contest over Ukraine and the Caucasus* (Oxford, Oxford University Press, 2017)

Tooze, Adam, *Crashed: How a Decade of Financial Crises Changed the World* (London, Penguin, 2019)

—, 'Is This the End of the American Century?', *London Review of Books*, 4 April 2019, pp. 3–7

Trachtenberg, Marc, *A Constructed Peace: The Making of the European Settlement, 1945–1963* (Princeton, NJ, Princeton University Press, 1999)

Trenin, Dmitri, *Novyi balans sil: Rossiya v poiskakh vneshnepoliticheskogo ravnovesiya* (Moscow, Al'pina, 2021)

Tsygankov, Andrei P., 'Crafting the State-Civilization', *Problems of Post-Communism*, 63/3, 2016, pp. 146–58

—, 'The Revisionist Moment: Russia, Trump, and Global Transition', *Problems of Post-Communism*, 68/6, 2021, pp. 457–67

—, *Russia and America: The Asymmetric Rivalry* (Cambridge, Polity, 2019)

—, *Russian Realism: Defending 'Derzhava' in International Relations* (London and New York, Routledge, 2022)

—, *Russia's Foreign Policy: Change and Continuity in National Identity*, 6th edn (Lanham, MD, Rowman & Littlefield, 2022)

Tsymburskii, Vadim, 'Ostrov Rossiya: Perspektivy Rossiiskoi Geopolitika', *Polis*, No. 5, 1993, pp. 11–17

Urio, Paolo, *America and the China Threat: From the End of History to the End of Empire* (Atlanta, GA, Clarity Press, 2022)

US National Intelligence Council, *Global Trends 2040: A More Contested World*, March 2021, https://www.dni.gov

Walt, Stephen M., *The Hell of Good Intentions: America's Foreign Policy Elite and the Decline of US Primacy* (New York, Farrar, Straus and Giroux, 2019)

Walt, Stephen M., and Dani Rodrik, 'How to Build a Better Order', *Foreign Affairs*, 101/5, Sep/Oct 2022, pp. 142–55

Waltz, Kenneth N., 'The Emerging Structure of International Politics', *International Security*, 18/2, 1993, pp. 44–79

—, 'Structural Realism after the Cold War', *International Security*, 25/1, Summer 2000, pp. 5–41

—, *Theory of International Politics* (New York, Random House 1979)

Wang Jisi, 'The Plot against China? How China Sees the New Washington Consensus', *Foreign Affairs*, 100/4, July/Aug 2021, pp. 48–57

Weber, Isabella M., *How China Escaped Shock Therapy: The Market Reform Debate* (London and New York, Routledge, 2021)

Weiss, Jessica Chen, and Jeremy L. Wallace, 'Domestic Politics, China's Rise, and the Future of the Liberal International Order', *International Organization*, 75, Spring 2021, pp. 635–64

Wertheim, Stephen, *Tomorrow the World: The Birth of US Global Supremacy* (Cambridge, MA, Belknap Press, 2020)

Westad, Odd Arne, *The Global Cold War: Third World Interventions and the Making of Our Times* (Cambridge, Cambridge University Press, 2007)

White Paper on German Security Policy and the Future of the Bundeswehr (Berlin, The Federal Government, July 2016), https://issat.dcaf.ch

Williams, A.J., *Failed Imagination? The Anglo-American New World Order from Wilson to Bush*, 2nd edn (Manchester, Manchester University Press, 2007)

Wilson, Andrew, *Ukraine Crisis: What It Means for the West* (New Haven, CT and London, Yale University Press, 2014)

—, *The Ukrainians: The Story of How a People Became a Nation*, 5th edn (New Haven, CT and London, Yale University Press, 2022)

Wohlforth, William C., and Vladislav Zubok, 'An Abiding Antagonism: Realism, Idealism, and the Mirage of Western–Russian Partnership after the Cold War', *International Politics*, 54/4, 2017, pp. 405–19

Yan Xuetong, 'Becoming Strong: The New Chinese Foreign Policy', *Foreign Affairs*, 100/4, July/Aug 2021, pp. 40–7

—, *Leadership and the Rise of Great Powers* (Princeton, NJ, Princeton University Press, 2019)

Yekelchyk, Serhy, *Ukraine: Birth of a Modern Nation* (Oxford, Oxford University Press, 2007)

Yong Deng, *China's Struggle for Status: The Realignment of International Relations* (Cambridge, Cambridge University Press, 2008)

Yurchenko, Yuliya, *Ukraine and the Empire of Capital: From Marketisation to Armed Conflict* (London, Pluto Press, 2018)

Zakaria, Fareed, 'The New China Scare: Why America Shouldn't Panic about Its Latest Challenger', *Foreign Affairs*, 99/1, Jan/Feb 2020, pp. 52–69

—, *The Post-American World: And the Rise of the Rest* (New York, Norton, 2009)

Zarakol, Ayşe, *After Defeat: How the East Learned to Live with the West* (Cambridge, Cambridge University Press, 2011)

—, *Hierarchies in World Politics* (Cambridge, Cambridge University Press, 2017)

Zhang Weiwei, *The China Horizon: Glory and Dream of a Civilizational State* (Hackensack, NJ, World Century Publishing Corporation, 2016)

Žižek, Slavoj, *Iraq: The Borrowed Kettle* (London, Verso, 2004)

Zubok, Vladislav, *A Failed Empire: The Soviet Union in the Cold War from Stalin to Gorbachev* (Chapel Hill, NC, University of North Carolina Press, 2007)

Zygar', Mikhail, *All the Kremlin's Men: Inside the Court of Vladimir Putin* (New York, Public Affairs, 2016)

INDEX

391

human rights (contd)
Charter international system 4, 5,
21, 24, 80, 144, 315
China and 115, 144, 209
Europe 21
Helsinki conference and 27–8
interventions 326
Russia and 115
sanctions and 297
spreading of 110, 115
state sovereignty and 5, 144
UNHRC members and 280
USA and 6, 109, 110, 118, 284,
291
Hungary 32, 73, 81, 132, 251
Huntington, Samuel P. 146
Hussein, Saddam 47, 94

IAEA 128
ICAN 221
ICC 282–4
Iceland 237
ideologies
absence of alternatives 62, 105
anti-communism 25–6
China 124, 136–7, 138, 143–4, 162
civilisations 327
Cold War II 276
communist 21, 30–1, 58, 136–7
competing blocs 9
confrontation 304
differences in Cold War II 278–9
divisions during Cold War I 1, 9, 21,
25–6, 36, 46, 105, 273
Europe 199
framework remaining 60, 90
globalism 160
innovations 39
liberalism 56
pluralism 38, 39
political West 143
primacy and 8, 23, 34
revisionism 40
Russia 101, 182, 188
socialist 319
third way 2
UN and 280
US hegemony 42, 43, 62, 114, 123
US offensive against China 163, 272

US Trumanite 274
USSR 138, 157, 158, 243
Ignatius, David 82
Ikenberry, John 61, 140, 142
IMF 25, 162, 286, 304
imperialism 55, 69–70, 77, 91, 116,
151, 169
India
Arctic Council 237
authoritarianism 287
BRICS 304, 305, 306
civilisation state 298, 312
D10 287
democracy and 91, 144
economy 169, 306, 310–11
environment and 236
FOIP and 161
multipolarity and 278, 321
neutrality on Ukraine war 164
nuclear power 223, 225
opposition to US hegemony 298, 300
Quad 155, 163
RCEP and 153
relationship with China 144, 163,
306, 309
relationship with Russia 188, 190,
298–9, 310, 311, 312
relationship with USA 309–11
SCO 309
sovereign internationalism and 322
UN Security Council and 301
Indonesia 144, 145, 190, 278, 306, 322
INF treaty 37, 224, 228, 229, 317
INSTC 311
Institute for Economics and Peace 9
internationalism
conservative 105
democratic
Afghanistan and the limits of 321
Atlantic power system 36
Biden's choices 123–4
communities of liberal
democracies 17
condemned by Russia and China
115, 148
definition 4
double standards in 302
embedding American globalism 6
false universalism and 301